Penguin Books

A Parents' Guide to the Law

Lesley Taylor is a solicitor who specializes in child-care, family and criminal defence work and is interested in civil liberties generally. She was born in Cheshire and has lived for the last sixteen years in London, where she is a partner in a firm of solicitors who concentrate on legal aid work. She is on the national committee of the Legal Aid Practitioners' Group and is a member of the Law Society's child-care panel.

Jeannie Mackie was born and educated in Scotland. Since graduating from Girton College, Cambridge, she has worked in private practice in London as a solicitor specializing in legal aid family work. She now works for environmental consultants. She has a daughter and a stepson.

A Parents' Guide to the Law

JEANNIE MACKIE AND LESLEY TAYLOR

PENGUIN BOOKS

PENGUIN BOOKS

Published by the Penguin Group
Penguin Books Ltd, 27 Wrights Lane, London W8 5TZ, England
Viking Penguin, a division of Penguin Books USA Inc.
375 Hudson Street, New York, New York 10014, USA
Penguin Books Australia Ltd, Ringwood, Victoria, Australia
Penguin Books Canada Ltd, 2801 John Street, Markham, Ontario, Canada L3R 1B4
Penguin Books (NZ) Ltd, 182–190 Wairau Road, Auckland 10, New Zealand

Penguin Books Ltd, Registered Offices: Harmondsworth, Middlesex, England

First published 1990
10 9 8 7 6 5 4 3 2 1

Filmset in Ehrhardt [Monotype Lasercomp]

Printed in England by Clays Ltd, St Ives plc

Contents

To Hannah, without whom this book would have been finished more quickly – J.M.

To John, to Holly, and to Jesse and Betty, who didn't need a book like this – L.T.

Acknowledgements

Many people have helped us in the preparation of this book although of course the mistakes remain our own. We would particularly like to thank Jan and Phil Adderley, Nick Carter, Phil Cutts, Owen Davies, Lisa Fairweather, Margaret Fernandez, David Leigh, Ken Macdonald, Brian Perman and Jane Turnbull, Christine Rossetto, Naomi Sack, Bob Sherman, Chris Studdert and Paul Nicholls.

Introduction

This book is a guide to the law for parents. The law is a vast and complex construction which regulates family life as much as any other area. We have been struck by how confusing the law and its language is for parents and their children, and how difficult it can be to get clear information in a straightforward form.

We have set out the basic rules and practice in what we hope is a readable way, and cover some of the main areas where parents might need help or information: money, employment, education, health, adoption and child-care as well as the more dramatic problems of children in trouble with the police, family breakdown and local authority intervention between parents and children. It is not a textbook nor a do-it-yourself guide to litigation for which personal professional help and expertise is needed. Nor can it cover every area which could affect parenting. But we hope it will provide a helping hand for people who need information for the most difficult and rewarding job they could have – bringing up their children.

The law is as at 1 January 1990 and is applicable only to England and Wales. Despite the commonly-held view that law is slow and unresponsive, it has changed greatly in this area and more changes are on the way. The Children Act 1989, which will not be fully implemented until late 1991 at the earliest, will make sweeping alterations to children's law. We have in most cases indicated in the text the changes this Act will make to present law.

Update

Since 1 January 1990, there have been some changes in the law. The most important changes are as follows.

- Children under eighteen can apply in their own right for legal aid to take civil actions, for example for personal injury, medical negligence or brain damage. It is their means which count for assessment, not their parents.
- In care proceedings, reports prepared by the guardian ad litem and the social worker can now be read by the court at the start of the proceedings.
- Parliament has voted in favour of the introduction of an upper limit above which abortions cannot usually be performed. This is now twenty-four weeks.

Chapter 1

Becoming a Parent

Giving birth or fathering a child is not the only way an adult in our society becomes responsible for a child, nor is 'natural' conception and labour the only route to parenthood. This chapter brings together the different ways in which people might become a parent. 'Parent' here means an adult who has a caring and responsible relationship to a child which is recognized as such in law.

The law relating to children has grown up piecemeal, with different Acts of Parliament passed to deal with differing circumstances. The result of this is a rather tangled proliferation of legal terms to describe the relationships adults have with the children in their care. Under the various statutes, people can have custody; actual custody; legal custody; custodianship; joint custody; and care and control of children. All these terms involve some degree of parental rights and duties towards the child. Happily, the law is changing and the new Children Act 1989 simplifies this, and introduces a general concept of 'parental responsibility' to replace the present confusion. 'Parental responsibility' includes all the rights, duties, powers, responsibilities and authority which by law a parent of a child has in relation to the child and his/her property.

The new terms do not alter the fundamental fact of family law, which is that single mothers and married couples have and keep parental rights and duties in respect of their own children, unless a court orders otherwise and makes orders giving these duties to someone else.

Under the new Act, married couples and single mothers will have 'parental responsibility' on the birth of the child; unmarried fathers and others can be given it by an order of a court.

Adoption

This is the process by which married or single people take a child fully into their family, with all the rights and powers they would have if the child was born to them. This is dealt with fully in Chapter 2.

Custodianship

Custodianship orders give legal custody of a child to the adult or adults they live with. They cannot be made in favour of natural parents. See Chapter 2.

Fostering

Fostering is when a person or family looks after another child in their home, for short or long periods, at the request of a local authority, voluntary organization or privately at the request of the parents. Note here, though, that if a child is looked after by anyone who is not a relative, under the rules about private fostering, after twenty-seven days the care-taker must tell the local authority that the child is living with them. This is dealt with fully in Chapter 7.

God-parents

Under the rites of the Church of England and the Roman Catholic Church the parents of a child can request other blood relatives or friends to stand as god-parents at the christening of the child. Under canon or church law, being a god-parent confers duties, particularly with regard to ensuring a Christian education, but no powers.

In family law, being a god-parent does not give any legal duty. However, in cases where the services of another adult are needed a responsible god-parent could be invaluable.

Examples of this follow.

● If following family breakdown access by one parent needs to be super-vised, judges of the family division have suggested that god-parents are suitable people to undertake this.
● If the court in divorce proceedings feels neither parent should have the care of the child, it can make a care order to the local authority if there is no other suitable person with whom the child can live. A sensible god-parent who knows and cares for the child could be appointed for this purpose by the court.
● If the family itself is temporarily unable to care for the child because of an

emergency it can ask the local authority to take the child into voluntary care. Rather than do this a god-parent, or indeed any trusted friend, could be asked to tide the family over.

Parental Responsibility Orders under the Children Act 1989

People who are not the parents of a child can apply for orders that give some security to their care of a child. They can be relatives or not.

Take the example of a grandmother who has looked after a child while a daughter or son was unable or unwilling to do so. She could have applied for a custodianship order to give her legal custody under the old law, if the child had lived with her for at least three months before the order was made and she had consent from the parent, or for at least three years without consent.

Under the 1989 Act she can apply for a 'residence order' (an order the child is to live with her):

- if the child has lived with her for at least three years (she does not need consent);
- if there is already a residence order in effect (for example, to either of the child's parents) and the parents consent to her having the child to live with her (the child does not have to be living with her at the time);
- where the child is in care to the local authority and the authority consent to this;
- whether or not there is a residence order in existence, with the consent of those who have parental responsibility for the child;
- where she has got the leave of the court to make an application for a residence order.

Finally, when a residence order is made to anyone other than a parent or guardian it carries 'parental responsibility' with it for as long as the order lasts.

Under the new law there seems to be more scope for people who care for children to get orders in their favour. But note that regulations could be made under the new Act which could, on the face of it, limit the categories of people who can apply for such orders.

Guardianship

People can be the guardians of a child by a court order, under a will or other written document, or for limited legal purposes. The term 'guardian' has various different meanings depending on the context.

An adult, usually but not always a parent, who acts on the child's behalf in litigation taken by someone else against the child is called a guardian ad litem. A social worker or probation officer appointed to make reports on the child in care proceedings is also called a guardian ad litem. Both these types of guardian are appointed for a specific temporary purpose, and are different from guardians whose role is to act more as parents.

Guardians Who Look After Children

Under section(s) 9 of the Guardianship of Minors Act 1971 the court can make an order giving custody of a child to the person who applies for it. This person then becomes the child's guardian.

Married parents who are in dispute with each other about who the child should live with can use this Act. This is useful in cases where the parents do not want to start divorce proceedings, which is the main forum where custody of children is settled.

The fathers of non-marital children can apply; so can the mothers. Although mothers automatically have full parental rights there are circumstances where an order to confirm this is useful.

People who are not the parents of a child can also become guardians, under the provisions of the Guardianship of Minors Act (GMA) 1971 and the Guardianship Act 1973.

Testamentary Guardians

Section 4 of the GMA provides that the mother or father of a minor (that is, a child aged under eighteen) may by deed or will appoint any person to be the guardian of the minor after her or his death.

Mothers can always do this, whether their child or children are marital or not. The fathers of marital children can use this provision, but the fathers of non-marital children can appoint a guardian only if immediately before their death they had legal custody of the child.

A will takes effect only when the person who made it has died, and a deed made to appoint a guardian on death would not come into operation until death.

With marital children, when a parent dies the other parent automatically becomes the child's guardian. This is the case even where the parents were divorced or separated and the dead parent had legal custody of the child. (For unfit parents orders which stop this see Chapter 10.)

Married parents can appoint testamentary guardians even though their spouse is alive and will care for the child. In such a case, the testamentary guardian acts jointly with the surviving parent. Parents who have been divorced or separated might prefer to appoint a testamentary guardian than have the other parent bring the child up alone. Even where the parents lived together happily, the mother or father might want a guardian when their spouse survives because they want the child to have the benefit of more than one concerned adult in their life; or because they consider the surviving parent might need help with making decisions or guiding the child; or because they want the certainty of knowing that if the surviving parent died, they have made arrangements for a guardian of their choice to take over.

In any case, if the surviving parent objects to the guardian he or she can apply to the court under the Act for a ruling on this. The court can either refuse to make any order, in which case the surviving parent will be the only guardian of the child, or can confirm the appointment of the testamentary guardian by ordering that they act jointly together.

Both parents can appoint a guardian – and if both parents die, the guardians act jointly together.

If the surviving parent and the guardian, or the guardians appointed by each parent quarrel about an aspect of the child's welfare, either of them can apply to the court for a ruling on the matters about which they cannot agree.

NON-MARITAL CHILDREN

The power to appoint a testamentary guardian is extremely important for the mothers of non-marital children. By appointing a testamentary guardian a mother can make sure that on her death her child is looked after by a person of her choice. She can appoint any person she wishes, including of course the father of the child. This will give the father the legal right to be the guardian which he would not automatically be given on the mother's death.

If a child is left without any surviving parent, guardian or custodian, anyone can apply to the court under s5 of the GMA for an order making him or her the guardian.

If a single mother dies without making arrangements, then the surviving father can apply under this section. The court will appoint the applicant 'if it thinks fit'. This gives some protection to single fathers but it would not be sensible for single mothers to rely on this. For a start, they might not want the natural father to bring up the child, and even if they did the court might not approve the application, or it could be disputed by another concerned relative or friend.

Where a natural father had legal custody of the child immediately before his death, he can appoint a testamentary guardian to act singly or jointly with the natural mother if she survives.

Step-parents

Step-parents are in an odd position where parental rights to a child are concerned. Without a court order giving them custody, they do not have automatic parental rights over the children of their dead spouse even if they have always treated them as full members of their new family.

Under this Act, without having some other kind of order giving parental rights a step-parent does not count as a parent, guardian or custodian if the blood-parent of the child dies. For the purposes of s5, under which anyone can apply to be the guardian of a child who has no other, an existing step-parent does not count as a guardian or parent at all – and there would be nothing to stop some other relative from applying for such an order. Where the divorced parent is still alive, they in a sense 'inherit' the parental rights of the dead parent. Where, therefore, the parent of the child wants the surviving step-parent to look after the child, he or she should appoint them as the testamentary guardian. If there is a surviving blood-parent, the step-parent will act jointly with them. If there is then a dispute about whom the child should live with, either can take it back to court for a decision on this.

The Powers of Guardians

Guardians are guardians 'of the person of the minor' and have powers and duties (under s7 of the Guardianship Act 1973) to look after any property the minor owns, in their own name but for the minor's benefit.

If the guardian thinks that the surviving parent is unfit to have legal custody of the child, he or she can apply to the court. The court can order that the guardian is the sole guardian of the child; or it can order guardian and parent to act jointly; or it may make no order, in which case the surviving parent remains the sole guardian of the child.

Where there is no surviving parent, the guardian has sole legal custody of the child.

Even where the child is being looked after by a surviving parent or another appointed guardian, a guardian is entitled to go back to court if he or she cannot agree with the other care-taker.

The Removal of Guardians

Apart from the powers of the county court to order that where there is a surviving parent he or she can act without the testamentary guardian – which effectively removes the dead parent's choice from the scene – the High Court can order the removal or replacement of any guardian of a child, if it considers this is for the welfare of a child.

This applies not only to testamentary guardians, but to all guardians appointed under or acting by virtue of the GMA. It could therefore include parents.

Where a parent has appointed a testamentary guardian who refuses to act, the court can appoint someone else to act with the surviving parent. This also applies where the guardian has predeceased the parent.

Practical Points

If a parent wants to appoint a testamentary guardian to act jointly with the surviving parent, it is only sensible to choose someone who gets on well with the other parent as well as with the child. In all circumstances, the parent must ensure that the testamentary guardian consents to being appointed and understands what the parent wants and expects him or her to do.

Making a will is a sensible step, not only to appoint a guardian but also to ensure some kind of financial certainty for the child and the surviving members of the family. If a parent has particular plans for the child's future, or specific wishes as to how they should be brought up, it is always possible to put these in the will itself, or in a letter to be read with it. These directions are not necessarily binding on the surviving parent or guardian, but because they would set out clearly what the parent had wanted they could either prevent disputes or help the court in deciding them.

Guardianship Under the New Law.

The Children Act 1989 repeals the two Acts described above, and re-enacts them in a simplified form. The basic law on guardians will be as follows.

When a child either has no parent who has parental responsibility for him or her, or has lived under a residence order with a parent or guardian who has since died, then anyone may apply to the court to be appointed as a guardian for that child.

A parent who has parental responsibility for a child can appoint a guardian to take over on his or her death in a signed, dated, written document or in a signed, dated and witnessed will. A document appointing a guardian is revoked by any later document unless the parent makes it clear the two guardians are to act jointly.

The appointment of the guardian takes effect on the death of the parent if there is no other parent surviving who has parental responsibility; or if immediately before death the parent had a residence order in his or her favour. If the surviving parent also had a residence order in his or her favour, then the appointment does not take effect and the child lives with that parent.

If the dead parent did *not* have a residence order in his or her favour, and there is a surviving parent who has parental responsibility, then the guardian chosen by the parent takes over only when the child has no one else with parental responsibility for him or her. This could happen either because the surviving parent dies, or gets rid of the parental responsibility. This can be done only in limited circumstances.

In other words, parents can no longer appoint a guardian who takes over responsibility for the child over the head of a surviving parent, if that parent has parental responsibility for the child.

People who are already guardians of the child can, on death, appoint another guardian to take their place. The rules for this are the same as for parents.

There can be more than one guardian of a child, acting jointly, each having parental responsibility. Guardians can choose not to act, if they do this in writing reasonably soon after they learn they have been appointed.

In any family proceedings, the court itself can appoint guardians under the powers given by this Act, even where no one has applied to be the guardian. It might do this where no one else seemed capable of caring properly for the child.

The new law does not change the current position on non-marital fathers who do not automatically have parental rights (parental responsibility). Non-marital fathers can get parental responsibility either by applying to a court for it under the new Act; or being given it by a written agreement with the mother. More details about this can be found in Chapter 11. If they do not have parental responsibility, they cannot appoint a guardian on their death, even where the mother does not survive them.

If step-parents want to protect their position on the death of their spouse, they should get parental responsibility by applying for a residence order with their spouse's consent. Otherwise, step-parents can be appointed by their spouses as guardians, and take over responsibility if there is no surviving parent with responsibility; or they can apply on their own behalf to be appointed as guardians by the court where their spouse had the only residence order before death.

BETWEEN THE ACTS

Where a guardian was appointed under the Guardianship of Minors Act and this appointment took effect before the new law comes into force, then the appointment is treated as having been made under the law when it does come into force. Appointments of guardians which have not taken effect by the time the new Act comes in will take effect under the provisions of the new law.

Assisted Reproduction

Assisted reproduction here refers to the situation where either or both of the child's biological parents – that is, the donor of the egg and the sperm – are not the same people who intend to bring the child up as their own within their family.

Approximately one in every seven couples has infertility problems which restrict or end their capacity to conceive and bear children as a couple. Although scientific advances have increased the ways in which medical intervention can help conception and successful gestation to full term, increasingly, couples who cannot produce children together resort to alternative methods of producing a child who is biologically the child of one of them. These cases can present serious legal and moral difficulties about the legitimacy of the children, who has parental rights over them, and in what ways parental rights can be transferred from the biological parents to the expected parents. Note that the term 'parental rights' used in this section means the same as 'parental responsibility', the new description under the Children Act 1989.

Artificial Insemination by Donor (AID)

AID cases are less controversial and difficult than 'womb leasing' surrogacy cases, because the method by which a woman chooses to conceive is more her private business than the law's. AID need not involve medical or other agency intervention if a woman chooses to use a privately-run sperm bank or come to a private arrangement personally.

Sperm banks can be run either by an area health authority located in hospitals or as private commercial concerns. While NHS sperm banks will be conducted according to professional standards, there is at present no licensing or regulating system for private sperm banks. There need not necessarily be any proper system for running health checks on the donors. It is likely that some form of licensing will be brought in.

Children conceived as a result of AID have at present no right to discover who their genetic father was, unlike adopted children who can apply for a copy of their original birth certificate on reaching age eighteen. If such a right was incorporated into law, there would have to be a system of matching donor with donee. Naturally, the right could not, for practical reasons, be retrospective.

AID is used by both married or single women, and the legal position of children born as a result differs.

Where women who are not married conceive and bear children they automatically have full parental rights in respect of those children. These rights cannot be taken from them unless a court orders it; they do not have to share rights with the biological father; in fact, they cannot surrender or transfer parental rights to any person, including the father, unless a court has ordered this to be done or sanctioned it.

A single woman can choose to conceive how she pleases without it affecting her legal position as the child's mother as far as the state is concerned. Women need not disclose the name or identity of the father of their children, or the method by which they conceived.

In a case where a woman has conceived by AID through a sperm bank, she will not know the identity of the donor, the donor will not know her identity or even whether the insemination resulted in a child being born. In these cases, to all intents and purposes the child has one parent, the mother, and a donor-father whose place in his or her life was purely technical.

However, maternal rights can be affected by the donor if his identity is known, his paternity can be proved and he chooses to involve himself with the child. This could apply where a woman comes to a private arrangement with a man whose background, health and attributes she knows, preferring this to the genetic anonymity of a sperm-bank donor. There is no reason in law why that donor could not at some point exert his legal rights. He will be in the same position as any father of a non-marital child – with the right to apply for custody and access under the Guardianship of Minors Act, and the right to apply for parental responsibility under the Children Act. It is not the existence of a social and sexual relationship with the mother which confers these rights, but the existence of the biological relationship between the father and the child.

A donor father can, like anyone else with an interest in the child, issue wardship proceedings which would be conducted on the same lines as any other wardship case.

Whether or not a donor would be successful in any of the above applications would depend on the facts of the case, and as in all custody and access cases the court would base its decision on what was best for the child. For further details on custody/access cases see Chapter 10.

The mother of an AID child where the donor's identity is known would have the same rights to apply for affiliation and maintenance as any single woman who can prove the child's paternity. The court would have to make an affiliation order if it considered the donor was the putative father; whether or not it would go on to make a money order, and if so for how much, could be affected by the court's sense of fairness to a donor.

With a married couple the normal legal presumption when the woman gives birth is that the child is fathered by the husband and therefore the legitimate child of the family. This presumption can be legally rebutted in court proceedings by evidence that the child was fathered by another man, for example in divorce when the husband, having discovered the child is not his, does not wish to have further financial responsibility.

This presumption would be removed by AID, and such children have been in a cloudy legal area where their legitimacy was in question. Now when married women use AID as a way of conception, the child's and the father's legal positions depend on whether or not the woman's husband consented to this being done. This is a new provision under the Family Law Reform Act 1987 which, when it comes into force, provides that a child conceived as a result of artificial insemination where the husband consented to this is to be treated in law as the child of both the husband and the wife, and not as the child of any other party, for example, the genetic father. The Act removes any rights the genetic father would have, replacing him by the husband who with his wife chose to have a child conceived in this way.

This seems to put a child born as a result of AID into the same position as all other children born in marriage: unless and until a dispute about paternity or consent is successfully proved, he or she is treated as the legitimate child of the husband and wife. This means that the husband and the wife share the parental rights and duties, in the normal way, and the husband, despite not being the child's biological father, is treated to all intents and purposes as if he were: the children are treated as legitimate with full family rights.

The only exclusion is that the new position does not affect succession to a title or dignity or allow the child to succeed to the husband's title if any. The child also cannot succeed to the mother's titles even if held in her own right, and is in the same position as a non-marital child in this.

Other than in this arcane area, the child would have the more usual rights on inheritance, inheriting money or property under a will in which he or she was a beneficiary and being able to claim a share of the estate in the intestacy both of the parents and other family members.

The consent given is to the artificial insemination itself. Where a husband did not consent to the AID and can prove this to a court's satisfaction, the child is *not* then treated as a child of both parties, but as the illegitimate child of the mother who would have sole rights and duties. The husband then would have no rights, duties or further legal responsibility towards the child. The consent issue here is to prevent husbands from having to take responsibility for a child they do not choose to have.

This provision clarifies the position of AID children within the family but applies only to married couples. People who live together, however stable and long-term this relationship may be, cannot benefit from this provision. A man in this situation who wished a legal status with the child would have to apply under the provisions open to unmarried fathers.

One expects that the majority of AID children are conceived with the full knowledge and consent of husbands who choose this option with their wives following medical tests on their own fertility. It is presumably envisaged that husbands who do not consent will take proceedings promptly. An interesting situation could arise if they do not but, knowing the child is not 'theirs', and knowing they did not consent to its conception, they still treat the child as if it were their own. In this situation, the husband could, in subsequent divorce proceedings, be made liable for the maintenance of the child.

In divorce, both husband and wife can be ordered to pay maintenance for the upkeep of a child even if they knew that the child was not theirs, as long as during the marriage they treated the child as if it was. In divorce, orders are made for the 'children of the family', and it does not much matter where they came from as long as they were accepted as children of the marriage, and treated as such, for example, financially supported by the other parent.

With children born as a result of AID without the husband's consent, there could be situations where, despite proving lack of consent in divorce proceedings, men are still made liable financially for the child, because they seemed to accept the child into the family. As this provision is new, it has not been yet tested in the courts.

Note that the provision applies only to artificial insemination, a technical process with remarkably little human contact. If a woman conceives as a result of sexual intercourse with a man to whom she is not married, during the course of a valid marriage, even with her husband's consent and even with just the intention to conceive, the child's position is unaffected by the new law: the child would be illegitimate, with no statutory rights to be treated as a child of the husband.

In practical terms this would make a difference to the child only if the father rejected him or her and the family unit broke down. A husband's consent to this method of conception would presumably precede an acceptance of the child as part of his family; if the conception was without his consent but he then accepted the child into the family and treated it as his own the child would be a 'child of the family' in any eventual divorce.

Egg Donation, Host Mothers and AID

Fertility techniques are now so sophisticated that eggs can be donated by the wife or another woman, fertilized in a laboratory by the husband or third party and placed in the wife or another woman to gestate.

Where the woman in a couple has healthy ova but cannot for some reason bear a child, an ovum can be surgically removed, fertilized by her husband or a third party, and placed in another woman to gestate. Equally, an ovum can be taken from another woman, fertilized and placed in the intending mother. Who then is the natural mother? There is no specific legal definition of a natural mother as, until scientific advances separating fertilization/gestation and labour from each other, there has been little need for one. Legislation on human fertility and embryo research is expected; but it appears from indirect references to 'blood links' in the existing legislation that the genetic link rather than the gestational link is the one which confers motherhood. In the above examples, the donor of the ovum would be the natural mother.

One could, technically, have court actions fought by the donor of the egg seeking to establish parental rights – but as custody law leans towards the concept of 'bonding' between mother and child and the creation of emotional ties between them following birth, one cannot quite imagine litigation over a child's future based on an emotional tie with a surgically removed unfertilized ovum. However, the rich variety of human behaviour might yet produce a test case on this.

Where the husband has fertilized the ovum, he is the father by virtue of that genetic link. That is common-sense. But where a couple decides to enter into a surrogacy arrangement with another woman who conceives by AID, common sense gets a battering. If the surrogate mother conceives with the consent of her husband the provision above would operate – and the genetic father's rights would count for nothing. The surrogate mother's husband by consenting to the insemination would become the child's legitimate father. As no one can transfer or surrender parental rights, any agreement made by the surrogate mother's husband not to do anything about this would be invalid. Technically one could get a situation where the surrogate mother agreed to hand over the child to the couple, while her husband refused to do so. As the child's legitimate father, his consent would be needed in subsequent adoption proceedings and he would have to be a party to any custody application. This cannot have been intended by Parliament and the provision needs to be amended.

Where the ovum taken from the woman in the couple was fertilized by a man other than the woman's partner, then the former would have parental rights – unless the fertilization was done by AID with consent, when the genetic link would be ignored.

In a case where neither of the couple had a genetic link with the child, they would be analogous to adoptive parents, with no parental rights of any kind unless and until awarded these by a court.

Surrogacy

Surrogate motherhood is when a woman gives birth to a child conceived by a man to whom she intends to give the child following birth, to be brought up by him. The surrogacy cases brought in the English courts so far have concerned childless couples who came to an arrangement with another woman to give birth to the husband's child with the understanding that the child will be brought up by the couple.

This section deals mainly with couples who cannot have children, but of course there could be considerable variations on this theme: for example, a woman might be physically capable of conceiving and bearing a child, but chose not to do so, preferring to arrange that another woman does it for her. Such an arrangement would be dealt with by the law in the same way as it deals with infertile couples – but the court in any subsequent custody case would consider the woman's temperament, mothering capacity and suitability for caring for the child, as it does in all cases, with a likely added concern about why she chose not to have her own genetic child.

Equally, a single infertile woman could enter into a surrogacy arrangement, but there would be no genetic link between her and the child which, when combined with her not having a 'standard' family, might well be seen as harmful to the child's interests.

Surrogacy as such is not illegal. To some extent, people who want children are able to come to whatever private arrangement they choose, but the law restricts who may organize surrogacy; it imposes safeguards for the child with particular reference to its future legal position; it gives guidelines for the local authority in the area concerned; and it continues to have regard to the natural mother's position despite any agreements the parties may have come to about her 'rights'.

When a baby is born as a result of a surrogacy arrangement, whether or not an agency has been involved, local authorities will need to consider whether the child will be at risk. This, of course, happens only if they know about it.

A surrogacy arrangement is defined as one in which a woman, whether for payment or not, has agreed to become pregnant with a view to handing over the baby to another couple, usually the child's father and his wife.

If the local authority after making inquiries think the child is at risk, their options are the same as for any other child in this position. In an emergency they can get a place of safety order from a juvenile court, or make the child a ward of court, or take care proceedings. In the well-publicized surrogacy wardship case of Baby Cotton, the Judge Mr Justice Latey recommended that wardship be used in such 'unusual and complex' cases. In that case, the biological father of the child was given custody of the baby whom he and his wife wished to adopt, to give them full legal rights.

Most surrogacy arrangements are made when couples who cannot have a child want to have one which has a biological link with at least one of them: in the nature of it, it will be the man's child and he has the rights, such as they are, of the father of a non-marital child. The father's wife or partner has no physical link with the child and therefore no full legal relationship until one is created by an order of the court. The natural mother has sole parental rights.

When what is required is a permanent extinction of the natural mother's parental rights and the creation of full parental rights for the woman of the couple, then adoption is the most effective way of doing both these at once. The father and his wife make a single joint application. Although he is adopting his own child, by doing so the father obtains full parental rights which he did not previously have. Adoption legislation allows for non-marital fathers applying to adopt their own children. Various judgments have also approved of adoption by a natural parent, considering that making the child legitimate is in his or her best interests.

An adoption order is permanent, conclusive and gives full parental rights; it also confers legitimacy on the child who, for all purposes including inheritance and succession rights, is in the same position as a child born naturally during marriage. From the date of the adoption order the natural mother's rights and duties are permanently extinguished. The procedure and requirements for the adoption of a child of a surrogate mother are the same as for more conventional cases. (For the procedure and law on adoption see Chapter 2).

However, there is one major difference between the adoption of a child of a surrogate mother and other adoption cases: the financial aspects of surrogacy arrangements. It is usual and indeed humanitarian for the couple to offer to pay the surrogate mother's expenses caused by the pregnancy. These may be considerable, including compensation for loss of earnings, private medical care, etc. There may also be an element of reward or fee for the surrogacy service. Even in cases where the surrogate mother has offered to bear the child for philanthropic and not financial reasons there is likely to be some payment made, out of the recognition that pregnancy is expensive.

Law and public policy are against the purchase of children: the Adoption Act 1976 states that a court cannot make an adoption order if money has been transferred to facilitate adoption. Parents who make payments to a surrogate might fall foul of this unless at the time they gave the money they had no intention of adopting the child. And that might be difficult to prove.

Adoption

Adoption is the process by which adults who are not necessarily a child's natural parents become that child's parents in law, from the date of the adoption order, with all the parental rights and duties relating to the child vested in them. Legal adoption is fairly new in the UK, as it was not until 1926 that the first Adoption Act was passed to give a legal status to people who brought up children who were not biologically their own. There is no common law on adoption, which is all based on statute.

When a court or an adoption agency makes any decision relating to an adoption it must give first consideration to the need to 'safeguard and promote the welfare of the child throughout his childhood'. It should, as far as is practical, find out the wishes and feelings of the child about the decision and give these due consideration, having regard to his age and understanding.

The present Act is the Adoption Act 1976 which came into force on 1 January 1988, and regulations still in force although they were made under earlier Acts. The previous – and radical – Act was the Children Act 1975 which was consolidated in the Adoption Act 1976 and is no longer relevant to adoption.

The Children Act 1989 does not fundamentally affect the Adoption Act 1976 although it will be amended to take account of the change from 'parental rights' to 'parental responsibility'. The principles remain the same – but after the Children Act 1989 comes in all references to parental rights should be read as meaning responsibility; references to non-marital father's rights to apply for custody, care and control should refer to rights to apply for parental responsibility and a residence order.

Adopted children are treated as if they were born to their adoptive parents. If the adoptive parents are a married couple, this applies whether or not the child was actually born before or after their marriage. If the adoptive parent is a single person the child is treated as if he or she had been born to that adoptive parent in marriage.

Whatever the married status of an adoptive parent, no adopted child is therefore illegitimate. All adopted children are treated as if they have no other parents.

The traditional – and stereotyped – view of adoption is that a childless married couple wishing to have a family, adopts either an orphan or a healthy baby whose single mother gives it up for adoption. The real situation is very different, altered partly by social changes which have 'dried up' the supply of babies for adoption, partly by a shift of emphasis from adults' rights to have children, to children's rights to have parents, and partly by the Children Act 1975 and the thinking which lay behind it.

Some babies are still adopted of course, and there is a small but apparently increasing number of babies being brought in to the UK from the 'Third World' by would-be adoptive parents. However, now that the 'stigma of illegitimacy' has mainly gone, recognized by the recent removal of legal differences between children born in or out of marriage, and women freely choose to bring up children on their own, most adoptions in this country are of older children, many of whom have been in institutional or foster care either because their parents cannot look after them, or because they were removed from their parents' care because of social services' concerns about their welfare.

All children under the age of eighteen may be adopted, unless they are or have been married. Even if a child was married under the law of another country, and would have been under-age for a British marriage, he or she cannot be adopted under British law. A child can be adopted even if he or she is already an adopted child. In England and Wales, unlike in Scotland, the child does not have to consent to the adoption, although the court should take the child's wishes and feelings into account depending on his or her age and understanding.

Before the Children Act 1975, research found that once children were in care, they were likely to stay there until they were eighteen. Because no child could then be adopted without the parents' consent, children who might have benefited from life in an adoptive family were trapped in children's homes. The Act made it possible for these children to be adopted, by means of a provision stating that in some circumstances the parents' consent could be dispensed with.

This has meant that children can now be adopted who otherwise would not have been, but it has also meant that the adoption of a child can be a harrowing process for the natural parents who may be fighting to keep the child, and for the adoptive parents who fear their application might fail.

Anyone involved in this situation must have proper legal advice and representation. Legal aid is available for both natural and adoptive parents if they qualify under the financial rules.

Adoption Agencies

Although some adoptions are organized privately, for example adoption by relatives of the child, most are organized through approved adoption societies and the social services departments of local authorities.

One of the ideas behind the Children Act 1975 was to set up a comprehensive adoption service, with adoption work becoming part of social services' duties towards children generally, with each local authority running a service in conjunction with approved adoption societies in their area.

Not all local authorities have set themselves up as approved adoption agencies, and use outside adoption societies for this part of their work. Adoption societies – which are called agencies in the Act and henceforth in this chapter – must be approved by the Secretary of State and are highly regulated under the Act. There are penalties for adoption agencies which work without approval, and it is also a criminal offence for anyone other than an adoption agency to make arrangements about or to place a child for adoption. There are exceptions to this, and 'private' adoptions where the child was not placed with a family through an adoption agency are not entirely ruled out.

Adoption agencies have duties to the child they want to be adopted; to the child's parents; and to the prospective adopters. Decisions are not made by one person, but by a panel set up by the agency to make recommendations to them. This panel – of at least five people – should include a doctor, social workers used to adoption work and at least two independent people who are not employed by the agency. The panel makes recommendations about accepting candidates as prospective adopters; whether or not adoption is in a particular child's interests; and with whom the child should be placed.

Prospective Adopters

Being accepted by an adoption agency as a suitable parent for a child in their trust is hard. The agencies can pick and choose, many set age limits above which they will not consider people, and many are so well off for potential adoptive parents that their lists are closed, or open only to families which have already adopted one child through them.

In order to make decisions about placing a child, the agency needs as much information as possible about the health, circumstances, character and suitability of the prospective adopter. Their investigations are full and detailed, and include information on the home the child would live in, the reasons for wishing to adopt, religion, interests and hobbies, marital history and family history, income and living standards and an assessment of personality. There must be an up-to-date medical report and examination of the prospective adopters, and references from two referees.

Adoption Procedures

Definitions of Parents and Guardians

Before the Children Act 1975 children could not be adopted without the consent of their parents. Now adoption orders can be made either with or without the natural parents' agreement. Where parents do not agree to adoption the question of their consent is still fundamental to adoption, and the court cannot make any adoption order unless and until the parents' agreement or otherwise has been fully considered. After a hearing the courts can now dispense with the parents' consent.

The definition of what a parent or guardian is under adoption law is therefore important: the court does *not* need to get the consent to adoption of any person who does not come under the definition.

MARRIED PARENTS

The parents of a child are the mother, in all cases, whether or not the child was born in marriage; and the father, if he was married to the mother of the child before or after the birth. If the marriage was after the birth, it legitimizes the child and gives the father full parental rights.

Both the mother and the father of a marital child are treated as parents after a divorce, regardless of who gets custody of the child. The non-custodial parent still has some parental rights, and must agree or have their agreement dispensed with to an adoption which would remove all parental rights permanently. This will be the same under the new law, when the parent who does not have a residence order will still have parental responsibility for the child.

Similarly, the consent of both parents must be obtained or dispensed with even if they have had their parental rights removed by a previous court order: e.g. orders in wardship, care and divorce, or by resolution of the local authority where the child was originally in voluntary care.

The adoptive parents of a child who is again being adopted are parents with full parental rights to be taken into account. A step-parent is *not* a parent in adoption.

NON — MARRIED PARENTS

Non-marital fathers have minimal legal rights and duties in respect of their children. An important right they do have is to apply to a court for custody or access under s9 of the Guardianship of Minors Act. A father of a child who does this and gets custody is then a 'guardian' within the meaning of that word in adoption law, and can be fully involved in the proceedings.

However, unless appointed guardian by a parent with parental responsibility as described on p. 22, a non-marital father is not a parent for adoption law. But his right to apply for custody (present law) and parental responsibility (new law) of the child must be taken account of where the mother is likely to agree to the child being adopted. In this case, the court through the reporting officer (see p. 23) must interview any person 'claiming' to be the father of the child, find out whether he wants to apply for custody and, if he does, assess his chances of success.

The court cannot make an adoption order by agreement unless this has been done. If the reporting officer finds the father has a good chance of success in applying for custody, the adoption hearing will adjourn until the father's case is dealt with.

Where the mother is fighting the adoption application, the putative father does not have to be involved in this way, but if he is already a part of the child's life, the child's guardian ad litem should include him in the investigations. His views about the adoption should be put to the court through the guardian, and the court will have to consider whether or not breaking an existing relationship with him is in the child's interests. The quality of the relationship might therefore be a factor leading the court to refuse an adoption order.

A non-marital father who is paying maintenance for the child – but only if there is an order that he do so or a legal liability to do so through a contract with the mother – must be included in the proceedings as a respondent in any application for a freeing order. This does not mean he is given any parental rights he did not already have, but he would be entitled to appear in court, be represented and be heard.

GUARDIANS

The guardian of a child is a person appointed by deed or will: either parent can appoint in their will what are known as 'testamentary guardians' for their child. The testamentary guardians effectively take over the dead parent's parental rights, and act in conjunction with the surviving parent, if any (see Chapter 1).

Under the new law, parents who have parental responsibility will be able to appoint guardians for after their death simply in a written, dated and signed document.

A guardian can also be appointed by a court order – for example after a successful application for custody under the Guardianship of Minors Act 1971. This will still apply when the law changes to the extent that orders made before it came into force will continue.

Under the new law, the court in family proceedings will have the power to appoint guardians to have parental responsibility for the child. The court in adoption will have to consider their consent or otherwise as with parents.

Conditions for Adoption

Before an adoption order is made the courts must be satisfied that:

1. the parents agree freely and unconditionally to the child being adopted with a full understanding of what is involved; or
2. the parents' agreement can be dispensed with; or
3. the child is 'free' for adoption (this means that a previous order has been made freeing the child for adoption).

1. PARENTAL AGREEMENT

The parent(s) must freely and unconditionally consent to the child's adoption. A parent who agreed to adoption on condition that he or she could still write to the child or have occasional access would not have given unconditional consent. Although the court can and occasionally does add terms or conditions to an adoption order, the parent's own consent must be total. Parents are entitled to state their preferences about the religious upbringing of their child but are not entitled to lay down other preferences about the adoptive parents. They should understand that adoption severs their parental relationship with the child who will become part of the adopter's legal family from the date of the adoption order, and that they will no longer have a relationship with the child.

Consent must be given with an understanding of the issues involved. If a parent cannot make a proper consent because they are under a disability (for example, they have a mental illness), then their consent can be dispensed with on that basis. The mothers of children less than six weeks old cannot make an effective consent.

Generally, agreement is written down in a properly executed and witnessed document, but it can also be made orally. It can be made at any time before the adoption order is made, and it can be withdrawn at any time before an order is made: the parent is not bound to an adoption by agreeing. However, although a withdrawal of agreement could be entirely reasonable and treated as such by the courts, it could also be evidence that the parent was not thinking of the child's best interests as a reasonable parent should. In that case, the court could use it as evidence that the parent was unreasonably withholding consent to the adoption (see 'Dispensing with Consent', below).

In one case, a young mother agreed to an adoption of her child but then changed her mind when she and the child's father decided to marry and bring up the child with help from her family. The courts decided that this was perfectly proper, and that her change of mind was reasonable.

Agreement can be made to the social services, adoption agencies and to reporting officers appointed by the court.

Social services are always involved in adoptions at some stage, either because the child is in their care and they have decided to place the child for adoption or because they must be notified of intended private adoption proceedings. Generally, where a child in care is going to be adopted, the social services will have worked with the parents and will know whether or not they are likely to agree.

Actual adoption proceedings are started by the prospective adopters themselves, and not the social services or adoption agency. When the papers starting the case are filed, the court appoints a reporting officer who is chosen from a panel of suitably qualified people, including experienced and senior social workers and probation officers. He or she acts independently of all the parties, and is responsible for:

- ensuring as far as possible that the parents' agreement to the adoption is given freely and unconditionally with full understanding;
- witnessing a written agreement to the adoption;
- investigating all circumstances relevant to the agreement; and
- reporting back to the court.

The independence of the reporting officer is a protection for the natural parents. Parents who could have been under intolerable emotional strain or confusion when they told their social worker they would agree to adoption are given the chance to discuss it with an independent professional who has no axe to grind and was not involved in any of the previous decisions about the child.

Where the agreement is given, and the reporting officer is satisfied it was properly given, the court can rely on this. There must still be a full adoption hearing in which the court decides if adoption is in the best interests of the child and if the adoptive parents are suitable.

2. DISPENSING WITH PARENTAL CONSENT

Where parents do not agree to an adoption the court can dispense with their agreement only after a full hearing of the evidence on both sides, where the parents can appear and be legally represented.

There are six grounds on which the court can dispense with their consent. They are, that the parent or guardian:

1. cannot be found or is incapable of giving agreement;
2. is withholding his or her agreement unreasonably;
3. has persistently failed without reasonable cause to discharge the parental duties in relation to the child;
4. has abandoned or neglected the child;
5. has persistently ill-treated the child;
6. has seriously ill-treated the child.

For ground 1 to succeed, serious attempts to find the parent should have been made. For grounds 3, 4, 5 and 6 to succeed there must be evidence of bad behaviour by the parent against the child. Ground 2 is the most commonly used.

For ground 2 to succeed, the court must be convinced that the parent is not behaving as a reasonable parent should: in this context, reasonable parents are expected to think seriously about what is best for the child. In adoption cases, what is best for the child might be not be being part of the parent's own family any longer and belonging to the adoptive parents instead. It is obviously painful for natural parents to contemplate that their child would be better off without them. The court can decide whether or not adoption would be in the child's best interests and, if so, whether the parent was unreasonable in not consenting to it. They investigate all the circumstances surrounding the adoption and refusal of consent to it, weighing up whether a reasonable parent could have acted as the parents in the case have.

It is not unreasonable in itself either not to consent to adoption in the first place, or to consent and then withdraw that consent. It depends – as all cases concerning children do – on the facts of each particular case.

In one case, a woman first of all consented to adoption, then remarried and withdrew her consent. The court found she had done this because her husband asked her to – presumably not thinking about the child's best interests but about her own situation – and dispensed with her consent on that ground. In another contrasting case, a couple left their child for years with a foster mother in England and refused consent to adoption on the basis they wanted the child to return to the country of origin. This was not considered unreasonable.

One very important factor is how long the child has been living with the prospective adoptive parents, and how attached the 'new' family is. As all adoptive parents must live with the child for a period before the proceedings start, the court does have some idea from reports and evidence of what the relationship between them is.

A 'reasonable' parent would be more likely than an unreasonable parent to appreciate, despite personal pain, that the child was secure and happy in a long-term placement with the new family and be reluctant to break this up.

If the court decides the parent was reasonable in withholding consent, the adoption proceedings cannot, obviously, go ahead. The court can then make other orders – for example, making a care order or making the prospective adoptive parents 'custodians' instead.

If the court decides the parents withheld their consent unreasonably, then they start the next phase of the hearing: investigating whether or not the applicants to the adoption should succeed.

If parents do not agree to adoption – or agree first of all and change their minds later – then the case must be contested at a hearing. The court in these cases must appoint a guardian ad litem to act for the child and represent his or her interests. The parents' interests are represented by their own lawyers.

The guardian ad litem's role is to investigate the facts of the case, including but not limited to the matters raised in the documents, reports and statements filed at court by the prospective adopters and the adoption agencies. Children can be present at adoption hearings, and the guardian advises the court on whether or not this is appropriate. The guardian makes confidential reports to the court for the hearing, but can also make interim reports if he or she thinks it is necessary. Guardians have a wide discretion to do what they feel is in the interests of the child to whom they have duties.

Guardians and reporting officers are chosen from the same panel of independent professionals and can be the same person: that is, if a parent agrees to adoption first of all and then changes his or her mind, the reporting officer appointed for that can then be appointed as the child's guardian for a contested hearing.

3. FREE FOR ADOPTION

A court can order that a child is 'free for adoption' at an early stage, even before there are any prospective adoptive parents. This means that the parents' consent to adoption has been dealt with beforehand, and the natural parents do not have to be involved in the adoption application itself.

Only adoption agencies can apply for a freeing order. They do not have to, and do not always do so. They can apply for a freeing order before or after they have placed the child with an adoptive family.

One advantage of a freeing order is that children free for adoption who are then placed with an adoptive family can make links and bonds with them without fear that the adoption itself might be bitterly contested by the natural parents or fail because of this. This is the theory – in practice, children are frequently placed with adoptive families without a freeing order being made, and the main hearing is the adoption hearing.

Once made a freeing order operates like an adoption order as far as the parents are concerned. The freeing order removes all parental rights and duties from the natural parents or guardians and transfers them to the adoption agency which made the application. Effectively, the natural parents are no longer the child's parents, and become, in law, 'former parents'.

Although a freeing order may be a preliminary step in the legal process of adoption for the child and any potential adoptive parents, it can be the end of the process for the natural parents.

For freeing orders, as with adoption orders, the parents can agree or not agree to the order being made. When agreement is given the court *must* be satisfied that consent was free and unconditional, and made with a full under-standing of what was involved. Consent to the freeing order is expressed as being consent to an adoption order – even if at the time of the freeing order the child is not yet placed with prospective adoptive parents. The natural parents should understand that consent means giving up all rights to see, contact or have the child returned to them, as finally as with an adoption order itself.

When parents do not agree with the order being made, the adoption agency must apply for their agreement to be dispensed with on one of the same six specific grounds as for adoption orders.

Unlike adoption orders, parents must also consent to the application for a freeing order being brought at all. This consent is just agreement to the adoption agency making the application, and does not bind the parent to agreeing to the freeing order being made. In practice, a parent who agrees to the adoption agency applying for the order is likely to agree to the order being made – but they can change their minds. If they do not agree to the application being made, the agency cannot even apply unless they also ask the court to dispense with the parents' agreement to the freeing order itself.

Again, the consent of a mother whose child is less than six weeks old is ineffective.

If an adoption agency applies for a freeing order before placing the child with a family, the court must be satisfied that placement of the child with a suitable family is likely before it makes the order. It would be wrong for children to be severed from their natural parents without a very real and immediate prospect of getting another family. If a freeing order is made, but the child is not then placed with an adoptive family within a year of it, the parents in some circumstances can go back to court.

The adoption agency can issue proceedings in

- the High Court – in which case the child must also be a party, represented by the Official Solicitor; or
- the county court in the area where the child or natural parents reside; or
- the magistrates' court in the area where the child or natural parents reside.

The agency must include the following as parties to the action ('Respondents'):

- each natural parent or guardian of the child (for definitions of parent and guardian see pp. 20–22);
- any local authority or voluntary organization which has parental rights or duties in respect of the child – for example, the local authority with whom a child was in care;
- any person liable under any order or agreement to contribute to the maintenance of the child. A parent paying maintenance following a divorce would be a party automatically because of being a parent, but this would also cover a step-parent paying maintenance following divorce from the child's parent.

Note that potential adoptive parents are not respondents to the action, and play no active part in applications for freeing orders.

In all cases, the adoption agency must supply the court with a written report they have prepared, giving full details about the child, the natural parents and any prospective adoptive parents they have in mind. The report indicates the parents' wishes and feelings about the child being adopted. What happens next depends on whether or not the parents are likely to agree.

If the report shows the parents are likely to agree, the court appoints a reporting officer on behalf of the parent or guardian of the child. His/her duties include interviewing the natural parents or guardians, with a particular duty towards the father of a non-marital child; investigating all the circumstances which are relevant to their agreement; ensuring as far as is reasonably practicable that their agreement is given freely and unconditionally and with a full understanding of what is involved; preparing a written agreement to the adoption order on a standard form and witnessing the parents' agreement to this (this document is filed at court and is accepted as evidence of the parents' agreement); and reporting back to the court.

Parents who agree to a freeing order at this stage must be given a chance to declare that they do not want to be further involved in future questions about the child's adoption. The reporting officer must discuss this option with them, and later confirm to the court that he or she has done so. Parents can also choose to make this declaration later on if they wish.

An important point here is that parents who *do not* make a declaration, and keep their limited right to be involved, must be told by the adoption agency within fourteen days following the end of twelve months from the date the freeing order was made whether or not an adoption order has been made and, if not, whether the child has been placed with a family for adoption.

Parents who *do* make this declaration lose their entitlement to get that information: they also lose their right to apply for revocation of the freeing order if no adoption order is made within the time limits.

Parents can change their mind about agreeing to adoption at all at any time until the freeing order is made. If after talking about it with the reporting officer and understanding the consequences of agreement they decide not to agree, then the adoption agency must apply for their agreement to be dispensed with in a full hearing before the court where the parents can put their case.

Where the initial report filed by the adoption agency shows that the parents are not likely to agree to a freeing order, the court must appoint a guardian ad litem, again a person independent of the agency and chosen from a panel of suitably qualified persons. In any case, the court can appoint a guardian for the child if it thinks the child's interests need this safeguard or the circumstances make it necessary.

The guardian ad litem's main role is to represent the interests of the child. No reporting officer is appointed in these cases, and natural parents or guardians who do not want the child to be adopted must get their own legal representation. Legal aid is available subject to means. The parents cannot represent the interests of the child in freeing orders – what they want may not be what the child needs.

The court must decide what is in the child's best interests independently of all the other parties' views. The court assesses what the child needs from the evidence and, importantly, from the opinions and evidence of the guardian ad litem who either appears in court or instructs solicitors for the child. Where the case is in the High Court the Official Solicitor will generally be asked to be the guardian ad litem, and appears through barristers at the hearing.

Other duties of the guardian ad litem include investigating: facts and allegations made by the adoption agency in its initial report; the documents (the originating process) which started the action; the 'statement of facts' which says why the agency is asking the court to dispense with the parents' consent to the adoption; and any other matters that seem relevant to him or her. The guardian ad litem performs any other duties he or she considers necessary or as directed by the court. He or she has a wide discretion in what is investigated because the circumstances of each case are so different, and everything material to the interests of the child should be made known to the court.

The guardian ad litem also advises the court whether or not the child should come to the hearing and makes a written confidential report to the court for use at the hearing (he or she can make interim reports before that if necessary).

Where parents who originally decided they could not agree to the adoption change their minds before the hearing, which they are entitled to do, the court appoints a reporting officer for them, with the same duties as above. The guardian ad litem already appointed for the child can be appointed as the reporting officer.

When the guardian ad litem's report is finished and the case is heard the adoption agency must then prove to the court that the parents' consent should be dispensed with. The grounds for this are exactly the same as for dispensing with consent in an application for adoption and is dealt with above.

If consent is dispensed with the court then orders the child free for adoption. The parents become 'former parents' from that point.

Revocation of a Freeing Order
Freeing orders can be revoked, but only in the following circumstances:

- no adoption order has been made; and,

- the parents did *not* make a s14 declaration (that is, they chose to keep their right to information); and
- the child has not been placed with an adoptive family for twelve months or more after the freeing order was made; and
- the parent wants to resume parental rights in respect of the child.

Applications to revoke freeing orders are rare, because the combination of circumstances needed to make them does not often arise.

However, this part of the Act gives natural parents at least a way of having the case looked at again by the court if their child is in the damaging situation of having no family at all for more than a year. Freeing orders break the child's legal relationship with its birth parents, but long-term institutional care or fostering is not what children are 'freed' for.

The parent in this situation applies to the court which made the freeing order. Until the case is heard, the adoption agency cannot place the child with potential adoptive parents without first getting the court's consent. Otherwise, this might be seen as a pre-emptive strike.

If the court does then revoke the freeing order, parental rights and duties which were vested in the adoption agency when the order was made are returned to the person who had those duties immediately before that happened. If a local authority had the parental duties before the agency, they go back to the person who had them before – who is likely to be the parent.

If the parents' application fails they cannot make another one unless the court gives them leave to do so. The court will not give leave unless either there is a change in circumstances or it seems 'proper' to give leave.

A parent who signed the declaration that they did not wish to be involved with the child's adoption in future has no rights to be informed if any adoption order is made, if the child has been placed with a family for adoption or to apply for revocation as above.

If a parent in this position discovers by accident that the child is still without a family more than a year after being freed for adoption, they cannot use adoption law to have the case looked at. They could make the child a ward of court, because anyone, including former parents, can use this jurisdiction as long as they state their relationship to the child in their original application.

The Procedure for Adoptive Parents

Get on the list of an approved adoption agency which will then thoroughly vet you, checking your health, financial circumstances, character, etcetera. If it thinks you are suitable, the adoption panel will recommend you as a prospective adoptive parent.

The agency then matches you to a child. They tell you about the child, including details of health, personal history and background. You meet the child. The child is placed with you in your home. You are then regularly visited by the agency which makes reports about how things are getting on.

You can apply to the High Court, county court or magistrates' court for an adoption order after the child has lived with you for at least thirteen weeks. The child must be at least nineteen weeks old before you apply. The adoption agency provides the court with full reports on you, the child, and the whole situation. The court either:

● makes the adoption order;
● refuses to make an adoption order; or
● makes an 'interim' adoption order which gives you legal custody of the child for a probationary period of not more than two years. These orders are rare: they could be made in cases where it was not yet certain to the court that adoption was the best or only plan for the child.

If the court makes an adoption order you have full parental rights from that date, and are the child's parent in law. The child is registered in the Adopted Children Register, and an adoption certificate is made.

If the natural parents were involved in the adoption hearing, they can appeal the making of the adoption order.

If the court refuses to make an adoption order you can appeal to the Court of Appeal (from the High Court and county court) or to the family division of the High Court (from the magistrates' court). The child should be returned to the adoption agency within seven days of the order, or within a longer period of up to six weeks if the court orders this.

WHAT HAPPENS IF IT ALL BREAKS DOWN?

Although the law can make a legal relationship between parents and children in adoption, emotional bonds and ties can be made only by the people involved. If the child and the prospective parents cannot settle down together with love and tolerance, then the parents should have the strength to admit this as soon as possible.

Part of the skill of an adoption agency is to place children with the right people, but placements can still break down. If this happens before an adoption order is made, prospective adopters can ask the agency to take the child back, giving at least seven days' notice. The agency can remove the child from the prospective adopters on the same notice if it is not happy with the situation. This can be done at any time up until an adoption order is made, but if an application to adopt has already been filed, the agency must get the court's leave to remove the child.

If the relationship between the parents and child breaks down after an adoption order is made, then the normal law about such family disasters applies. The child can be taken into care; be put into voluntary care; be made a ward of court; be re-adopted by another family.

If the adopters were a married couple, on divorce or separation the court can make custody orders in favour of either of them.

Right to information

Adopted children have a right to copies of their original birth certificates once they are eighteen.

When an adoption order is made, it is registered in the Adopted Children Register. The details on the register are: the birth date of the child; the name and surname and sex of the child; name, surname and occupation of the adopters; and the date and place of the adoption order. Each adoption has an entry number, which is linked – secretly – to their original registration of birth.

An adopted person can apply to the Registrar-General for the information needed to find the original birth entry. He or she can be counselled if they want to be, and by the agency which placed them if they choose. Counselling is obligatory for people adopted before 12 November 1975 but voluntary for people adopted after that date.

Adopted children who want to find their natural parents can use the basic information on the register of their birth to try to trace them. The quickest method of doing this would be to get information from the original agency which placed them for adoption: but there is no legal requirement or practice that agencies need help on this at all. On the contrary, they preserve the confidentiality of the original parents and the privacy of the records.

INFORMATION UNDER EIGHTEEN

If someone does not know who their parents were, they cannot know who they might be related to. In order to avoid marriage to a relation an adopted person under eighteen who intends to get married can apply to the Registrar-General, giving his or her name, address and adoption details and the name and details of the person they wish to marry. The Registrar-General will say whether or not the couple are within the 'prohibited degrees of consanguinity'. The effect of these degrees of consanguinity is that a marriage to someone within them is void. They include sister, aunt, mother, grandmother and the male equivalents. People who knowingly have sexual relationships with close relations commit the offence of incest.

The regulations refer only to intended marriages. To be realistic, information should be given as of right to anyone under eighteen who is having or contemplating a sexual relationship. However, the applicant for the information does not have to 'prove' intended marriage or produce an engagement ring.

WHAT SHOULD ADOPTIVE PARENTS TELL THE CHILDREN?

The legal right to information is sparse. Whether or not the adopted person can trace and find their parents depends on luck and determination. How much the parent tells the child is up to them, but research has shown that even happily adopted children have a real need to know where they come from, who their parents were, and what the circumstances of their lives were.

Good social-work practice includes giving the child information about their original family, perhaps in the form of a family book with photographs and a family tree. Children who know they are adopted are likely to ask questions about why they were adopted, and what happened to their own family, and parents should know what it is best to tell them. It might be damaging for a child to be told the full facts of a tragic or cruel background at an early age – this has to be balanced against the child's need to know something of his or her background. Adoption societies and social workers can counsel the family about this.

In the end, the decision about what to tell the children depends on the adoptive family. In one case, a prospective adoptive mother who had brought the child up from an early age told the court that she absolutely refused to tell the child that she was not the natural mother. Although this was contrary to current social-work practice and held potential pain for the child, it did not affect the outcome and an adoption order was made.

PRIVACY AND CONFIDENTIALITY

Adoption hearings are heard privately, either in chambers or in a closed domestic court depending on the court that is used. 'Private' here means that only the people directly involved can go into court, and the press and public are not admitted. If a case is reported in law reports only initials are used and the privacy of the families and child is preserved.

Reports made to the court – for example, by the guardian ad litem – are confidential and seen by the judge and professionals only. They are not shown even to the applicants, as they contain confidential information about the child's natural family.

In some cases, the identity of the applicants can be kept secret from the child's own parents. If this is required, the case is given a serial number and all the documents the parents can see – for example, the statement of facts in cases where their consent is to be dispensed with – are worded so that the identity of the applicants is not disclosed. Note here that a parent is not asked to consent to an adoption by any particular person but to adoption generally. The parent has no right to 'vet' or approve of the person who will care for the child, which is the responsibility of the agency and ultimately of the court.

Where the natural parents are involved at the actual adoption stage – that is, where they do not agree to the adoption – the two families do not slug it out in court or cross-examine each other as is done in disputed custody cases between parents. There are two issues: the first to be dealt with is whether or not the natural parents' consent should be dispensed with; if it is decided it should be, the court then deals with the second issue – the suitability of the prospective adoptive parents. It is not a contest between opposing parents.

The confidentiality of the hearing and adoption process is preserved for ever, and the adopted child is not entitled to get any adoption records disclosed to them under the Access to Personal Files Act 1987, which gives some right to see social work and health records.

The Adopters

Married Couples

Only one application can be made to adopt a child. Married couples make a single joint application. Both husband and wife must be over twenty-one, with at least one of them domiciled in the UK, Channel Islands or Isle of Man.

The Children Act 1989 will introduce a lower age limit of eighteen if the eighteen-year-old is either the father or mother of the child who is to be adopted; or his or her spouse is twenty-one; and they are married.

'Domiciled' means having the UK as one's home, either through choosing to live there permanently or through marrying someone who does. Domicile is a difficult legal concept, but in practical terms problems would arise only if the applicants to adoption had homes in more than one country and had decided not to live under UK law or were of foreign nationality.

Two people living together cannot make a single joint application, nor can each make a separate application. Cohabitees or friends living together cannot therefore adopt a child together.

Single Applicants

Single people can apply to adopt if they are over twenty-one, domiciled in the UK as above, and either not married or if married able to satisfy the court that the spouse cannot be found or that they have separated and this is likely to be permanent or that the spouse is incapable through mental or physical ill-health of making an application.

These restrictions would prevent applications to adopt where one partner wants a child and the other does not, a situation unlikely to benefit a child. A single person can apply to adopt a child of either sex. Being divorced counts as 'not married'.

Blood Relatives

Children can be adopted by their relatives, and by their own natural parents. Adoptions by near relatives are still possible but rather frowned upon – adoption for example by an aunt or grandmother can mask the real family relationships, and be either confusing or unnecessary for a child. As adoption must actively promote or safeguard the child's welfare the court would have to be convinced that having a grandmother as a legal parent is in the child's interest and does not merely muddy the waters. There are other orders that can give a secure relationship between the child and the adult who looks after him or her, for example a custodianship order which under the present law the court can make if it decides not to make an adoption order. Custodianship orders will be abolished by the Children Act 1989 which introduces 'residence orders' (where children live with the person named in the order) and 'parental responsibility' orders. There seems to be no reason why in future the court could not give a relative parental responsibility and make a residence order instead of an adoption order.

Adoption by Parents

There is of course no need for married parents to adopt their own child.

Although it might seem unnecessary for a parent to adopt a non-marital child there could be advantages;

- a 'putative' father could adopt to give himself full parental rights;
- a natural mother could adopt to legitimize her child.

The courts have spoken warmly of legitimation being one of the advantages of adoption. However, as adoption by one parent cancels out the parental rights of the other, the courts have to be convinced that this is either a desirable consequence of the adoption, or cannot be helped.

The rule therefore is that when a parent applies to adopt his or her own child, the court must be convinced that the other parent is either dead, cannot be found or there is some other reason that justifies their legal relationship with the child being extinguished.

Reasons to justify cancelling parental rights should be quite strong – for example, that the other parent has seriously ill-treated or abandoned the child. However, if cancelling out the other parent's rights is the only or main reason for trying to adopt the child, the matter could be better dealt with by other orders (for example, a no access order in matrimonial proceedings under the present law or a prohibited steps order under the new law).

Step-parent Adoptions

When legal adoption was first introduced into English law, it was not intended to help step-parents but became widely used by them. Step-families applied personally in the magistrates' courts to give the child and step-parent a new legal status, to enable the child's surname to be changed to the step-father's, and to give emotional or psychological security to the new family.

Parliament did not think this was particularly desirable, and the law now states that where a parent and a step-parent apply to adopt a child, the court should dismiss the application if it thinks the matter would be better dealt with by an order for joint custody made in matrimonial proceedings. Under the section they suggest should be used (s42 of the Matrimonial Causes Act 1973) step-parents can apply for a custody order, sharing this jointly with the parent they married. This can benefit a step-parent only in cases where the parents of the step-child were married and divorced, and the parent with whom the step-parent now lives has custody of the child.

The reasoning behind this is that it might not be good for a child to lose all contact with his or her biological father or mother, even where they are happily settled in a new family with one of their parents and the new partner.

The rule that the court should dismiss an adoption application by a step-parent if it considers the matter would be better dealt with elsewhere is not changed by the Children Act 1989. Instead of step-parents applying for a joint custody order in divorce, they would apply for a residence order with the consent of their spouse.

Although the court must consider the alternatives to adoption, it can still make adoption orders in favour of step-parents only where it is obvious the child will not suffer from losing a parent, and there are tangible benefits to the child from the adoption.

The Court of Appeal, when hearing the first case of step-parent adoption after the 1975 Act came in, found that although *both* parents and the step-parent were agreed on adoption, making an adoption order would provide little for the children that they did not have already in their new family. The order was not made.

This was a fairly strict interpretation of the Act: there are other interpretations of it, including a recognition that even where the legal ties have been cut, emotional ties can continue if the parents and step-parent are prepared to allow this. For example, there is no bar to a step-father and a mother adopting a child while encouraging or allowing the father to keep in touch. The court can give access to the natural parent as a condition of the adoption.

As always with family cases, the court's decision depends on the facts of each case and the characters and personalities of the people involved.

Non-agency Placements or 'Private' Adoptions

There is no such thing as a completely private adoption, and there are strict rules on who can place children for adoption. Generally, it is a criminal offence to arrange an adoption unless it is done by an adoption agency, a relative of the child or following a High Court order. In other words, although families can arrange among themselves to look after and adopt a child of that family, no one else can. If X arranges with Y to adopt Y's child, who is no relation, then this is against the law.

Where a family member – including a parent or step-parent – wants to adopt a child, the social services must be closely involved to check the child's interests. The rules are that where the applicant is a parent, step-parent or relative of the child, an adoption order cannot be made unless the child is at least nineteen weeks old by the time the order is made and has lived with the applicant for the past thirteen weeks, and the local authority have been given 'sufficient opportunities' to see the child at home with the applicants. The local authority report on the home and family to the court, which must as with any other adoption be satisfied that the applicants are suitable.

Before the family adopters even apply to adopt they must tell the social services department that they intend to adopt the child, giving three months' notice. The local authority then has duties towards the child, who becomes 'a protected child'. The local authority must visit at home and check the home environment and the suitability of the potential adopters; and they must make a report to the court about this.

When a child becomes protected, the local authority have real powers to intervene if they do not like what they see. They can insist on getting entry to the home to see the child (it is a criminal offence not to let them in); they can remove the child from the home and get a place of safety order from the court; or they can take the child into care.

Children are protected in this way until an adoption order or other order settling his or her future is made or the application to adopt is withdrawn or the child becomes eighteen.

When a child is placed for adoption by an agency the applicants are checked and vetted thoroughly before any child is allowed near them, and the agency has power to remove the child the instant it becomes worried about suitability. It is only right that children placed 'privately' should have the same protection.

The law on consent is the same: the parents of the child must either have agreed to the adoption, or have had their consent dispensed with on the usual grounds. With family adoptions, it might well be that the parent is dead, so consent would not apply. With family adoptions, there must still be a reporting officer to deal with agreement – and a guardian ad litem for the child where there is a dispute.

It is possible that a child could be formally 'placed' with relatives by the adoption agency, where for example the child had been removed from the natural parents and the relatives had stepped in to help and offered to be the prospective adoptive parents instead of strangers. In such a case, the rules for time etcetera would be the same.

Overseas Adoptions

An increasing number of couples appear to be turning overseas for adoptive children, and there is now an organization which gives assistance and advice to those who wish to do this.

This is a politically and ethically complex area, partly because of the debate about whether or not it is moral to adopt children from a poor country and bring them up in the West, and partly because adoption by a British citizen gives British nationality to a child from another country. Some countries forbid international adoptions and others appear to welcome it. In those where it is welcomed or at least possible, the child is generally adopted by the UK family under the law of that country and then brought into the UK by the new family.

As countries have different adoption rules and laws, there can sometimes be conflict where there is an overseas adoption. Britain recognizes the overseas adoptions of children from some Commonwealth countries and UK-dependent territories, and some other territories, e.g. France, Austria, USA. The full list is found in Adoption (Designation of Overseas Adoptions) Order 1973, SI 1973 No. 19.

This order does not recognize overseas adoptions from South America, India, Pakistan or Bangladesh, and British citizens who adopt children from those countries will have to adopt them again under British law to have their parental rights recognized in Britain.

ADOPTION AND NATIONALITY

Adoption gives British citizenship to a child if one or both of the applicants – mother or father – are citizens themselves. However, no adoption abroad, even if recognized by Britain, can give a child British nationality which is automatically conferred by an adoption order made in Britain. This affects children adopted abroad since 1983 when the British Nationality Act came into force.

However, the Home Office can register as British citizens children brought in after any overseas adoption. This is not a right but a discretionary power. Applications to be registered as a British citizen are made after entry to the UK.

ADOPTION AND IMMIGRATION

The adoptive parents will have to get 'entry clearance' for the child. This should be done before the child leaves the country of origin, but with some countries it can be done at the port of entry in the UK.

The clearance is for leave to enter and remain for a set period, generally six months, which can be extended. If it has to be extended, the adoptive parent must apply for an extension *before* six months are up.

The Home Office deals with entry clearance, either on the spot or after making inquiries. It can contact the local authority of the area where the potential adoptive parents live, and ask them to investigate whether adoption would be in the child's best interests, and whether or not there is an obvious reason why an order should not be made.

How easily the clearance is given depends on the circumstances. It seems that some adoptive parents have no trouble and are barely asked questions at all; but for others, the task is impossible. Some press reports – anecdotal but interesting none the less – found that immigration officers were likely to wave white, middle-class couples through and give entry clearance without difficulty. Asian families seeking to bring in a child from the Indian subcontinent are not likely to be treated with such understanding, however.

ADOPTION HERE

Once the child is in the country, the adoptive parents must notify the social services, giving three months' notice as for family adoptions. From this point the child becomes a protected child, as above. The local authority must investigate and report to the court.

The adopters must live with the child for twelve months before an adoption order can be made; the shorter period of nineteen weeks applies only to agency placements, relatives' adoptions and placements following a High Court order.

The adoption process is much the same as for ordinary adoptions except that consent is shown by the adoption order from the child's country of origin, with evidence about the law in the country of origin being given to the court. The High Court should be used as the child will get the adoptive parents' nationality on adoption, and become British. This matter must be dealt with at a high level.

The court can refuse to make an adoption order altogether unless it is convinced that the child *could not* have been looked after by his or her own parents. This was decided in a case where an Asian family wanted to adopt the child of close relatives. The natural parents were alive and consented to the adoption. The court found that, although in bad circumstances, they were capable of bringing up the child.

This discriminates seriously against adoptive parents of children from overseas, as there is no requirement in ordinary adoptions that the parents must be too poor, too sick or too incompetent to care for the child.

The question of nationality is also dealt with at the adoption hearing, as the court can refuse to make an adoption order where they consider the only point of the application was to give citizenship. A cynical interpretation of this is that the immigration laws are racist, and operate unfairly against non-white applicants.

THE LEGALITY OF OVERSEAS ADOPTIONS

It is an offence to make arrangements for adoption unless it is done either through an agency or by relatives of the child. Parents who find their children overseas come into neither of these categories, but as the arrangements were not made in the UK they do not commit an offence under English law.

Adoptions by Overseas Applicants

It is against the law to take children who are British subjects out of the country to be adopted under the laws of another country, unless that adoption is to be by a parent, guardian or other relative. The penalty for this is a fine or imprisonment up to three months.

To avoid breaking the law, people who want to take children out of the UK to adopt them elsewhere can apply beforehand to the court for a provisional adoption order which gives them parental rights. The rules and procedure for this are broadly similar to ordinary adoption applications.

The court must be satisfied that the applicants intend to adopt the child under the laws of their own country. The child must be at least thirty-two weeks old, and have lived with the applicants for the twenty-six weeks before the application is made.

Local authorities are allowed to arrange for children in their care to emigrate but this must be approved by the Secretary of State.

'CONVENTION' ADOPTION ORDERS

The Hague Convention on Adoption is an effort to rationalize the adoption laws of different countries and make the recognition of adoption less complex. At the moment only the UK, Switzerland and Austria have ratified the convention, so it applies only to adoptions by nationals of those countries.

Adoptions and Money

People are not allowed to buy children. When anyone applies to adopt a child, the court will not make an adoption order unless satisfied that no money has been exchanged and that no one has been paid to arrange the adoption, to give their consent or to hand the child over to the adoptive parents.

Some payments are lawful – but only if made to or by a properly authorized adoption agency, for reasonably incurred expenses. Payments made between the members of a family who arrange a private placement for adoption are not exempted, and people should be careful that they make no agreement to pay money in connection with the proposed adoption.

Parents who adopt a child overseas must also be aware of this part of the law. When the court is asked to make an adoption order on a child from overseas, it must still investigate the financial aspects which took place abroad. Medical and legal expenses paid to a properly authorized person abroad, for example a lawyer, would be permitted, but payments made directly to a mother would be prohibited.

Custodianship

Custodianship orders were introduced into law by the Children Act 1975, but the relevant sections came into force only in 1983. These orders will have a short life, as the entire Children Act will be repealed by the Children Act 1989.

A custodianship order gives the legal custody of a child to the person in whose favour it is made. The custody can be shared with another person. These orders give a legal relationship with the child to the person with whom the child is actually living at the time the order is made. They do not change the fact of where the child is physically, and no application can even be made to court unless the child has lived with the applicant for at least three months.

Relatives, step-parents and anyone with whom the child is living can apply for this order. Natural parents cannot apply.

Custodianship orders can be made, under the present law, instead of adoption orders in some circumstances. This is done where the court does not feel that adoption is the best course to promote and safeguard the welfare of the child, perhaps because the child's links with the natural family should not be broken.

Relatives and step-parents can apply if the child has lived with them for the three months before the application and if the person who has legal custody of the child consents to the application being made. Anyone else may apply if the child has lived with them for at least twelve months, including the three months immediately before the application, and they have the consent of the person who has legal custody of the child.

Where the applicant does *not* have consent, they must have lived with the child for at least three years, including the three months immediately before the application was made. If the person who should give consent cannot be found, consent can be dispensed with. Unlike adoption, this is the only ground for dispensing with consent.

These provisions were useful for people who lived with the child as part of their family, without any legal rights to keep them, for example in a private fostering arrangement, or as local authority foster parents. Getting a custodianship order could give the child a measure of security with the de facto parent.

There are equivalents to custodianship orders under the Children Act 1989. Put simply, the courts can give security to people who live with children even if they are neither parents nor guardians. For a description of this, see Chapter 1.

Chapter 3

Other People's Care of Your Child

Child-care provision for the under-fives is piecemeal, better in some localities than in others and, for the vast majority of children, is organized and paid for privately. Finding a good and happy situation for a child whose parent works is a mixture of luck and judgment and entails an endless juggling of time and money. Under-fives provision ranges from state-run nurseries to full-time, live-in nannies, taking in childminders, extended families and parents doing each other favours. The average parent has to find and pay for a suitable person to look after the child, and there is a limited choice.

Finding a good system depends on what is available in your area, and what you can afford. Childminders are listed by the social services as are private nurseries which are covered by the same legislation. State nurseries can be found through the social services: places there are at a premium and priority is given to children with social needs, for example either those who are at risk in some way or the children of single parents. Nursery classes and nursery schools run by the local education authority are also in short supply in some areas and may give priority to children in social need. You can get details from the council about these. Finding private child-care – nannies, au pairs, mother's helps, babysitters – is up to you, either by advertising in local papers and the nanny's bible, *The Lady*; or by approaching a specialist employment agency. Agencies charge fees to the employer, but the best ones should provide competent staff who have been vetted and interviewed by the agency before they are sent to you.

Childminders

The current law on childminding is found in the Nurseries and Childminders Regulation Act 1948 which contains the bare bones of registration and responsibility. But as from January 1991 the old Act will be replaced entirely and replaced by new provisions in the Children Act 1989.

The new law has not made sweeping changes to childminding, but has tightened up and clarified the position. Where the law makes significant changes this is made clear in the paragraphs below. Both the old and new Acts provide for:

- registers of childminders to be kept by the social services
- applications by potential childminders to be put on the register
- checks to be made by the social services before granting an application
- cancellation of a childminder's authority to look after children
- inspections to be made by the social services
- penalties for looking after children without being registered.

The new definition of a childminder is a person who looks after one or more children under the age of eight to whom s/he is not closely related; s/he spends more than two hours a day doing this for reward. Under the old law a childminder looked after children under school age who were not close relations in her/his own home for reward for more than two hours a day.

The changes have made one important difference. Under the old law, there was little to stop a childminder looking after unlimited numbers of children after they got out of school, which might prevent proper care of the younger children or babies in her/his care all day. Now, children under eight have to be included in the calculations made by the social services in deciding how many children the minder can lawfully care for.

Nannies and nanny sharing were not mentioned in the old Act, but are specifically excluded from the new. A nanny is someone who looks after a child or children wholly or mainly in the child's own home, or if she has two employers in either home. Nannies therefore do not need to be registered or have any dealings with the social services.

Child-care arrangements with other parents or friends, even where some payment is made, do not come under the Act as long as the friend or parent does not spend more than two hours a day looking after unrelated children for reward.

Foster parents, parents and people with parental responsibility for a child are also not childminders. A member of a family is 'closely related' to a child if they are a grandparent, brother, sister, uncle or aunt by blood or marriage, or a step-parent. That is, you can lawfully pay granny for looking after your child without her having to register as a childminder.

Registration

The social services must keep a register of all childminders in their area. The register is open to inspection by members of the public at all reasonable times – under the new law it can be held on computer.

Registration makes the difference between lawful and unlawful childminding. Unlawful childminders can be prosecuted and fined. However, registration is no guarantee of quality. 'Unlawful' childminders can provide lively, stimulating and safe care for children where registered minders do not. But apart from avoiding prosecution, registration does have advantages for the minder, parent and, one hopes, the child.

In order to be registered, the childminder's premises have to be checked for safety and suitability by the social services who also screen the minder, any employees and immediate family. The social services, through their childminding officers, provide help for the minder, putting her/him in touch with playgroups, other minders and toy libraries. The minders' own organization has been crucial in raising the image of childminding from Dickensian-type 'baby-farming' to a proper system of child-care.

Social services can refuse an application for registration if they are satisfied that the place where the children would be looked after is not fit for children – 'not fit' here really means not adequate, rather than not conforming to ideal nursery-type conditions. Or they may decide that the potential minder is not fit to be in the proximity of young children (i.e under eight according to the new law; under school age according to the old).

The social services will inspect the premises, and either refuse an application outright because of unsuitability, or make conditions for improvement. Improvements could be minor, for example getting fire screens or making play equipment safe.

Under the old law, childminders had to include in their application details about whether or not they, their employees if any, and immediate members of their family aged over sixteen had had orders made against them which effectively barred them from looking after young children. For example, certain criminal convictions, orders forbidding them to foster children, and orders arising from neglect or ill-treatment of a child. The new law continues this type of screening, but the detailed regulations are not yet available – it is highly likely they will be if anything stricter than the old regulations. The local authority can refuse an application on this information. If a childminder does not disclose information which should be added to the application, and this is discovered, the social services can cancel the registration and remove the authority to look after young children.

As well as this 'self-screening' process, the social services have the power to check whether the minder or adult members of the family who will have contact with the children have criminal records.

Childminders are registered for a fixed number of children, for example one baby and two toddlers. In fixing the number of children, the social services take account of how many other children there are likely to be in the house: the minder's own young children for example, or members of an extended family.

Minders have to keep records of the name and addresses of the children they look after, and details of people they have living in the house or helping with child-care. These records must be shown to the social services and any changes notified to them.

The social services can fix requirements for registered minders: for example that the house is properly and safely maintained or that necessary repairs are made. They can change or vary these if they feel the need. They have the power to visit the minder at home and inspect the premises. They must visit at a 'reasonable time', such as during the day when children are there rather than barging in at midnight. When they visit, they can inspect the children, the records kept by the minder, and obviously the house itself. If anyone obstructs the social services' visits, they can be prosecuted for obstruction and fined.

Under the new Act, the social services must visit childminders once a year.

CANCELLATION OF REGISTRATION AND PENALTIES FOR UNLAWFUL
CHILDMINDING

Under both the old and new Acts, the social services can cancel a minder's registration by giving written notice.

The social services can do this under present law if the childminder has failed to comply with their conditions or requirements made on registration, or that should have been made when he or she was registered. This would cover the situation where the house was unsafe, or the children were not properly fed, or proper records were not kept.

The new law also entitles the social services to cancel registration if requirements and conditions are not met or broken, as well as entitling them to two general powers: they will be able to cancel registration where they would be justified in refusing to register the childminder (for example, they discover something about the minder or the house which would have stopped them registering in the first place); and they can cancel registration if the care provided by the minder for a child is 'seriously inadequate having regard to the needs of that child'.

The new Act provides a further emergency provision. The social services can apply to court for an order cancelling registration in an emergency without notice to the childminder. The court can cancel the registration only if they consider that a child in the minder's care is suffering or likely to suffer significant harm. This is the same test that will be used to decide whether or not children should be taken into local authority care.

Childminders have a right of appeal to the social services against written notice. If court proceedings are used, they can appeal within those.

People who mind children without being registered, or after their registration has been cancelled, face criminal proceedings. Parents who use unregistered minders do not commit a criminal offence.

The Benefits of Childminders

These rules and regulations about childminding cater, as they must, for worst-case scenarios, and could give an entirely misleading impression of this sort of child-care.

The advantages of childminders for parents and children are legion. The children are looked after in a family, with companionship, in the minder's own home. They can feel part of another family as well as their own, looked after locally in a stable environment with continuity of care – childminders are more likely to stick around than nannies or au pairs. Where the childminder has an active involvement in local play centres, the child can get the best of both worlds: the fun of playgroup and the cosiness of a family. Childminders with their knowledge and experience of children can also actively help parents.

Contracts

Childminders are not employees of the parents nor are they employed by the social services. They are, however, in a contractual relationship with parents – they provide child-care in return for payment. It makes sense for both parties to have a simple written contract setting out the main terms of the relationship. The social services department can provide childminders with simple form contracts. Otherwise, the minder and parent can agree a basic contract setting out:

- the hours of child-care
- the fees paid
- the arrangements about food (is it to be brought by the parents or provided by the childminder?)
- conditions about collection and delivery of the child by the parents
- rates charged for 'overtime' if the parents are late
- period of notice for ending the arrangement, on both sides
- any retainers paid during holidays, etc.

Clarity is what matters here. The contract is not a legal weapon to be used in court if the relationship breaks down in acrimony but a sensible way of sorting out rights and obligations to prevent dispute.

Responsible parents should ensure that the childminder knows how to contact them wherever they are in case of accident or illness, and has all relevant medical details including allergies to drugs and details of the child's GP.

Childminders choose and set their own rates, which traditionally tend to be low. They are self-employed and responsible for their own tax and insurance payments. Parents cannot get tax relief on child-care costs.

There have been cases of parents suing childminders for a child's injuries caused by their negligence or lack of care. The only possible point in doing this is if the childminder can pay compensation for a child through insurance. Some minders are insured for this – ask what the position is or speak to the social services.

Private Nurseries

These are controlled by the same Acts as childminders, and are subject to the same type of screening process, which covers the premises and employees. Lists of registered nurseries are kept by the social services in the same way. Ask the child-care advisers at the social services for advice, and ask for recommendations from your friends, health visitors or any other professional or experienced parent. Like childminders, some nurseries are better than others and you should make sure you are allowed, and preferably encouraged, to visit the nursery with your child before choosing, to see all areas where the children go, and that all your questions are properly answered.

Nannies

Nannies are employees of the parents. They look after the child or children in their home with agreed conditions, hours and wages. Nannies are – or ought to be – entitled to the same employment conditions as other employed workers:

- a written statement of the terms and conditions of their employment, given within thirteen weeks of starting work
- observance of the law on sexual and racial discrimination
- national insurance (NI) contributions paid by the employer
- PAYE deductions
- statutory sick pay (SSP) paid by the employer
- after one year's continuous employment, protection from being sacked without notice.

Where the nannies are part of a large enough domestic staff and qualify by length of service (two years), they should get maternity leave and unfair dismissal protection.

That is the theory. The specific practical position is as follows.

Written Statement of Terms and Conditions

Under the Employment Protection (Consolidated) Act 1978 all employers, regardless of how many other people they employ, must provide an employee with a written statement of the terms of their employment. This should be given within thirteen weeks of the job starting. It must contain:

- names of both parties
- job title
- date work started and expected length of employment
- hours of work
- how much money, when and how it is to be paid
- periods of notice on both sides
- what the employee can be sacked for, and disciplinary procedures
- pension rules
- 'receipt' by employee of this document.

The conditions of work thus laid down can be changed at any time by agreement.

The statement is meant to give some degree of protection to an employee: without it, an employee could be uncertain of his or her exact role or be in a poor position to argue with an employer who unilaterally changed the terms of their employment. In industry, employment statements are used to show what the agreed position was in disputes and unfair dismissal cases. Practically speaking, such a document is hardly an industrial weapon for a nanny who is not protected by the unfair dismissal legislation unless she is part of a staff of more than ten employees. It is, though, a legal requirement *and* a useful basis for a contract between the parties.

Employers do not have to pay pensions; nor have a settled disciplinary procedure; nor do they have to write down the absolute nitty-gritty of the nanny's work. (An exhaustive list of what nannies or parents do for children would take hours to write: 'child-care' would be enough.)

Sexual and Racial Discrimination

Until the Sex Discrimination Act 1986 private households and employers of less than five people were exempted from sexual discrimination legislation. This exemption was removed by the 1986 Act – but a new 'Genuine Occupational Qualification' (GOC) was introduced for private households. A GOC is an allowance to choose the sex of the employee you want because the gender is in some way vital to the job; e.g. male models, female rather than male actors to play Cleopatra, etc.

This allows for sexual discrimination in private households (e.g. advertising for or choosing a female rather than male nanny) where there could be 'reasonable objection to someone of the other sex having the degree of physical or social contact with a person living in the home, or the knowledge of intimate details of a person's life'. As nannies are up to their necks in intimate details of the family and social contact with small children it is therefore perfectly proper to specify the sex you want.

Racial discrimination, while repugnant wherever it occurs, is not unlawful under the Race Relations Act 1976 for sifting through applicants for a job in a private household. This exemption does not cover victimization on the grounds of race once someone has been employed.

National Insurance and PAYE

An employee – in tax terms – is anyone who works in Great Britain with earnings which should be charged to schedule E. Schedule E covers people working under a contract of service, which need not be written but spoken or implied. In other words, it covers practically everyone except the genuinely self-employed who hire themselves out on a freelance basis under a contract *for* services.

Nannies can be self-employed, running themselves as small businesses, perhaps working for several employers and taking responsibility for their own tax, self-employed NI contributions, and claiming expenses against tax. This is unlikely: if you have a nanny you are almost certainly an employer, she is an employee, and you have responsibilities to operate a PAYE system with deductions.

Failure to deduct tax and national insurance contributions is an offence committed by the employer. Failing to make NI contributions can open the nanny to penalties for not doing so and leave her with either no or a reduced rate of benefits if she becomes unemployed, sick or pensionable.

HOW IS IT DONE?

Working out NI contributions and deductions for tax can be complicated and time-consuming until you get the hang of it. The first requirement is a relationship with your local tax office which should advise you; a supply of explanatory leaflets and the forms you will need to operate the system.

When you start employing someone, get in touch with the local tax office and fix an appointment with an officer for general and specific advice. It is after all in their interest to guide you, as you are collecting tax and NI contributions for them.

National insurance contributions are made up of two parts: the employer's contribution, an 'extra' sum paid by the employer on top of wages paid to the employee; and the employee's contribution, deducted by the employer from the wages paid. There is a lower earnings limit below which NI contributions do not have to be paid either by the employee or the employer. As a guide, this is currently £41 per week. Contributions must be paid by employee and employer on wages over this limit, and paid on the whole amount even if it just scrapes past: e.g. gross pay of £45 per week should have contributions made on the whole amount, not just the 'extra' £4.

Employer's and employee's NI contributions are worked out as a percentage of the gross wages paid: i.e. the amount before income tax is deducted. Gross pay includes bonuses, subs or advances on salary and travelling expenses to work.

The contribution rate can vary with each financial year. It also goes up in steps or bands as the salary increases, with a larger percentage of the whole salary having to be deducted on larger salaries.

NI contributions are due on the first date when wages over the lower earnings limit are paid. Start deducting and setting aside the money for a quarterly payment from the first payment of salary to the nanny.

You will need:

- the nanny's national insurance number (if she does not have one, because this is her first job, or has forgotten it, then she should apply to the local social security office taking proof of her identity and date of birth.)
- *Employer's Guide to N.I. Contributions* (Ref. NP15) available from the tax office
- the latest leaflet giving lower earnings limits, contribution rates, and statutory sick pay and maternity pay rates (currently this is leaflet NI208 but ask for the most recent one)
- contribution tables (*Tables for Employees*, not contracted out Form CF391) – see below
- deduction working sheets – see below
- payslips (booklet P30 BC [Z]) to record the sums you send to the Collector of Taxes.

There are two methods of calculating what contributions are owed: from tables or a more exact percentage system. The most commonly used and easiest are contribution tables. New tables are published when the rates change, showing the period when they should be used. Make sure you have got the most up-to-date set. If NI contributions are underpaid because the wrong rates are applied, you will have to make up the difference.

The deduction working sheet is a record of what contributions have been deducted and made; the long form is P11 87 with columns for recording earnings, contributions, sick pay, statutory maternity pay, totals and income tax payable. Leaflet P8, *Deductions Guide*, gives instructions on how to complete the sheets.

At the end of each income tax month, or quarterly if this is agreed with the tax office, you should send the following to the Collector of Taxes:

- payslip, showing details of the payments
- employee's contributions
- your contributions
- any PAYE deducted.

The financial year begins on 6 April and ends on 5 April: income tax months follow this, so the end of one month is the 5th of the next.

At the end of each year complete an end of year return (Form P14) and send this with the completed deduction sheets to the Collector of Taxes. Complete a P60 form (annual certificate of pay and tax) for the employee showing the total deductions made on salary over the year.

Tax is paid on salary over the personal allowance. The tax office should tell you what tax-free sum your employee is allowed, which depends on her earnings during the current tax year; and her coding, which determines what rate of tax she should pay. Tax codes are available for the PAYE system, and should be obtained from the local office.

Statutory Sick Pay (SSP)

It is the employer's responsibility to pay sick pay directly to the employee. The maximum period this is paid for is twenty-eight weeks' absence in any one period of sickness. You can agree how many weeks of sick pay go with the job when you hire the nanny: if she is just off work for a day or two with minor illnesses, then it is obviously far less complicated just to pay her wages as normal. Paying SSP is more economic for the employer if the nanny is unwell for a long period, as the employer can recoup SSP from the NI contributions made. If paying SSP, contributions have to be paid on the gross amount of sick pay just as with salary. The employer can recoup sick pay, and her NI contributions paid on it, from the quarterly or monthly amount sent to the Collector of Taxes. If there are not enough NI contributions to repay you in one month, you can recoup it from the next; if that does not cover it, apply in writing to the Collector of Taxes for repayment of the whole amount of SSP and your employer's contributions on it. Leaflet NI227 (*Employer's Guide to Statutory Sick Pay*) and SSP555 *Rates and Notes* available from the local social security office give information about how this is done.

In the real world of nannies and employers, a nanny who cannot work for long periods because of illness is more likely to be asked to leave than to be paid SSP. When employees have employment protection, being sacked either because they have exhausted their sickness entitlement or are using it to the full would be unreasonable, and could fuel an unfair dismissal claim. Nannies are not protected by unfair dismissal legislation unless they are part of a staff of over ten: and would have no recourse against an employer who asked them to leave because of illness.

Dismissal

Employment legislation, as has been seen, does not really impinge on the normal nanny–employer relationship, but wrongful dismissal could apply.

A dismissal is wrongful if it is without notice or without payment in lieu of notice. Employees get this protection after fifty-two weeks' continuous employment. If an employee is sacked without notice, a successful wrongful dismissal action would result in the employer having to pay the wages due for the period of notice. The period of notice is worked out by reference to the period wages are paid for – by the month or by the week. Within a year, a nanny can be sacked without any notice period at all.

Contracts between nanny and employer, like contracts between parent and childminder, are more aide memoires to them both than weapons in an employment war. It makes sense to be clear about what the nanny's duties, hours, wages, holiday entitlement and conditions are. It can also prevent problems in future if you set out the bad news as well: what would make you sack her instantly, what kind of behaviour would lead to being warned you might sack her, what period of notice you will give her, and the period of notice she will give you when she decides to leave. Any contract should be clear, unambiguous and in writing, with each of you keeping a copy.

Accidents

Make sure that all insurance policies you have cover the nanny. Car insurance should be checked – in particular that there is not an age restriction on your policy. Ask to see the nanny's licence if she is to drive. A provisional driving licence will not do and penalty points on a licence will increase your premium on the policy.

Check that house contents insurance covers the nanny's possessions as well, to replacement value if destroyed, and that you are properly covered by insurance against accidents caused by negligence. As a lawful visitor to your house, she should be protected. (See also Chapter 12.)

Poll Tax

Anyone living in your house who is aged over eighteen and not a student or otherwise exempted is responsible for paying poll tax. You do not have a legal liability to pay the poll tax for an employee if she does not, but as a householder you do have responsibility to fill in the community charge form correctly.

Au Pairs

Au pairs are foreign girls and young women who live in and do a maximum of five hours' work a day in return for board and lodging, pocket money and the chance to learn English.

Under the immigration rules which control who is allowed to come into Britain and for how long, unmarried female au pairs from certain countries between the ages of seventeen and twenty-seven can come for a maximum period of two years. They have to be female – the exemptions from immigration control do not apply to males. They do not need work permits and are given leave to enter the UK under the au pair arrangements conceded by the Home Office. These arrangements cover young women from the following countries: Andorra, Austria, Belgium, Cyprus, Denmark, Finland, France, Germany, Greece, Iceland, Italy, Liechtenstein, Luxemburg, Malta, Monaco, the Netherlands, Norway, Portugal, San Marino, Spain, Sweden, Switzerland, Turkey and Yugoslavia.

Several of these countries are full members of the EC. EC citizens are allowed to live within other member states in any event, and can enter for up to six months without a problem. Note here that although Spain and Greece are now in the EC they are not full member states until 1993 and until then Spanish and Greek au pairs will continue to be treated under the au pair arrangements and not the comparative freedom of EC arrangements.

Women from non-EC countries will need confirmation that they are coming here to work for you as an au pair. If you use an agency to find an au pair they should advise you what is required and smooth the girl's entry through immigration by giving her a full and detailed letter of why she is coming here and for how long.

Au pairs are allowed to stay for a maximum of two years – this can be all in one go, or separate stints which are added together. Leave to enter is generally given for six months and extensions can be applied for once they are here, up to the two-year limit. Extensions must be applied for before the first six months is up. After six months non-EC au pairs turn into 'aliens' and have to register as such with the Special Aliens Registration Office at 10 Lamb's Conduit Street, London WC1. The fee for registration is £27. If they do not register, and are discovered, they can be removed from the UK.

There are strict rules about non-EC nationals working in Britain – but au pair duties as defined by the Home Office are 'light housework' and do not count as employment for this purpose.

EC au pairs should be given entry for six months automatically. If they want to stay for longer, they can apply for residence permits by applying to the Home Office *before* the original six months expires. They should send their passport and a form EC1 published by the Department of Employment.

There is no reason why male EC nationals should not work with children in the UK – they would though not be official 'au pairs' and would have to enter under the EC provisions.

Citizens of the Commonwealth are, technically, allowed into Britain to work as part of a tour to the mother country if they are aged between seventeen and twenty-seven, come for a maximum of two years and originate from Canada, New Zealand or Australia (which have working schemes set up). They will need to apply for a working holiday visa in their own countries.

Citizens of other countries need work permits before getting leave to enter the UK and work here. Without Home Office permission to work, anyone who comes to the UK on a limited visa (for example on holiday, or as a student) who then takes up employment is in breach of their terms of entry and illegal. The penalties for discovery involve being taken into custody by immigration officials and deportation to the country of origin.

Tax and National Insurance

Au pairs – who are not officially 'employed' – do not need to pay tax or NIC and neither do you on their behalf.

EC and Commonwealth nationals who work full- or part-time do, technically, need to pay tax and national insurance. If they are here for short periods their wages might be less than the annual personal allowance and would therefore be 'tax-free', but they are still liable to pay NI contributions on earnings over the earnings limit current for the tax year in which they are employed.

If you are employing someone who under immigration rules is not allowed to work here, then attempting to pay tax and NI on her behalf would be equivalent to trying to get a minor into an over eighteen film at half price.

Babysitters

The law on babysitters is sketchy to say the least. There is no minimum age for babysitters as such but note:

● leaving unguarded fires where there are children under fourteen who suffer injury as a result is an offence
● adults have responsibilities not to neglect children in their charge: a babysitter in your house at your request who is a minor could be in your charge
● the restrictions on employment of minors (see Chapter 5) – obviously, a few hours' evening babysitting is not 'employment' as such but anything longer or more formal can be
● leaving a child alone is not an offence on its own – but if as a result of this the child suffers, then abandoning her would be straightforward evidence of neglect.

As with any lawful visitor to your home you have liability to the babysitter for injuries caused by your negligence. And of course you continue to have full responsibility for your own child — selecting a patently bad babysitter who neglects or ill-treats the child while you are out could again be a sign of your direct neglect.

Chapter 4

Education

'No person shall be denied the right to education.'
Article 2, 1st Protocol to the European Convention on Human Rights.

Education is a duty as well as a right, and is compulsory for children aged between five and sixteen. It is the parents who have the duty to provide education for their children between these ages: the 1944 Education Act sets out this duty as ensuring that children receive efficient full-time education suitable for their age, aptitude and ability and any special educational needs they may have. The duty is discharged either by sending the child to a school, or by educating them 'otherwise' than at school, for example at home, or in a small group with friends. Education 'otherwise' is dealt with later in this chapter.

'Full-time' education is not precisely defined, but regulations for state schools provide that they should meet for at least 400 sessions in each year, reduced by no more than twenty sessions for occasional holidays. The school day must be in two sessions separated by a mid-morning break.

Within the school day classes of children mainly aged under eight should have at least three hours of secular instruction, which can include time out for playtime, medical and dental examinations and treatment. This rises to at least four hours' secular instruction per day for classes mainly over eight. Time spent filling in the register of attendance is additional to this.

State Education

Schools are run either by the state or privately. This section deals with the state sector.

Education is the responsibility of the Department of Education and Science (DES), headed by a Cabinet Minister – the Secretary of State for Education and Science. Parliament passes the laws which relate to education, which are then administered by the DES and the local education authorities (LEAs) which deal with each area of England and Wales.

Education at a local level is the responsibility of local government: LEAs correspond to the non-metropolitan county councils and the metropolitan county councils. Inner London's education was run by a unified, directly elected body, the Inner London Education Authority (ILEA), but this was abolished in the 1988 Education Reform Act which handed education over to each individual London borough. ILEA handed education over to the boroughs in April 1990.

The education authority is run by a committee chosen from the elected councillors who then appoint a chief education officer, a professional who advises the councillors and manages the education system for that area. The DES has some measure of control over who is appointed as chief education officer, and can veto the appointment if they are not fit and proper persons.

The Education Acts give local education authorities both duties and powers. The difference between these is that they *must* carry out their duties, but they have a wide range of discretionary powers which they *can* carry out if they so choose. While LEAs are responsible for carrying out the ideological duty of the radicalizing 1944 Education Act – to contribute towards the spiritual, mental and physical development of the community by ensuring that efficient education is available to meet the needs of the community – in practice their primary duty is to provide educational facilities and institutions for those who must under the law be educated.

In law, people for whom educational provision must be made are children of compulsory school age, and then up to nineteen if they choose to stay on at school. LEAs have no duty to provide pre-school education, adult or further education. When an authority does provide nursery education or further education, it does so under its discretionary powers. The extent to which these powers are used depends on the policies, management and funding of each individual authority, and there is wide national divergence. To put it bluntly, some local authorities are better than others.

Each LEA pays for and runs its own schools within its area. The schools are run on a day-to-day level by the head teacher and governors.

Historically, LEAs inherited a piecemeal collection of educational institutions following the 1944 Act which, while charging them with providing suitable education for all, did not fund them to build a new network of schools. So while many new schools were built, LEAs also took over and started to fund existing schools founded by charitable organizations and churches.

Within the present system, all state-sector schools are called 'maintained'

schools, but schools which were originally set up by the LEAs or their pre-
decessors are called 'county' schools, and those set up by anyone else are called
'voluntary' schools.

Within the 'voluntary maintained' group of schools, there are separate categories of 'aided', 'special agreement' and 'controlled' schools. While all are
maintained financially to some extent by LEAs, there are levels of financial
maintenance and control. Voluntary aided and special agreement schools have
more independence from the LEA as they get some of their funding needs direct
from the DES and other sources (such as parents or church foundations), and
controlled schools are entirely funded by LEAs.

'Independence' in this context means more control of internal organization,
different composition and functions of the governing bodies, and different
selection procedures to take account, for example, of the religious purpose of the
school. In this chapter where there are differences between voluntary and county
schools, these will be pointed out. Otherwise, the law is the same.

'Special' schools provide education suitable for children with learning difficulties who are not, for educational reasons, integrated into mainstream
schools.

What Sort of School?

NURSERY SCHOOLS

Nursery schools and nursery classes attached to primary schools take children
under the age of five, generally from rising three years old for part-time and full-
time informal play-based education. A good nursery school is a lovely place, with
children playing and learning together at their own pace, but despite good
intentions there is inadequate nursery provision within the state sector.

Before the Second World War, LEAs and voluntary bodies between them
provided severely limited pre-school education – there were only thirty nursery
schools in 1931. During the war there was a large expansion in provision, because
women were needed for war work. When the 1944 Act was passed it took account
of the under-fives and positively required LEAs to 'have regard' to the needs of
under-fives.

The 1967 Plowden and Gittins Reports strongly recommended expansion of
under-fives provision, and in 1973 the then Secretary of State in 'Framework for
Expansion' put forward plans to implement Plowden properly, aiming to have
mainly part-time nursery provision for 90 per cent of four-year-olds and 50 per

cent of three-year-olds by 1982. This never happened. The fact that nursery provision is little better than it was pre-war, and considerably worse than in other European nations, is shameful.

The 1980 Education Act then formally abandoned both the good intentions of 1944 and social needs by repealing the LEA's duty towards the under-fives, leaving them only the power to establish and maintain nursery schools and classes.

The Plowden Report had envisaged that until there was an extensive network of nursery schools and classes, gaps would be filled by voluntary-run schemes and playgroups. Ironically, thirty years later that is now the case – without the extensive government-funded network.

While some LEAs do run pre-schools and classes, provision is piecemeal and inadequate, with priority given to children with social needs. There is by no means a place for each child.

In choosing a nursery school or class, apply first to the local education office, find out what provision there is, and put the child's name down as soon as possible.

With playgroups, contact the local outpost of the National Federation of Playgroups or the national office.

In choosing pre-school education for your child, look at both what is on offer in the nursery, and how the children are playing together. Ideally there should be both indoor and outdoor play going on, both supervised quite closely, with a range of activities like sand and water play, puzzles, painting, drawing, modelling, all on offer to the children at the same time; a quiet room or place for children to sit, sleep or read quietly; and enough staff to ensure the children are both safely supervised, and if not playing with each other are engaged with an adult in various small groups.

Nursery classes attached to primary schools are feeder groups for the school, so in choosing these, you also must look at the school itself. The advantage of nursery classes is that by the time your child goes up to 'big school' she is familiar with the buildings, fellow pupils and some of the staff and can make the transition from play to more formal learning easily. The disadvantage can be that if the child did not take to the nursery class, she may take even less to the school and if labelled naughty or difficult may find it hard to make a fresh start.

Always when choosing schools or pre-education it is a good idea to talk to the children and the parents about their views of the school – parents will give you the dirt where schools may not, and children will tell you things even their parents do not know!

PRIMARY SCHOOLS

These take children from five to eleven in Infants and Juniors. An infant pupil is aged between five and eight, and a junior pupil eight but not yet twelve.

The LEA have to provide a place for your child from statutory school age, which the child reaches in the term following her fifth birthday. Children whose birthdays fall early in the academic year or the summer before will therefore go to school when just five. Children with birthdays at the beginning of the summer term may be five and a half. There is no legal duty to accept your child before the fifth birthday, although some LEAs operate a reception class system for rising fives, and can offer part-time places until statutory school age. This ensures that your child joins in with the rest of the school mates she will have for the next six years at the beginning, and will not have to be one of a few new children mid-year, and gets three full years in the Infants which lay the foundation for academic learning.

What is best for the child is something only you can tell. Traditionally, it was thought that children who started school young had an academic advantage over older children, being exposed to learning at the time they soak up knowledge like sponges. Now, however, teachers' unions and some educationalists query this, feeling that a young child can suffer academically by being over-pushed, or not being allowed to progress at her own pace through the developmental stages necessary before she can tackle numeracy and literacy. A good primary school head will talk to you about this, but again, only you know if your child is ready for the exciting rigours of school life.

MIDDLE SCHOOLS

These are a fairly new innovation, recommended by the Plowden Report in 1967 which saw the need for children to have a broad-based non-specialized type of education, like the primary schools offer, rather than the more selected and exam-oriented provision made in secondary schools.

Children are taken from between eight or nine and twelve or thirteen. Following Plowden, about fifty LEAs operated middle schools, but the number is not increasing, and some authorities have either already abandoned the concept or are doing so.

With falling school rolls and the current debate about educational standards, benchmarks and the national curriculum, middle schools with their emphasis on child-centred learning are not likely to prosper.

The district education office will tell you the area's policy.

SECONDARY EDUCATION

Secondary schools accept children from the age of eleven until statutory school-leaving age or the end of sixth form. Statutory school-leaving age is the Easter following the sixteenth birthday if this falls before January, or the first Friday following the sixteenth birthday if later. Pupils who stay on after their sixteenth birthday can leave as they choose between then and the age of nineteen when the LEA's duty to educate ceases.

In the state sector, secondary education may be either comprehensive – that is, accepting children without reference to their academic ability; or selective – that is, choosing them for the school on that basis.

The old division between grammar school and secondary modern exists in that there are still approximately 150 grammar schools, although they are now classified as independent schools and no longer receive 'direct grant' funding from the DES.

Some LEAs operate a non-comprehensive system of education by paying for children to attend these schools. The comprehensive/selection debate has raged since 1965 when the then government published a circular (10/65) asking LEAs to publish their proposals for the reorganization of schools on comprehensive lines. The LEAs were ordered under the 1976 Education Act to reorganize into comprehensives, but this Act was repealed in its entirety in 1979 and 1980.

The present position is that LEAs can select or not as they choose, although in practice most do not. Comprehensive education is still a political issue, and the issue of selection on academic merit is very live, particularly as schools which opt out from LEA control can after five years apply to change their admission procedures.

Where LEAs do operate selection as a basis for admission to a school, they must tell you on what basis this is and there is a right of appeal on refusal of a place (see below).

Sixth-form Colleges

Because of falling school rolls and other factors, many LEAs have abolished the sixth form in maintained schools, setting up sixth-form colleges for the area which cater for the sixteen plus children from local schools. As a direct alternative to staying on at school, admission to these is by local borough. A big enough sixth-form college is able to offer a range of A-levels and vocational courses, but they are in direct competition with tertiary colleges.

Tertiary Colleges

These are run by the LEA. In metropolitan districts, they are inter-borough and as such can draw on a wider consumer population with correspondingly larger choices.

They provide education for the sixteen to nineteen age group, and further education beyond that both in academic and vocational training. A child wishing to transfer to a tertiary college needs the permission of the local LEA to do so.

City Technology Colleges

These are schools within the state sector, introduced by the present government to provide technical education. At present there are about twenty but plans for expansion are mooted. They can select on ability, and are funded directly by central government.

FURTHER EDUCATION

This comprises universities and polytechnics operated by themselves, with their own academic and qualification selection procedures, and further education colleges operated by LEAs, which are open to all.

Education Otherwise

Children have to be educated, but this does not have to be at a school.

As we have seen, under the 1944 Education Act parents have the duty to ensure their children receive efficient full-time education either by regular attendance at a school or otherwise. 'Or otherwise' means that parents can choose how to educate their child. This is backed up by the general principle that 'so far as is compatible with the provision of efficient instruction and training and the avoidance of unreasonable public expenditure pupils are to be educated in accordance with the wishes of their parents'.

If therefore a parent decides either not to enter a child into the school system, or to take them out after trying it, he/she can fulfil their duty by providing alternative education at home alone, or jointly with other parents.

Parents who do this – an estimated 8000 – while opting out of the school system, cannot be fully independent of the state and are still bound by the duty to ensure that their children's education is efficient, full-time and suitable to their age, abilities and aptitudes and to any special educational needs that they may have.

The quality of education at home is checked by officers of the local education authority who have powers to inspect the child's system of working, attainments and syllabus – which is of course compared with what children learn in school and with current educational opinion about what they should do and know.

If the court has to decide upon how efficient an education at home is, according to an aged but leading case in 1911 magistrates do not have to decide the case on whether the education was as efficient as it might have been at school, but can relate it to how it suited the particular child they are dealing with. However, one of the judges in that case said that this method of deciding efficiency was all right in the absence of 'any bye-laws' providing that a child of a given age shall receive instruction in given subjects. In other words, given 'bye-laws' for what should be taught, what was 'efficient' would be tailored to those. Under the national curriculum which sets specific targets for children at certain ages we do now appear to have exactly such 'bye-laws'. It seems likely therefore that parents who try to ignore or circumvent the national curriculum will have a tougher job in convincing LEAs that the education they provide at home is efficient.

If the LEA believe that the parent is failing in his or her duties under the Act, then they can require the parent to satisfy them that the duty to educate, as above, is fulfilled. If they are not satisfied, their ultimate deterrent is to order the child to attend a named school, with prosecution of the parent if they do not. The actual procedures are dealt with later in this chapter.

Parents who keep their children out of school and see to their education themselves obviously have strong views about the type of education schools offer, or may disagree with the accent placed on literacy and numeracy at an early age, at the possible expense of creative or practical skills. Parents can get support and advice from Education Otherwise, a membership organization of parents in similar situations.

Education authorities themselves have power to arrange for children to be educated otherwise than at school in what the Education Act 1944 calls 'extraordinary circumstances', for example where the child is in hospital or ill at home. Their duties to provide education do not cease when a child is sick or even when a child has been excluded from school. LEAs run a home tuition service for children in such circumstances.

How Schools are Organized

All maintained schools in England and Wales are organized and controlled by the

LEA, the head teacher and the governing body which must include representatives of parents, under a constitution and constitutional rules.

Every county, voluntary and maintained special school, both primary and secondary, has as its constitution an Instrument of Government; the rules under which the school is to be conducted are called the Articles of Government.

The rules under which a school is controlled cannot be inconsistent either with any of the Education Acts or with any trust deed under which the school was originally set up. For example, in the case of a denominational school founded by a church there will be an original constitution setting out who was to manage it, and how, with proposals for appointment of suitable governors, referred to as 'foundation' governors.

Any county, controlled or maintained special school with less than 100 pupils must now have as its governing body two parent governors, two governors appointed by the LEA, one teacher governor, the head teacher unless he/she chooses not to be a governor, and either two foundation governors and one co-opted governor if it is a controlled school, or three co-opted governors in any other case.

Any county, controlled or maintained special school with over ninety-nine but less than 300 pupils must have three parent governors, three governors appointed by the local education authority, one teacher governor, the head unless he/she does not want to be a governor, and either three foundation governors and one co-opted governor in controlled schools, or four co-opted governors in any other case.

Schools of the same type with between 299 and 600 pupils have four parents governors, four LEA appointed governors, two teacher governors, the head unless he or she does not want to be a governor, and either four foundation governors and one co-opted governor in a controlled school or five co-opted governors in any other case.

Aided and special agreement schools must have one governor appointed by the LEA, as many foundation governors as is permitted by the original deed or instrument setting up the school, at least one parent governor, with schools of less than 300 at least one teacher governor, and at least two if more pupils, and the head unless he or she chooses not to be a governor.

With such schools the foundation governors must outnumber the other governors by two or three depending on the size of the body, and at least one of the foundation governors must also be at the time of appointment a parent of a child at the school.

The fundamental difference here is that maintained and controlled schools can have only the maximum number of parent governors, but aided and special agreement schools technically can have as many as they want as long as the foundation governors outnumber the others.

WHAT DOES A GOVERNOR DO?

Governing bodies have been given more influence in how a school is run, and made more accountable to parents in recent legislation. Effectively, they work with the LEA and the head teacher in running and managing the schools, dealing with internal finance, discipline problems, and now, importantly, having a wider say in what is actually taught in schools. A parent can be a governor either by election as a parent governor, appointed by the LEA, or co-option either by the LEA or as a foundation governor. Training courses are run by LEAs, and there is financial reimbursement of necessary expenses. Governors' meetings have to be held at least once a term, and governing bodies must give parents an annual report about the school and its develop-ment which can be discussed and questioned at an annual meeting of parents. Resolutions can then be passed by parents which governors are bound to consider and report back to the parents – although they do not have to do this until a year later at the next meeting.

Choosing a School

If you want state education at primary or secondary level, the first step is to contact the LEA's district office for a list of all maintained schools in the area and information about the policies they carry out.

Parents have to decide what sort of school they want, taking into account how far it is from home, religious beliefs, and the type of facilities they want for the child.

In practice parental choice is limited by the availability of the type of school in their area – there may be dozens of schools in cities and far fewer in the country. This causes particular problems for parents who choose a school out of their borough or area. Once you have picked a school or schools, you are entitled under the Education Act 1980 and the Schools Information Regulations 1981 to get information about that school, either from the LEA or the governing body. This will be in the form of a prospectus.

LEAs must tell you what sort of school it is; what its religious affiliation is; admission and transfer policy; transport to and from school policy; meals and refreshments policy; the authority's policy about grants; entry for public examinations; and provision for special needs in detail.

In addition, the governors of an aided or special agreement school must tell you its classification; particulars of the curricula for different age groups; subject choices; how sex education is given; and with secondary schools, the level to which subjects are taught and the kind of careers advice given. They must include details of religious affiliation; the rights to withdraw children from religious worship or instruction; arrangements made for children with special educational needs; details of grouping or streaming; homework; pastoral care; discipline; dress; and arrangements for visiting the school; for pupils aged fifteen and over, details of public examinations entry, how many pupils sit exams and in what subjects.

Schools in Wales must also detail their policy in respect of Welsh-language teaching. The LEAs and governors must also in the same document publish the details of admission to the school, the arrangements made for appeals against refusal of a place, how many pupils are to be admitted in each year, and how admissions are organized for children out of the area. The LEA must also publish their criteria for offering places for children at schools which they do not maintain – that is, their policies on funding places at independent schools.

LEAs must lodge this information in public libraries, make it available on request to all parents, and ensure parents of all primary school children have it before transfer to secondary schools. Governors at schools must make it available on request to parents. Parents whose first language is not English have a right to have this information, free of charge, in their first language.

Heads and LEAs may have different policies about parents visiting the school – phone and ask. Ideally, you should be shown freely round the school and given an interview with the head teacher where both you and the child can see what the school is like. Remember, the head will also be interviewing you; even in primary schools where selection on academic merit does not operate, a popular school can effectively choose who they want as long as they properly fulfil their own admissions criteria. Once you have made your choice, formally apply for a place by notifying the school itself if it is voluntary or special agreement, or the LEA direct for others. With some schools there is a waiting list – make sure your child is still on this by regular checks and letters.

When do you choose and apply? It is best to do this as quickly as the school will allow. Some will not entertain applications unless the child is rising five, and not permit visits or interviews until around the Easter before September admission. Others leave it later still – the information published by the school does not have to be out for each school year until six weeks before the school takes applications, so you may not have long to decide.

Once you have decided which school you want, the Education Act 1980 gives a legal right to express a preference for a particular school and to give your reasons for the choice. This is a newish right intended to increase the amount of influence parents have over their child's education, which in any event is dictated by the general principle that pupils are to be educated in accordance with the wishes of their parents as far as is compatible with the provision of efficient instruction and training and avoidance of unreasonable expenditure.

LEAs and the governors of county and voluntary schools must comply with this choice unless doing so would prejudice the provision of efficient education or the efficient use of resources – for example if the school was oversubscribed and full; or the chosen school was an aided or special agreement school and the choice was incompatible with the arrangements made for admission to that school by the governors – for example church schools of a denomination the child did not belong to; or the school selects by ability or aptitude and the child did not fit the criteria.

APPEALING AFTER REFUSAL OF A PLACE

If your child is refused a place at the school of your choice, under s7 of the Education Act 1980 you have a right of appeal. The appeal is heard by an appeals committee set up by the LEA for county and controlled schools, and by the governors of aided and special agreement schools. LEAs and governors have to make arrangements for appeals, publishing this information in the prospectus as above.

When you get written notification that a place has been refused, you should also get written reasons why, be told you have a right of appeal, and told the time limits (generally fourteen days) within which you can appeal, and to whom. You make the appeal in writing, giving reasons for appealing and detailing why you feel your child should be offered a place. You should by then have got all the information you need about the school's criteria for admissions, and it is sensible to peg your reasons why you want a place round these criteria. For example, some schools will give preference to children with older brothers and sisters at the school, or children with social needs, and if these form part of your reasons for wanting that school, go into as much detail as you want about them. You must keep a copy of your reasons, which form the basis of the appeal.

The appeal committee of an LEA school has three, five or seven members nominated by the authority. They can be authority members, or people who although not members of the authority know about educational conditions in the area or are parents of children at the school. Authority members can outnumber the other members by one, but members of any education committee of the authority cannot be the chair: so the smallest committee could have two LEA members and one parent or local person experienced in education chairing the appeal. Teachers at the school cannot sit on the committee, nor can anyone who decided in the first instance that your child should not be given a place.

Appeal committees for special agreement and aided schools also have three, five or seven members nominated by the governors. Half the appeal committee, excluding the chair, must be appointed by the LEA which maintains the school, and may include one or more governors, although they must not be the chair.

People who cannot sit on such committees are non-teaching employees of the authority, anyone who took part in the decision not to admit the child, and teachers at the school. The smallest committee therefore could be one LEA appointment, one school governor, and a teacher at another school chairing.

The grounds of appeal are made in writing. The appeal can be decided only on this if you wish, but you must be given the opportunity of going personally to the appeal hearing. You can speak, and the committee have discretion to allow you to take a friend or to be represented. The committee take into account your original reasons for choosing the school and the arrangements made and published by the LEA or governors for admission to the school. That is, they go back to first base: why do you want the school and does your choice fit with their admissions policy? The members decide by voting: if the vote is equal, the chair can have a second casting vote. The decision must be communicated to you, the LEA and the governors in writing.

The procedure outlined above is the bare bones contained in the Act: the conduct of appeals is outlined in a code of guidance which has no statutory force. This code says that authorities should see the desirability of having parents on appeal committees; should consider in setting up appeals committees and ad-mission procedures how to avoid conflict of interest or bias in the event of appeals; should provide parents with written guides to appeals, or proforma appeal forms at the time they notify refusal of a place, and should organize the appeal hearing so that it is accessible to the parent and takes place at least fourteen days after the parent is told of the venue and time; and that at least seven days before the hearing the parent should get a written statement summarizing the admissions policy and giving reasons for the decision not to admit. Further, their discretion to allow a friend to attend should be in parents' favour unless there are good reasons why not, in which case they should tell the parent the reasons.

What happens at the appeal is up to the committee, but the code of guidance sets out an order for events, which follows the order of legal cases and court appeals. It is a quasi-legal event and the principles of natural justice operate: that is, you should have a right to speak, to question, to state your case, to see the evidence relied on by the LEA or governors, with respect for your right not to be surprised in the middle of the proceedings by information previously kept secret from you.

The order of events therefore ought to be:

1. you open the proceedings by going through the grounds of your appeal, adding or amplifying your reasons;
2. the local authority then question you through their representative conducting the appeal on their part;
3. the LEA or governors then put their case, which you are entitled to question;
4. the LEA or governors sum up, and you finish by summing up your case;
5. members of the appeal committee may question you or the LEA representative.

Either you or the LEA/governors can produce written evidence: this could include school medical or psychological reports. If the authority produce these, you should have a right to see them before you are expected to argue against them, and if anything is sprung on you then apply for an adjournment to prepare your case in the light of this new material. The code of guidance says the committee can adjourn for this.

On the other hand, if you have evidence you want to bring, put it in either with your written grounds of appeal or send it to the appeal committee before the hearing. If you cannot, suggest an adjournment for the LEA to think about it. The purpose of this is to allow them time to consider your evidence properly, which may be crucial.

If you realize during the appeal that there is something you could produce which you did not realize would be helpful, then again ask for an adjournment.

How you conduct the appeal depends of course on the circumstances, and the reasons for refusal of the place. If it was based on selection at secondary level and your child's previous school reports showed a less than startling academic attainment, you can always argue – if this is the case – that they do not reflect his potential, producing other educational evidence of his abilities.

If the school is oversubscribed and the LEA or governors argue that giving your child a place will prejudice the efficient use of resources, meaning that one more child will be the straw to break the camel's back, then they have to prove this – the fact a school has reached its fixed number of registered pupils does not automatically mean they cannot extend it.

If the school operates 'banding' at secondary level – where they accept a certain quota of Band 1, 2 and 3 children depending on their academic perform- ance – then you can either argue your child was wrongly banded, or that one more will not affect the school adversely.

Practical Tips for the Conduct of Appeals
First, do take a friend, phoning first to check you can. Not only can a friend provide you with moral support, but he or she can take notes for you of what is said, and the answers to your questions. You should be able to read these over before you submit your case at the end.

Secondly, prepare the case as thoroughly as possible. As the appeal is based on the admissions criteria of the school, know them backwards. Practise what you are going to say: make notes to read from if necessary. Don't be afraid to take your time – the appeal affects your child's future, so do not feel you have to rush it, or deal with all your points in two minutes. If you have a good point, repeat it as much as the committee can stand – you obviously do not want to bore them into submission but make sure they do get all your points down clearly.

Third, try not to get angry or aggressive even if you feel it is going badly – although schools cannot refuse a child a place because they do not like the parent, if they take against you it might influence them. Be positive: you obviously like the school, and think it is right for your child, so say so.

Finally, there is nothing in general principle or the code of practice to say you cannot tell the committee how terrific your child is and what an asset they would be to the school: if she has musical or athletic ability, the school would like to know.

The decision of the appeal committee is binding on all parties. If it is unsuccessful, technically you can take it further, directly to the Secretary of State who under s68 of the 1944 Education Act can, if satisfied by a complaint by any person or otherwise that the LEA or governors have acted unreasonably in the exercise of any of their powers or performance of any of their duties, give directions to them as to the exercise of the power or performance of the duty. To translate: if they get it badly wrong, he can right it. Under s99 of the 1944 Act he can declare the LEA or governors in default of their duty, give directions about what they should do, and get an order from the High Court to make them do it. This sounds wide, but in practice the Secretary of State is reluctant to interfere at all and there is practically no chance of getting the decision of an appeal committee reversed in this way.

Special Educational Needs

Children with handicaps or disabilities used to be classified according to the disability itself and segregated into special schools which specialized in the care or 'educational treatment' of that problem. This concentration on the handicap and not on the child tended to ignore the individual needs and potential of the children, and the consequent segregation removed children from the educational mainstream and ordinary life.

The Education Act 1981 which came into force in April 1983 abolished the old classifications of children into such subgroups, and set up a structure whereby LEAs, parents and schools could co-operate in assessing what the child's problems and educational needs were. It provided for the integration of children with learning difficulties into mainstream schools.

The Act followed a five-year investigation by the Warnock Committee into special schooling and special needs. As the ideal behind the Act is to call a halt to siphoning off children from the rest of educational life, it may be illogical to have a separate discussion of learning difficulties in this chapter, but the law relating to special needs is detailed, difficult and needs space to itself. How children with special educational needs are catered for is important to education and society as a whole. The Warnock Committee found that while 2 per cent of children were likely to need the full range of educational provision, about one in five of all children was likely to have some special educational need during his or her school days.

Vitally, the Act's philosophies reflect in microcosm the compelling need for education to adapt itself to the needs of the children it serves rather than adapting children to fit in with it.

WHAT THE ACT SAYS

The law on special needs is mainly found in the Education Act 1981 and Regulations made under it, both of which have equal force. The DES issued an important circular 1/83 which is not part of the law but advises LEAs on how they should operate the Act.

The Act was passed to provide that children with special educational needs are identified, that the nature of their needs is understood, that relevant extra help is provided for them where they are found to need this, and that children with complex and severe learning difficulties who might otherwise have been allocated to special schools get this extra help in ordinary schools where this is possible educationally and financially.

The basic definition of the Act is 'learning difficulty'. A child has a learning difficulty if:

- he or she has a significantly greater difficulty in learning than other children of his or her age; or
- he or she has a disability which prevents or hinders him or her from making use of the educational facilities generally provided in schools for children of his or her age; or
- he or she is under five years old and is likely to be in either of the above groups when he or she reaches five.

The definition of 'learning difficulty' specifically excludes problems children may have at school because the language or form of language in which they are taught is different from the language they speak at home.

Not all children with learning difficulties as defined above have special educational needs. Children with special educational needs are those whose learning difficulty needs special educational provision of some sort. For example, a child in a wheelchair might be prevented by this from participating in some school activities and to that extent have a 'learning difficulty', but special educational provision need not necessarily be made for him or her.

Special educational provision is very approximately defined in the Act as additional or otherwise different provision than is generally made in the local area. This definition applies only to children over the age of two. For children under two, special educational provision means any provision at all. Basically, special education provision means extra help that other children in the school do not get.

The governors of county or voluntary schools and the LEA running nursery schools are under a duty to use their 'best endeavours' – somewhat short of an absolute duty – to secure that any pupil they have whose special educational needs requires extra provision to be made gets the required help. They must also make sure that the teachers understand how important it is to identify children who have special educational needs and are told what the needs are.

The question of precisely what kind of provision is needed and how it is to be given is left to the LEA to organize and not stated in the Act, which sets up a framework where children's needs can be worked out between the LEA and the parents, and the experts and other agencies they involve.

WHAT THE ACT DOES

The Act sets up a procedure through which children's special needs can be identified and assessed, and a decision is made about what kind of different or additional educational provision they need. Where children are found to have learning difficulties which call for different or additional provision to be made for them, the LEA issue a 'Statement' of their needs. A statement of this kind is a formal document in a form prescribed by regulations setting out the child's special educational needs and what sort of special educational provision is to be made, and by whom, to meet those needs.

Circular 1/83 talks about the protection of a statement for a child – and expects all children with severe or complex learning difficulties which need the provision of extra resources in ordinary schools to have this protection. Children in special units attached to ordinary schools, and all special schools, state or independent, must have statements.

The Act gives an LEA a further duty to arrange for special educational provision to be made for the children assessed formally as needing it, and to keep 'under review' the arrangements they make for this.

Where a child is the subject of a statement for whom extra help is arranged, the LEA has a duty to arrange that he or she is educated in an ordinary school, as long as they have taken account of what the parents want and as long as educating the child in an ordinary school fits in with the child getting the special educational provision he or she needs, the efficient provision of education for the other children in the school, and the efficient use of resources. These conditions effectively mean that an LEA can decline to integrate children into ordinary schools if they can show this would cost too much, or hinder how efficiently the rest of the school runs. Generally speaking, authorities which are committed to integration find a way around limited budgets, and those which are not committed do not.

Once a child with a statement is integrated into an ordinary school, there is a further duty on LEAs to make sure that he or she mixes in activities with children who do not have special needs. This provision is to make sure that schools themselves do not separate off children from the mainstream all the time, although the provision made for the child might properly call for some time spent being taught alone or in a smaller group. This duty to integrate internally in schools is dependent on it being reasonably practicable and compatible with the child getting the provision he needs, the other children being efficiently educated and the efficient use of resources, as above.

Experts agree that if a child has or might have learning problems, it is best that these are discovered early, and the Act provides for this.

Health authorities, who through child health clinics and health visitors are in frequent contact with the under-fives, are given a duty under the Act to tell parents if they think a child of this age might have special educational needs. The health authority must then allow the parent a chance to approach the education authority and talk this over, before they themselves notify them. At this stage the health authority also has a duty to give the parent information about the voluntary bodies who might be able to help them.

Children's special needs may also be identified early if they go to a state nursery school: the Act says LEAs should ensure that nursery school teachers are aware of the importance of this.

ASSESSMENT

Assessment is how the LEA find out what learning difficulties children have so that they can understand how to meet their educational needs. Assessment can be informal in schools, with LEAs making their own arrangements for this, or formal under procedures laid down by s5 of the Act. The range of problems that can affect a child's capacity to learn is extremely wide, from permanent complex multi-disabilities to temporary illness, and every school is therefore likely to have some pupils with special educational needs.

Many of these needs are catered for by provision, like remedial teaching, which is available as part of the general education facilities supplied by the LEA and individual school. If a child needs extra help of the sort generally and normally available in schools in the area, then he or she need not be formally assessed under the Act's procedures, but can and should be assessed informally in the school.

The DES in their guidance circular 1/83 advise that normal assessments are a continuing process, and that teachers should notice and understand when a child has a learning problem, and try out different ways of dealing with it. It urges all the different professionals, including the school medical staff, to keep in touch with each other about the child. The circular advises that parents should also be kept closely involved.

Involving parents in informal assessment is not, however, a legal duty under the Act and, unhappily, some teachers and schools do fail to inform parents that their child has a problem in class, or leave it to the end of term or year report. This is despite the circular's statement that with assessments in schools 'the aim should always be to provide assistance before the situation becomes critical'.

With formal assessment parents have a statutory legal right to be kept fully informed and involved, and to get copies of all reports and information. The intention is that LEA and parents work together in a partnership to help the child. The circular goes further than the Act in this and suggests, although it is not a legal requirement, that the child's own feelings and perceptions should be taken into account and that older children themselves should be involved in the partnership.

Who Decides on Assessment?

The LEA should formally assess children for whom they are responsible when there are grounds to suggest that the child needs more help than is generally available in ordinary schools in the area under normal arrangements. The DES accept that what is generally available differs from place to place – in other words, some authorities provide more than others for the benefit of all children.

The LEA are responsible for children in their area who are at schools they maintain, or for whom they have arranged education, or who are being educated at other schools whom they know to have special needs, or who are aged between two and sixteen and do not go to any school.

Parents have a right under s9 of the Act to ask the LEA to assess their child if they are worried about him or her having any learning difficulty, and the LEA must do this unless they think the request is 'unreasonable'.

However, with children under two LEAs must carry out an assessment if the parents ask for this. If it is the LEA themselves who want to assess such a young child, this can be done only with the parents' consent. With children aged over two, the LEA do not need parental consent.

Once the LEA decide to assess they must in writing:

- tell the parents that they propose to make an assessment
- tell the parents the procedure they will use for doing this
- give the name of a contact in the LEA who can give the parents further information
- allow the parents twenty-nine days minimum to put in their own written evidence and make representations.

At this stage the parents should, if they have not already done so, get as much information and advice as they can. LEAs have a legal duty to provide detailed information about their special needs policies and provision, as do individual special and ordinary schools. Ask freely about the assessment itself, which experts will be used, what examinations will be made and how closely you can be involved in discussions. The named LEA officer is a source of information, as are independent voluntary agencies – some of which are listed in the back of this book.

Representations

Parents' representations at this stage can be written or verbal. If verbal they should be minuted in writing and agreed between the parent and the LEA.

Parents can send in independent experts' reports on the child or the written views of health visitors, doctors, etc. All parties involved have a right to see every document submitted to the LEA, so parent representations or other evidence are passed on to all the professionals involved. The best advice this book can give is *seek independent advice as quickly as you can*, unless you feel entirely sure that assessment is in the child's best interests, and you and your child agree with the authority's plans. Because the child has no independent rights to put in his views or evidence, parents are the spokespersons for him throughout.

The LEA must consider and take into account all the evidence submitted to them and, once the set period has passed, must tell the parent in writing that they will make an assessment, and their reasons for doing so. They must notify the health authority and the social services at the same time. They can decide at any point after serving the notice not to carry out the assessment, informing the parent in writing. The parent has no right of appeal against decisions at this stage.

Making the Assessment

An LEA must seek written medical, educational and psychological evidence, and any other advice that they consider desirable, for the purpose of arriving at a satisfactory assessment.

The educational advice must be from a head teacher at the school the child has attended for the last eighteen months – the head can consult with those who actually taught the child. If the child has not been at school, the advice must come from a teacher experienced in special needs. If the child is partially or fully deaf or blind and his teachers are not suitably qualified in that field they can again consult with those who are.

The medical advice must come from a fully registered medical practitioner, either already treating the child or asked to do so for the assessment, and the psychological advice must come either from an educational psychologist already employed by the LEA or engaged by them for the assessment.

Other advice sought by the LEA can come from anyone in a position to advise – and other health authorities or social services can submit their contributions also.

The circular advises the professionals on what to aim for in the assessment: a picture in the round of what that particular child can do, his strengths and weaknesses, how he relates at home and school and his past history. They should also give their professional views of what the intended extra provision will aim at in terms of helping the child's educational development and growth of independence, and what facilities and resources are recommended for the achievement of these aims.

The 'checklist' for professionals provided in the circular covers a wide range of strengths and weaknesses the child could have, from physical functioning to self-image and interests, and a wide range of help from physical environment at school to the need for individual attention.

The LEA can, under Schedule 1 of the Act, arrange for the child to be medically or otherwise examined for purposes of assessment. They must serve the parent with a notice setting out the time, date, place and purpose of the examination. The parent has a right to be present but can also be prosecuted and fined £50 if he or she fails to take the child to the examination without reasonable excuse. As the vast majority of parents will already be doing everything in their power to help their child it is unlikely that this draconian power would need to be used – but threatening a parent with criminal proceedings if they do not consent to a medical examination of their child raises the question of how free that consent actually is.

Parents have the right to submit whatever evidence or reports they choose – organizations like the Centre for Studies on Integration in Education (CSIE), set up by the Spastics Society, and the Advisory Centre for Education (ACE) have lists of independent experts who can help (for addresses see p. 404). As experts can differ as widely in their views about a child's potential and attainments as anyone else, the basic rule is to get a second opinion if you feel any aspects of your child's needs have been misunderstood or missed.

When all the evidence has been submitted, the LEA must decide whether or not the child's needs are such that they should determine special educational provision for him or her.

If they decide either that the child does not have special needs or that he does but they are not so severe or complex that the LEA should do anything extra about this, the LEA must notify the parents in writing and inform them of their right of appeal direct to the Secretary of State. Such appeals rarely succeed, because the Secretary of State will interfere in the LEA's decision only if he finds that they have behaved unreasonably. If he does, he can direct them to reconsider their decision.

Where the LEA decide they should determine special educational provision – which calls for a statement to be made under s7 of the Act – they serve a copy of the proposed statement on the parents. The statement must contain:

- copies of all reports and advice given to the LEA
- details of the extra educational help recommended
- details of the extra non-educational help recommended
- details of the agency (such as a health authority) which will supply the above
- details of the type of school appropriate for the child – named if this has been decided.

The LEA must also send written details of the rights parents then have to make representations to the LEA about the statement, to have a meeting to discuss it with the LEA and to have further meetings to discuss any parts of the assessment advice with the people who gave it.

The first representations and first request for a meeting must be given within fifteen days of receiving the statement. Further meetings after that must be requested within fifteen days of the previous meeting, with further representations having to go in within fifteen days of the last meeting in the series.

After considering the representations made, the LEA may keep the statement as it was, modify it, or decide not to make a statement at all. They must tell the parents of their decision and if making a statement must serve on them a copy of the statement, the name of an LEA contact who can give information and advice about the child's special needs, and details of the parents' right of appeal under s28 of the Act.

These appeals are against the type of special educational provision recommended in the statement. They are heard by a committee of three, five or seven people nominated by the authority, and are run in the same way as school choice appeals. The committee can only either confirm the statement, or after making observations remit it to the LEA for reconsideration.

Parents can have one further appeal in writing to the Secretary of State. This is either against the appeal committee's confirmation of the statement, or against the LEA's final decision after the case has been remitted to them. On appeal, the Secretary of State can confirm or amend the statement, or direct the LEA to cease to maintain one at all. There is then no further appeal procedure.

THE NEW CURRICULUM

Children educated at special schools are not automatically exempted from the new national academic curriculum, but may be individually exempted in whole or part in their statements. Children with special needs educated within

mainstream schools can be exempted from the curriculum on the recommendation of the head teacher. For further details, see 'The New National Curriculum'
p. 95.

THE CHILDREN ACT 1989

Under the Children Act 1989, LEAs have been given a new power to benefit
children who are statemented under s7. They will be allowed to send and pay for
children to go to establishments *outside* England and Wales which specialize in
providing for children with special needs. They can cover the cost of travel, fees
and maintenance there, including parents' reasonable expenses. This enlightened
provision could, for example, cover sending a child with cerebral palsy to the
Peto Institute in Hungary which specializes in that field.

What Happens if Children are not being Educated?

The LEA can prosecute parents in the magistrates' court for failure to educate
their children; or bring care proceedings in the juvenile court; or do both at the
same time. When the LEA are considering prosecuting the parents, they must
also consider whether it would be appropriate to bring care proceedings as well,
and even if they decide not to, the magistrates' court that hears the prosecution
of the parents can direct them to bring care proceedings in the juvenile court.

Parents can fall foul of their duty to educate children:

- by failing to make sure the child goes to school regularly, which is known
  as truancy or absenteeism;
- by failing to register them as a pupil at a school at all; or
- by educating them otherwise than at school, but not matching up to the
  LEA's ideas of what is suitable and efficient education (see pp. 65–6).

Regular Attendance and Truancy/Absenteeism

'Regular attendance' as set out in the 1944 Education Act probably has the
common-sense meaning, although it is not legally defined. There are, naturally,
times when children do not have to go to school, either because they are
prevented from going (e.g. by illness or any other 'unavoidable cause') or because
they have been given permission to stay off.

With any absence from school it is good practice to let the school know why the child did not attend as soon as possible. If a child is frequently or inexplicably absent, a good school will want to know why, and in any event state and independent schools are required to tell the LEA if a child is off for more than two weeks without a medical certificate or is frequently absent. Always get a medical certificate when appropriate. With some illnesses, the school will not thank you for sending the child back within any quarantine period, so check their policy on infectious diseases.

Schools also have the power to exclude children temporarily if they have head lice or verminous infestation.

Other 'unavoidable causes' cover the natural disasters to which families are prone and basically means a temporary but real reason for not going to school. Snowed in, yes; something fascinating on television, no.

RELIGIOUS DAYS OF OBSERVANCE

A child need not attend school on a day exclusively set apart for religious observance by the religious body to which his or her parents belong. As these are known in advance, again it is good practice to let the school know at the beginning of term. It is the parents' religion that counts here, not the child's.

TRANSPORT

If you live more than a set walking distance from the school and the LEA either have made no arrangements for transport to and from school or not provided boarding accommodation or a place at a more local school, and you can prove all of this – then you cannot be found guilty of not sending the child to school. Official ideas of how far a child can walk twice a day may astonish many parents: for children under eight it is two miles, over eight it is three miles.

LEAVE OF ABSENCE

A parent or person in charge of the child can apply for leave of no longer than two weeks per year for the child to participate in an annual family holiday or to go on his or her own holiday.

Generally, no leave can be given to a school pupil to work, whether for pay or not, during school hours and children under fourteen should not work at all, but a child aged between fourteen and sixteen can have leave to take up 'work experience' placements which are arranged through the school and LEA.

Under the Education (Work Experience) Act 1973 children can have leave to take part – with licences – in theatrical performances at home or abroad. For fuller details see Chapter 5.

UNJUSTIFIED ABSENCE

Truancy or absenteeism is unjustified absence from school. There is no legal definition of how much absence actually constitutes 'absenteeism'. Schools vary in how quickly they report absenteeism to the LEA, or even notice it, especially when children leave school for the session after registration. According to the DES, school attendance rates especially among the fourteen to sixteen age range are 'worryingly low', and because of concern about this the procedures whereby LEAs deal with absenteeism are currently being reviewed. There is a British tradition of absenteeism from school – when some degree of compulsory education was first introduced in 1880, the attendance rate for the next decade was only 60 per cent.

LEAs have a responsibility to provide support services for schools – the Education Welfare Service – and have powers to take legal action to enforce school attendance. Education welfare officers (EWOs) are social-work trained and in theory should have a good knowledge of the school's curriculum, policies, advantages and problems. The DES recommend that EWOs are brought in at an early stage when there is absenteeism, and that they devote their social-work skills to the main objective – getting the child back into school – rather than the family's problem as a whole.

EWOs visit the home, talk to the family and try to negotiate a return to school with the children. If unsuccessful at this stage they will consider court action.

Failure to Provide any Education, or Inefficient Education

If an LEA have reason to believe that a child is not registered as a pupil at a school or is getting an 'unsuitable' home education, their first step is to write to the parents asking them to satisfy the authority within fourteen days that the child is getting a suitable education.

If the authority are unhappy with the parents' explanation or lack of it, they will send out another notice saying they want to make a school attendance order which obliges the parents to send the child to a school. At this stage the LEA must name the school they intend to specify in the order. They can, if they want to, name several schools. If they name voluntary and special agreement schools the governing body of those schools must first agree to take the child.

The parent then has another fourteen days to do one of the following:

● to accept the LEA's choice of school, or one of the alternatives if offered; or

● to apply for a place at another maintained school – telling their local authority about the application if another LEA maintain that school; or

● to apply to the LEA to pay the fees at an independent school, also applying direct to the school for a place.

If the child gets a place at another maintained school, that school is named in the order which is then made. If the child is refused a place at the maintained school, then the parents can appeal to the tribunal, in the same way as with any other school choice refusal. The LEA wait for the result of the appeal hearing: if it is successful, then that school is named in the order. If the appeal fails, the order names the school chosen by the LEA.

If the child gets a place at an independent school, and the LEA have agreed to pay the fees there, that school is named in the order. If the LEA are not going to pay the fees, they still name the school in the order if they agree it will provide a suitable education for the child.

School attendance orders last until the child reaches school-leaving age, but parents can at any time ask the LEA to substitute another school for the one named in the order, or revoke the order altogether because the child is being suitably educated otherwise than at school. If the child gets a place at the new school – which can be maintained either by the local authority or another one – the LEA will amend the order to show that school.

The LEA can revoke the order if the parents persuade them they are giving the child a proper and suitable education out of school.

Penalties

Once a school attendance order has been made, a parent who still does not register a child at a school faces prosecution by the LEA under s37(5) of the Education Act 1944.

If you are facing prosecution under the Act you should get legal advice as soon as possible. You may be eligible for legal aid or initial advice under the green form scheme (see Chapter 13). Even if you do not have lawyers for the trial, it is sensible to get some initial advice on how to represent yourself and what your defence, if any can be.

The magistrates' court issue a summons which is sent to the parent by post, fixing a day for going to court. As with any other charge, the parent can plead not guilty and fight it, in which case the hearing will be put off to another date.

With this offence – failing to comply with a school attendance order – a parent is entitled to be found not guilty if he proves that he/she is providing the child with efficient full-time and suitable education. For parents fighting for education 'otherwise', this is another step in the battle.

If the court finds that the quality of education is acceptable, they will not convict, and can direct that the school attendance order stops.

However, even if a school attendance order is demolished in this way, the LEA still have a positive duty to carry on checking the child's education, and can take further action if the situation changes.

If the parent pleads guilty or is convicted, the penalties for a first offence are fines and for a further offence imprisonment. However, the Children Act 1989 removes imprisonment as a penalty for the parents, although they can still be fined.

If a child does not attend school regularly, the parents can be convicted of an offence under s39 of the Education Act 1944. As with any other magistrates' court hearing, if the parents decide to plead not guilty at the first hearing, the magistrate will fix another date. When the case is heard the LEA must prove that the child was not attending school regularly, for example by producing the school's attendance register.

The parent can defend himself by showing the child was legitimately absent, either with leave or because one of the reasons set out above applies. If the court accepts this, the parents must be acquitted. While the court may be sympathetic to a parent they have to be strict in how they interpret the defence – in one case they acquitted when a child was kept off school because of the parent's illness, not the child's. The LEA appealed this decision and won.

The parents can be convicted even if they did not know the child was missing school – it is not enough to send them off in the morning or drop them at the school gates: the child must get to school, be registered as present, and stay there.

If found guilty, the parent can be given a conditional or absolute discharge or fined.

If convicted, the parent has an automatic right to appeal to the crown court against conviction, sentence or both. 'Automatic' here means that if the parent fills in the appeal forms setting out what he is appealing against and why, and lodges them at the court within fourteen days of the conviction or sentence, the court must hear the appeal.

An appeal against conviction is a re-hearing of the whole case by a judge – not a jury – sitting with one or two magistrates. Both the parent and the LEA can produce the same or extra evidence as heard in the magistrates' court, which can be oral or through properly produced documents.

An appeal against sentence involves the parent accepting he was guilty of the actual offence but arguing that the punishment was too harsh, either because the sentence did not take his personal circumstances sufficiently into account, or was unreasonably heavy in relation to what he actually did. The court has power to decrease the sentence after hearing the basic facts and the arguments of both sides, but can also increase it if it thinks the magistrate was too lenient – a power which is rarely used, but is a nasty sting in the tail of this automatic right to appeal.

There is another method of appealing against the magistrates' court decision: appealing direct to the divisional court in the High Court if the magistrates have got their law wrong.

If the High Court finds the magistrates have wobbled in interpreting or understanding the law, it directs the case back to them for re-hearing often with directions to convict or acquit. This is not an automatic process at all, and unless you are highly legally skilled yourself, lawyers are vital – particularly as the choice of appeal is either/or, and not both.

The two offences detailed here are found in s37 and s39 of the Education Act 1944. The Children Act 1989 does not repeal them, and education authorities will still be able to get school attendance orders and prosecute parents who do not comply with their terms.

Care Proceedings for Non-Attendance at School

PRESENT LAW

Under the present law, the court can make care orders on children who do not go to school. Under the Children and Young Persons' Act 1969 a local education authority – not the social services – can take care proceedings under the separate 'education ground' if they reasonably believe a child is not receiving efficient full-time education *and* is in need of care and control.

Frequently, not going to school is only one part of a child's wider social problems, and the education welfare officer can ask the social services to step in if they are not already involved with the family.

Only an education authority can take care proceedings on the education ground alone, but before taking proceedings they should consult fully with the social services, partly because the social services administer supervision orders – although they can ask an EWO to supervise the child for them – but mainly because if a care order is made the social services take legal responsibility for the child.

Technically, all proceedings in the juvenile court are care proceedings but a care order is only one of the orders that can be made. Generally, education authorities will ask for a supervision order only, and the DES advises that care orders for absenteeism should be applied for only as a last resort. Even so, approximately 5 per cent of the children in care are there under the education ground alone.

If the case is proved, the court can:

● make no order at all; or
● bind the parent over to exercise control and take proper care of the child; or
● make a care order committing the child to the care of the social services; or
● make a supervision order; or
● make a hospital or guardianship order.

Supervision Orders
The child is allocated a social worker who is responsible for checking all is well, sorting out any family problems that might influence truancy, and basically keeping tabs on the child and the family. The child lives at home.

Binding Over
This order is made when a parent binds him- or herself in a sum of money to exercise proper control of the child. This is really a promise to send the child to school and to pay up if you do not. The money is paid to the court if and when the parent is summonsed back to court for 'breach' of his promise. This order can be made only if the parent agrees to accept its terms.

Educational Care Orders
Once a care order is made on any ground neither the court nor the parent can tell the social services what to do with the child, and they have a very wide discretion in how they then deal with the child. What the social services decide to do will depend on the individual circumstances of the case but the options they have are:

1. Allowing the child to live at home and go to a local school. If this is not satisfactory, the social services can later remove the child from the home without having to return to the court for another hearing as the child is already in their legal care.
2. Taking the child to live in a social services children's home either with education on the premises (Community Home with Education – CHEs) or at a school. The quality of such homes is highly debatable.
3. Sending the child to a boarding school, spending school holidays either with the parents or at a local authority children's home.

Educational care orders last until the child has attained school-leaving age; or until they are revoked or discharged.

Hospital and Guardianship Orders
These are used where children have a serious degree of psychiatric or mental disorder.

THE NEW LAW

The Children Act 1989 has abolished failure to go to school as a ground on its own for care, and educational care orders will be done away with from that date.

Under the new Act, the sole ground for a local authority to take care proceedings is that the child is suffering or is likely to suffer significant harm. The harm must be attributable either to the parents' care, or to the child being beyond parental control, and includes ill-treatment or impairment of physical or mental health or development. 'Development' is wide – it covers physical, intellectual, emotional, social and behavioural development.

Looking at this definition – which has not yet come into force and is therefore untested – it seems that a care order could still be made because a child's intellectual or social development was being harmed by not going to school. However, that course looks likely to be used only in extreme cases as the Act sets out education supervision orders to deal with educational problems.

The main difference between a supervision order and a care order is that with supervision the child is *not* removed from his or her parents.

Education Supervision Orders
The main points about these are:

1. They are brought only by the education authority, and not by the social

services. However, the two authorities should still liaise and discuss the child's needs as a whole.

2. The application is for an education supervision order. It is made if the court is satisfied that the child is of compulsory school age and is not being properly educated. Proper education is as usual: efficient, full-time and suitable to the child's needs, ability, aptitude and any special educational needs he may have.

Once a supervision order is made, the LEA 'assist and befriend' the child, allocating an officer to do this. Supervising officers where possible should find out the wishes and feelings of the child and the parents about the child's education, including any views they have about where the child should be educated. The officer should 'give due consideration to' what the child wants, depending on his or her age and understanding.

The officer can then make directions about the child's education, again considering the parents' and child's wishes and feelings as far as these can be found out.

The supervision order lasts for a year only, unless extended. An LEA can apply to the court for an extension, as long as they do this three months before it would have expired. The extension can be for longer than a year, but not for longer than three years. What this means is that education supervision orders cannot drift on, and must be regularly reviewed by a court. They stop automatically when the child is over school-leaving age.

Education supervision orders cannot run at the same time as a care order – education authorities are not allowed to apply for them where a child is already in care.

They can be done away at any point if the child, or the parents, or the local education authority successfully apply to the court for the order to be discharged. In other words, a child now can apply personally to the court for the order to be lifted and has the same rights in this as the authority itself.

Dovetailing with Other Orders

It is assumed that if there is an attendance order (under s37 of the Education Act 1944) which is not being obeyed, or where the child is not attending a school regularly under s39, then the child is *not* getting a proper education (the ground for education supervision orders).

This assumption can be beaten down by the parents proving the child is getting a proper education, for example by showing they are educating him or her at home to an acceptable standard. Where they cannot prove this, a supervision order would be made. If a supervision order is made, any attendance order made before lapses and the supervision order takes over.

Penalties

Where the officer has made directions about the child's education and these are persistently flouted, the ultimate deterrent for the parent is to be charged with the offence of failing to comply with the directions. The penalty for this is a fine only.

There are defences for parents laid down in the Act. These are to prove that:

- they took all reasonable steps to ensure the direction was complied with; or
- that the direction was unreasonable; or
- that they had complied with another requirement or directions in a supervision order and it was not reasonably practical to comply with the education directions as well. (This appears to be the 'can't be superhuman' defence: for example, where a child is under an education supervision order and another supervision order, and the provisions clashed.)

The Act makes a difference between parents' actions and children's, understanding that while parents might do all in their power to comply with the directions, they cannot entirely control what a child does.

Where the child fails to comply with a direction made by the supervising officer, the LEA can tell the social services who then investigate the child's circumstances. As the child does not commit a criminal offence by flouting directions, there are no 'defences' – but it should always be open to a child at least to tell the authority that she felt the direction was unreasonable or did her best to comply with it. There could be circumstances where a child decided not to comply with a direction on perfectly reasonable grounds: e.g. not going to a school where there was bullying. A properly-run education service would investigate such allegations and, one hopes, would not penalize a child or family who had good cause for not obeying directions.

Independent Schools

An independent school is one which provides full-time education for five or more pupils of compulsory school age but is not maintained either by a local authority or by the DES through grants. Sometimes called public schools, they are funded through the payment of fees, bequests, endowment trusts and other private means, although those which have been granted charitable status get state help through tax benefits.

The independent system of education runs separately from the state system, and the schools within it organize their own affairs including selection and entrance policies, curriculum, discipline and all other forms of management. The independent system does not have a central authority like an LEA, and has no statutory duty to provide education for your child. Generally speaking, such schools are run by their governors and head teacher.

Independent schools which provide accommodation for children (boarding schools) have a duty under the Children Act 1989 to safeguard and promote the child's welfare. The local authority responsible for the area has a duty to check children's welfare at school, and they have powers to enter and inspect. If concerned, the LEA can report the school to the Secretary of State.

There are over 2200 independent schools in the UK, educating about 550,000 children or 7 per cent of the total school population. The system covers education from pre-school to leaving age and beyond. The DES used to keep a list of all registered independent schools which parents could apply for, but now do not. The Independent Schools Information Service (ISIS) keeps a list of about two-thirds of such schools which can be obtained from them.

Unlike the state system, independent schools do not by law have to provide information about themselves. Nor is there any general formal appeal system against refusal of a place.

Parents should apply directly to the chosen schools for a prospectus and details about selection and entrance. Although schools do not have to give you detailed information, as they are in the market place they would be foolish not to. If in doubt about their academic results or standards – ask. If a place is refused, ask what the school's policies are about reapplication or informal appeal to the governors.

Independent schools have power to select their pupils on whatever basis they choose. At secondary level the academic selection process is either through the Common Entrance examinations which children take at thirteen or through the school's own academic testing. Increasingly at primary and junior level schools are 'assessing' children for academic aptitude through interviews and tests.

CONTROL

Independent schools are controlled to some extent through statute and regulations laid down by the Secretary of State for Education. All independent schools must be registered with the Registrar of Independent Schools, an official at the DES. It is a criminal offence for anyone to run a school that is not so registered. New schools setting up must apply for registration, giving details, and then must be fully inspected before the registration is made final.

After registering, independent schools must provide annual information to the DES about the numbers, sex and age of the pupils; the numbers of children doing courses for public examinations; detailed information about what subjects are taught for A-level or equivalent grade; the numbers, names, ages and qualifications of teachers, including what if any degrees they hold; and other details including fees charged and fire precautions. Although parents have the right to see the register – and about two a year take this up – most of the above information is confidential and not on it.

The Registrar of Independent Schools must also be told immediately if the proprietor or head teacher changes or the school moves or shuts down, and told within one month that a teacher has been sacked for misconduct or resigned before he probably would have been sacked. If a school does not give the required information, the Secretary of State can order its name to be deleted from the register, and it cannot lawfully continue operating.

STANDARDS

'Independent' means that the content of the curriculum, the level and quality of staffing and type of education offered is not controlled or even advised on by the LEA. However, a parent's duty to provide efficient education for their child is not discharged by sending a child to just any school and theoretically the LEA has a continuing duty to take action against the parent if they consider that a registered pupil at an independent school is being inefficiently educated. The practical difficulties of such supervision by an LEA mean that they will worry about the quality of the education only if they are closely involved with the school, e.g. through paying the fees or when, rarely, the child is the subject of a school attendance order naming an independent school.

Independent schools have a duty under the Pupils' Registration Regulations 1956 to report irregular attendance of a registered pupil to the LEA, who can then deal with truancy as with maintained school pupils.

Educational and physical standards of the school as a whole are regulated through Her Majesty's Inspectorate (HMI) of Education in England and Wales, an arm of the DES. There are approximately 400 inspectors of education, although this number may be increased. They work in local areas with responsibility for local schools in their patch. If concerned about a school, either through their own knowledge or after complaints have been made to them, they have power to enter, inspect and report on the school. Their reports are published and freely available from the DES. A school which has been the subject of an inspection and report is not necessarily educationally inadequate – it could have been a matter of temporarily bad fire precautions or not enough toilets.

Much of HMI's work is research and advice for the Secretary of State on general education issues. As an advisory national body they do not take up parents' individual complaints about minor matters to do with education or disputes with the school.

The Secretary of State can close down bad schools if he is satisfied from an HMI report that they are 'objectionable'. Approximately four or five schools close in this way each year. Schools can be found objectionable on one or more of the following grounds:

- the premises are unsuitable for a school
- the accommodation is inadequate or unsuitable for the numbers, age and sex of the pupils
- the school is not providing efficient and suitable instruction for the pupils
- the proprietor or any teacher employed at the school is not a proper person to be so employed.

The Secretary of State issues a notice of complaint to the school setting out what is wrong and giving a time limit to remedy the faults. If the school puts its house in order after getting a notice of complaint, then no further action is taken. If it does not, the Secretary can eventually order the school to be struck off the register. It cannot lawfully continue to operate and must close.

Schools can appeal the notice of complaint to the Independent Schools Tribunal, which can uphold or dismiss the complaint. The tribunal has wide powers to strike schools off the register, disqualify proprietors from running an independent school or disqualify teachers – e.g. those who have been convicted of or confessed to criminal abuse of children.

Independent schools are exempted from the national curriculum and each school can decide what to teach and how to teach it. Independent schools are treated differently from maintained schools in other educational areas as well: they are not bound by the rules against 'political indoctrination'; and as they are not run by local authorities are free from the provisions against promoting homosexuality found under s28 of the Local Government Act 1988. The professionals who run independent schools seem to be treated as less in need of regulation than professionals in the state sector.

The New National Curriculum

Until recently, the curriculum was a matter for the local authority, head teacher and governing body; what children are to study at different ages is now to be laid down by law.

Schools, in consultation with their local authorities and governing bodies have traditionally been allowed considerable scope to organize their own curricula and methods of teaching them. This apparent liberty was, of course, modified at secondary level by the syllabus requirements of exams such as GCSE and A-levels, but secondary school pupils and their parents have had a good deal of choice in what subjects to take or drop.

Radical changes have been made by the Education Reform Act 1988, which has introduced a standard national curriculum with attainment targets and assessment for different age bands of children. The imposition of a standard curriculum gives more power to central government to control what is to be taught and, in practice, is likely to affect how teaching is to be done.

The new law does not apply to maintained special schools nor to independent schools which can continue teaching as before. Independent schools are likely to bear the national curriculum in mind when preparing their own, but are not bound by it.

The Education Reform Act describes the curriculum in exceedingly solemn and weighty words: it is to be 'balanced and broadly based, promoting the spiritual, moral, cultural, mental and physical development of pupils at the school and of society; and to prepare pupils for the opportunities, responsibilities and experiences of adult life.'

Parents might feel this is rather a lot to bear for a five-year-old just learning to read – but the practical purpose of the new law appears to be to raise standards of education nationally and to increase basic scientific and technical knowledge. Whether it will succeed in its aims is not for speculation here.

Basically, the national curriculum comprises ten subjects. Maths, English and science are the three 'core' subjects. In Welsh-speaking schools – i.e. when more than half of the subjects will be taught in Welsh – Welsh is a fourth core subject. There are seven 'foundation' subjects: history, geography, technology, music, art, physical education, and, at secondary level, a modern foreign language. Schools in Wales which are not Welsh-speaking schools have Welsh as a further foundation subject.

The curriculum is not a matter of choice for schools, parents or pupils. All local authorities, governing bodies and head teachers have a duty to secure that the curriculum in their schools falls in line with the national curriculum.

The national curriculum must be taught between the ages of five and sixteen. It does not apply to school students who stay on after the age of sixteen who will, presumably, have a wider choice of subjects for A-level, but as some disciplines – like classics – depend on a grounding which may not have been available below sixteen because of the pressures of the curriculum, parents will have to wait and see what the full effect of these changes are.

Students under sixteen who have a particular interest in or aptitude for subjects not on the curriculum will have to fit these in according to the demands of the compulsory subjects. Artistic or musical children will not be able to study these as a 'core' subject but only as a foundation subject; children who have a particular flair for languages will not be able to drop, say, geography in favour of another language.

The Act does not specifically write in penalties for refusal by a child or parent to comply with the national curriculum. It is possible, though, that any such refusal or non-compliance could be treated in the same way as non-attendance: the parent being liable for failing to ensure that the child has a suitable education as defined by this Act.

Schools will be able to choose their own timetabling, and decide when and for how long the curriculum subjects will be taught: the Act says that the Secretary of State cannot make orders laying down specific timetables for schools.

Schools will still be able to provide education in other subjects. How much time they will have to do this is a matter of dispute. The government's present estimate is that the national curriculum will take up approximately 70 per cent of the pupils' time. Other commentators consider this is too low, and the real figure is around 95 per cent.

How the National Curriculum is Organized

The vocabulary of this Act is new and worth explaining.

Under the Act, school children are divided into four age groups called *key stages*. Key stage 1 is from beginning school until age seven; key stage two from then until eleven; key stage 3 from then until fourteen; key stage 4 from then until school-leaving age.

A child is treated as being in a key stage if the majority of children in his or her class have reached the necessary age for it. What is to be learned in each subject and in each key stage is called a *programme of study*. What the children are meant to have learned by the end of each key stage is called an *attainment target*; and the method whereby the school finds out if they have learned it or not is an *assessment arrangement*.

The Act itself does not set out what it is that children should know by a certain age; that is the task of various working parties presently convened by the Secretary of State who will eventually make regulations and guidance circulars setting out the nitty-gritty of the new curriculum.

The curriculum is being introduced gradually, starting from September 1989 when programmes of study and the targets in maths and science were prepared for key stage 1 children. It is expected that the entire curriculum will be in place by 1993, although some commentators do not expect it to be completed for several years after that. As it is being introduced piecemeal, some classes will use it and others will continue in the old form, but all teachers will probably plan their teaching to take account of it before formally introducing it into their classes.

ASSESSMENT

Like the details of the programmes of study, exactly how assessments will be carried out on children is not known at the time of writing. The Act leaves the question of what sort of assessment is to be done to be decided later by the Secretary of State. It is likely to be done internally by the school. There are suggestions that assessment is primarily an aid to the school rather than a test for children, to indicate how much more help a child might need to reach the attainment targets.

The Act does refer to the different abilities and maturities of children within each key stage, with an indication that this will be taken into account, perhaps with varying attainment targets within each age group. That could show an intention to take the whole child into account, not just how they measure against a standard – but as any parent knows, children have an acute sense of the academic pecking order in their class and their own positions within it, and there must remain a fear that children who do not do well in their assessments will feel they have failed in some way.

Once up and running, assessments and school examinations generally will be reviewed by a new body made under the Act, the Schools Examination and Assessment Council. The composition and duties of this body are the same as for curriculum councils below except that they will deal with assessments and examinations and not the curriculum itself.

WHO DECIDES THE CURRICULUM?

Programmes of study and attainment targets for the different age groups are decided by working parties set up by the Secretary of State. Their conclusions are then thrown open to consultation by other experts and interested parties and can be amended at that stage. Once they are settled and agreed, regulations will be passed by Parliament and they will become law.

The Secretary of State has a duty to revise the curriculum if he thinks it is necessary to do so – this means that if some of it does not work well in practice it can be altered, again by regulation.

The Act sets up Curriculum Councils for England and Wales. Each council will have between ten and fifteen members. The job of the councils is:

- to keep the curriculum under review
- to advise the government on anything to do with the curriculum that they see fit
- to publish information about the curriculum (this information will be available to parents).

They can also do research and development work on the curriculum if asked, and generally aid the DES on the whole area of what is taught in schools.

The members of these councils are neither elected nor appointed by schools or local authorities but appointed directly by the government. The persons appointed must include people who have relevant knowledge or experience in education – they do not all have to be directly concerned with education in their professional lives.

One advantage for parents and pupils is that when the curriculum is in force it will be a matter of public record what children are taught under it. The councils' duty to publish information about the curriculum could result in parents having a much clearer view of education than at present.

EXEMPTIONS

Generally the curriculum applies to all pupils aged between five and sixteen in the maintained sector, but there are exceptions.

Special Needs

The most important exception concerns children who have special educational needs. Special schools are exempt from the religious education provisions of the curriculum but are not automatically exempt from the national curriculum itself. However, a child's statement of special educational needs can now include a provision either excluding the national curriculum or applying it to them with modifications. This provision should be open to appeal in the same way as other special educational provisions.

Individual Children
Head teachers in any maintained school can take a pupil out of the national curriculum for a special temporary period which must not be more than six months.

The main reason for doing this envisaged by the Act is where the head considers that a child has or probably has special educational needs which should be assessed. It could also be used where a child was disruptive and needed a 'cooling off period', or required intensive language teaching for a period.

If a head makes this decision, then he or she must give the following information to the school's governing body and the parents of the child:

- the reasons he or she has made the decision that the national curriculum does not apply to the child and the likely effect of this;
- what education the child will receive in the meantime; and
- either a description of how the child will be got back into the system after the period of time has expired or, where this applies, his or her opinion that the child might have special educational needs for which the local education authority should determine special provision.

Where the head thinks the child might need special educational provision, the local authority have a duty to consider assessment of the child. Assessment here is, of course, special needs assessment and not target testing under the new Act.

Parents have a right to request a head to make such a direction about their child, and a right to ask the head to vary or revoke a direction he or she has made. If the head then either does not make the direction as asked by the parent, or does not vary or revoke one when asked, the parent has a right of appeal to the governing body of the school.

Parents might consider asking the head for a direction like this if, for example, the child was floundering after a period of absence, and they wished some other kind of provision made for them for a short period. The practical benefit of this for parents would depend on the resourcing of the school and what was on offer for the child.

This provision applies to maintained special schools as well and could be used where the head thinks the child's special educational provision should be reviewed.

Whole Schools
The Secretary of State can direct that an individual school can be taken out of the curriculum system for experimental development work on education. This

needs the agreement of the local education authority and the governing body and in some cases the Curriculum Council.

What Must Not be Taught in Schools

Maintained schools must not either promote homosexuality or indoctrinate their pupils politically.

Section 28 of the Local Government Act 1988 provides that a local authority shall not intentionally promote homosexuality or publish material that does this; and shall not promote the teaching of the acceptability of homosexuality as a pretended family relationship in any maintained school.

Where politics are concerned, LEAs and head teachers of maintained schools must actively forbid 'partisan political activity' by junior pupils of their schools when at school, or in activities arranged by members of staff for the pupils. How head teachers are meant to do this is not made clear: perhaps they have to sniff out the radicals in the reception class!

Senior pupils are exempted from this prohibition, but not from the general onus put on head teachers and governing bodies to provide balance when political subjects are discussed, either in school or in extra curricular activities to do with the school.

Sex Education

How sex education is taught, and whether it is taught at all, is now a question to be decided by the governing body. If the governing body decide it ought to be a part of the curriculum, they have to keep a written statement of their policy about this, and how the content of the subject should be organized. The head teacher should have up-to-date copies of the governors' policy about sex education, which any parent can inspect. If the governors decide not to teach sex education, they must say so in the written statement.

Before making their statement about sex education the governing body should consult the head teacher and LEA and take account of what people in the community feel about it. They can determine how the education should be given – in set lessons or spread throughout other relevant subjects – what the content is to be, and how much information is given.

This is subject to an over-riding legal requirement: when sex education is taught, it has to encourage the pupils to have due regard for morality and family life. The DES advice to schools on this is partly to encourage the positive aspects of morality – restraint, respect for self and others and the responsibilities of parenthood – and partly to inform senior pupils of the illegality of some forms of sexual activity: buggery, indecent assault and under-age sex.

In the current climate, AIDS and health are important in the teaching of sex education. The DES advice to schools is that senior pupils should be told clearly and factually of the risks of promiscuous sexual activity and drug-taking; teachers should themselves be properly informed and prepared to answer questions on AIDS; and schools should raise pupils' level of awareness of risks.

SEXUAL COUNSELLING

Where a teacher is asked for direct personal advice from a pupil, he or she is advised to limit their role to encouraging the pupil to talk to their own parents. This caution is for a reason: the Gillick case highlighted the problems in giving advice to under-age girls (for more about this see Chapter 12). While it is in some circumstances ethical for a doctor to advise on or prescribe contraceptives to a girl under the age of sexual consent (sixteen) there is no such professional protection for teachers. A teacher could technically be accused of assisting the commission of under-age sex if he or she did advise on contraception in specific rather than general terms. Teachers are advised to warn pupils where they know they are embarking on a sexually risky course of action. Whether they tell anyone else of the pupil's disclosures is left to their own professional judgment.

HIV POSITIVE PUPILS

Schools have been advised on the precautions necessary where a pupil is HIV positive. The DES see no reason why an HIV positive pupil should not take part in all activities of school life, with some sensible exceptions such as not swapping blood samples in biology lessons and any spilled body fluids being cleared and disinfected promptly.

Discipline in Schools

Discipline in schools is a matter for the head teacher who has the right under the 1986 Education Act (No. 2) to determine what rules there should be and what disciplinary measures are suitable for the school. He or she has the power to suspend or expel pupils who infringe those rules, and has a duty to promote self-discipline, regard for authority and good order in the school.

School rules must be reasonable; they should not be racially discriminatory or otherwise unlawful, and in state schools there must now be no form of corporal punishment for their infringement.

Teachers are 'in loco parentis' (in the place of parents) to the children in their charge, and parents are taken to have delegated powers to them to discipline their children reasonably. This delegation carries on until it is formally withdrawn by the parent: in the 'detention' case discussed below, the court said that if the father had clearly withdrawn authority from the school to detain his child for minor indiscipline then the accusation he made of wrongful imprisonment would have stood up.

Teachers are expected to behave towards their pupils as a reasonable parent would who had that number of children in those circumstances. This includes the power to chastise them, within the rules and articles of the school.

Within these parameters, head teachers have discretion to decide what is best for their school, in consultation with the governing body and in accordance with any written advice on principles the governors make.

Parents and pupils are taken to have agreed with the fundamental rules of a school by sending the child to it: unless through parents' pressure or litigation it can be shown that the rule itself was unreasonable or otherwise improper. For example, the head of a private school had a rule that turbans were not allowed to be worn in the school; this was found to be racially discriminatory and struck out. Otherwise, heads can insist that uniform is worn and suspend children who infringe this until they conform.

The authority of the school extends to what the pupils do on their journeys to and from school – in one case boys who were forbidden to smoke at school were disciplined for smoking when out of school, and the school's action was held as reasonable by a court.

Punishments

When school rules are broken the traditional sanctions are verbal chastisement, detention, suspension and expulsion.

The 1986 Act abolished corporal punishment for all schools maintained in any way by a local authority, and for all pupils who were funded at independent schools by public funds (through assisted places schemes and local authority payments). Corporal punishment is physical punishment which includes caning, slapping or hitting a child, or throwing things at them including chalk.

Teachers are entitled to use physical force to prevent immediate danger of personal injury or immediate danger to property. The force used should be only what is reasonably necessary to prevent damage to person or property – a teacher who hauls pupils away from a fight is justified in laying hands on them. If he then loses his temper and slaps the errant pupil, he would have gone over the line. Teachers are protected by the general law on self-defence: if attacked by a pupil they would also be entitled to use whatever degree of force was necessary to protect themselves, or another, from injury.

Corporal punishment is forbidden in independent direct grant schools, and in schools run by the Ministry of Defence. In those independent schools which still allow corporal punishment it must be 'moderate and reasonable'. However, independent schools seem to be phasing out corporal punishment following the reform within the state sector.

VERBAL CHASTISEMENT

In the general criminal law, putting someone in fear of an imminent physical attack is an offence (technically this is assault – letting rip with physical violence is battery). A teacher who intimidates a child and puts her in well-founded fear of attack would therefore be committing an offence. A teacher who tells a child off for a misdemeanour in a controlled and reasonable way appropriate to the offence and the understanding of the child is carrying out the proper discipline of the school.

DETENTION

Improperly used, detaining a child after school against their will is wrongful imprisonment and/or trespass to the person. When reasonably used – for example, keeping a child behind during playtime to re-do work or as a punishment for disrupting a class – when this fits in with the ethos of the school and the disciplinary measures generally accepted there, it is lawful. There are questionable areas of discipline which, if tested in the courts, might not be fully upheld.

In one case an entire class was kept behind for ten minutes because of disruption by some members of it. In the subsequent court case, the court warned of the dangers of 'indiscriminate' punishment when children who had not actually offended were lumped in with those who had, and considered that blanket detention of a whole class was a last resort. But in that case the teacher's action was found to be reasonable in the circumstances.

The general rule is that disciplinary actions by teachers are likely to be reasonable if they come within the type of disciplinary measures used by the school and are not inappropriate for the children dealt with. This is a matter of fact in each disputed case – the detention of a child who then had to walk home alone in the dark worryingly late is a different issue from a child kept in class during break.

EXCLUSION FROM SCHOOL

Head teachers have the right to exclude a child from school on disciplinary grounds. The exclusion can be temporary suspension from school for a set number of days; indefinite suspension, for example where a condition has to be fulfilled before the child can come back; or permanent exclusion or expulsion.

Exclusion of any sort is bound by set rules laid down in the 1986 Education Act (No. 2) which have also to be incorporated into the articles of government of schools. Articles of government are the 'constitutional' basis upon which schools are internally managed and controlled.

Exclusion has to be on disciplinary grounds, for breach of the rules or measures decided on by the head teacher and governors. Although only the head can decide to exclude a child, the governors and in some cases the LEA have a role to play also, particularly in ordering reinstatement of the pupil and in appeals against exclusions.

The basic rules are:

1. If a head teacher does exclude a pupil aged under eighteen from school, he or she has a duty to tell the parents without delay that their child has been excluded, the reasons for it, and the time-scale of the exclusion. The head has only to take reasonable steps to get this information across; and does not have to tell the parents if the excluded pupil is over eighteen. Obviously the pupil himself has personal knowledge of the exclusion.
2. If a head teacher decides, after a pupil has been excluded, to change the suspension into expulsion, then again he or she must take reasonable steps to tell the parents of this change and the reasons for it without delay. Heads might do this if, after investigation in the school about the incident that led to the suspension, it turned out to be a more serious offence than it had appeared before.
3. In any exclusion, the head must take reasonable steps without delay to tell the parents of under-age pupils (and the pupils themselves if aged over eighteen) that they have a right to make representations to the governing body and the LEA about the exclusion.

The head teacher has to tell either the governing body or the LEA about the exclusion if it is for more than five days in any one term, or for less time than five days if because of the exclusion the pupil misses the chance to take a public examination at the school. Exclusions for under five days do not have to be notified to the LEA or governing body at the time. The head does have to include general details of exclusions during the term to the governing body at their meetings.

If a pupil is excluded from school, then the pupil and parents can either sit it out and go back to the end of any temporary suspension from school, or make representations about the exclusion to the LEA or governing body who can order reinstatement (i.e. countermand the suspension).

Where the exclusion is permanent, and a bid for reinstatement is not successful, the pupil or parents can appeal to the LEA and governing body who, under the articles of government, have appeal committees for this purpose. Pupils over eighteen can take action themselves; if under eighteen the parents act on their behalf.

Reinstatement

The LEA and governing bodies have the power to order reinstatement of a pupil excluded for a fixed period, indefinitely or permanently.

Theoretically, LEAs and governing bodies can intervene and reinstate a pupil of their own accord, and do not have to be 'appealed' to for reinstatement to order it. On the other hand, they do not have to involve themselves in any temporary suspension for a fixed period.

The DES advice is that this power should be used with careful consideration and not too hastily, presumably because reinstatements challenge the wisdom of the head in suspending in the first place, and could undermine his or her authority over the school.

Where the suspension is for a short period, the DES hint in their advice that they might just be content to 'note' the position. If, however, the LEA or governing body does order reinstatement of a pupil excluded for a fixed time, the head has to accept the pupil back when they say.

The LEA can order reinstatement of a pupil excluded for a fixed period in any sort of maintained school, but should consult with the governing body before making directions. Where both the LEA and the governing body order reinstatement but use different dates, the head accepts the pupil back at the earlier time. The point of these rules is that pupils should not be deprived of education for longer than is absolutely necessary.

In more serious cases than temporary exclusion, either the LEA or the governing body has to be involved.

INDEFINITE EXCLUSIONS

LEAs always have to involve themselves where a pupil is excluded indefinitely. This is so whatever type of school is involved – county, controlled, voluntary aided, maintained special schools and special agreement schools.

Obviously, indefinite exclusions should not drag on. The LEA must consult with the governing body and fix a date for the pupil to be allowed back into the school. They issue a direction to the head with the date – the head has to comply with this, unless he or she decides to make the exclusion permanent, in which case the head's decision carries more weight.

EXPULSIONS

In county, controlled and special maintained schools (where the LEA has more control than the governing body), when the head decides to expel a pupil (permanent exclusion) LEAs must consult with the governing body and consider whether or not the pupil should be reinstated. If they decide he or she should be allowed to go back to school, they direct the head accordingly; if they decide he or she should not go back to school, they must inform the pupil (if aged over eighteen) and the parents (if under eighteen). At that point, the pupil or parents have a right of appeal to an appeal committee.

In voluntary-aided and special agreement schools, the governing body itself has the duties above. They must also tell the LEA if they decide the pupil should not be reinstated.

Appeals

If a pupil is expelled, they must be given details of their right to appeal. Appeals against expulsion are to an appeal committee. Technically, these are appeals against not being reinstated after permanent exclusion from a school. Appeals are made in writing, setting out the grounds of the appeal. This is done either by the parent or a pupil personally if aged over eighteen. There should be a hearing where oral arguments can be made, and the committee can decide to let the pupil or parents have a friend with them or be represented.

Where a pupil is reinstated by the LEA and the governing body object, they too can appeal against the decision. In such a case the unfortunate pupil or the parents can also make written representations, or appear personally to argue their case.

If a pupil is not reinstated at the end of the day, the LEA still have a duty to provide him or her with an education – the school may have washed its hands of the student, but he or she still has rights to an education.

Heads can suspend pupils on conditions: e.g. not allowing them into schools unless and until they conform to the school's rules or reasonable measures to promote discipline. In one case a pupil ran away from school to avoid a caning. The parent did not insist the child go back to school and was convicted of not ensuring the child's regular attendance at the school. In defence, the parent said the child, being suspended, was 'lawfully absent' and they should not be convicted. Not so, said the court, failing to comply with reasonable conditions is not lawful at all. Although that case pre-dated the 1986 rules on suspensions, and the criminalization of caning children in schools, courts are likely still to uphold efforts made by a head to promote discipline even if, as in this case, it led to some degree of double jeopardy. The advantage of the new rules is that with a reasonably well-run authority indefinite suspensions will not drag on without resolution.

If following expulsion a parent made no effort to find alternative education for the child, there is no reason in law why he or she should not be prosecuted for it.

Opting Out

Opting out – properly known as 'acquisition of grant-maintained status' – is a new provision under the Education Reform Act 1988. It is now in force.

Schools maintained by the local education authority can decide to move out of LEA control and become self-governing. Schools might choose to do this if they were at odds with the LEA on policy for the school or plans for education in the area.

Once a school has decided to seek grant-maintained status, their detailed plans have to be approved by the Secretary of State. Once approved, the school changes from being maintained and funded by the LEA to being maintained by the DES through grants paid directly to them.

The DES recoups the cost of the school from the LEA which has already raised the money for the maintenance, salaries and running costs of the school through the rates system. The exact sums which are paid and recouped are estimated from information the LEA has to provide about the present costs of each individual school in their area, and the costs of central services that the school benefits from.

The school's assets – such as buildings and equipment – pass from the LEA to the governing body of the school. If the school has money or assets from sources other than the LEA – as church schools do, for instance – they keep these without change.

Financially, the aim is that schools which do opt out have the same levels of funding as they would have had while maintained by the LEA.

Large primary schools with more than 300 registered pupils, and all secondary schools, can apply for grant-maintained status. Small primary and middle schools, which are treated as primary where there are no more than 300 registered pupils, are not eligible. A middle school treated as secondary would be eligible despite numbers. Nursery and special schools are not eligible. A school which is eligible cannot opt out if it is due to be closed down by the LEA.

WHO DECIDES TO OPT OUT?

The decision to opt out is made by the parents of registered pupils at the school who vote in a secret ballot. The ballot can be called for either by the governing body of the school after they have passed a resolution to do so in two governors' meetings (the meetings must be no less than twenty-eight days and no more than forty-two days apart); or the governing body, after a percentage of the parents have given a written request to them to do so. The number of parents who request this must match the number of at least 20 per cent of the registered pupils.

If a ballot is called for, it is conducted by the Electoral Reform Society. The costs of the ballot are paid by the DES. The ballot must be taken no earlier than twenty-eight days and no later than three months after the governors' last resolution or the parents' request for a ballot.

A parent has a vote in such a ballot if they have a child who is a registered pupil in the school and they are down as a parent on the admissions register of the school.

This last provision limits the number of voting parents a child can have: in some extended families following divorce or separation a child might have several adults in a parental role, but only those whose names are entered on the register of pupils at the school can vote. These registers must contain the names of every person known to be a parent of the child, and governors must take reasonable steps to find out who they are.

The vote is decided by a simple majority of those who vote. If the turnout is low, and less than 50 per cent of the parents eligible to vote have, then there must be another ballot. If the majority of those voting in the second ballot vote for opting out then the proposals go ahead for approval to the DES. This happens even if the turnout at the second ballot was lower than at the first.

If the parents vote for grant-maintained status, then the governing body must publish their proposals for the school within six months of the vote. These proposals must be put up in conspicuous places around the school and published in a local newspaper. Any member of the public can then comment on or object to these proposals directly to the Secretary of State in the period when he is considering his approval of the school becoming directly funded. Parents who were out-voted can put forward their views at this stage also.

The proposals should cover: admission policies to the school; who the governors are and for how long they will serve; what provision the school will make for special educational needs; staffing levels; plans for in-service training for teachers.

WHAT DIFFERENCE DOES IT MAKE?

Getting grant-maintained status means that the governing body of the school manages the school rather than a local authority, employing the staff, dealing with finance, ordering policy and running it in all aspects. The school becomes self-governing within the limits of the law on maintained schools.

Becoming grant maintained does not mean the school becomes independent, and there are restrictions on the power of the governing body to make immediate sweeping changes. No grant-maintained school is allowed to alter its character for five years following change-over: it cannot change from comprehensive to selective on ability or vice versa; or become single sex if mixed originally or vice versa; nor can it decide to stop providing special educational provision. Note these restrictions last only for five years.

The governing body continues to be bound by the law on maintained schools: for example they cannot charge fees for education they provide apart from extras like music lessons, and they have a duty to enforce the national curriculum. The governing body must still carry out the relevant functions they had as governors before opting out, and in addition, they take over the LEA's duties, for example as employers.

THE ROLE OF THE LEA

After a school has opted out of local government control, the education authority must still carry out certain duties in connection with the welfare of pupils at grant-maintained schools. Briefly these are:

● to ensure there are sufficient schools for the area, taking into account the contribution made by any grant-maintained schools in the area
● to ensure that parents comply with the law on school attendance. This means that the LEA when notified that a child is not attending a grant-maintained school when they should be must still investigate and take proceedings if necessary
● to make free transport available to and from schools as required by law
● to pay for children's board and lodging if they attend a grant-maintained school where this would have been paid if the school was still maintained by them
● to carry out their duties in respect of special educational needs and provision.

The LEA have power to make certain grants for clothing, etcetera, even when children go to the grant-maintained school: they are put specifically under a duty to carry out their functions so that they treat children at such schools no less favourably than others. They also have to run their careers service as a central one for all pupils in their area.

School Closures

LEAs faced with falling school rolls and the need to run their service economically have the power to close schools if there are surplus school places in their area. They must publish detailed proposals, allow a two-month period for objections to be made and considered, and then either apply to the Secretary of State for approval of their plans, or where they do not have to do this at least tell him that they have decided to carry out their plans for closure. Schools cannot avoid being closed down by a last-ditch attempt to apply for grant-maintained status, but they can get in at the beginning of the closure process.

The local authority must consult the governing body before publishing proposals to close down the school, and at that time the governing body should decide whether or not to call a ballot of parents. The DES suggest that the governors should aim to publish their application for grant-maintained status before the end of the two-month period allowed for objections to the LEA's plans to close down the school. The two applications will then be decided by the Secretary of State, taking the application for grant-maintained status first.

Chapter 5

Employment and YTS

Employment

As far as the law relating to employment is concerned, children and young people under eighteen fall into three different groups:

1. under thirteen years old
2. those aged between thirteen and the end of compulsory school age (this can be from fifteen years eight months to sixteen years four months)
3. those aged between the end of compulsory school age and eighteen.

The law protecting children and young people is mostly health and safety legislation and, in that context, the definition of 'employment' is wide. It means helping in a trade or profession which is carried on for profit and it need not be paid, but this still excludes a considerable amount of work commonly done by youngsters which falls outside the various legal definitions of 'employment' (and therefore outside the restrictions in law). Some examples of this are babysitting, doing odd jobs and gardening on a casual, non-regular and self-employed basis.

Law in this area is still a tangle of Acts of Parliament which cover the whole country, and local authority bye-laws which cover only their own areas. Responsibility for enforcement is split between government departments, including the Health and Safety Executive and the DSS, local authorities and local education authorities, and the police.

Research has indicated widespread breaches of the law and generally poor enforcement of it.

1. UNDER THIRTEEN YEARS OLD

The law here is straightforward: no child under the age of thirteen may be employed.

There are only two exceptions. First, where a local authority bye-law permits it: for example, a local authority can permit children under thirteen to be employed by their parents in light agricultural or horticultural work and can permit them to do such work for up to an hour before school. This must not involve driving or riding on a tractor or similar machinery. (It is an offence to allow a child to ride on an agricultural implement of any kind.) Second, where a child is employed in the entertainment business and a licence has been obtained (see below).

2. THIRTEEN TO END OF COMPULSORY EDUCATION

For children in this age group, part-time and temporary full-time work is allowed but it is subject to restrictions. Basically, these are that the child cannot work:

- during school hours
- before 7 a.m. or after 7 p.m. on any day
- for more than two hours on a school day or on a Sunday
- in a job involving lifting, moving or carrying anything so heavy as to be likely to cause injury
- in factories, mines, quarries, construction sites, UK-registered ships and other undertakings.

On top of these, local authorities can make bye-laws imposing more restrictions. These will vary from borough to borough. Often they impose minimum age restrictions for certain types of work or they regulate the number of hours which can be worked and specify the frequency and length of holidays, meal breaks and rest periods.

Local education authorities have further powers to extend the controls on child employment. In particular, LEAs can prevent or restrict the employment which would otherwise be lawful of specific children in the interests of their particular health, well-being or educational needs. This is done by serving a written notice on the employer preventing the employment or placing restrictions on it. This is backed up by penalties if the notice is contravened.

Girls (and women) and boys under sixteen cannot be employed underground, for example in mines, unless the periods underground are not a large part of the job.

An under sixteen-year-old cannot be employed in a factory workshop unless only members of his or her family are employed in the particular undertaking, or unless the workshop is for training and part of a technical school or college. Under sixteen-year-olds must not operate dangerous machinery or handle poisons.

Farming has quite different, more lax, sets of rules and, perhaps as a result, children account for a quarter of all fatal agricultural accidents. Amazingly, children over thirteen are allowed to drive a tractor on private land and ride on agricultural equipment. They are not permitted to operate circular saws or remove guards from equipment of any kind.

3. SIXTEEN TO EIGHTEEN-YEAR-OLDS

The rules governing this age group will not only cover young people working part-time out of school or college, but also teenagers who have left school and are working full-time. The law for sixteen to eighteen-year-olds used to be similar to that for children. The 1989 Employment Act has, however, cut huge swathes through legislation developed over the years to protect this vulnerable group from exploitation. Most of this protective legislation has now gone, the rest can be dismissed at the stroke of a government minister's pen. The Employment Act 1989 has an appendix of seven pages of protective legislation dumped on the scrap-heap, much of which related to sixteen to eighteen-year-olds.

Generally, people in this category used not to be able to work in industry or shops for more than a maximum number of daily or weekly hours. Gone are the provisions preventing young people from working for more than forty-eight hours a week, or limiting overtime and providing for regular meal and rest breaks. Restrictions on night work remain for the time being, but the Secretary of State has the power to repeal this protection by an order. Sixteen to eighteen-year-olds must not, for the present, work after 10 p.m. or before 6 a.m. and there must be a break of at least eleven hours in each twenty-four hours. Sunday working is now permitted.

Sixteen to eighteen-year-olds must receive full instruction and training before working with most machinery and be adequately supervised. They are not permitted to use power presses or circular saws or repair or maintain machinery or work on unguarded machinery at all. There are still a number of prohibited occupations such as blasting or working with various chemicals. All employers must notify the local careers office within seven days of employing a sixteen to eighteen-year-old, detailing full information about themselves, the job and the young person.

Under seventeen-year-olds cannot work as street traders unless the local authority allows it where, for example, they work for their parents.

Under eighteen-year-olds cannot work as street traders on a Sunday. No one under eighteen can work in licensed premises, including off-licences and betting-shops.

Children in Entertainment

Where children want to take part in performances, the general rule is that a licence must be obtained. This part of the law applies to children who do this type of work professionally. It would not apply, for example, to children who take part in school plays or church concerts and receive no money for doing so apart from expenses.

Children under sixteen need a licence obtained from the local authority if

- there is to be an admission charge for the performance; or
- the performance is to take place on licensed premises or in a club; or
- the performance is to be broadcast or filmed (this includes rehearsals).

A licence is also required for a child who has been in other performances for more than three days in the last six months. For children under fourteen, there are more regulations covering the granting of licences. They will be granted only for acting a role which has to be played by someone of that age, or for participating in an opera or ballet or a mainly musical event.

The local authority must be satisfied that the child is fit enough to do the performance, that proper provision has been made to safeguard the child's welfare and health, that his or her education will not suffer and that his or her parent or guardian agrees.

If the local authority refuse the application then the parent can appeal to a magistrates' court.

Any person, including the parent, who allows a child to take part in a performance without a licence, or who lies when applying for the licence, commits a criminal offence and can be fined or imprisoned.

There are stricter rules covering more dangerous performances such as an acrobat or a contortionist. Under-twelves cannot be trained for these performances and under-sixteens only can be trained if a licence is granted.

Under-eighteens who wish to perform abroad must first apply for a licence to the magistrates' court. This does not apply if the person is only temporarily resident in this country.

Earnings

A child's earnings belong to him or her. This is quite clear. What is not so clear is whether a parent is entitled in law to deduct anything towards the child's keep.

A child of any age is taxed on his or her income in exactly the same way that an adult is. This income need not be from work. It can be from investments or maintenance paid by either parent to the child. It is important to remember, though, that grants and scholarships do not normally count as income and therefore the child does not pay income tax on them. A child is always entitled to claim the single person's tax allowance.

A person's national insurance record, which eventually entitles them to a state pension, starts at age sixteen. A child is then allocated a national insurance number. If the child is working then NI contributions are deducted from pay by the employer provided that the child earns more than the statutory lower earnings limit (this can change each year). If a child is not earning then he or she is credited with contributions up to their eighteenth birthday; for example, this would cover students. If the child does not pay contributions because he or she earns sufficiently low pay to be below the lower earnings limit then there is no credit but voluntary NI contributions can be paid. YTS trainees get credits or if their training allowance is above the lower earnings limit, then contributions are deducted.

Employment Protection Rights

After twelve weeks at work, everyone is entitled to a contract of employment setting out their right to holiday and holiday pay, their wage rate, hours of work, pension entitlement and disciplinary procedures. If you do not get a contract after twelve weeks and are still not given one after asking for it, you can go to an industrial tribunal which will order one to be provided or declare the terms of your contract. Surprisingly, there is now no minimum holiday entitlement but if your contract is silent on this point, a court would 'infer' holiday entitlement equivalent to that usual in the industry.

There are laws protecting employees against being unfairly dismissed, entitling them to be paid if made redundant, or to have maternity leave and pay if they become pregnant. The bad news, however, is that most of these rights pass young employees by because almost always they depend upon length of service. Often the crucial period is two years. For example, if a full-time employee (of any age), that is, someone who works more than sixteen hours a week, is sacked or made redundant then he or she cannot make a claim for unfair dismissal or for redundancy pay unless they have worked continuously for their employer for two years. Part-timers, who work between eight and sixteen hours a week, have to work for five years to get these rights.

Similarly, if a woman wishes to claim leave to have a baby and receive maternity pay she must, if she works sixteen hours a week, have worked for her employer for two years by the eleventh week before her baby is due. If she works between eight and sixteen hours per week she must have worked for her employer for five years.

If an employee is dismissed and is not paid any holiday pay which is owed, or is not paid his or her full entitlement to pay in lieu of notice, then he or she can sue the employer for wrongful dismissal to recover that notice or holiday pay. This is quite distinct from unfair dismissal and it does not depend upon length of service, it depends on the terms of the employment contract.

It is also important to note that a young employee can, at sixteen, join a trade union.

Discrimination

The race and sex discrimination laws do not require any 'time serving' and children and young people are protected by this legislation if there is an employment contract, on YTS or most other training, for education and in respect of the provision of any service. You are entitled not to be treated any differently because of sex or colour, race, etcetera. The remedies under the legislation are, however, very limited and it often takes a very long time to enforce your rights.

Youth Training Schemes (YTS)

If a young person leaves full-time education before the age of eighteen and cannot find work, he or she is not normally entitled to claim income support. They are supposed instead to find a place on a YTS. While in youth training, they are paid a training allowance. If this is lower than the amount which the Department of Social Security says a young person needs to live on then their income is topped up by income support even though they are under eighteen. Certain young people are exempted and can claim income support when they are sixteen or seventeen – for details see Chapter 6. Nobody *has* to do YTS – it is just that they cannot claim income support if they do not find work in some other way.

What Choices Does a Trainee Have?

WHAT IS YTS?

YTS is a training programme for sixteen and seventeen-year-olds which lasts for up to two years. If a young person leaves full-time education before eighteen and is unemployed the government guarantees them the offer of a place. Programmes vary in content but a trainee receives work experience, supervision and training with an employer, and further education or training at a college for at least twenty weeks on a two-year programme and at least seven weeks on a one-year programme.

IS YTS COMPULSORY?

The answer is no, *but* ... if a school leaver who is under eighteen cannot find some other form of work he or she cannot claim income support. Although the government guarantees each applicant the offer of a place they do not guarantee that every applicant can have the exact training and work experience that they want.

HOW IS YTS RUN?

YTS is supervised by the Manpower Services Commission who appoint approved training organizations to act as managing agents and actually run the schemes. These organizations are generally companies, local authorities, colleges of further education or voluntary organizations. There is one appointed for each area, and they supervise the individual firms and employers who offer work experience to trainees. It is the responsibility of the managing agents to provide training and skilled instructors; to enforce health and safety regulations; and to ensure that equal opportunities are offered regardless of race or sex.

WHO IS ELIGIBLE FOR A YTS?

● Any sixteen- or seventeen-year-old school leaver who has not found a job.

- Some young people who are already working, for example in apprentice-ships.
- Disabled school leavers who are aged eighteen to twenty-one.
- Eighteen-year-olds who could not start YTS earlier because of pregnancy, because they needed to improve their English, or because they were serving custodial sentences.

HOW LONG DOES YTS LAST?

This depends on how long a trainee stays on in full-time education and how soon after leaving school or college he or she joins YTS.

In general, if a prospective trainee leaves school at sixteen and joins YTS within twelve months, then they are entitled to a two-year programme. Their entitlement will be cut by one month for each month they delay joining YTS after the first twelve months are up.

If they stay on an extra year, leaving at seventeen, and they join YTS within a year, then they are entitled to one year on it. They cannot go on YTS if they do not join it within a year of finishing full-time education.

Eighteen-year-olds who could not start earlier and disabled young people are entitled to a two-year programme.

DOES YTS LEAD TO A JOB OR A QUALIFICATION?

YTS does not necessarily lead to a job, and the government are careful not to guarantee that it does. Obviously the idea is that employers will be attracted by the idea of employing youngsters and will take them on if they do well. It has been suggested, however, that some employers look upon the scheme as a source of cheap labour with no obligation to provide long-term jobs. In general, though, it is likely that youngsters who have taken part will be at some advantage in the job market over their contemporaries who have no work experience or training.

Increasingly, those who administer the scheme are trying to persuade participating employers to offer 'employed YTS' rather than non-employed training. The distinction is that employed trainees are full employees of their employers with normal terms and conditions rather than the truncated ones which apply to non-employed trainees. They also receive rather better pay than the normal training allowance. In the past, the majority of trainees have been non-employed, but this is changing. In some parts of the country, as many as 30 or 40 per cent of trainees are employed.

It is possible to gain vocational qualifications, such as City and Guilds Certificates, on YTS. If a trainee stays on a YTS programme for more than twelve weeks, they receive a YTS certificate when they leave which records what they have achieved. It is also possible to do an apprenticeship as an employed trainee.

MONEY AND YTS

A trainee either receives a training allowance if he/she is a non-employed trainee or a wage if he/she is an employed trainee. This must not be lower than the minimum training allowance.

Trainees who are not employed may be entitled to claim their travel expenses and a lodging allowance where the training takes place away from home. The rates for the training allowance go up periodically and can be obtained on inquiry at a local careers office or jobcentre. They are, however, not high.

Income tax and national insurance contributions are not usually paid by YTS trainees unless they are employed trainees or they have an extra source of income. Frankly this is because the training allowance is so low that they do not reach the threshold of the personal allowance for tax or the lower earnings limit for NI. If this is the case, they are credited with NI contributions.

Income support can be claimed to top up the income of trainees whose allowance is lower than the amount that the DSS says you need to live on. This might apply, for example, where a trainee has a family or dependents living with him or her.

If a sixteen- or seventeen-year-old has had a job or been a YTS trainee since leaving school but leaves, they can claim a bridging allowance of income support. This is payable for up to eight weeks in any twelve-month period. This is intended to tide them over while they look for work or a YTS place and they must register for work or YTS at a careers office or jobcentre.

Parents of sixteen- and seventeen-year-old school leavers who are registered for work or YTS will continue to receive child benefit and income support dependency additions for their children for:

- sixteen weeks after the first Monday in September when the child leaves school in the summer;
- sixteen weeks after the first Monday in January when the child leaves school at Christmas;

● sixteen weeks after the week following Easter Monday when the child
leaves school at Easter.

WHAT RIGHTS DOES A TRAINEE HAVE?

Training Agreement
All trainees get a training agreement at the start of the programme setting out
their rights and responsibilities and giving details of the terms and conditions,
such as pay, holidays and sick leave.

Working Hours
These are at least thirty hours a week but not usually more than forty hours a
week, excluding meal breaks. If the trainee is required to work outside normal
hours, for example, in the hotel trade at weekends or in the evenings, then this
has to be accepted as part of the job, but parental consent is needed if the trainee
is under eighteen.

Holidays
A trainee gets at least eighteen days' paid holiday per year plus bank and public
holidays or time off in lieu.

Sick Leave
Trainees get three weeks' paid sick leave but must inform their scheme straight-
away that they are sick and get a doctor's certificate if they are off for more than
seven days. Their money will stop after three weeks' absence until their return.

Other Time Off
Trainees get time off without loss of money in order to take tests or exams
connected with the programme, and to attend job and career interviews if they
are not already employed. This time off must be arranged in advance with their
supervisor or training officer.

Health and Safety
This is the responsibility of the managing agent and the employer providing
work experience who are supposed to ensure that trainees are never exposed to
danger. However, the health and safety laws which apply to adult employees do
not apply to all trainees. If a trainee, or parent of a trainee, has a complaint or
worry it should be made to the scheme supervisor or the trade union or health

and safety representative. Trainees are supposed to receive training in health and safety and in their duty to avoid injury to others as well as themselves. They are supposed to be issued with protective clothing and equipment if it is needed.

There is some concern at the number of injuries sustained by trainees, which have unfortunately included some fatal accidents. Major accidents or fatalities are some two and a half times higher per 100,000 YTS trainees than they were four years ago. Unguarded machinery and lack of supervision is a contributory factor. Injuries to fingers account for some 26 per cent of accidents. Employers can be fined only a maximum of £2000 under the Factories Acts.

All accidents must be reported immediately to the supervisor. The trainee should ensure that it is entered in the accident book which the employer must maintain. It is the duty of the managing agent to investigate and report to the training agency which is part of the Manpower Services Commission. A trainee who is injured or who contracts an industrial disease might be entitled to claim industrial injuries benefit. Advice can be obtained from the managing agent, the trade union representative or from a citizens' advice bureau (CAB). All activities on the YTS have insurance cover and it may be that an injured trainee should claim against the scheme. Again, seek the advice of the union representative, the CAB or a solicitor. A YTS trainee would qualify for free advice from a solicitor under the green form scheme (see Chapter 13).

Trade Union Membership
A trainee has the right to join any union which will take him or her as a member. A union with whom the employer or work-experience provider deals can represent trainees in grievance and disciplinary procedures.

Complaints and Grievances
The training agreement should explain the procedure in detail. Complaints or concerns should be raised with the training officer or union representative in the first instance. If the trainee is at college then the students' union representative should be able to help. All YTS trainees at college are automatically members of the students' union. If this does not work then the grievance can be raised with the careers office or the area office of the training agency.

IS IT POSSIBLE TO CHANGE TO ANOTHER PROGRAMME?
The answer is yes. A trainee can apply for a transfer to complete his or her training on another scheme. The managing agent can help to arrange this. If a trainee leaves before completing the programme they have the option of

re-entering YTS later for a further period of training. The disadvantage is that
they might not be able to get back on the same programme and re-entry is
possible only if they are still within the time allowed for completion of their
training. This means within three years of leaving school if they have a two-year
entitlement, and within two years of leaving school if they have a one-year
entitlement.

CAN A TRAINEE BE ASKED TO LEAVE?

The answer is yes, but only in cases of serious misconduct. This would probably
include stealing and persistent bullying of fellow trainees. Every effort is supposed
to be made to help trainees stay within YTS. If a trainee feels that he or she has
been treated unfairly in being asked to leave they can invoke the grievance
procedure laid down in the training agreement. Trainees do not have employment
protection rights (see above) unless they are in employed training and have
acquired rights through their contract of employment or their length of service.

Recent Changes to the Law

The Employment Act 1989 continues an unfortunate trend of trimming back the
rights of young employees which began in 1986 with the removal of their right
to a minimum wage. The protection of the Wages Council was then removed
from young people.

The Act ends the protections which formerly applied to the working hours and
holiday rights of sixteen- and seventeen-year-old employees. The restrictions on
night work will eventually disappear – they will legally be able to work at any hour.
They will be treated like adults, but there is no proposal to pay them an adult wage.
The changes will mean longer hours, fewer breaks and less money. They will have
fewer rights and protection than their contemporaries who are on YTS.

The restrictions on working with dangerous machinery or substances have
been kept as have the limits on hours worked by school students. Young people
are protected by the Health and Safety Act like all employees but lose those
safeguards which were specific to them. It is likely that as a result young people's
hours will be extended and they will be allowed to work at any hour. This comes
at a time when there are 15 per cent fewer factory inspectors who will inevitably
be spread over more work. The fear is that young people will be at greater risk of
accident and injury if they are working at night when core management is not on
hand to provide supervision.

Chapter 6

Benefits and Tax

This chapter describes in outline the financial aspects of bringing up children, the benefits that can be claimed for them, the position following family breakdown and the rights parents have under the tax and social security systems to get some financial assistance or advantage in the expensive business of having a family.

Money breeds law – and the volume of legislation, regulations and cases on all aspects of family finance means that this chapter cannot be exhaustive and can only be a guide to the area. Parents with detailed or specific problems should seek further advice and information from the sources at the end of the book.

A guiding principle of family finance is that parents support their own children, whether they do this through their own employment or resources or by claiming their entitlement to state benefits through the social security system. Social security law places parents under a legal liability to maintain their children. This includes unmarried fathers who have been adjudged to be the fathers of their non-marital children, and the mothers of non-marital children.

Social security is the system of cash benefits payable by the state to people who can and do claim them. The system began in 1911 as an insurance scheme, when the employed paid compulsory contributions from their wages into a fund which provided pensions on retirement. As a contributory scheme the amount and extent of cash paid out depended on the amount of cash paid in, and the employed worker's contribution record. The idea was that most financial needs would be dealt with through national insurance (NI) as they arose, but that there would have to be some form of financial supplement for people who for various reasons did not have a full record of contributions. The 'supplementary' benefit scheme was intended to work in tandem with the NI scheme, to top up the amounts paid through NI and protect people with insufficient or no contributions – and therefore reduced or no pay outs – from poverty. Supplementary benefit is now called income support (IS). 'Social security' is the term that covers NI benefits and income support, family credit and child benefit.

Income support, although intended to be just a safety net for a few, now supports far more people than NI benefits. Whatever the sociological reasons for this, the fact is that increasing numbers of children live on or near the poverty line, and that family breakdown forces more parents into the social security system every year.

Although NI is basically a contributory insurance scheme, the system has developed and expanded, and some benefits have now been introduced under it which are not linked to the payment of contributions. However, because of the basic insurance principle – getting money back because you have paid money in – claimants for benefits under the NI scheme whether contributory or not are not means-tested. Being poor is not one of the conditions of eligibility.

As income support is paid to supplement a low income, and poverty is a condition of entitlement, claimants are means-tested to see if they qualify.

Child benefit (CB) is different from other benefits in that it is neither means-tested nor dependent on contributions paid during employment, and this and the other social security benefits specifically for children will be dealt with in detail further on.

National Insurance Benefits

NI benefits are payable on retirement, on unemployment and in sickness. The amounts paid out are not high and if claimants have no other source of income they may be entitled to income support and other means-tested benefits.

The scheme is funded by contributions from those in work, whether they are employed by someone else or working for themselves, employers' contributions and a top-up from government funds. Workers' contributions are divided into four classes, which give different entitlements to benefits.

CLASS I

Class 1 contributions are a graduated percentage of earnings compulsorily deducted from salary at source. They are paid by earners employed under a contract of service, aged between the school-leaving age (sixteen) and pensionable age (sixty for women; sixty-five for men). The contribution is paid on earnings between the lower earnings limit and the upper earnings limit (these change each year).

Payment of Class 1 entitles you to the full range of contributory benefits:

- unemployment benefit
- sickness and invalidity benefits
- widows' benefit
- retirement pension.

In addition, child's special allowance and maternity allowance can be paid but the former is on the way out and the latter now limited by recent legislation.

CLASS 2

Class 2 contributions are flat-rate weekly contributions. They are paid by all self-employed people who must arrange payment themselves, either through National Giro, direct debit through a bank or buying stamps for a contribution card.

They give entitlement to:

- sickness and invalidity benefits
- widows' benefit
- retirement pension

Child's special allowance and maternity allowance are payable as under Class 1.

CLASS 3

These are voluntary flat-rate weekly contributions that can be paid by people who want to keep up their rights to some entitlements although not working. They may be paid by anyone between sixteen and pensionable age, and should be paid either by the end of the year or within the end of the second year following that. They give entitlement to widows' benefits, retirement pension and child's special allowance – as above.

CLASS 4

These are compulsory contributions payable on the profits or earnings of the self-employed between certain levels which are set each year. They give no entitlement to benefits – the self-employed who have to pay Class 4 will already be paying Class 2 and be entitled to that range.

Eligibility Conditions

For most contributory benefits there are two conditions – the first is that in any year the claimant has made or had credited to him a fixed amount of contributions; the second that in the relevant year before the claim is made the claimant has actually paid a fixed number of contributions. For long-term benefits – like pensions – this condition has to be satisfied for a number of years. If a claimant is eligible under the first condition, but has not paid enough contributions under the second condition, or with long-term benefits was not paid up for the full number of years, the benefit can still in some cases be paid, but at a reduced rate.

Benefit years run from the first Sunday in January – the tax year runs from 6 April. The 'relevant year' for the second condition is the last completed tax year before the benefit year in which the claim is made.

Unemployment Benefit (UB)

UB is paid at a fixed rate, reviewable annually. Some people over pensionable age can claim UB and are paid at a higher rate for themselves and adult dependents, and can also claim an addition for dependent children under sixteen. People under pensionable age are paid a weekly rate for themselves, and for adult dependents. They cannot claim anything for dependent children.

Broadly, people are entitled to UB if they lose their employment and they are under pensionable age.

UB is a short-term benefit paid for each day of unemployment that forms part of a period of interruption of employment.

The amount of UB is fixed at two rates, with higher benefits for people of pensionable age. People under pensionable age can claim additions for adult dependents but they cannot now claim any increases for child dependents – as in the nature of things the majority of unemployed people with young children will fall into this age group, if they have no additional income they must then apply for income support for their children.

UB is administered through unemployment offices. The claim is made by personal attendance at the office to fill in a claim form and questionnaires about availability. Claimants must sign a declaration saying that they were unemployed in the period for which they are claiming, were capable of and available for work on each of those days, and satisfy and continue to satisfy the conditions for receipt of benefit for themselves and any dependents. After the initial claim you will be told to attend the office every week or fortnight to sign the declaration after that. To be available means not only physically around to take up employment if offered, but prepared to do so – for example, any statement that indicates you might have to delay accepting an offer of work because of having to make child-care arrangements could be construed by an adjudication officer as showing you were not genuinely available.

The sort of work you are expected to be available for is, to begin with, the sort of work you have been doing in the past, and claimants are allowed to place some reasonable restrictions on the type or conditions of work they are prepared to do. The restrictions have a better chance of being seen as reasonable by the department if you can prove your restrictions do not rule out work in your field – for example, if you want to work only in school hours, show that employers in your area operate flexi-time or that part-time working suits their situation.

CREDITING CONTRIBUTIONS

Contributions are credited to increase the contribution record of people who are unable to pay them either because they are unemployed or cannot work because of other responsibilities. They protect future benefit rights.

Credits are given automatically with no need to make a claim for them to

- the unemployed who are signing on
- people who cannot work because they look after an invalid
- people over sixty
- widows
- divorced women.

The credits of particular relevance to families are home responsibility protection credits and starting, education and training credits for young people.

Home Responsibility Protection
This credit allows people to stay at home looking after children without affecting their rights to the long-term benefits of retirement pension, widows' pension and widowed mother's allowance.

No specific claim for this protection need be made. You get it if you are entitled to CB – but note that although CB can be paid for children in full-time education up to nineteen, HRP lasts only until the child is sixteen.

Starting Credits
Entitlement to the long-term benefits of retirement pensions and widowed

mother's allowance is based not only on the amount of contributions paid in each tax year, but on the number of years during which these contributions should be paid. The number of years is calculated on how long a claimant's working life was, and for this purpose 'working life' starts at sixteen.

Young people who stay on at school after the school-leaving age of sixteen, when technically they could start work and pay contributions, would therefore be penalized when their entitlement to benefits was calculated on retirement.

A year's worth of Class 3 credits is therefore given to young people for the tax year in which they are sixteen and for two years after that.

Class 1 credits are given to people for the year in which they become seventeen, going towards unemployment and sickness benefit only. Before any entitlement to UB arises for a young person they must have actually been employed and actually paid enough contributions to qualify.

Education Credits

Students on a course of full-time study, or approved training or an apprenticeship get Class 1 credits for the tax year in which they finish the course as long as they started it before they were twenty-one. These count towards UB and sickness benefit only.

Training Credits

Those taking part in training courses run by the Manpower Services Commission or their successors can get Class 1 credits.

YOUNG PEOPLE AND THE INSURANCE SCHEME: BARRING FROM BENEFIT

Young people under eighteen must not only sign on at the unemployment office like adults to get benefit, but must also register for employment either at a job-centre or local education authority careers office. If they do not, their benefit can be stopped.

Income Support

Income support is part of what used to be called the supplementary benefits scheme. This system was radically changed in April 1988 when supplementary benefits disappeared to be replaced by family credit (formerly family income supplement) and income support. Family credit is dealt with later in this chapter.

Income support is administered by the Department of Social Security through local offices. It is a means-tested benefit. As with all social security benefits, be they means-tested or otherwise, there is an enormous amount of law, but there is help through the maze for claimants. Post offices and DSS offices have a range of leaflets that briefly describe what benefits are available and citizens' advice bureaux (CABs) give free advice on social security. There are excellent publications from the Child Poverty Action Group (CPAG) which cover all social security benefits.

The basic rule about entitlement to income support is if in doubt ask, and ask firmly. As the regulations lay down what can be claimed, ask which regulation applies to your case, and why. If you do not get clear and satisfactory answers, get further help or information as above. This is particularly important because at present the system is creaking severely under the strain of coping with the numbers of claims made each year, and offices are understaffed and subject to industrial disputes.

Claims are administered by adjudication officers who make the necessary decisions about entitlements. If an adjudication officer decides against you, there is a right of appeal to a social security tribunal. The right to appeal is automatic in that you do not need to show a point of law is involved. If the tribunal decides against you, you can appeal on a point of law to the social security commissioner. Unless you know the regulations and law thoroughly, you should consider getting professional help for any appeal.

IS is a cash payment made to those whose income is not enough to live on. It is the safety net of the welfare benefits system in that you need no NI contributions or credits in order to claim it. Crudely, your income is deducted from the amount you need to live on and the result is the amount of income support you will get.

Eligibility

Like unemployment benefits, entitlement to IS is intimately linked with availability for work, and people in full-time work, however badly paid, cannot claim it.

Full-time work is twenty-four hours per week done either for payment or in expectation of payment – if the number of hours worked per week varies, then the test is how many hours per week are normally worked. There are exceptions to this rule; for the disabled who are allowed to work longer hours without being disqualified from benefit; for childminders working from home; and for people on government or Manpower Services Commission training courses (including YTS and re-training for adults).

Parents working full time for a low wage may be able to claim another means-tested benefit, family credit.

As well as those working more than twenty-four hours per week, people *cannot* claim IS if they are:

● under nineteen and still at school or in full-time non-advanced education
● students in advanced education
● not resident in UK
● married to or the cohabitees of claimants (either partner can claim but not both)
● married to or the cohabitees of people in full-time work
● in custody
● involved in a trade dispute at the time of the claim (strikers are not entitled to IS for the first seven days of the dispute)
● in possession of capital which exceeds the allowed amount
● out of work, having left a job voluntarily without good reason
● out of work, having been sacked for misconduct
● out of work, having failed without good reason to apply for or take a suitable job
● unemployed, having failed without good reason to take up government training.

People *can* claim IS if they are not in one of the above groups *and* they are available for full-time work and sign on at an UB office or jobcentre.

Regulations provide that certain categories of claimant are exempted from having to be available for work. The list includes the blind and disabled, those looking after severely disabled people at home, and people over sixty. The exemptions of particular relevance to families are:

1. A single person who either has a dependent child under sixteen living with him or is fostering an under-sixteen-year-old for a local authority or a voluntary organization. (A single person here means a man or woman living on his or her own – the exemption does not apply to partners in a married or unmarried couple, where one should be available for work unless exempted under another category. The child must be under sixteen. Note that for this exemption the person taking care of the child does not have to be getting child benefit for him or her.)

2.   A person who is looking after a child under sixteen because the child's parent or usual carer is ill or temporarily away.
3.   A person who is looking after either their partner or another member of the family aged nineteen or younger who is ill.
4.   A woman who is pregnant and who the DSS accept is unable to work, or who has eleven weeks or less to wait until the birth, or a woman who has had her baby but whose baby is less than seven weeks old.
5.   A YTS trainee whose training allowance is topped up by IS.

Calculating Income Support

The formula for doing this is simply expressed as follows: deduct the claimant's income (this includes earnings from part-time work – less than twenty-four hours a week) from the amount that he or she needs to live on and the result is the amount of IS claimable.

The claimant's needs are called the 'applicable amount'. They are divided up into three categories:

1.   Personal allowances – the amount which the DSS decide that you need for basic living expenses; this differs from personal allowances in income tax law
2.   Premiums – the amounts given for extra needs
3.   Housing costs – the amount given towards housing overheads.

1. PERSONAL ALLOWANCES

These are very low. They are reviewed each year. They vary according to the age of the claimant and whether he or she has a partner or is single. The personal allowance for a child varies according to the age of the child.

2. PREMIUMS

These are extra payments on top of personal allowances to help claimants cope with family responsibilities, age or ill-health. There are no longer any additions to benefit to help claimants cope with particular expenses incurred by their families, such as high heating costs, extra laundry or special dietary needs. Claimants who face these difficulties may be able to obtain assistance from the social fund, and are referred to that section of this chapter.

Premiums of particular relevance to families are:

Family Premium

This is payable if there is a child in the household for whom the claimant is responsible. The premium is payable per family, not per child. It can be paid even if you do not get a personal allowance for the child, for example because he or she has capital of more than the current limit. If the child lives with you only for part of the week, you can claim a proportion of the premium.

Lone-parent Premium

This is for single parents and is payable even if the claimant receives no personal allowance for the child, for example because the child has too much capital.

Disabled Child Premium

The claimant receives this if his or her child is receiving attendance allowance or mobility allowance or is blind. This premium is paid for each child who satisfies the condition. There is no entitlement if the child has capital of more than the current limit.

3. HOUSING COSTS

This includes mortgage interest payments if you are buying your home. However, repayments of capital off the mortgage are not covered, nor are insurance premiums for endowment policies which are often linked to mortgages. If the home is a flat with a long lease of more than twenty-one years, then you can claim for ground rent and service charges. If you are renting your home, then this should be paid for by housing benefit (HB) which you claim from your local council if you are on IS. Any costs which are not included in the 'applicable amount' and paid by the DSS should be covered by the HB scheme.

HB is a separate claim which is made to the local authority. It is paid either direct or in the form of reduced rent. Water rates are unfortunately not covered by HB; you are supposed to pay them out of your IS.

What about Rent Paid to You?

If you have a grown-up son or daughter living with you then the whole of their contribution to the cost of the accommodation and the living expenses will be ignored, but there will be deductions made from your housing costs.

Rules on Capital

You can have up to £3000 and still get IS. You can not get it if you have more than £6000. (The rates applied at the time of writing but they change each year. It is advisable to check with your local DSS office.) If your savings or capital fall in between those two figures, you can still get benefit, but it is reduced by the income that you are deemed to earn from your capital. This is called tariff income. It is set each year.

When calculating your capital the value of your home is disregarded. Savings from your past earnings are taken into account only when all the debts of that period including tax have been deducted. Money put aside for current bills is counted as capital.

Any money which you receive from the social fund (see later) or from social services under Section 1 of the Child Care Act 1980 will be ignored. 'Section 1' money is sometimes paid by social services to help a family where this will prevent a child from being taken into care. It is also sometimes paid to help a child to leave care.

HOW IS MONEY IN TRUST TREATED?

The rules are complicated and if you are in this position you are advised to seek expert advice. Broadly, any money held in trust for you will be taken into account if you are absolutely entitled to it. Payments may be treated as capital or income depending on the circumstances. Sometimes money is put in trust following the receipt of damages for a personal injury suffered by the claimant or a member of the family. In this case the value of the fund is usually ignored for two years. If the beneficiary of the trust is a child, the value is ignored until the child leaves non-advanced education. However, the payments made from the trust will be treated as capital or income as appropriate.

Income Support and Couples

A couple generally fare less well than two single people in terms of IS. They receive a couple rate which is less than that for two single people. A couple is two people of the opposite sex living together and sharing the same household. This does not apply to gay couples of either sex who will be paid benefit as two single people.

Either party can be the claimant provided that he or she satisfies the conditions of entitlement. They can swap the role between them if they wish. It is the needs, income and capital of both parties which are assessed. If either is in full-time work, the other cannot claim.

If the DSS decide that a couple are cohabiting and reduce or disallow benefit, the decision can be appealed.

If the couple argue that they are not cohabiting, they should appeal. In any situation where the claimant does not share the benefit the partner who is being deprived can ask the DSS to direct that all or part of the benefit is paid to them. Alternatively, he or she can apply for a 'crisis loan' from the social fund. This would usually cover them for up to two weeks only. Whether they get any money depends on the seriousness of their situation and on how much money is left in the fund. For further details on the workings of the social fund, see 'One-off Payments and Emergencies'.

COUPLES WHO ARE NO LONGER TOGETHER

Where couples are married, they are liable in IS law to maintain one another and their children, even if they are separated. Once they are divorced, former spouses are not liable in IS law to maintain one another, but they are liable to maintain their children. Where couples have not been married, they are not liable to maintain one another under IS law if they separate. However, if such a couple have a child, then the parent with whom the child does not live is liable to maintain the child. The person liable to do the maintaining is known as the *liable relative*.

Claimants are obliged to divulge the amounts of maintenance, whether official through a court order or unofficial, that they receive. The DSS are hot on this at present because they want to discourage state dependency in favour of private family dependency.

If either the DSS or the claimant cannot secure voluntary maintenance from the former spouse or partner, then either they or the claimant can apply for a court order. Claimants who have been married should note, however, that if the DSS get the order then it lasts only as long as the claimant is on IS, at which point the claimant would have to get their own order. This anomaly does not apply to single mothers who were not married to the father of their child. If the DSS applies for a maintenance order, it can be transferred to the mother if she ceases to claim benefit. A claimant, whether divorced, separated or never married, can always get their own order and then make it over to the DSS by registering it at their local magistrates' court. The point of getting the DSS to apply for the order or assigning your order to them is that the DSS will pay you your benefit regularly even if the maintenance is not paid. Otherwise they will deduct the amount of your maintenance from your benefit, regardless of whether you are actually receiving it. Note, though, that as a result of an efficiency scrutiny the DSS are tending now to scale down their collection of maintenance on behalf of claimants.

It follows from this that the DSS will try to encourage the liable relative to support his or her dependents. The claimant should not however be refused IS for refusing to divulge the relative's whereabouts, so long as there is a good reason for not doing so *and* the claimant is living below the IS level. Equally, a claimant should not be penalized by being refused benefit if they cannot give information about the relative because they do not have it. A claimant caught in either of these situations and refused benefit can appeal.

Income Support and Single Parents

SINGLE MOTHERS

As mentioned above, single mothers who were never married to the father of their child can have a maintenance order applied for by the DSS transferred to them when they come off benefit. A single mother can sign over her own order if she has one to ensure regular money.

ONE-PARENT BENEFIT

This is a flat-rate weekly payment which can be claimed by single parents. It is not means-tested. It will however come off your IS if you decide to claim it. You are not obliged to claim it. If you receive only a small amount of IS it may be better for you not to claim one-parent benefit because it may disqualify you from IS altogether and therefore lose you the benefits that go with IS such as free school meals.

YOUNG SINGLE MOTHERS

Although under eighteen-year-olds cannot usually claim IS, single parents who are under eighteen but over sixteen can. Young mothers who are under sixteen cannot claim IS but they can claim child benefit and one-parent benefit. If they are living at home with their parents who are on IS, the parents can claim IS for their daughter and the baby until the mother is sixteen and can claim for herself and her child.

Additions for Children

A claimant can usually claim benefit for a child or young person who is living as a member of their household. The child concerned must be under sixteen, or under nineteen and still at school or a college of further education. Students must be studying full-time and in non-advanced education, that is up to and including A-level or its equivalent.

If your dependent child is sixteen or seventeen you can continue to claim for them if they are in full-time non-advanced education. If they have left education you can claim IS and child benefit for a period, then they are expected to take part in YTS if they cannot find work elsewhere. On YTS they are paid a training allowance.

A child who has left full-time education and is not working can claim IS in his or her own right at the age of eighteen if they meet the entitlement conditions. However, the parent's benefit for housing costs may be reduced on the basis that the child is expected to contribute to the household.

Some young people under nineteen who are still at school or college can claim IS in their own right, for example a girl with a child of her own.

Young People and Income Support

Until recently, young people in the age group sixteen to twenty-five were entitled to the same amount of social security as anyone else. Over recent years their rights have been steadily eroded because, in an effort to reduce dependency on the state, the government has decided that young people should become more dependent on their families.

Most under-eighteens are now not entitled to receive IS. Those in the age group eighteen to twenty-five receive less IS than other adults. There are some concessions to vulnerable groups but the basic premise seems to be that those under eighteen must take part in YTS or go without, and those aged eighteen to twenty-five must remain dependent upon their families.

Young people who leave school at sixteen or seventeen are not usually entitled to claim IS in their own right. They are expected to take a place on the youth training scheme, indeed the government states that it guarantees them a place. It should be said, however, that the guaranteed place will not necessarily be on the course which they most want, and they may well be expected to compromise their choice. Young people on YTS receive a training allowance.

If the training allowance is lower than the amount which the DSS say that you need to live on then you are entitled to claim IS to top up your income, even if you are under eighteen.

For more about YTS see Chapter 5.

WHAT HAPPENS IF A YOUNG PERSON BECOMES UNEMPLOYED?

If a sixteen- or seventeen-year-old has had a job or has taken part in YTS since leaving school but is no longer employed or has left YTS, then he or she is entitled to a bridging allowance of IS for up to eight weeks in any twelve-month period while looking for work or a YTS place. He or she must register for work or YTS at a careers office or jobcentre in order to qualify.

CAN PARENTS CLAIM INCOME SUPPORT FOR THEIR CHILDREN?

Parents of sixteen- or seventeen-year-old school leavers will continue to receive child benefit and IS dependency additions for their children for a period after the child leaves school.

The child must register for a job or for YTS, and the benefits will be paid for sixteen weeks beyond the first Monday in September; or the first Monday in January; or the first week after Easter Monday – depending on whether the child leaves school in summer, at Christmas or Easter.

CAN ANY UNDER-EIGHTEENS CLAIM INCOME SUPPORT?

There are broadly three categories of young people who can claim IS under the age of eighteen in their own right.

1. Young people for whom severe hardship would result if they were not paid IS. They can claim for as long as the severe hardship lasts. An example would be young people seeking emergency accommodation at night shelters. Severe hardship is a tricky test to meet and young people are likely to find it easier to claim if they fall into either of the other two categories described below. Young people cannot appeal a refusal of IS in this situation.
2. Young people who do not have to sign on for work as a condition of getting benefit. This includes those who are single parents, who are registered

blind, who are incapacitated through physical or mental disablement or
illness, women who are pregnant (they need not sign on for eleven weeks
before the birth and for seven weeks after), and those who are receiving a
training allowance.

3. Certain young people who are living away from home. This category
includes those who are genuinely estranged from their parents; who have no
living parent or guardian; who have been in care within the last two years;
who are on bail, or under the supervision of a probation officer or a social
worker and are placed away from home; who cannot live at home for fear of
being physically or sexually abused; who are handicapped or mentally ill and
away from home because their parents cannot cope; whose parents are in
prison, or in hospital or unavoidably absent abroad (this would include
parents prevented from coming to this country by the immigration rules);
and those who are married. Young people in this category are entitled to
benefit for a set period only. This is from the week following the first
Monday in September for sixteen weeks if they are summer school leavers,
or if they leave at Christmas or at Easter for twelve weeks from the week
following the first Monday in January or from the second week following
Easter Monday.

One-off Payments and Emergencies

If a claimant needs extra income support to meet one-off expenses or emergencies,
an application can be made to the social fund. This is administered by the DSS.
It is the safety net of the IS system, which is itself the safety net of the social
security system.

It is also possible to get an urgent case payment of IS. This is a reduced rate
of IS payable in emergencies to people who are not entitled to IS. It is possible
to claim this if you are treated as receiving income but for some reason it has not
been paid to you. The DSS must be satisfied that if you do not receive a
payment you or your family will suffer hardship. All capital and income available
to you will be taken into account.

Payments from the social fund will be budgeting loans or crisis loans, which are
repayable, or community care grants which are not. The fund is cash-limited,
which means that each office has a budget which is has to stick to. If the money
for that year has run out then you will not get your loan or grant. These types of
payments from the fund are discretionary only. If they are refused, then there is
no independent appeal, only internal reviews.

The DSS will look carefully at all the circumstances and will make a payment only if the application fulfils all the criteria, and if the payment cannot be obtained by the applicant from any other source.

BUDGETING LOANS

The applicant must have been on IS for twenty-six weeks to qualify for one of these. Applications are supposed to be decided within twenty-eight days. They are classified as high, medium or low priority. High priority would be a loan for essential furniture and household equipment or for bedclothes. Medium priority covers non-essential furniture and household equipment or redecoration. Items classed as low priority would be rent in advance where the applicant already has secure accommodation and the move is not essential, or removal expenses where the move is not essential. You cannot get a loan of this type for domestic assistance, for legal or medical expenses, or for repairs to a council property.

CRISIS LOANS

These are given to meet expenses arising in an emergency or because of a disaster. They are usually given to provide a specific item, or service, or to provide living expenses for up to fourteen days. You do not need to be claiming IS already to qualify for this type of loan, but you must be without sufficient resources to meet your family's immediate short-term needs. The loan must be either the only means by which serious damage or serious risk to your health or safety or that of someone in your family may be prevented, or it must be for rent in advance required by a private landlord and the payment is being made to help the recipient to re-enter the community after a stay in institutional or residential care.

Applications should be dealt with as soon as possible, and it is advisable to apply in person at the local DSS office. All the family's resources are taken into account, except for the value of the home, business assets and personal possessions. Loans of this type are given for disasters such as fire, flooding, being stranded away from home, loss of money, or living expenses for up to fourteen days. They are not given for holidays, housing costs, telephone charges or car expenses unless for emergency travel expenses.

There is no minimum, and the loan cannot be so high that you would be unlikely to be able to repay it. Payment is usually by giro, but it can be in food or accommodation vouchers, or travel warrants.

Loans in General

Because these are loans, you are under an obligation to repay them. The repayments will be deducted from the benefit. They still have to be paid even if you come off benefit. The DSS can take court proceedings to recover the debt. The maximum repayment period is usually seventy-eight weeks, but this can be extended to 104 weeks, for example if you take out another loan from the social fund.

COMMUNITY CARE GRANTS

These are not repayable. There are a number of situations in which people on IS can claim them. The ones of most relevance to families are grants given to ease exceptional pressure on families; to ease domestic crises; and to help a parent to visit a child who is with the other parent pending the outcome of a custody case. Any capital that the applicant or partner has over a small base limit can affect how much they get. The priority groups for receiving grants include families under stress and young people leaving care or custody.

Young people leaving custody who cannot go to live with their parents may get a grant to set up home and buy clothing. They can also claim living expenses if they are on short home leave. Similarly, young people leaving care can receive grants to set up home and pay fuel connection charges. This would include young women in care who have had babies and are leaving mother and baby homes. Parents can apply for a grant where a child up to the age of nineteen is returning home after being in care for at least four months. This would be to provide essential furniture and clothing. Grants can be used to help women and children who have been subjected to domestic violence. This would be given to help them to move, to set up home elsewhere, and to replace lost clothing and footwear.

The parents of disabled children or children with behavioural problems brought about by mental handicap or illness can be assisted by grants. These could be obtained to purchase washing machines, tumble driers, replacement clothing where there is excessive wear and tear, or security items such as barriers for stairs.

Where there have been domestic crises, priority is given to those with the most acute needs, such as single parents too ill to care for their children. Grants can be given here where a child is returning home from the care of relatives or friends, or going to their care, or to help the parents to visit their child in such a situation. This does not apply where the care is provided by the local authority.

Grants are never given for phone expenses, housing costs which cannot be met by a budgeting loan, or expenses which the local authority must meet. Applications should be decided within twenty-eight days.

Reviews and Complaints
These can be applied for within twenty-eight days of the decision, in writing, giving the reasons. The DSS must look at all the circumstances, the guidance issued and the directions given. They must in addition look at new evidence and at relevant changes in circumstances. If you are in this situation and are not satisfied with any aspect of a grant or a loan, we suggest that you get advice from a CAB or a law centre.

THE FAMILY FUND

If you have a severely handicapped child under the age of sixteen, and you are unable to get a grant or a loan to meet the need you have, it may be worth looking into the possibility of a payment from the family fund. This is a government fund administered by the Rowntree Trust. It exists to provide help in the form of goods, services or a grant of money to families with severely handicapped children under sixteen. Local authority foster children are, however, excluded. Help can be provided to pay for family outings, holidays, washing machines, clothing, bedding or furniture. There is no income test, but the family circumstances are taken into account.

Child Benefit

This is governed by the Child Benefit Act 1975 and Regulations. The benefit is neither means-tested nor dependent on payment of national insurance contributions and is paid to people responsible for one or more children. It is paid at a fixed weekly rate per child, and is reviewed annually: the rate cannot go down from year to year, although it does not have to be increased, only considered.

Although CB is not means-tested and is paid to everyone regardless of their income if they are not otherwise disqualified, it is treated as a resource for income support purposes and if it is claimed it is deducted from the weekly allowance given for the child. The rationale behind this is that the DSS IS payments are intended to cover all the child's needs. Even if this applies to you, it is still advisable to claim CB because getting it at all qualifies you for certain other benefits.

Although technically CB is a social security benefit it is dealt with separately from local DSS offices at a central base in Newcastle. The address is Child Benefit Centre, PO Box 1, Newcastle-upon-Tyne, NE88 1AA.

Eligibility

Parents or other people who are responsible for children can claim CB if in the week for which it is claimed the child was living with them or they were contributing to the cost of providing for them at a weekly rate not less than the current rate of child benefit.

If you are temporarily separated from the child and not therefore 'living with' him or her, CB can still be claimed unless you have been separated from the child for more than fifty-six days – eight weeks – out of the sixteen weeks before the week in which you claim CB. You will not lose benefit under this rule if during those fifty-six days the child was absent from you solely because he or she was

● being educated full-time at a recognized educational establishment; or
● receiving medical or other in patient treatment; or
● in residential accommodation for medical purposes; and,
● if the absence is longer than eight weeks, you are supporting the child.

The effect of these rules is that if your child attends boarding school or has to go into hospital you still get CB for those periods away from you.

You can still claim CB for the first eight weeks of your child being in care.

How to Claim

You will have to get forms CB2 and CB3 from the local DSS office and make a written claim, enclosing the birth or adoption certificate. If you claim late, after the child was born or came to live with you, you can still get benefit for the six months before you made the claim, without having to explain yourself. This may be extended to twelve months' arrears if you have 'good cause' for your late claim.

CB is paid for all children under sixteen, and children between sixteen and nineteen who are getting full-time education. It is not paid for children of whatever age who are:

● married
● claiming IS in their own right

- being educated in the course of their employment – e.g. apprentices or on YTS except for approximately four months after they leave school (see Chapter 5)
- in custody
- in care longer than eight weeks.

RESIDENCE QUALIFICATIONS

You and your child should generally be resident in the UK. Until recently, families could absent themselves from the UK for a period of twenty-eight weeks and still claim CB for that time, but this has been reduced to eight weeks. This bars from benefit families who go abroad, e.g. to visit relatives in Asia, where a short visit makes no economic sense at all.

One-parent Benefit

This is a flat-rate weekly payment, paid in addition to CB, and paid in respect of the eldest child who qualifies. It is not taxed, but it counts as a resource when IS is claimed.

The claimant

- must be living with the child and entitled to claim child benefit for the child
- must not be cohabiting, or if married residing with his or her spouse
- must not be residing with a parent of the child unless the claimant is entitled in respect of another child and is not residing with the parent of that child.

Cohabitees are classed as still residing together during any period of temporary absence. Married couples are classed as still residing together until they are legally separated or divorced, or until they have been apart for at least thirteen weeks and the separation is likely to be permanent. They are also classed as residing together even if one or both are temporarily or permanently in a hospital or an institution.

This benefit does not require an NI contribution record, nor is it means-tested. It is not payable when the recipient is receiving guardian's allowance, widows' benefit or invalid care allowance for the child. If the recipient gets an increase of any other benefit in respect of the child, the increase will be reduced by the amount of one-parent benefit.

Guardian's Allowance (GA)

This is a flat-rate weekly payment made to those looking after children who are effectively orphans. It is paid in respect of each child if there is more than one. It does not depend on a NI contributions record, and it is not means-tested.

1. The claimant must be entitled to child benefit for the child.
2. The child must be an orphan, or if only one parent has died the surviving parent must have disappeared or be serving a long prison sentence (over five years).
3. The residence conditions must be satisfied – at least one of the child's parents must have been born in the UK or have spent a total of at least one year here in any two-year period since reaching the age of sixteen.
4. The child must be living with the claimant or be maintained by him or her at the rate of at least £8.40 per week (the figure at the time of writing) in addition to any payment being made to qualify the claimant for child benefit.

This benefit can be claimed by step-parents. Adoptive parents may continue to receive it if they were entitled to do so immediately before the adoption. Where adoptive parents die, or where one dies and the other has disappeared or is in prison, GA may be payable if all the other conditions are met. If a single person adopted the child, then it is payable if that person dies.

If a child's parents were not married, GA is payable if the mother dies and paternity has not been clearly established or admitted by the father.

If a child's parents, whether natural or adoptive, get divorced, one of them dies and the other parent does not have custody of the child, was not maintaining the child, and was not obliged by a court order to do so, GA is payable – but not to the surviving parent.

Family Credit (FC)

This is a means-tested benefit paid to low-income families in work. It was introduced in 1988 and it replaced family income supplement (FIS). It is assessed according to income on a sliding scale, as was FIS. It is tax-free.

The differences between FC and FIS are as follows:

- FIS gave a right to free school meals whereas FC does not
- FIS was paid irrespective of savings whereas FC is reduced by savings over an annually reviewed limit (£3000 at the time of writing)

- FIS was paid for a one-year period once assessed whereas FC is awarded for six months at a time
- FIS gave automatic entitlement to free milk and vitamins whereas FC does not
- FIS had a thirty-hour working week as the minimum threshold with a twenty-four hour week for single parents, whereas for FC it is twenty-four hours for everyone
- FIS was calculated on gross income whereas FC is based on net income.

To qualify, a family must include at least one child whether the family is headed by a couple or by a single person. The claimant or her partner (FC must usually be claimed by the woman) must usually work twenty-four hours or more per week and jointly their capital must not exceed an annually-reviewed limit (£6000, at the time of writing).

How much they get depends on the family's income and capital. A family does not qualify if the bread-winner's earnings come from working abroad.

If two people of the opposite sex are cohabiting, they will be treated as a couple and only one of them will be able to claim on behalf of the family. Their joint income and capital are assessed. It is possible to appeal against an assessment of cohabitation. Separated couples are not treated as cohabiting.

CHILDREN

In order to claim FC for a dependent child, the child has to be under sixteen, or under nineteen and in full-time education. A young person does not count as a family member if they are receiving IS in their own right.

Where the parents of a child are separated, if the child spends part of the time with the non-custodial parent, then it is the parent who receives child benefit in respect of the child who can claim FC, provided that they qualify on other grounds. If neither parent claims child benefit, then the child is classed as part of the family of the parent with primary responsibility.

FC can be claimed for a child who is at boarding school or in temporary care; but not for one who is serving a custodial sentence, or who is being fostered for a local authority, or for the purposes of adoption; or who is in hospital or residential accommodation on a long-term basis and who is no longer in regular contact with his or her family. (Once a child is adopted, FC can be claimed provided that the family qualifies in every other way.)

CAPITAL

A family cannot claim FC if their capital amounts to more than the annually-reviewed limit (£6000 at the time of writing). If their capital amounts to between £3000 and £6000 then they are deemed to have income from it which will affect the assessment of their income. These parameters change annually and it is advisable to check with the local DSS office.

In a family headed by a couple, it is the capital of both parties which is assessed. A child's capital can affect FC; a family will not get FC for each child who has more than the capital limit (£3000 at the time of writing) unless it is a trust fund set up with the damages or compensation awarded in respect of a personal injury that they suffered.

Certain forms of capital are disregarded, for example the value of the family home if it is owned. There is no provision to disregard money put aside to pay bills. Tax owed from past earnings can be disregarded. Money paid out by an insurance company for compensation is ignored for six months, as is the surrender value of life, endowment and pension policies. Fixed-term investments will be ignored if they really cannot be realized but the claimant must show that they have made every effort to obtain any asset that they can, for example could they sell the asset or could they raise a bank loan using the asset as security? Redundancy money counts as capital. Payments from the social fund do not. Business assets will be disregarded, but they will be counted if they are sold. Income tax refunds count as capital. The value of trusts set up will be ignored for at least two years if they are set up from compensation paid for a personal injury. The value of trusts which give the beneficiary a life interest only, or a reversionary interest (an interest which comes into being if someone else dies) are ignored.

INCOME

This includes earnings, social security benefits and most maintenance payments. In a family headed by a couple, the income of both parties is assessed. If a child of the family has income, that is included unless the child has more than the capital limit, in which case he or she comes out of the calculation altogether, or the child has income in excess of the amount of credit awarded for someone of their age, then they are taken out of the calculation and their income does not count unless it is maintenance payments.

The same disregards that apply to adults apply to children's income too. If a child has income which is earnings, it does not count. It is net earnings, after deduction of tax, national insurance and half of any payments into occupational or private pension funds, that count. They are assessed in the five weeks or two months immediately before the week in which the claim is received, depending on whether the earner is paid weekly or monthly. If the earner is self-employed they look at net profits.

There are special rules in the following situations.

Childminders
Their earnings are classed as one-third of their receipts from childminding, less tax, NI and half of any payment they make into a self-employed pension plan.

Taking in Boarders or Lodgers
The earnings from this count only if it forms a major part of the total weekly income. Payments by grown-up children living in the home towards 'board' are also ignored.

Benefits
Those which are ignored as income include:

- income support
- housing benefit
- social fund payments
- child benefit
- one-parent benefit
- attendance allowance
- Christmas bonus.

Those which are counted include:

- state pensions
- all other NI benefits including statutory maternity pay and statutory sick pay (these two benefits count only if they have been received for a continuous period of more than thirteen weeks).

Adoption Allowances
These are counted in full up to the amount of the adopted child's credit used in calculating the maximum FC payable. Over that amount, they are ignored. If the child has capital over the current limit then the entire adoption allowance is ignored, but no FC is payable for the child.

Custodianship allowances paid by the local authority are treated like adoption allowances. If the natural parent pays maintenance, then it is counted in full.

Fostering Allowances
If the foster child is placed by the local authority or a voluntary organization the allowance is ignored. If the arrangement is a private one, any money paid by the parents counts as maintenance.

Training Allowance
These allowances received from the Manpower Services Commission by YTS trainees are ignored in so far as they are to reimburse travelling expenses or meet the costs of living away from home.

Maintenance
Payments for an adult or a child count as income whether they are made voluntarily or under a court order. If payments are made sporadically only, the DSS make the assessment on what was received in the thirteen weeks preceding the claim.

Instalments of Capital
If a claimant is receiving instalments of capital and receiving them will bar him or her from getting FC, for example because they go over the capital limit, then the instalments are treated as income not capital.

Tariff Income
If a claimant has capital of between £3000 and £6000 then he or she is deemed to have income from it. The parameters are reviewed annually and should be checked with the local office of the DSS.

The Calculation of Family Credit

This is done by reference to the threshold or 'applicable amount' which is set each year, and the credits awarded to each member of the family. The amount of the credit for children varies depending upon the age of the child.

If the family's income does not exceed the threshold, then they will receive maximum FC. If their income does exceed the threshold, then they receive the maximum FC reduced by 70 per cent of the excess of their income over the threshold.

'Passport Benefits'

These are the extra benefits which flow from receiving FC. It can be worth a family claiming FC even if they are entitled only to the minimum, which is 50p, in order to get these extra benefits.

● The family may be entitled to housing benefit.
● They will probably qualify for the community charge rebate scheme.
● They may be entitled to financial help with school uniforms.
● They will qualify for free legal advice under the green form scheme.
● They will get free or at reduced charge: prescriptions, dental treatment, glasses or contact lenses, and fares for attending hospital.
● They can apply to the social fund for non-repayable grants for maternity expenses or funeral expenses.
● They may get severe weather payments, that is grants from the social fund to meet fuel bills in times of exceptional cold.
● They will qualify for a grant from their local authority towards loft insulation.

Health Benefits

Free Prescriptions

The following groups of people are entitled to free prescriptions:

● people over state retirement age
● children under sixteen
● young people aged sixteen to nineteen in full-time education
● pregnant women and mothers up to twelve months after the baby is born
● people suffering from certain sicknesses and disabilities (details from doctors or the DSS)
● people (and their families) who get income support or family credit
● people on low income.

Low income is determined by comparing the claimant's requirements to his or her income resources. 'Requirements' are the equivalent of 'applicable amounts' for IS purposes, less housing benefit. 'Resources' are the equivalent of income and capital calculated according to IS rules. It is the resources of the whole family which count. 'Low income' means that the requirements of the family exceed its income resources *and* they have less than the current capital limit. The claim is made on DSS form P11, available from post offices and social security offices.

Dental Treatment

The following people get free dental treatment:

- those under eighteen, or under nineteen but in full-time education
- pregnant women, or mothers with a child up to twelve months old
- those on income support or family credit (the whole family qualifies)
- those on low income (see above).

Those who are on low income, but not low enough to get free treatment, may be able to pay reduced charges. Their income resources must exceed their requirements by less than one-third of the charge *and* they must have less than the current capital limit. They will then be entitled to remission of the difference between the charge for one course of treatment and three times the amount by which their income resources exceed their requirements.

Opticians' Charges

Sight tests are no longer free to all. Children under sixteen and those on IS can still have a free eye-test. Many people may have to pay, although it is expected that some opticians will offer free eye-tests as part of a package including the purchase of glasses or contact lenses.

The following are entitled to free glasses or contact lenses:

- those under sixteen, or aged under nineteen and in full-time education
- those on income support or family credit (the whole family qualifies)
- those on low income (see above)
- those whose eyesight is constantly changing and who therefore need frequent changes of lens prescriptions.

The glasses or lenses will be paid for by a voucher. If you think you may qualify for free glasses or lenses on low income grounds, do not pay for them before applying to the DSS for help because you cannot usually get a refund.

Those who need powerful or complex glasses or contact lenses may be entitled to help with part of the cost if they do not qualify for free help. We suggest that you seek information from the DSS or a CAB or law centre.

If you are entitled to free glasses or contact lenses or help with the cost, the

optician gives you a voucher. In order to get a voucher you must need glasses or
contact lenses for the first time, or need a new prescription, or need new glasses
or contact lenses because the old ones have worn out through fair wear and tear.

Travel to Hospital

It is possible to claim fares to hospital if you need to attend for treatment. You
must travel by the cheapest form of transport. You can claim the fares of a
companion only if it is medically necessary to be accompanied.

Those on income support or family credit and their families qualify, as do
those on low income (see above).

You have to pay the fares and you are then reimbursed by the hospital recep-
tionist.

It is possible to claim part of your fares where your income resources exceed
your requirements by less than one-third of the travel expenses and you have less
than the current capital limit. You are entitled to a payment for the difference
between the travel expenses incurred in any one week, and the amount by which
your income resources exceed your requirements.

Free Milk and Vitamins

The following people are entitled:

- handicapped children who cannot go to school because of their disablement are entitled to milk tokens
- pregnant women on income support get milk tokens and free vitamins
- nursing mothers, that is women who have had a baby within the last
  thirty weeks and who are breast-feeding, get free vitamins if they are on
  income support
- children under five in families who are on income support get milk
  tokens and free vitamins.

Milk tokens can be exchanged for seven pints of milk per week, or, for a child
under twelve months, 900g of dried milk.

Free vitamins are obtained from child health and maternity clinics, and consist
of two bottles of vitamin drops every thirteen weeks for children, five containers
of vitamins to nursing mothers and two containers of vitamins every thirteen
weeks during the pregnancy to expectant mothers.

Children in day-care with a registered childminder or a day nursery can get free milk for each day that they spend in day-care. This is additional to any other entitlement which they may have. They get one-third of a pint per day, provided by the childminder or the nursery who claim reimbursement.

People on family credit or on a low income are not entitled, but those on family credit with children under twelve months can buy reduced-price dried milk from maternity and child health clinics.

Education Benefits

LEAs have some statutory duties to provide financial help for the needs of school children either in the form of cash benefits or services, and have a wider range of discretionary powers to do so. As their powers are discretionary, parents cannot make them give assistance for their children's needs, and each LEA can decide through their own administrative channels what, if any, benefits they will give, how they allocate their funds and what form the help will take.

A word here about powers. If any public body, like a local authority, set up by Act of Parliament exceeds the powers given to it by statute it opens itself to actions in court under the 'ultra vires' rule (literally, 'beyond their powers'). To enable it to carry out the full range of functions that it could choose to have without being challenged it is given specific powers to cover a very wide range of activities. Having a power, though, does not mean it has to use it.

For the full range of what your local authority does provide ask at the local education office or school.

School Meals

Although the law gives LEAs only the power to provide all registered pupils at maintained schools with meals, it lays a duty on them to provide meals for any pupil whose parents are on income support. There is no nutritional standard laid down for these meals, nor any set method of administering it – schools can use a ticket or voucher system if they wish.

If children bring their own packed lunches, schools must provide a place for them to eat without making a charge for this. One LEA did attempt to charge a fee for this service – which was quite wrong.

Where LEAs do provide meals for all pupils, they can charge for this, as long as pupils whose families are on income support are exempt. They have power to remit all or part of the charges that they make depending on the circumstances of the pupils or the class.

Many schools now have a canteen system rather than school lunches and children buy their food either at normal or subsidized prices depending on whether or not the authority has remitted some of the charges.

School Uniforms

Whether or not a school has a uniform and how strictly they enforce what is to be worn at school depends on the wishes of the governors. LEAs have a discretionary power to help parents with the cost of buying the uniform, either by cash help or a voucher system for use at certain shops. There can therefore be schools which insist on a uniform in an area where the LEA does not help parents with the cost. Unfortunately for parents on income support whose children attend schools where a set uniform must be worn, the DSS social fund specifically bans loans or grants made for any educational or training need and distinctive school uniform or sports clothes and equipment.

This ban probably does not cover the purchase of non-distinctive school uniform like chain-store grey or navy skirts and trousers, which can be worn as normal clothing – so you might be able to get a budgeting loan from the discretionary social fund (see 'One-off Payments and Emergencies', above).

LEAs can provide 'necessitous' clothing for children who would otherwise be inadequately or unsuitably dressed or shod for school.

School Transport

Under s55 of the Education Act 1944, LEAs have a duty to provide school transport which must be free of charge – but this duty does not cover all children and can be limited properly by the LEA to doing what they think is necessary as long as they do provide transport for children who live further than two or three miles from school. This means they *must* provide transport for some children, and can provide for all.

When they do provide transport, it can be through using school buses or paying for bus passes.

The two- and three-mile rule in full is: transport must be provided for children under eight who live more than two miles from school and children over eight who live more than three miles away. The distance is measured by the nearest available route. This does not mean the shortest route available, as the safety of the route must be considered as well. One case in 1985 held that a route was not to be seen as 'available' at all if it was dark, unlit and a danger to a young girl in winter, and it was held in that case that saying the child could be accompanied by a parent was unreasonable.

The two- or three-mile rule can be strictly enforced: a child who lives only a few yards beyond this limit can be ineligible, and eligibility for transport over two miles can stop on the eighth birthday.

The sting in the tail of this concession is that if parents exercise parental choice and have their child educated outside the catchment area the LEA can decide not to pay for the transport.

LEAs can if they choose pay the whole or part of the reasonable travelling expenses of school pupils for whom no other arrangements have been made. However, this power is rarely used.

Charges Generally

The Education Act 1944 set out the then prevailing belief that education should be free. Section 61 says: 'No fees should be charged in respect of admission to any school maintained by a local education authority ... or in respect of the education provided in any such school.' The courts have upheld a wide definition of 'education', and in one case held that an LEA were wrong to have charged fees for a field trip in school holidays taken by a school student as part of an A-level geography course. However, there are proposed legislative changes to allow LEAs and schools to charge for 'extras' not on the basic curriculum.

Scholarships and Bursaries

LEAs can make maintenance grants to children staying on at school after their sixteenth birthday. These grants are:

- discretionary;
- made for the purpose of relieving financial hardship;
- payable to children over sixteen attending a school or sixth-form college;
- means-tested on parents' income; and
- dependent on the LEA being satisfied that the child is on a suitable course, and on the child continuing to attend and progress.

As a means-tested benefit, this is open to parents on income support. As to the eligibility of others, this will depend on the local authority concerned.

In some circumstances LEAs can make grants to help students on further education correspondence courses, as long as the course is suitable and the grant is needed to relieve financial hardship.

LEAs also have the power to pay boarding school fees of children, either where the boarding school is maintained by them to prevent hardship or at independent boarding schools where, for example, the education is suitable for their needs. This can include payment of fees at schools which cater for the especially gifted child, or those with particular musical or dramatic talents. It also covers payment of fees at special schools where daily travel is impossible or inadvisable.

Assisted Places Schemes

The assisted places scheme allows some children to take up places they have been offered at independent schools at secondary level which they could not otherwise do because their parents could not pay the fees. It is a means-tested scheme, with a sliding scale of financial help according to the parents' income.

It is simple in principle: the parents' means are assessed, and depending on their income they pay either a proportion or none at all of the tuition fees charged by the school. The DES pays the school the remainder of the tuition fees that the parents cannot afford. Boarding fees are not included in the scheme.

Not all independent schools operate the scheme. It is operated only by those which have gone into 'participation agreements' with the Secretary of State.

Children are eligible for assisted places if:

* they have been resident in the UK for two years before 1 January of the year in which, if they got an assisted place, they would go to the school; and
* they are at least eleven years old, or if not yet eleven would reach that age by the August of their first 'assisted' school year and were in a class of mainly eleven-year-olds; and
* are of the age which under the participation agreement is a normal age of entry to the school; and
* their parents had, when applying for an assisted place, given the school full details of their income for the preceding financial year; and a projection of their income for the financial year before the child would take up any assisted place offered, and any other information required by the scheme; and
* the child qualifies for a place under whatever academic procedures the school itself finds appropriate.

Sixth-form students can be eligible for the scheme: if the school's participation agreement extends to selecting their sixth form, or if the pupil is already at the school and applies for an assisted place for the sixth form.

The children of European Community nationals working in the UK can also be eligible for the scheme, as are the children of refugees. There are less stringent residence qualifications for these pupils.

Schools have to publish details of their assisted places schemes including how many they offer and what arrangements they make for remitting fees to parents and admitting pupils. They should publish the details in whatever ways they think should reach the people who need this information. It would be adequate to put these details on a prospectus, for example. Assisted places can be given to children who come from other independent schools – but at least 60 per cent of the places in any one school should be allocated to pupils from publicly maintained schools.

As well as remission of the tuition fees, the scheme also covers incidental expenses and allows for grants for clothing, uniform and travel to and from the school. The school also remits the costs of field study trips in scientific subjects for assisted pupils, and the cost of school meals at day schools if the parents are on income support during the relevant school year.

The school recoups the grants and 'lost' fees from the Department of Education and Science.

The actual method of working out who owes who what is fiendishly complicated and contained in regulations made under the Act which started the scheme, s17 of the Education Act 1980. The school to which you apply should provide you with the application forms and financial requirements necessary.

MUSIC AND BALLET SCHOOLS

There are five such schools which have adopted an aided scheme for pupils which is similar to the assisted places scheme at ordinary independent schools. They include the Royal Ballet School and the Yehudi Menuhin School. The regulations are very similar with two important differences: they accept children at eight, and the residential schools remit boarding fees as well as tuition fees.

Help from Social Services

Under section 1 of the Child Care Act 1980, social services departments are under a duty to give financial assistance or assistance in kind where this would prevent a child from being taken into care, or help a child to leave care. This help can cover many different things, for example, clothing, equipment, help in the home, and fares to visit children in temporary care. Policy on what can be offered varies widely between authorities. It is always worth asking the social worker.

The Children Act 1989 has modified this duty somewhat. After its full implementation, the emphasis will be on help in kind rather than cash, and on loans rather than grants. Recipients of IS or family credit cannot be required to pay.

Inland Revenue

Although you might not immediately associate tax as being a source of income, *tax relief* can be. The 1989 budget brought in far-reaching changes in tax law which were implemented gradually. This section covers the new and the old law because tax is usually assessed retrospectively.

Personal Allowances

Everybody, whether they care for children or not, is entitled to a certain amount of tax relief. This is called the *personal allowance*. It means that you do not pay tax on that part of your income. Indeed, you may not pay tax at all if your income is not higher than the amount of the personal allowance. This amount is set each year by the government in the budget.

If you are a single parent with at least one child living with you, then you can claim the *additional personal allowance*. To qualify as a single parent you must be unmarried, divorced, a widow or widower, and your child must be either under sixteen or in full-time education or training. Your child need not be your own son or daughter as long as he or she is under eighteen at the start of the tax year (6 April) and is looked after at your own expense. The point of this allowance was to bring the tax relief for single parents up to the level of the *married man's allowance*. Until April 1990 this allowance could be claimed by any married man, whether he was a father or not, so long as his wife lived with him. It is higher than the personal allowance. There was also a special allowance for working wives which applied whether or not they were mothers. This was called the *wife's earned income relief* and it was equivalent to the personal allowance.

The effect of these allowances was that income tax law discriminated against cohabiting couples who both worked. They would receive the benefit only of two personal allowances whereas married couples who both worked received the equivalent of two personal allowances plus the additional amount by which the married man's allowance exceeded the personal allowance.

In April 1990, a system of independent taxation for husbands and wives was introduced. Husbands and wives are taxed on their own incomes whether earned or unearned. Each is responsible for their own tax affairs and for paying the tax due on their separate incomes. Each spouse has a personal allowance equal in size to the single person's allowance under the old system. However, married couples will continue to do better than cohabitees because the husband is allowed an additional allowance called a *married couple's allowance* which is equal to the difference, under the old system, between the single person and married man's allowances. If he has insufficient income to absorb the whole of the additional allowance, the unused part can be transferred to his wife and set against her income.

Tax Relief and Investments for Children

Children are entitled to the single person's allowance for income tax purposes from birth. This means that if they have income, they will only pay income tax on the difference between their total income and the personal allowance.

They are obliged to make income tax returns and they also have the right to claim repayments of over-paid tax. In general, it is the responsibility of the parent or legal guardian to make returns and to claim repayments while the child is still at school. Once a young person starts work, or in any other case where a minor has the full direction, management and control of his or her own affairs, the responsibility to make returns and to claim repayments passes to him or her.

In the case of most trusts the position is the same – claims and returns are made by the parent or legal guardian. Where the trustees themselves have direct control or management of the trust income of the minor and may either apply it for the minor's benefit, pay it to the parent or legal guardian or retain it for accumulation on the minor's behalf then the trustees must make any claims and returns. This, however, depends on the exact terms of the trust concerned, and professional advice should be sought in cases of doubt.

Children can have accounts at many building societies and banks, including the National Savings Bank. With some of these accounts, the money is 'locked in' and cannot be withdrawn until the child reaches the age of seven and can draw money on the strength of his or her own signature. Before opening an account it is advisable to check the arrangements for withdrawals, and whether they can be made on the parent's request.

Children's building society and bank accounts have the disadvantage that tax is deducted automatically from the interest earned before it is credited to the account. This takes no account of whether or not the child has any unused personal allowance for the tax year in question. If a child has income of less than the personal allowance, it is advisable for money to be invested in an account in which the interest is credited gross, that is without deduction of tax. Such accounts are available at the National Savings Bank. Other institutions should be asked whether they run similar schemes.

It is possible for children to own unit trust investments. It is advisable for the units to be registered in the joint names of the child and a responsible adult. This means that the investment can be sold to realize the investment money while the child is still a minor. A particular advantage of unit trusts is that the tax on the income from them can be claimed back, if for example the child's income is not over the level of the personal allowance. The disadvantage of any investment of this type is that the value of the investment will fluctuate with the market and cannot be guaranteed to go up only. Independent financial advisers should be consulted before complicated or risky investments are entered into.

MAINTENANCE PAID FOR AND TO CHILDREN

Until a change in the tax laws in 1988, if a child's parents separated and one parent was paying maintenance to the other under a court order or agreement, it was better that payments for the benefit of the child were made direct to him or her rather than to the recipient parent. The child was then able to claim the personal allowance against the payments. The alternative was that the payments were made to the recipient parent who would generally end up paying tax on the amount by which the payments exceeded the personal allowance, because it was likely that he or she had other income as well. In practice, as long as the payment was expressed to be to the child it could in actual fact be paid to the parent. It is obviously inappropriate for money to be given directly to children too young to manage it.

The tax position on maintenance payments was changed drastically in the 1988 budget. Basically they were taken outside the tax system. Up to that time, there was a distinct tax advantage to maintenance payers in paying under a court order, because they got tax relief. The child recipient was liable to pay tax on maintenance received, but could use his or her personal allowance and so paid tax only on maintenance over the amount of the personal allowance.

The old rules have now gone, *except* for those whose orders were applied for by 15 March 1988, and made by the court by 30 June 1988. For people in this category, the maintenance rules continue as before, with two exceptions which are described below.

Under the old rules the payer had to deduct basic rate income tax before making the payment unless these were small maintenance payments. If the payee's income was less than the personal allowance then he or she would receive a refund of the tax paid. If his or her income was more than the level of the personal allowance then an assessment of the additional tax payable was received. Where the maintenance fell into the category of a small maintenance payment, by a special concessionary arrangement, the Inland Revenue allowed the payer to make the payment gross, and the recipient did not have to pay or claim a refund.

From 6 April 1988, the first £1490 of maintenance paid to a former spouse was exempt from income tax in the recipient's hands.

From 6 April 1989, the payer of maintenance which came under the old rules had to make the payments gross and the tax relief was limited to that received in the tax year 1988–89. The recipient is responsible for paying the tax due over and above the personal allowance and the exemption mentioned above.

If the order comes under the new rules, the payer simply pays over the maintenance gross, without deduction. The payee is not taxed on the maintenance received. Small maintenance payments have thus become redundant. The payer will get no tax relief on payments to a child, and on payments to an ex-spouse, he will get relief only on payments up to an amount equal to the difference between the single person and married man's allowance.

There is nothing to stop those who come under the old rules from electing, as from 6 April 1989, to convert to payments under the new rules. This election would be made by the payer, and is unlikely to be beneficial until such time as the tax relief pegged in 1988–89 is less than the maximum relief available under the new rules. Payers should consult their accountants and solicitors.

Because the main difference is that the payer no longer gets a tax advantage from paying maintenance under a court order, it seems likely that the levels of maintenance orders made will be less than previously, as less money overall will often be available when a marriage breaks up. Although the payee will not have to pay tax on maintenance, he or she may well get less in the first place and be worse off than under the old rules. Unfortunately, this seems to have been the effect of simplifying the tax laws. The personal allowances of recipient ex-spouses and children may well be unused, and the payer ends up paying more tax to the Inland Revenue.

Tax Relief on Payments to Children

DEEDS OF COVENANT

Until 1988 there was a tax-saving advantage in paying money under a deed of convenant, in other words, under a legally-binding agreement. This has now gone. Where a deed was already in place by the time of the changes, it continues to be effective for as long as it lasts. A deed had to provide for regular annual payments over a minimum period of four years to be valid for tax purposes. As with maintenance payments, the payer deducts basic rate income tax from the payment and the recipient recovers tax deducted if his or her income falls within the personal allowance, in other words if more tax has been deducted than he or she is liable to pay.

To be effective, a covenant had to be made before 15 March 1988, and lodged with the Inland Revenue by 30 June 1988.

Where the Child is Under Eighteen

A parent cannot make a tax-effective covenant to his or her own child aged less than eighteen years, but until 1988 a grandparent or other relative could. The money could be paid to trustees, such as the parents, for the benefit of the child. This tax-saving device has now gone, but covenants in place by the dates mentioned above continue to be effective for as long as they last.

Where the Child is Over Eighteen and in Full-time Education

It used to be possible for a parent to make a tax saving by executing a deed of covenant, and indeed it was so widespread for parents to use this method to pay their contribution to their son's or daughter's student grant that the Inland Revenue published a form giving an acceptable form of wording. This went in the 1988 budget. For covenants in force by the dates given above, tax relief is still available as long as the covenant lasts.

Capital Taxes

So far we have dealt with taxes which affect your income. However, this is not the whole story. The taxes covered below are levied on capital assets.

CAPITAL GAINS TAX (CGT)

CGT is a tax on capital profits. It is generally paid when an asset is sold. The rate of tax is the same as the highest rate of income tax paid by the individual concerned. There is an annual exemption, which changes each year. This means that that portion of gains in the year is exempt from tax. Not all assets attract CGT – some notable exceptions are your home and your car. Transfers of assets between married couples do not attract CGT.

CGT can affect families in a number of ways. Here are two examples.

1. What happens if you give an asset to a close member of your family, other than your spouse, or sell it to them at a nominal value? A market value is substituted in order to work out the tax payable.
2. Supposing you own a second home in which a dependent relative lives rent-free and, on selling it, you make a profit? The gain is tax-free.

From 1990, a married couple's assets will be treated separately. They will not lose the exemption from CGT where they transfer assets between them, but they will gain by each being entitled to the annual exemption, rather than sharing one exemption between them.

CGT is not particularly straightforward and there are many exemptions and regulations. This is a very basic explanation and you must see an accountant for more detailed advice.

INHERITANCE TAX

Despite its name, this does not apply only to money given away under your will – it can also apply to gifts or transfers made during your lifetime. Transfers between spouses are exempt.

Certain other gifts are also exempt of tax altogether. These are called potentially exempt transfers (PET). They fall into three categories.

1. An outright gift to an individual.
2. A gift into a trust known as an accumulation-and-maintenance settlement.
3. A gift into a settlement for the benefit of a disabled person.

No tax is payable if the donor lives for at least seven years after making the gift. Where death does occur within seven years, there is a reducing scale of tax payable depending on when the donor dies. The percentage of tax payable tapers over the seven-year period from 100 per cent in the first three years to 20 per cent between the sixth and seventh years.

If you make a lifetime gift which is not a PET, then the rate of inheritance tax is half that which it would be on death. An example would be a transfer of money or property into a trust where the trustees have a discretion as to how to distribute the income of the trust fund.

If you make a gift with a reservation, in other words if you continue to enjoy some benefit from the gift, then it still counts as part of your property and your estate would pay inheritance tax if you died still owning it. This would apply if you

gave your house to your grown-up children but continued to live there rent-free.
There are exemptions. The main ones which affect parents are as follows.

- you can give away up to £3000 tax-free in any one year, and carry this forward, if unused, to the next year;
- you can give sums of up to £250 to as many people as you like;
- you can give money away as marriage gifts. The amount you can give away depends on your relationship to the bride or bridegroom and is as follows under the current rates (note that all these figures were up-to-date at the time of writing but are subject to annual review; it is best to check with an accountant):
    £5000 by either parent
    £2500 by a grandparent or great-grandparent
    £2500 by the bridegroom to the bride or vice versa
    £1000 by any other person.

Capital taxes, like income taxes, discriminate against cohabitees since transfers and gifts between spouses are tax-exempt.

Capital taxes of both types apply to trusts. The law on trusts and their taxation is very complicated and we advise that you seek the expert help of an accountant if you wish to set one up.

Maintenance

Married Parents

There is a general duty on men to maintain their wives and children. This does not end on separation or divorce. A man is under a duty to maintain his children even if their mother remarries or cohabits with someone else, but he is not, in such a situation, under a duty to maintain his ex-wife.

The types of orders which the court can grant on family breakdown and divorce are described in detail in Chapter 10. The courts which can make orders concerned with money and property are the High Court, the county court and the magistrates' court. The laws under which they can make these orders are the Domestic Proceedings and Magistrates Courts Act, the Guardianship of Minors Acts, the Matrimonial Causes Act, and the High Court's general powers in wardship proceedings.

DOMESTIC PROCEEDINGS AND MAGISTRATES COURTS ACT

Under this Act, the magistrates' court can make maintenance orders in the form
of periodical payments and lump sum orders to a spouse or child.

THE GUARDIANSHIP OF MINORS ACTS

Under these Acts, the magistrates' court, the county court or the High Court can
make maintenance orders for periodical payments or for lump sums to children.

WARDSHIP

In wardship proceedings, the High Court can make maintenance orders in the
form of periodical payments, but only for marital children.

MATRIMONIAL CAUSES ACT

Under this Act, the county court or the High Court can make maintenance orders in
the form of periodical payments or lump sums in favour of spouses and children.
The court can also make property adjustment orders transferring property.

THE CHILDREN ACT 1989

This Act re-states the law relating to financial provision for children and makes
some alterations to it. It replaces the powers that the courts have to make
financial orders under the Guardianship of Minors Act.

A parent, guardian or person with whom a child resides by order of the court
will have the right to apply for financial provision for the child from the parent.
Such an application can be heard by the High Court, the county court or the
magistrates' court. In the High and county courts, the orders which can be made
will be maintenance by periodical payments, secured periodical payments, lump
sum orders, and property settlements and transfers. In the magistrates' court, the
orders will be periodical payments and lump sums up to £500. The magistrates'
court can specify that the payer of maintenance must give notice of any change of
address to anyone whose name is specified in the order. Failure to give notice can
result in a fine being imposed. Periodical payments orders and secured periodical
payments orders can be varied or discharged. This is largely as it is at present.

Orders for maintenance should not usually last beyond the seventeenth or eighteenth birthday unless it seems likely that the child will be undergoing education or training, or there are special circumstances, for example the child is handicapped or disabled.

Under the new law, young people over eighteen have the right to apply to any of the three courts for maintenance in the form of periodical payments or lump sum provision if they are in education or training or if special circumstances apply. This does not apply if there was a periodical payments order in force immediately before their sixteenth birthday. Once a young person reaches sixteen, he or she can apply for variation. A young person can also apply to revive an order for periodical payments if it ceases on or before their eighteenth birthday. The court has the power to revive it if the child is still in education or training or there are special circumstances.

Periodical payments orders cease if the parents live together for more than six months (unless they were applied for by an over-eighteen-year-old), or if the paying parent dies. A young person in this situation may have an action against the parent's estate under the Inheritance Act if insufficient provision has been made. (See 'Death of a Parent', below).

THE PROCEDURE

When making orders the court has to have regard to:

- the income, earning capacity, property and other financial resources which the payer and the recipient have or are likely to have in the foreseeable future
- the financial needs, obligations and responsibilities which the payer and the recipient have or are likely to have in the foreseeable future
- any physical or mental disability which the child has
- the manner in which the child was being, or was expected to be, educated or trained.

If the potential payer is not the parent, but a step-parent, the court must consider:

- whether the person had assumed responsibility for maintenance of the child and the extent to which and the basis upon which responsibility was assumed and the length of the period during which the responsibility was met
- whether he did so knowing that the child was not his
- the liability of any other person to maintain the child.

If an order is made that the child should reside with someone who is not the parent or step-parent, the local authority can make contributions towards the cost of accommodation and maintenance. This does not apply if the child lives with the parent or step-parent.

Unmarried Parents

Where the parents of a child are not married to one another, different but complementary rules apply regarding financial provision for their child. It used to be the case that only the mother could apply for a court order for maintenance or a lump sum payment for the child. The father had no right to do so even if he was caring for the child. The mother had to apply in the magistrates' court under affiliation proceedings. There was, however, nothing to stop the parents agreeing to make arrangements for maintenance whichever of them was looking after the child and therefore needed the maintenance.

The Family Law Reform Act of 1987 changed the law relating to unmarried parents. The changes came into force in 1989. It abolished affiliation proceedings and put children born outside marriage on an equal footing with those born inside marriage where claims for financial provision are concerned. Unmarried fathers who are caring for their children can apply for maintenance from the mother, just as divorced fathers can.

The Children Act 1989 has superseded the Family Law Reform Act on financial matters and incorporates its provisions. It enables courts to make the same orders for the children of married and unmarried parents alike.

Affiliation proceedings will still be relevant for those mothers who have orders made under their provisions. These orders will remain in force and can be enforced by the magistrates' court if the man is not paying. Affiliation proceedings could only be heard in the magistrates' court, whereas proceedings under the new law can be heard in the High Court, the county court or the magistrates' court. The old proceedings had to be started within three years of the child's birth. There is no such restriction in the new proceedings. The mother had to be a 'single' woman when she applied for affiliation or she had to have been when the child was born. This is not the case under the new law, so a mother who has subsequently married another man can claim.

Legal aid is available for these proceedings under Assistance by Way of Representation if the hearing is to be in the magistrates' court or under civil legal aid if the hearing is to take place in the High Court or the county court (see Chapter 13).

The applicant parent asks the court to make financial provision. There is not the same presumption that exists where parents have been married that the other party is the child's other parent. The court will not consider what order to make until the applicant has first proved that the other party is the parent. Often the other party will not dispute this in which case the court goes on to consider the money aspect.

If the other party disputes parentage then the court must hear evidence. Women applicants often find it frightening and distasteful to have to give this sort of verbal evidence in court. The man may be represented by a lawyer and she may well be cross-examined on what she says. The court does sit in private, though, so there will be no spectators.

The woman's evidence must be corroborated, or supported, by other evidence. This can take a variety of forms. Some examples are, the name of the man being shown as the father on the birth certificate, or other people giving evidence that the man and woman were living or sleeping together at the relevant time.

The court has the power to order blood tests to be taken. If this happens then a sample is taken from the man, the woman and the child and they are analysed. If either of the parents refuses to give a sample, the court cannot force them to do so, but inferences can be drawn from a refusal. Blood tests do not show conclusively that the man is the father but they can show that he is not, or that he could be. DNA fingerprinting can now be used which is absolutely conclusive either way.

Once the court establishes parentage, it then goes on to consider what type of order to make.

The High Court and the county court have wider powers in this respect than the magistrates' court. The latter can award maintenance only by periodical payments or lump sum orders, whereas the other courts can award periodical payments, secured periodical payments, lump sum orders, and property transfers and settlements.

PERIODICAL PAYMENTS ORDER

In theory there is no upper limit on this and it should be at the same sort of level as for the children of married parents who are divorcing. In practice the magistrates' court does tend to make lower orders. The orders can be paid weekly or monthly. The payments generally last until the child reaches seventeen but can be continued until eighteen or older if the child is in education or training. The order can be varied on the application of either parent or by the child once he or she reaches sixteen. If the payer dies the order ends (but the child can apply for provision from the payer's estate, see p. 169). If the recipient parent dies, or marries, the order remains. It ends if the child is adopted. A child who reaches eighteen can apply for maintenance by way of a periodical payments or a lump sum order if he or she is still in education or training or if special circumstances apply. This does not apply if the parents are living together or if there was a periodical payments order in force at the time of the child's sixteenth birthday.

LUMP SUM ORDER

This cannot exceed £500 if the proceedings are heard in the magistrates' court. The court can order a lump sum to cover the expenses of the birth, such as the cost of buying clothes and a pram. A further lump sum could be applied for later if the means of either parent changed.

As stated above, the magistrates' court often in practice makes lower orders than the county court or High Court, but in theory it considers the same factors in setting the level. These are:

- the income and property owned by the parents
- their financial needs and expenses
- the child's income and property (if any)
- the child's financial needs including any special needs such as a disability
- how all this affects the benefit position.

As in all matters involving children, the court should put the child's needs first. Unfortunately, once the order is made it is often not paid. There are, however, enforcement procedures and these are the same as for married parents.

Legal aid is again available for enforcement and the applicant applies for a summons. This is sent to the other parent who must go to the court hearing and explain why he or she has not paid. If the other parent still does not pay he or she can at worst be sent to prison although of course this does not pay the maintenance. If the payer is employed, the recipient can ask for an attachment of earnings order. This means that the employer deducts the maintenance from the payer's wages and sends it to the court. Alternatively the court can make an order that the payer's goods be seized and sold to raise the money owed, or that any money he or she may have in a bank account be used.

Tax relief is only available for the payer if the order was in place by the end of June 1988. It is in the interests of the recipient for the maintenance to be by court order rather than voluntary so that the order can be enforced if the payments stop. The impracticality of voluntary payments applies to married and unmarried parents and it is why solicitors generally advise that a court order is applied for.

Death

Of a Parent

When someone dies, control over their possessions passes to the executors they appoint in their will. If the person dies leaving no will he or she is classed in law as *intestate* and the law applies rules as to who inherits the property. Usually the next of kin applies to become the administrator of the estate.

When making a will it is best to seek professional advice because money or property left to a child under eighteen in a will can create difficulties. A child can own money or belongings but not land. This includes houses, flats and other buildings. It is usual to leave land or property to trustees who will administer it for the child until he or she reaches the age specified in the will for taking control. The trustees must usually follow the instructions laid down in the will. If none is specified then the law imposes certain duties, obligations and instructions upon them. These imposed instructions do not always result in the best use of the money, land or property available. Hence the importance of consulting a solicitor and an accountant when making the will.

The law interprets children to include non-marital children in this situation. So unless specified to the contrary, property left to children under a will includes non-marital children.

Children, whether marital, non-marital, or step-children, can apply to the High Court under the Inheritance (Provision for Family and Dependents) Act if it is felt that their parent's will has made insufficient provision, or no provision at all, for them. The court then looks at the whole picture, that is the child's financial needs and resources as well as those of the people who benefit under the will. The court can order maintenance payments or lump sums or a transfer of property, if it decides that provision is not adequate.

If a parent dies intestate then the rules of intestacy are applied. At present this means that their spouse inherits the first £75,000 of the estate and all the personal goods. The children inherit the rest but this is subject to the surviving spouse having a 'life interest' in it. This would mean that if the property produced an income, the spouse would get it. If there is no surviving spouse, then the children, marital or non-marital, get the lot.

If parents divorce, then any will made by either of them is affected but *not* in so far as it provides for the children. If either parent marries again then the will is automatically revoked. It is therefore crucial to make another will. If you do not then you are treated as dying intestate and the rules apply to the surviving spouse and children.

It cannot be stressed too much that it is far better for and more considerate towards relatives to make a will. The rules for intestacy are strictly applied and take no account of the particular needs of those left behind. Another reason why parents often prefer to leave a will is that they can nominate in it the person or persons to whom they wish to entrust the care of and/or legal responsibility for their children. These are known as testamentary guardians. There is no legal obligation to consult these people before naming them, but it obviously makes sense to do so. There is equally no absolute legal obligation on such people to assume responsibility – if the parent dies they can refuse to act. Guardianship, in this context, vests all parental rights and duties in the guardian. However, the guardian can be removed by a court order and the court can appoint a guardian if none is named or if one is named but declines to accept the appointment.

A guardian may be the trustee of the child's property and must account for it to the child when the guardianship ends – when the child reaches the age of eighteen or marries under that age.

If a guardian accepts the responsibility then they cannot later withdraw except by making an application to court. A testamentary guardian's appointment does not take effect until the surviving parent dies, if the parents were married. If they were not married then the law vests parental responsibility in the mother only. She could therefore appoint a guardian who would take over her rights in preference to the father. Equally, she could appoint the father as the guardian. In order for an unmarried father to take over automatically on her death, he must acquire parental responsibility by making an agreement with the mother or by applying to a court. Parents can each appoint a different guardian or guardians, in which case they act jointly after the death of the second parent.

If parents die without appointing guardians, and the children are cared for by relatives, then the relatives can apply to the court for guardianship. They can equally not apply and act without any formality or court order.

If no one is appointed and/or no one is willing to act, then the local authority are under a duty to take the children into care.

If a parent is killed due to the fault of another, then his or her dependents can make a claim under the Fatal Accidents Act 1976 against the person who caused the death. Dependents can include a surviving spouse and children. The court, in estimating damages, decides what financial benefit each dependent would have derived from the relationship if the parent had lived. This can cover the situation where the parent killed was the bread-winner and/or the one who had the day-to-day care of the child.

Of a Child

If a child dies then his or her estate passes to the parents because a will cannot normally be made by anyone under eighteen.

If the child is killed due to negligence on the part of somebody who is not the child's parent then a claim may be brought on behalf of the child's estate and/or on behalf of the child's dependents. Dependents here is a wide term and can include parents even though the child was probably dependent upon them.

In either case, damages are usually very low; lower for example than where a child is injured but survives. This is because the child's estate cannot benefit from loss of future earnings, only for pain and suffering during life. Further, the child's dependents can usually claim only for bereavement and distress. This is limited to £3500. A parent finding him or herself in this awful situation is strongly advised to seek expert advice from a solicitor.

Appendix

The best source of information on social security benefits is contained in the publications of the Child Poverty Action Group: *The National Welfare Benefits Handbook* and *The Rights Guide to Non-Means Tested Social Security Benefits*. The DSS also publish leaflets on each type of benefit, and these can be obtained from the local office.

On tax, the Inland Revenue publish many leaflets on all aspects of tax and these can be obtained from the office of the local Inspector of Taxes or from a citizens' advice bureau.

For more complicated problems it is advisable to seek professional advice from a law centre or CAB on benefits, and from an accountant on tax.

Chapter 7

Foster Parents

This chapter is for people who are or want to become foster parents and for people whose children are placed with foster parents.

Foster parents are in great demand at the moment. There has been a move away from placing children in care in community homes or institutions and in favour of placing them with foster parents. There are several reasons for this trend. Children who grow up in homes run the risk of becoming institutionalized and of missing out on building up special relationships with their carers who may change frequently. Moreover, children whose only experience of family life may have been a negative one desperately need the positive experience of life in a happy and secure family and the opportunity to enjoy the rewards of having a one-to-one relationship with an adult carer. For many children in care, whether permanently or temporarily, care now means foster care.

The law governing this area is contained in the Foster Children Act 1980 and the Boarding Out of Children Regulations 1988. The Children Act 1989 repeals the Foster Children Act. It is dealt with below.

The Boarding Out of Children Regulations 1988

These regulations have replaced earlier regulations which came into force in 1955 and they cover the conditions and the circumstances in which foster children should live.

The stated aim of the regulations is to provide a framework for current practice, while still allowing local variations in organization and policy.

Foster parents must be approved before children can be placed with them. The idea is to build up a fostering service with provision for recruitment, assessment, training, support and review of foster parents.

The law defines a foster parent as a person who has the care and maintenance of a child of whom he or she is not a relative, guardian or custodian. Although foster parents are often a couple, either married or living together in a stable relationship, many single people can and do foster children.

A foster child is one whose care and maintenance is undertaken by someone who is not a relative, guardian or custodian of the child. To fall within the provisions covering foster children, a child must be younger than the upper limit of the compulsory school age unless he or she is still a foster child at this point, then it extends to when he or she leaves the person caring for him or reaches the age of eighteen, whichever occurs first.

Fostering can be arranged by the local authority for children in care or privately between the parents and the person they choose to look after their child because they for some reason cannot care for him or her. The law covers both situations.

It is not usually fostering if someone cares for a child who is a relative of theirs. There is, however, provision in the new regulations for a child to be placed with a relative in an emergency. For more long-term stays, it is also possible for a foster parent to be approved to foster a particular child, and it is envisaged that this will be used by relatives.

A child is not a foster child if he or she is in care to a local authority or a voluntary organization and is placed to live in a community home, at a boarding school or in a hospital. It is not fostering if you are not a regular foster parent, but you look after someone else's child for them, provided that the child does not stay with you for longer than twenty-seven days. If you are a regular foster parent and you care for someone else's child it does not become fostering until they have been with you for six days. It is also not fostering if you are a prospective adopter and a child is placed with you by an adoption agency with a view to you adopting. The definition of fostering does not cover the placement of children who are the subject of place of safety orders nor does it cover temporary 'respite' care placements made under the NHS legislation. The latter usually involves relieving the parents of handicapped children by temporarily taking the children off their hands and into care. However, in both these situations authorities are supposed to apply the principles of the regulations as a matter of good practice.

The Foster Children Act 1980 talks about 'regular foster parents'. The definition of a regular foster parent relates to the period in the previous year during which he or she cared for a child. It is very complex. It is someone who is not a relative, guardian or custodian of a child and who cares for the child in question and who in the preceding twelve months cared for a child or children for at least three months (this can be continuous or aggregated) or for at least three continuous periods, each of which was of more than six days.

If you are a regular foster parent, you could have to notify the local authority if you care for the child of a sick friend or neighbour, or you take a friend's child on holiday, or you have a child from abroad on an exchange, if any of these situations lasts for more than six days. You could have to notify this as private fostering.

You cannot foster a child if one of the following situations applies:

- there has been an order made removing a child from your care
- you have been convicted of an offence involving children
- you have had your parental rights removed by a local authority under a parental rights resolution (PRR)
- you have been refused, or had cancelled, registration as a nursery or child-minder.

You also cannot foster a child if a member of your household falls into any of these categories.

Under the new fostering regulations you cannot have a child placed with you by a local authority unless you are an 'approved' foster parent. It is the local authorities or the voluntary organizations who approve foster parents. (For details see 'Approval of Foster Parents', p. 181.)

Private Fostering

Under the Foster Children Act 1980 there are various rules covering fosterers who work privately.

If you are proposing to foster privately you must give written notice to the local authority in whose area you live. This must be given at least two weeks before but not more than four weeks before you receive the child, unless you received the child in an emergency in which case you must notify them within forty-eight hours of receiving the child. The information you give must include the date of reception and your address.

Where the arrangement is private the local authority can request the name, sex, date and place of birth of each child and the name and address of the parents and/or guardians or the person who acts as guardian.

Remember that a child can 'become' a foster child if, for example, parent and child were staying with you and the parent left leaving you looking after the child. In such a situation, if you want to continue to look after the child you should notify the local authority within forty-eight hours.

If you are fostering privately and you move you must give written notice to the local authority. The same time limits as above apply, that is not less than two weeks before or more than four weeks before unless it is an emergency and then within forty-eight hours. If you move to a new area with a different local authority then you still inform the former authority who notify the new one. This rule also applies to foster parents who work for a local authority or a voluntary organization.

If you stop fostering privately you must notify the local authority in writing. This could occur, for example, if the child was taken away. You are supposed to do this within forty-eight hours. You are obliged to tell the local authority, if they ask, the name and address of the new carer.

There is no need to notify the local authority if you intend to resume fostering within twenty-seven days. If this does not in fact happen then you must notify them within forty-eight hours.

The Children Act 1989

This Act repeals the Foster Children Act 1980 and simplifies the law. The definition of a foster parent will be someone who fosters for a local authority or a voluntary organization, or by private arrangement.

The aim is to bring private fostering more in line with 'public' fostering, that is fostering for a local authority or a voluntary organization. A foster parent will not usually be able to foster more than three children unless their local authority exempts them or unless the children are all brothers and sisters.

The local authority will have a welfare duty towards privately fostered children. They will have to be satisfied that the children's welfare is being safeguarded and promoted. They will have a duty to advise private foster parents and visit private foster children. They will be able to inspect premises and children in them.

The power to remove a foster child from a foster home will be repealed because the Children Act creates new powers to protect all children. (See 'Place of Safety Orders', p. 177.)

A child becomes a private foster child if placed with private fosterers for more than twenty-eight days. Anything less than this will not be private fostering even if the person is a regular foster parent. If a child under eight is placed for less than twenty-eight days, it will be classed as childminding. (see Chapter 3). In future a private foster child will be one who is:

● under sixteen, or under eighteen if disabled
● cared for and who lives with someone who is not his or her parent or relative and who does not have parental responsibility for him or her

- with the carer for more than twenty-eight days
- not looked after by a local authority
- not in the same household as his or her parent, or person with parental responsibility, or relative who has assumed responsibility for him or her.

The foster parent will have to notify the local authority of the placement, as will any other person involved in the arrangement, such as the parent.

The local authority can impose requirements and prohibitions on private foster parents, such as the number of children they can care for, and the arrangements for their care. They can also prohibit fostering from taking place if they feel that the fosterer or the home are unsuitable, or the child's welfare would be prejudiced.

The private foster parent can appeal to a court within fourteen days of the decision. Failing to notify local authorities of private fostering will be a criminal offence, as will breaches of requirements or prohibitions imposed. A local authority will have a power of entry to private foster homes (see 'Search Warrants', p. 178) and it will be a criminal offence to obstruct the entry. The local authority can apply for a search warrant to enforce their power of entry.

Local authorities will have responsibilities towards private foster children when they leave foster care. Those who have left their foster home and are aged sixteen to twenty-one qualify for advice and assistance from the local authority. This enables the local authority to advise, assist and befriend the former foster child. Assistance may be in kind, or exceptionally in cash, but this can be a loan rather than a grant. Those on income support or family credit cannot be made to repay. The local authority is enabled to provide these services but it does not have to, which may well mean that hard-pressed councils do not offer them.

The Foster Home

The local authority can impose requirements as to the conditions in which foster children live. They can, for example, stipulate the number, age and sex of the foster children, the accommodation and equipment provided for them and the medical arrangements for protecting their health. They can, in non-private fostering, control what and how much information is given to the person in charge of the children. They decide how many people should be employed in looking after the children, and what their qualifications and experience should be. They decide what records should be kept, and what information and particulars should be given or received. They stipulate what fire precautions should be observed to protect the children. If there is a change in the number or identity of the children, they decide whether the arrangement can be allowed to continue.

The local authority have the power to prohibit fostering if the premises are unsuitable, the foster parent is unsuitable to have the care and maintenance of a child, or it would be detrimental to a particular foster child to live with a particular foster parent. The local authority must notify the foster parent in writing. They can cancel a ban of this sort of their own motion, or if the foster parent requests it, because, for example, there has been a change in circumstances.

A foster parent has the right to appeal against the imposition of a requirement or a prohibition to the juvenile court. This must be done within fourteen days of the notification of the refusal of an application to cancel a prohibiton. The court can cancel the requirement or prohibition, or vary the requirement, or allow more time for compliance with it. It can also substitute for an absolute prohibition, a prohibition to run from a specified date unless specified requirements are complied with.

There is a right of appeal against the decision of the juvenile court to the crown court.

Place of Safety Orders

A place of safety order can be sought by a local authority from the juvenile court if the court is satisfied that a foster child is, or is about to be:

● received by a person unfit to have his or her care; or
● received by a person who is disqualified from being a foster parent under the Foster Children Act 1980 or received by a person who is contravening a prohibition; or
● received to live in premises or in an environment likely to be detrimental to him or her.

These orders last for up to twenty-eight days, after which the local authority must not continue to detain the child in a place of safety without bringing him or her before a juvenile court.

The child is removed until he or she can be restored to the care of a parent, relative or guardian, or until other arrangements can be made, i.e. the child can be received into local authority care. If it is practical to do so the local authority must inform the parent or guardian or the person who acts as guardian; this includes the person from whom they are removing the child.

The local authority official who visits the foster home will generally be a social worker. This person can apply direct to a single magistrate for an order if there is proof of imminent danger to the health or well-being of the child. This could, for example, be done at the magistrate's home outside the hours that courts sit.

The order can be executed by a local authority official or by any police officer.

If a place of safety order is made because a prohibition has been contravened then the order may cover all foster children who live with the particular foster parent.

The New Emergency Protection Order (EPO)

When the Children Act 1989 is implemented, the place of safety order will be replaced by the emergency protection order. The EPO can be used to protect all children, not only those being fostered.

A court may make an EPO if it is satisfied that there is reasonable cause to believe that the child is likely to suffer significant harm. The order can last for eight days and can be extended only once for a period of seven days. There is a presumption of reasonable contact between the child and the person from whom the child was taken, and the social worker can return the child, if satisfied that it would be safe to do so, while the order is in force.

An EPO can be granted if there is a suspicion of significant harm coupled with an unreasonable denial of access to the child by an authorized person. (For further details of emergency powers under the Children Act, please refer to Chapter 9.)

Search Warrants

A single magistrate can grant a search warrant to the local authority if satisfied that there is reasonable cause to believe that a foster child is being kept in a household, and that admission by the local authority's representative has been refused or is likely to be refused, or that the occupier is temporarily absent. The magistrate must be shown any information or document setting out the brief facts which is sworn to by the person making it. The warrant authorizes the local authority to enter the premises, using force if necessary, at any reasonable time, in order to inspect the premises. The warrant must be executed within forty-eight hours of its issue otherwise it is invalid.

A refusal to allow a foster child to be visited by or to allow premises to be inspected by the local authority can be regarded as reasonable cause for suspicion that unnecessary suffering is being caused to, or offences are being committed against, a child. On the strength of this, a warrant can be issued under section 40

of the Children and Young Persons Act 1933 authorizing the police to search for
and remove a child.

The Children Act will change the law on powers of entry and search in this situation.

When making an emergency protection order, the court can authorize the
social worker to enter the foster home and search for the child. Obstructing this
power is an offence. The social worker can also search for and remove other
children in the home.

The police can assist the social worker to remove the child if he or she is
prevented or refused entry. The social worker and the police can be accompanied
by a doctor, a nurse or a health visitor.

The police have separate powers to remove a child and keep him or her in
police protection for up to seventy-two hours. This will be in local authority
accommodation.

When Things Go Wrong

Offences Relating to Foster Children

It is an offence to:

- fail to give notice or information regarding fostering if required to do so
  by the local authority
- fail to give notice or information within a reasonable time
- make a false or misleading statement in a notice or in information
- refuse to allow the local authority to visit
- refuse to allow the local authority to inspect the foster home
- have a foster child to live with you if disqualified from doing so under
  the Foster Children Act
- fail to comply with a requirement imposed by the local authority or keep
  a foster child in contravention of a prohibition
- refuse to comply with an order for the removal of a child or to obstruct
  anyone who is executing such an order
- deliberately obstruct a person entitled to enter the premises with a warrant.

The maximum penalty for any of these offences is six months' imprisonment or a
fine.

Accidents to Foster Children

It is important for foster parents to realize that they may need to insure to cover accidents to foster children in their care and for claims against them. In a recent case it was decided that they are not, in law, the agents of the local authority and so the authority is not liable for their negligence. This means the foster parents are liable and may have to pay out damages. This position is very unsatisfactory for foster parents and to alleviate this, the new regulations will provide for them to receive a notice from the local authority when they are first approved as foster parents. This will contain, among other information, the authority's arrangements for meeting claims by or against foster parents for damage, loss or injury or legal defence costs.

There is a number of options:

- local authorities can indemnify foster parents, accepting responsibility for damages and expenses incurred as a result of fostering and of the actions of any foster child
- foster parents can be covered by an extension of the local authority's own insurance
- foster parents can be covered by a block policy arranged by the National Foster Care Association, an organization for foster parents and those involved with foster care
- local authorities can pay an increased allowance to enable foster parents to pay for their own insurance.

Becoming a Foster Parent

Recruitment

How foster parents are recruited depends on the individual local authority. Some fostering is arranged by voluntary organizations but this is less common. For the purposes of this chapter we have assumed that the agency will be a local authority.

Frequently local authorities run publicity campaigns in order to recruit foster parents. These sometimes focus on fostering generally, but increasingly they concentrate on specialist schemes or needs, such as teenaged children, handicapped children or children who have lived in community homes for many years and who risk becoming 'institutionalized'.

In recent years, there has been a growth in advertising for foster parents for specific children, who have perhaps proved 'hard to place'. Largely these advertisements appear in the specialist press, such as the newsletter of the British Agencies for Adoption and Fostering (BAAF), and will be read by established foster parents who may be interested in new challenges.

Steadily, however, there has been a growth in advertising in the national and local press with the aim of interesting new recruits by focusing on individual children who are in some way typical of the children needing foster parents. The new recruit may not be allocated that particular child but the aim of the advertising is to alert potential candidates to the large number of children needing foster parents.

Many local authorities hold open meetings at which inquirers can learn more about what fostering entails by talking to experienced foster parents. Potential foster parents can contact their social services department, asking to speak to the adoption and fostering unit or its equivalent. Alternatively, the National Foster Care Association (see p. 405) can assist by putting candidates in touch with the right department of their local authority and by supplying literature on a wide variety of topics of interest to fosterers.

Approval of Foster Parents

The regulations provide for foster parents to be approved before children can be placed with them. It is possible, if required, for this approval to be in relation to a specific child only. The regulations require the local authority to visit the applicants and they provide for the following matters to be taken into account by local authorities when approving persons as foster parents.

1. HEALTH

The proposed foster parents should expect to undergo a medical examination in the same way that prospective adopters have to. If a potential fosterer has some sort of health problem this does not necessarily mean that he or she cannot foster. It obviously depends on the nature and seriousness of the problem, and the extent to which the applicant's health may deteriorate.

2. MARITAL STATUS

This is not just nosiness – the authority need to know as much detail as possible about the fosterers in order to form a complete picture of them, including particulars of any previous marriages. In particular, the guidance on the regulations issued by the then DHSS directs authorities to check marriage certificates as marital status becomes significant if adoption is considered later.

3. OTHER ADULTS LIVING IN THE HOUSEHOLD

It is important to know who the child will be living with along with the foster parents, who will participate in the care and the daily life of the child, and the demands made on the foster parents by other members of their household.

4. ACCOMMODATION

The suitability of the accommodation should be checked and also access to amenities such as schools and public transport, bearing in mind visits from natural parents. This becomes even more vital where a child has special needs or handicaps, and may need to be within easy reach of special schools or hospitals.

5. CHILDREN

The social worker who investigates the family should communicate with the children of the proposed foster parents to explore their feelings about a foster child living in their home. It is obviously important for the fosterers to consider very carefully the effect that having a foster child or children will have on their family and social life. Where the foster parent has children by a previous marriage or relationship who do not live in the home, the extent of contact should be looked into.

6. ANY OTHER CHILD LIVING IN THE HOUSEHOLD

Where the foster parents are approved by other agencies, their views must be sought, and approval should be given only after consultation between the authorities. Obviously it is important for fosterers not to be over-stretched by looking after more children than they can cope with.

7. RELIGION

The authority will need to consider the extent to which religion influences family life, whether the applicants are familiar with other faiths and denominations, and whether they have an insight into, or an understanding of, any other religions and the capacity to care for a child of a different religion or from a more or a less religious background. Where possible a child is placed with foster parents of the same religion or who undertake to bring the child up in his or her own religion. Also, the extent to which a foster child will be expected to participate in the foster parents' religious activity.

8. CULTURAL BACKGROUND AND RACIAL ORIGINS

There is an acute shortage of foster parents from ethnic minorities and many local authorities are running recruitment drives to try to remedy this. Foster parents, like any other group, should reflect the community as a whole, and some local authorities have a policy that children should wherever possible be placed with a foster family of the same race or culture as the child. Because it will always be difficult for exact 'matching' to take place – and many people would not feel that this was always necessary or desirable – the authority will want to know whether the fosterers have any special experience and knowledge equipping them to care for children from different racial or cultural backgrounds. The local authority will need to know whether the applicants have links through marriage, family or friendship with a particular group, or a special understanding of a particular culture and knowledge of language. They will also want to know the extent to which the prospective fosterers are prepared to develop such links and understanding.

The Children Act 1989 places local authorities under a duty to take into account the different racial groups to which children in their area who are in need belong when making arrangements for people to act as foster parents.

9. EMPLOYMENT

The authority need to know how the employment or occupation of the fosterer or his or her partner affects their family life. For example, is shift-work involved? How much time is available for family activities? Where the main carer in the family works outside the home, the authority will need to know the child-care arrangements to cover daily care and 'emergencies' such as sickness.

10. LEISURE ACTIVITIES AND INTERESTS

Details will be sought on the applicants' hobbies and the extent to which these involve the whole family, including any foster children.

11. STANDARD OF LIVING

The general lifestyle of the family will be examined with a view to 'matching' the child as far as possible with a family similar to his or her own in terms of standard of living.

12. PREVIOUS EXPERIENCE

It is clearly of crucial importance to know the applicants' experience and capabilities in terms of caring for children of different age groups, especially other people's children. Apart from interviewing the applicants at length, the social worker will probably speak to the family's health visitor about this.

13. CRIMINAL CONVICTIONS

The police will be asked to check their records of criminal convictions. The applicants and all other adult members of their household will be asked to give their permission for this to happen. Even convictions which are 'spent' under the Rehabilitation of Offenders Act 1974 must be disclosed. (For further details of the provisions of this Act, see Chapter 8.) A refusal to give permission for the record to be checked will mean that the application is not considered further. In making these checks the local authority will particularly be safeguarding against the child living with people who have been convicted of sexual offences, offences of violence or ones involving drugs. This covers a wide variety of offences, some of which are a great deal more serious than others. It should be stressed that the possession of such a conviction will not necessarily bar an applicant of itself. The offence may have been committed a long time ago, and may have involved a trivial infringement of the law, for example, possession of a small amount of cannabis for personal use. It is up to the local authority to decide.

Local authorities will check their own records in respect of all adults in the household. They may have records if any member of the household is known to social services, for example because they have had a social worker. The social worker should visit at least once when all members of the household are in. The object of this is for the social worker to observe and explore with the family their relationship to one another and the extent to which family members will be included in the care and the day-to-day life of the foster child. The social worker must also inquire into the demands made on the fosterers by other family members, e.g. elderly relatives, who may need to be cared for.

14. PREVIOUS REQUESTS

The views of any other authority or agency to which the applicants have applied to foster or adopt will be sought by the local authority. This includes unsuccessful applications. Where the prospective fosterers live in the area of another authority, the views of that authority will be requested. If the applicants are already approved by another agency, then approval will be given only after there has been consultation between the authorities.

The fourteen points listed above are included in the regulations but are not intended to be an exhaustive list, nor are the questions intended to be a checklist to which there are right and wrong answers. The idea is to identify all the factors which make up the general picture of the potential fosterers, their family and way of life.

The DHSS guidelines specifically direct local authorities to form a view of the applicants' attitudes and expectations in relation to the following matters: child-rearing, discipline, looking after someone else's child, understanding and perception of fostering, and working with parents; the applicants' capacity to provide a foster child with protection, nurture and opportunities for development; the applicants' preference and suitability as a foster parent for any particular group of children or for any particular type of fostering.

There is no prescribed procedure for reaching these decisions; each agency should arrive at its own. However, all applicants are required to provide two referees, and the agency should interview both of them. It is further recommended that the social worker interview a member of the applicants' wider family to determine the importance of the extended family to the foster family, and to determine the attitude of the whole family towards the applicants' having a foster child.

What a Local Authority Should Tell Approved Foster Parents

AS A REQUIREMENT OF THE LAW

1. The local authority's policies and procedures for the review of approval as a foster parent, including the procedures for reconsideration.
2. The local authority's procedure for dealing with complaints made by foster parents.
3. The arrangements of the local authority for meeting claims by or against

fosterers in respect of damage, loss or injury or legal defence costs. (See 'When things go wrong', above.)

4. The local authority's arrangements for paying foster parents including information on scales, special payments enhancements and the method of payment.

AS A MATTER OF GOOD PRACTICE

1. The matters which will be covered in the placement agreement between the foster parents and the local authority.

2. How the local authority deal with the agreement all foster parents must make regarding medical and dental treatment.

3. The local authority's duties to visit the child, and to review his or her progress, and to provide support to fosterers, and to notify them of any variations to the fostering arrangements.

4. Foster parents are expected not to apply to other fostering agencies for approval, nor to foster privately, nor to apply for registration as childminders without first notifying the local authority for whom they foster. This is meant to give the local authority time to consult the other agency and to discuss the proposals with the foster parents. This is something which is expected of responsible foster parents but in the regulations themselves the onus of notification rests with the agencies.

5. The local authority's powers and duties, and the policies they operate, when terminating a foster placement. It should be explained to foster parents that except in an emergency they will not remove a child in an arbitrary or unplanned way without first discussing this with the foster parents and coming to an agreement.

6. The training available to foster parents and whether this is voluntary or compulsory.

7. Vital practical information such as emergency telephone numbers and essential advice such as the liability to pay income tax which can arise on payment for fostering.

Review of Approval

Local authorities are required to review their approval of foster parents periodically. It is up to them to formulate their own policy, including how often the reviews take place. The policy should be notified to all approved foster parents.

The intervals between reviews should not necessarily be uniform for all foster parents: foster parents caring for children on a long-term basis can be reviewed less frequently than those who care for children in a series of short-term placements.

There should also be reviews when there is a change in the foster family's circumstances. Some examples of such a change would be a change of address, the death of one of the foster parents, the separation, divorce or remarriage of foster parents or a change in health of one of the foster parents or of a member of their family. A review may also be needed where a complaint or allegation has been made against a foster parent.

The review should be conducted by a social worker attached to the authority's fostering service. It should include a visit to the home, discussion with the foster parents, and meeting other members of the family. Experiences and difficulties on both sides should be aired, including the reasons why a foster home may have been under-used or not used at all.

It may be that the 'review' should in fact be a complete reassessment if the foster parents are seeking to be approved for a different kind of fostering from that which they have undertaken previously. They may, for example, wish to foster older or younger children than before, for longer or shorter periods than before, or care for children who need special help to recover from physical or sexual abuse.

The review and the decision arising out of it should be recorded by the local authority. The decision and the reasons for it should be discussed with the foster parents and they must be notified in writing. They should also be reminded of the procedures for appealing against the decision. It is likely that if approval is terminated this may have happened at the same time as the removal of a foster child from their care. The foster parents may be challenging the ending of the placement as well as the ending of their approval as foster parents. If so, these two decisions can be reconsidered at the same time.

Often fostering will end because that is what the fosterers want. If foster parents decide to give up, then notice of termination of their approval should be given to them by the local authority, unless they intend to resume within the foreseeable future, say within a year.

The guidance issued under the 1988 regulations urges authorities to terminate approval formally when it is decided that a foster parent is no longer suitable to foster. It is not considered to be appropriate simply to avoid placing children with them.

The Training of Foster Parents

There is a move towards foster parents being seen in a more professional light and towards creating a fostering service. Integral to this is the training of foster carers.

The guidance issued under the new regulations advocates training at three levels:

1. support, discussion and evaluation in the home;
2. participation in foster parent groups; and
3. participation in formal training with other foster parents and social workers.

There is no national scheme as to how things should work – it is up to each individual authority to devise their own scheme. Some themes, however, should be common to all preparation and training programmes, such as working with natural parents. This is of crucial importance, whether the fostering is to be long or short term. It is vital to the child that his or her own family should continue to be involved, and in practice a lot will depend on how much they are encouraged to be so by the substitute family. Foster parents often provide an opportunity for parents to learn about good parenting by example. Of course there will always be some parents who are hostile and who may have little insight into why their child has been taken away and resentful of the fact that the local authority have chosen to place their child with foster parents whose care they may unfavourably and unfairly compare with their own. These cases are not that frequent but fosterers need to be prepared for them, and need to know how to deal with such situations as they arise.

There should be a clear understanding of the support which a local authority has a responsibility to provide if difficulties or crises arise. Fosterers need to be alert to the possibility that previously undisclosed abuse, including sexual abuse, may come to light during the placement. Also there is the increasing problem that some children will be HIV positive (that is, carrying the AIDS virus) and foster parents need to have clear and accurate information on the circumstances and factors which suggest that a child might be at risk, and the implications for family life and the child's care.

As well as receiving training at the beginning of their career as foster parents, there should be opportunities for continuing training available to all fosterers.

Local authorities should provide support to their foster parents in recognition of the difficult job they do. Fostering sometimes causes stress in family relationships, the fosterers may find it acutely difficult to handle children who are disturbed in their behaviour because of their past experiences. This in turn can lead to problems for fosterers with their own children who may at first resent the special attention needed by the foster child.

The foster child's own social worker can provide advice, support and assistance to the foster parents. In some cases, however, it will be helpful for foster parents to have their own social worker, or if this is not possible, an experienced foster parent with whom they are 'linked' so that they have a source of support. This can be useful where, for example, the foster parents are isolated from foster groups perhaps because of lack of transport, or where they specialize in short-term placements which do not give them the opportunity to form relationships with the children's social workers.

Reports

The 'visitor' assigned to check on the foster family by the local authority or the voluntary organization must report in writing when he or she sees the child and when they visit the foster home.

The authority or organization must keep up-to-date written records on children fostered out by them and by other agencies in their area for whom they provide supervision of the foster family. These records must be retained for at least three years after the child attains the age of eighteen or dies if that occurs earlier. The records are open to inspection by any person authorized to see them by the Secretary of State. In practice, however, the discretion as to who sees them tends to be exercised by the local authority. This does not necessarily mean that the persons about whom the reports are written – the child, the parents, or the foster parents – get to see the reports. It is up to the local authority. There can often be particular difficulties about getting access to medical reports.

Registers

Each local authority must keep a register of children fostered out in their area whether they are fostered by them or by another agency. This must include each child's name, sex, date of birth and religion. It must also include the names, addresses and religion of the foster parents. The register should also include the name of the agency which has responsibility for placing the child, the date that the foster placement starts and finishes, and the reason why it finishes.

Any local authority can ask the local authority in whose area the child is fostered to perform any of their supervisory duties and to provide a report as often as agreed on the welfare, health, conduct and progress of each child. If this is done, a note of these arrangements must be entered in the register. Similarly, if the child is boarded out by a voluntary organization, and the area local authority is performing supervisory duties, a note of this must be entered on the register.

The register entry for a particular child is kept for at least five years after the child reaches eighteen, or would have reached eighteen if he or she dies before attaining that age.

Like the records kept by visitors, the register is open to inspection by people authorized to see it by the Secretary of State. In practice, it depends on the local authority concerned as to whether the child, the parents or the foster parents have access to it.

Where a local authority or voluntary organization foster a child in another area, and end the placement, they must tell the area local authority that this has happened, the date it ended, the reason why, and whether it is intended to place another child in the foster home.

If the area authority receive information that a placement is no longer in the child's best interests, then they must tell the placing local authority or voluntary organization immediately.

Each local authority must satisfy itself as to whether or not a voluntary organization fostering out children in the area can satisfactorily discharge the duty to supervise the placement. If satisfied that it cannot, it must take the duty over. This situation is quite rare, but the regulations provide that where this does happen there must be a review every three years. The responsibility can be transferred back to the voluntary organization if the area local authority become satisfied that they can properly supervise again.

Where a child is in care to a local authority but in the charge of a voluntary organization and the organization fosters the child out, then it is the organization's responsibility to notify the local authority of this fact, and of the name and address of the foster parents. If the placement ends, the organization must notify the local authority of the reason for this. If the area local authority has to take over supervision, then they must tell the local authority who have care of this fact.

Visits during Fostering

Where the foster parent is single and there are no other members of the household, the local authority must visit within the first two weeks, and then again within the following two weeks. Following this, as a minimum, there should be a visit once every six weeks in the first two years, then once every three months. There must be a visit within one month of a move by the household, and immediately if there has been a complaint, unless it appears unnecessary.

In all other cases, there must be a visit within one month of the start of the placement, and thereafter, as a minimum, every six weeks where the child is under five and the placement has not yet lasted two years. Where the child is over five, the rule is every two months. In placements which last longer than two years, the visit should be every three months. All these are minimum requirements, and children should be visited more often where it is necessary and desirable. There should always be a visit within one month of a move, and there should always be an immediate visit if there has been a complaint, unless action appears to be unnecessary.

Different minimum visiting requirements apply once the child ceases to be of compulsory school age. First, there should be a visit when this event occurs, or within three months of it. If a new placement starts after the child reaches this point, then there should be a visit within one month of the placement starting. Thereafter there should be a visit every three months and there should always be visits within one month of a move, and immediately on receipt of a complaint unless action appears unnecessary.

REVIEWS

There should be a regular review covering the welfare, health, conduct and progress of the child. This review should consider the reports prepared by the local authority visitor. It must take place within three months of the start of the placement, and there should be a further review thereafter, as a minimum, at least once every six months. The review should be conducted by someone other than the local authority visitor, for example another social worker. A note should be entered in the case record, together with a note of any action recommended.

Emergency Placements

These will arise where there has been an urgent admission to care. In an emergency, the regulations allow a child to be placed with a person who is not an approved foster parent. The person must be a relative or friend of the child.

The authority should nevertheless make the fullest possible checks, including checks with the police to satisfy themselves that the relative or friend is a suitable person to be entrusted with the child. Where possible the parent's views or those of other relatives should be sought. The proposed carer should be interviewed, the home visited and information obtained about the other members of the household.

Placement with an approved foster parent should, however, be the general rule even when admission to care is unplanned.

The purpose of this exception is to avoid the unnecessary and sudden removal of a child from the care of a familiar figure in reassuring surroundings.

Such a placement should last no longer than six weeks. The social worker must visit the child weekly. If the child has not been medically examined and assessed within the preceding three months then this must take place within two weeks of placement. The relative or friend can of course always apply to be an approved foster parent if it is envisaged that the stay be longer than six weeks. The provision that a foster parent can be approved in respect of fostering one particular child was designed with this in mind.

Where the placement is an emergency one, the fosterer should sign an abridged form of the agreement that would be signed in any other situation. The 'emergency' foster parent must undertake to:

- care for the child as if he or she were a member of the foster parent's own family and must promote the child's welfare
- allow access to parents and other relatives and friends as arranged by the local authority
- allow the authority to visit the child in the foster home, and allow them to remove the child if they consider it necessary
- maintain confidentiality and not disclose, without the consent of the authority, information about the child and family acquired through the foster placement.

The local authority must make sure that the temporary foster parents have the information they need to look after the child.

The Agreement between the Local Authority and the Foster Parents

Each time a child is placed with foster parents, the regulations require that the authority and the fosterers must enter into an agreement which sets out the arrangements for the child's care. There is no set form for these agreements but they must all contain the following elements.

1. An undertaking by the foster parents covering five areas:
    *   to care for the child as if he or she were a member of their own family, promoting the child's welfare which includes safety, health, education and general development
    *   to notify the local authority immediately if the child is seriously ill or has a serious accident or if any other circumstances arise which seriously affect the child
    *   to notify the local authority of any change of address or change in the foster parents' own personal circumstances or when anyone joins or leaves the household
    *   to allow any person authorized by the local authority to visit the child in the foster home and to remove the child
    *   not to disclose without the consent of the authority any confidential information on the child or family.
2. The arrangements for access to the child by the child's parents and family.
3. The frequency of the visiting and reviews by the authority.
4. Arrangements for the foster parents to get medical and dental treatment for the child.
5. The details of the payments by the local authority.

The regulations also state that the agreement should cover any particular arrangements for the child's care, development and upbringing, including health and education. This means that the agreement can be tailored to the individual needs of the child and can be flexible. The agreement might be very simple where the placement is short term. It can be more detailed where the placement has a specific aim and the foster parents have pledged to work towards this aim with the child and possibly also the parents. Some examples are where the foster parent is training an older teenager for independence, or is working towards a change in the child's behaviour. The agreement should in this type of situation include the promises made by the local authority, for example to provide access to specialist services or other support.

The Natural Parents' Position

The agreement should be signed by the foster parents and the local authority but not by the child or the parents. The parents should however be given the details of the placement agreement which relate to and affect themselves and the child. If possible the parents should have consented to these parts of the agreement. The parents should be given written notice of the foster parents' name and address, the agreed access arrangements, the plan for the child and the aim of the placement, and any other matters relating to the care and welfare of the child.

The guidance issued under the regulations makes it clear that the only circumstance in which the written notice may be withheld is where the parents' whereabouts are unknown or where the authority has decided that to give such information to the parents would not be in the child's interests, that is where they do not want them to visit the foster home. These cases should be exceptional and the reasons should be recorded on the child's case record.

Parents should be involved as much as possible in the plans for their children and should be kept informed of their progress and health. All discussions and agreements should be recorded and written details sent to the parents.

Payment

All foster parents receive a fostering allowance towards the cost of caring for the children placed with them. These payments are not uniform: they vary from agency to agency. These are paid by the local authority's adoption and fostering unit or its equivalent at a voluntary organization. There is a minimum fostering allowance recommended by the National Foster Care Association (NFCA) but this has not been adopted by all local authorities and voluntary organizations.

In some cases, extra costs are incurred by the foster parents and they are paid an enhanced allowance to take account of this. Examples might be where additional heating is needed for a delicate child or extra clothing for a hyperactive child who wears clothes out more rapidly.

Both these sorts of payments are a reimbursement of expenses and as such are not treated as income by the Inland Revenue when assessing how much income tax the foster parent must pay.

Often foster parents are paid an additional payment over and above the reimbursement of expenses. These are sometimes called reward payments or professional fostering allowances. They are paid in recognition of particular fostering tasks, such as caring for difficult, disturbed or handicapped children who require a greater input of time, skills and experience over and above the norm. These payments are taxable.

The paying agency should give the foster parent a statement at the end of each tax year which sets out any payments received on which tax ought to be paid. The foster parent can then send this to the Inland Revenue with his or her tax return. There is no need for the foster parent to include in the return any payments which are for expenses, i.e. the normal or enhanced fostering allowance.

If the foster parents think that the paying agency are calculating too high a proportion of their payment as the reward element then they should take this up with the agency concerned. If this does not work then they must keep detailed records of income and expenditure and notify the Inland Revenue when their income tax is assessed.

Foster parents receiving a reward element in their payment are classed as self-employed as far as those earnings are concerned. Tax assessments are made on the 'preceding year basis'. This means that the tax for the year will be based on the receipts of the previous year. The tax itself is paid in arrears, and in two instalments, on 1 January in the tax year of assessment and on 1 July following. The tax year runs from 6 April each year to 5 April the following year. So, for example, where a person makes his or her annual accounts to 31 July each year, their assessment for the tax year 1987–88 will be based on their income for their accounting year ending on 31 July 1986. The tax assessed will be payable on 1 January 1988 and on 1 July 1988.

Because they are self-employed no one will be deducting tax from their earnings from fostering before they receive it. This means it is wise for them to make provision for the expected tax bill by setting aside money to meet it. How much they need to save depends on the level of payments and the prevailing tax rate. The NFCA can assist on this and annually publish a pamphlet on fostering allowances and income tax which includes a table setting out yearly tax based on weekly income. For foster parents with complicated tax affairs who may already employ an accountant to help them, it is wise to seek expert advice.

NATIONAL INSURANCE

Foster parents who are not being paid reward or professional payments need not pay NI contributions on their receipts from fostering. However, foster parents receiving fees or professional allowances or reward payments are classed as self-employed for national insurance purposes as well as income tax purposes and must pay contributions. There is, though, a small earnings exception below which contributions are not payable. This changes each year and should be checked with the local DSS office.

Private Foster Parents

It is likely that the tax and national insurance consequences of fostering will be the same for private foster parents as they are for those who foster for local authorities or voluntary organizations. In other words they should not have to pay tax or NI contributions if the money they receive is merely to reimburse expenses already incurred. If it is more than this then they will be liable to pay tax and NI contributions and in their case it will be essential to keep detailed records and accounts since it is less likely that the parents whose children they are caring for will do this.

Welfare Benefits

The rules covering entitlement differ according to the benefit being claimed. The benefits commonly claimed by fosterers are dealt with below.

CHILD BENEFIT

Fosterers *cannot* claim child benefit unless they are fostering privately. Child benefit cannot be claimed twice, however, so foster parents can claim it only if the natural parents are not. In order to claim, the natural parents must be paying towards their child's upkeep, and the amount must be at least the equivalent of the child benefit rate. Parents with children in local authority care can claim child benefit if their child lives with them for at least one day a week.

UNEMPLOYMENT BENEFIT

Fostering payments are not taken into account when entitlement to unemployment benefit is calculated unless they include a reward element. If they do, then this may affect entitlement.

INCOME SUPPORT (SUPPLEMENTARY BENEFIT)

The rules here differ according to whether or not the fostering is private. When calculating entitlement, fostering payments are ignored even if they include reward payments. This is not the case with payments for private fostering which are taken into account.

Foster children are not treated as a member of the claimant's household so there is no extra payment made in respect of them, unless the arrangement is private and the foster parents are receiving the child benefit in which case the foster child counts as a dependent and the claimant receives extra income support.

Single foster parents are not required to be available for work when caring for a foster child in order to qualify for income support.

FAMILY CREDIT (FAMILY INCOME SUPPLEMENT)

The rules for disregarding fostering allowances are the same as for income support.

HOUSING BENEFIT

Any fostering allowance paid is disregarded as income when calculating entitlement. There is an extra element paid for the dependent foster child.

ATTENDANCE ALLOWANCE

This is tax-free and does not affect fostering allowances. Entitlement does not depend on the means of the claimant, but on satisfying certain medical conditions. It is paid to the carer for the benefit of the child.

MOBILITY ALLOWANCE

This does not affect fostering allowances and, like attendance allowance entitlement, depends on medical conditions rather than financial criteria.

Your Child at Sixteen

Sixteen is a significant age in a child's life. A number of important rights are acquired, and in many respects the law treats him or her as an adult. Here is a summary of the main changes.

- A sixteen-year-old can leave school.
- He or she can work full-time and get a national insurance number.
- He or she can join a trade union (some unions admit members below the age of sixteen).
- A sixteen-year-old can marry with parental consent. If consent is not forthcoming the child can apply to the court for authorization.
- Sixteen-year-olds can probably leave home without their parent's or guardian's consent. In law they remain minors until they are eighteen, but in practice courts are unlikely to force a young person to return home against their wishes, unless things are going badly and it is felt that they are at risk.
- Girls can legally consent to sexual intercourse.
- A young person can consent or refuse consent to medical, surgical or dental treatment. This includes contraceptive treatment. They can also choose their own doctor. A child under sixteen cannot normally consent and consent is given through the parents. The law states, however, that the consent of a child under sixteen is sufficient provided that the doctor is satisfied that he or she understands the implications of their decision.
- A sixteen-year-old can apply for a passport with the consent of one parent, and will be deleted from a parent's passport at sixteen. A child under sixteen can be issued with a passport but it is the parent who applies.
- A boy can join the armed forces with parental consent; girls have to wait until they are seventeen and a half.
- Sixteen-year-olds can hold a licence to drive a moped.
- They can buy cigarettes and tobacco.
- They can consume certain alcoholic drinks — beer, cider or wine — with a meal in a restaurant, or in a room used for meals in a pub or hotel.

- They can buy fireworks.
- They can buy premium bonds (they can hold them at any age if someone buys them on their behalf).
- They can go into a pub without an adult but they cannot buy alcohol.
- They must pay full fare on trains and on tubes and buses in London (in other areas they may have to pay full fare at fourteen).
- They must pay for prescriptions unless one of the exemptions applies.
- They can take part in a public performance without a local authority licence.
- They can apply for legal advice and assistance under the green form scheme, and it will be their income on which eligibility will be assessed. There will be no need for the application to be made through the parent or guardian. They can apply for legal aid in a criminal matter in their own right and eligibility will be assessed on their income rather than their parents'. This contrasts with legal aid in a civil matter where a young person must usually apply through their parent or guardian until they are eighteen. (See Chapter 13 for further details.)
- They remain juveniles in the eyes of the criminal law until they reach the age of seventeen.
- At sixteen they can be sentenced to a period of community service.
- At sixteen they can be sentenced to detention in a young offender institution. The maximum term is six months in the juvenile court or twelve months in the crown court. The minimum term depends on the sex of the child; for boys it is twenty-one days, for girls it is four months and one day. (See Chapter 8 for further details.)
- Child benefit ceases to be payable to the mother of a young person who reaches the age of sixteen, unless he or she is receiving full-time education at school or college.
- Income support is not usually claimable by sixteen- or seventeen-year-olds who have left school. They are expected to find a place on the Youth Training Scheme, where they receive a training allowance. There are some exceptions (for details see Chapter 6).
- Maintenance orders for children do not cease until they reach the age of seventeen unless the order provides for them to continue while the child is still receiving full-time education. Even if the original order did not include this possibility, an application can be made to the court if the young person stays in school or college.

Chapter 8

Children in Trouble with the Police

Your child does not have to be a criminal to be involved with the police. In urban areas where there is a policy of high-profile policing on the streets, and at events patronized by young people, the chances of your child having some contact with the police are fairly high. That encounter could become hostile if handled badly. Sometimes it starts as hostile – a suspicious police officer stops your child for questioning. Your child does not have to answer questions but a refusal and a strict adherence to his rights may not be respected by the police officer who could believe he has something to hide. If the police officer is not fully satisfied by your child's answers then he can arrest him on suspicion of having committed a crime. The legal basis for arrest is that the police officer suspects – he does not have to *know* – that a crime has been or is about to be committed and that your child is involved.

Sometimes when children are stopped and questioned or arrested there is an innocent and plausible explanation or the offence is extremely minor. The police are not particularly geared towards expecting or believing innocent explanations or turning a blind eye to trivial transgressions. While they have a wide discretion in how they approach a minor breach of the law and can and do choose not to take action, police function, training and ideology is to fight crime, make arrests and get convictions. Images of paternalistic bobbies who are closely connected with the community, who know local children's parents and might have a word in their ear and leave it at that, fit badly with inner-city life and the techniques of modern policing. Childhood misdemeanours which can be dealt with by the whole subtle range of parental control are increasingly treated as a breach of the criminal law. To be blunt, what you might think of as 'scrumping', a young and enthusiastic police officer might see as an offence under section 1 of the Theft Act 1968 relating to apples. Train-spotting on a railway line could be a breach of either British Rail regulations or, if the child is warned off and returns, an offence of criminal trespass. Borrowing a friend's bike and failing to return it can be theft. Shouting abuse at a rival school can be 'insulting words' under the Public Order Act. In case you feel we exaggerate, the authors have experienced a case where an eleven-year-old boy who had never been in trouble took a milk bottle from a neighbour's doorstep. He was arrested, held in custody for four hours, convicted of section 1 theft in the juvenile court and fined £1.

A child of any age can be picked up by the police but only children of ten and over can be prosecuted, ten being the age of criminal responsibility. In law, a child is someone under fourteen, and a young person is someone aged fourteen to seventeen. In the eyes of the criminal law, a person becomes an adult at seventeen, though not all of the penalties which can be imposed on an adult can be imposed until someone reaches twenty-one. Often the term 'juvenile' is used to describe anyone up to the age of seventeen.

Arrests

The way in which the police should operate when dealing with suspects is governed by the Police and Criminal Evidence Act 1984 and the codes of practice issued under this Act by the Home Office. This law applies to all people, of whatever age, who are in contact with the police but some rules apply to juveniles only.

There is now a nationwide power allowing the police to stop and search people and vehicles for stolen goods or prohibited articles. There are some safeguards – the police must identify themselves and their police station, inform you of the object of the search and the grounds for it. They must have reasonable grounds for suspecting that you have what they are looking for. They are not supposed to act on prejudices of their own or just hunches and if you are searched in public, they can require you to remove only your outer garments. They must make a written record of the incident and you can ask for a copy of it.

'Prohibited articles' is a wide term and includes not only obvious weapons, but otherwise innocent items which can be used as weapons or in a dishonest way. This, of course, can apply to almost everything.

Arrest means that someone is detained and is not free to leave at will. If you are arrested you must be informed of this fact as soon as possible and the reason for it. Often a suspect is not arrested but is asked to go to the police station. This is sometimes called 'helping with inquiries' and means that you are there voluntarily and can leave unless you are arrested. If your involvement with the police starts off on a voluntary footing and then changes, they must tell you at once that you are under arrest.

The police have the power to search someone on arrest. Once someone is arrested, they must be taken to a police station as soon as possible unless the police need to take them somewhere else first to carry out reasonable investigations.

Everyone under seventeen has the right to have their parent or guardian informed of their arrest, and must be interviewed only in the presence of a parent, guardian or another responsible adult (not a police officer). The police should contact you first by phone or a visit. It may be some time since your child's arrest, so get to the police station as soon as possible. If you cannot be found then they should contact a solicitor or an independent person, usually a social worker. A solicitor should act as an aid and support to the child and give legal advice. The effectiveness of social workers in this situation depends upon the individual but they may have no practical experience of police stations.

You may want a solicitor to help at this stage. Many solicitors who do criminal work are willing to go to the police station and free legal aid is available to suspects being held in a police station. Your local citizens' advice bureau or law centre can recommend solicitors who work in this field. Out of office hours you may have an emergency service in your area, perhaps run by a law centre, and some solicitors have emergency numbers. Also there is a twenty-four hour duty solicitor scheme whereby a solicitor is available on call to give free legal advice and assistance at the police station. You can ask the police to contact the duty solicitor. If you go to the police station on your own, remember to take a pen and lots of paper, a watch and something to read (perhaps this book!) as you may have a long wait. If you have other children, make arrangements to have them looked after rather than take them with you. A word of caution – in our experience of dealing with the police it is better to be calm and reasonable than angry and aggressive, even though you will undoubtedly be extremely anxious. A person who becomes wildly hysterical is likely to find themselves thrown out of the police station or arrested. However, try to be firm.

The Police and Criminal Evidence Act gives you authority for being there. The benefit to your child comes from the presence of a trusted adult. He is probably very frightened already and needs to feel supported, otherwise he may feel pressured to make admissions which are not true. Remember the incredible degree of psychological pressure put on a suspect in custody. Police stations are bleak and uncomfortable buildings, delays are endemic, and detention in these circumstances may reduce the morale and confidence of children to the extent that they can confess to things that they have not done. In addition, research has shown that someone being interviewed in custody may have an overwhelming desire to please the questioner by saying what the questioner wants to hear.

Even if your child has committed an offence it is just as important for you to be at the police station. He may feel guilty as well as frightened, have fantasies of going to prison and, not knowing the law, may confess to a serious offence when he is guilty only of a lesser one.

When you arrive at the police station ask to speak to the custody officer who is responsible for the welfare of suspects in custody. Ask what has happened, whether they want to interview your child and what, if anything, the child has said. Make a written note of who you speak to, what you are told and when. In later court hearings your notes could be crucial. Ask to see your child in private. This is your right. If you are not allowed to, ask why and make a note of this.

When you see your child in private, ask him what has happened. If you are angry, try to reserve it for later. Remember *you* might be in a state of shock and need to control your reactions. Check with your child that he has not been pressured or threatened by the police or anyone else and that he has no injuries. If he has, ask for a doctor to be called immediately. Find out how the injury happened, make notes yourself and tell the doctor. Find out what happened, letting your child tell you in his own words.

Your child may confess all to you and, if it is straightforward, might want to make a clean breast of it to the police. Your child may deny any involvement with the offence and be able to prove his innocence, and sometimes in these circumstances it is better to give details of his defence at this stage. However, these decisions are very hard to make on the spot, and if you are in any doubt, ask to see a solicitor.

In any event, your child has the right to remain silent. The police have to tell him this, using the following words: 'You do not have to say anything unless you wish to do so, but anything you do say, will be written down and may be used in evidence' (the caution). Tell your child this yourself and make sure he understands.

You might advise your child to remain silent in the following circumstances: if the police do not have a lot of evidence (a confession would be the strongest evidence they could get, and without it there may not be enough even to charge); if you feel your child is under so much pressure he will make a false confession; if you feel you are not being told the whole truth of the situation and your child may be protecting someone else; if you are unsure whether he has a defence; or if you feel he is himself confused and uncertain about what really happened.

If you are not allowed to see your child in private, something is going seriously wrong. If you are then allowed to sit in on the interview, without a private word before, you should advise him that as he does not *have* to answer any questions, he should stay silent. If you stick your neck out like this, make sure you have told the officer why you have advised silence and ask him to make a note of your reasons and make a note of that conversation yourself. If you make a note as soon as possible after any conversation or event, then you are allowed to produce that note in court to refresh your memory of what took place. This is more effective and more persuasive than relying on memory – police evidence is generally based on written record. Even if you make it clear to the police that your child does not wish to answer questions, they will probably try to put them anyway in an attempt to draw him into an interview. Be prepared for long silences.

In an interview there will normally be two officers present – one asking questions and one making a verbatim note. If you interrupt, a note will be made. If you later correct something, both the original and the correction will appear in the record of the interview. Try to keep notes of the interview yourself, so that there is an independent record.

The interview may seem interminable, as everything will be written down, and after the questions have ended, you and your child will be offered the chance to read through the notes to check and/or correct them and then initial each answer and sign at the bottom of each page. This is your opportunity to challenge anything which has been inaccurately recorded, as you check the police version against your own notes. Hence the importance of keeping your own notes. If they refuse to change something, you should refuse to initial and sign.

So far, we have dealt with the situation where the police record the interview on paper because that is still the norm. However, at several police stations there is an experimental scheme whereby they are tape recorded and this is likely to be extended. The obvious difference is that a tape recorder records not just what is said but the manner in which it is said. It is therefore important that answers are given as clearly and confidently as possible. It is, for example, easy to misinterpret shyness and hesitation in speaking as shiftiness. Of course, this applies to the police too and bullying should be obvious to detect. The main advantage to the suspect is that the recording of false answers will be more difficult to do on tape than it is on paper.

The interview will be conducted in a room intended for that purpose. There will be a table and chairs and very little else. It will not be comfortable, and may be bare and badly ventilated. There will be no home comforts and the effect may be demoralizing for both of you. If the interview is long, there may be a break for refreshments, canteen tea or coffee brought by an officer.

The interview is likely to start formally and correctly. After some time it can become more relaxed and you may find yourself chatting to the officers. At the risk of being cynical, watch this – if you are unguarded and give information of advantage to them, they will use it. In practice, nothing *you* say is off-the-record, but the officer will probably deny in court that he made any helpful, unguarded comments about your child's case. Some officers are scrupulously fair and disinterested, but at a police station always bear in mind the risk we have described. Similarly, watch your reactions and especially those of your child. If he fidgets or appears bored, as teenagers often do, the police may write this down and interpret it as callousness or lack of interest in the seriousness of the situation.

If you feel your child is being bullied, do not be frightened to object and if necessary stop the interview there and then. Particular things to look out for are offers to release your child if he helps the police or threats to detain him if he does not. Things which sound innocuous, for example a suggestion that once he has made a statement the child can be out of the police station in no time, are, in law, improper inducements to confess. If your child has been arrested with other people, the police are entitled to show him statements made by his co-accused which implicate him. They are meant to hand the statement to the child without any comment. If a police officer suggests that, as the child's friends have put him in it, he should come clean, that is improper. Bear in mind that the co-accused could be lying, and particularly that the statement itself is not evidence against your child at court. If at court a co-accused says that your child was involved then that is evidence, but there are safeguards attached to this which are dealt with later in this chapter.

Nobody expects your child to enjoy being in a police station and the police have no duty to be positively nice but there are basic humanitarian principles which should not be broken. If your child is treated so badly that he confesses, it may be possible to argue at court that that evidence was obtained by 'oppression' and should be excluded. This argument is extraordinarily difficult and rarely successful. If you suspect from your child's behaviour that he has been oppressed, do all you can to find out from him what has happened and demand to see a senior officer immediately. Ideally, the best way to prevent oppression is to be with your child throughout, but this is rarely possible.

Pressure can work wonders. Consider a complaint by telephone to the complaints department at the nearest police headquarters, or to department CIB2 at New Scotland Yard in London, in an effort to put pressure on the police handling the case.

Sometimes the police ask to take body samples from suspects to help in their investigations. These can be blood, semen, urine, saliva, genital or rectal swabs;

or samples of nails, footprints or hair. Consent has to be given in writing by you if your child is under fourteen or by you and your child if he is over fourteen.

Non-intimate samples can be taken without consent if a police superintendent authorizes it, but he must suspect your child of a 'serious arrestable offence' and believe the sample will tend to prove or disprove their involvement.

Intimate samples cannot be taken without consent and must be taken by a doctor. However, if you or your child refuse then this can be brought up later in court and used against your child.

The police may ask your child to take part in an identification parade. The object of such a parade is to test the ability of a witness to pick out from a group the person, if he or she is present, whom the witness has claimed to have seen previously on a specified occasion. Every precaution should be taken to ensure that they are fair and that the witness's attention is not directed specially to the suspect instead of to all persons on the parade. There is a Home Office circular (No. 109/1978) governing the conduct of parades.

If you find yourself in this situation we strongly advise that you contact a solicitor. Under Rule 2 of the circular a suspect has the right to have a solicitor or a friend present. A juvenile should not be put on a parade unless his or her parent, guardian or solicitor is present (Rule 3). You must be given a leaflet explaining the procedure (Rule 1). No one is obliged to take part in a parade but if you refuse the police may allow the witness an opportunity to see the suspect in a group of people. They are supposed to exercise care not to direct the witness's attention to the suspect – but in this situation you have less control and the same strict rules that apply to parades do not apply here. Sometimes they threaten to have a confrontation between suspect and witness for the purposes of identification. They should not do this unless it is impracticable to arrange for an alternative method such as a parade or a group setting, for example where the suspect is of singular appearance.

Sometimes the police suggest that they will be unable to muster enough volunteers – there should be at least eight in a parade, and a pool of volunteers of more than this number from which the suspect and solicitor can choose who to have on the parade. They then suggest allowing the witness to see the suspect in a group setting such as in a railway station or walking by on a street.

A request by a suspect for a parade to be arranged should always be complied with unless it is impracticable, so always insist that they attempt to arrange one. If it really is impracticable to arrange, then a 'walk past' in a group setting is next best, provided of course that there are sufficient people there of similar age, appearance and dress to the suspect.

Never agree to a confrontation. In that situation there is a risk that the witness will claim to be able to identify the alleged offender even if he or she is not sure. The witness is, after all, not being given any choice or comparison and will guess that this is the suspect.

Identification parades are run by senior officers *not* involved in the investigation. They must keep a careful note of everything that happens. The witness or witnesses should be given no information on the suspect, they must not see the suspect or anyone involved in the parade before it is held. They should not talk to one another while waiting to view the parade and must not be shown a photograph or description of the suspect before seeing the parade. The witnesses view the parade individually and once each one has seen the parade they are not allowed to talk to those who have not. Nor must they be told whether a previous witness has made an identification. The witness must be told that the person whom he or she saw may or may not be in the line-up and it should be pointed out that if he or she cannot make a positive identification then they should say so. The witness must identify by touching or clearly pointing out the person.

The suspect can choose where to stand in the line-up and can choose which of those volunteers in the pool he or she wishes to be included in the parade. After each witness has viewed the parade, the suspect may change position in the line-up.

Once the police have completed their inquiries, your child will either be released or detained. If their inquiries are not completed, he can be detained until they are, or released to return at a later date. If he is charged, he can be bailed or held in custody. The police could decide to do nothing else and let your child go home.

If your child is detained without being charged, the police can keep him only for as long as is necessary to enable the custody officer to determine whether or not he has enough evidence to charge. If he does not, your child can be detained in order for the police to secure or preserve evidence relating to the offence for which he is under arrest or to obtain such evidence through questioning. However, the police can normally hold your child only for a maximum of twenty-four hours without being charged unless your child is suspected of a 'serious arrestable offence' and a senior police officer believes that detaining your child is necessary to obtain evidence. In that case, a police superintendent can authorize detention for up to thirty-six hours. Detention beyond thirty-six hours is possible but can be authorized only by a court. Examples of 'serious arrestable offences' are murder, rape, serious indecent assaults and offences which cause serious injury or serious financial loss to any person.

If he is charged, he can be held in custody before he goes to court only if the offence is serious, or if the police do not have the person's name, or believe they will not attend court. The custody officer must try to make arrangements for him to be held in the care of the local authority rather than police custody.

Sometimes the police will release your child to come back to the police station at a later date. They may require you to stand surety for your child. This is a serious commitment as, if he does not turn up, he can be arrested again and you can lose your money. The police can always decide to release your child and then summons him to attend the juvenile court rather than charge him.

If the police decide not to charge because your child has not been in much trouble before, they can refer the matter to the juvenile bureau or youth and community section, a special department of the local police force, who will make inquiries into your child's circumstances, perhaps by speaking to his school and/or social worker and usually by visiting you at home. They will decide then whether to caution your child or have him charged or issue a summons. The caution in this context is a stern telling-off at the police station in your presence. The use of the caution is discretionary and practice varies from area to area. It is mostly used for younger people who admit property offences. The child has to agree to being cautioned and should never agree if he has a good defence, as although the caution is not a criminal conviction, the police can refer to it in court if your child is prosecuted for something else. If he does not agree to be cautioned he can be charged.

If they decide to charge your child the procedure is that an officer not involved in the investigation, a sergeant, reads out to you and your child the essence of the accusation and the law which it breaks, e.g. 'You are charged that on the 4th day of September 1989 you stole a bar of chocolate the property of Woolworths, contrary to section 1 of the Theft Act of 1968.' He will then ask if your child has anything to say. It is usually advisable to say nothing. The reply, whatever it is, will be recorded in writing.

After the charge, and sometimes before, the police will want fingerprints and photographs of your child. They cannot fingerprint a child under ten. In order to take fingerprints the police need your consent in writing if your child is aged ten to fourteen, and both you and your child's consent if he is between fourteen and seventeen. They can dispense with this only if a superintendent authorizes it because there are reasonable grounds to suspect that your child is involved in a criminal offence and that fingerprints will tend to prove or disprove this; or if your child is charged with a recordable offence and he has not already had his prints taken in the investigation of the offence. A recordable offence is one that the Secretary of State authorizes as suitable to be stored on national police records; in practice, this means most offences. If your child is cleared of the offence or the offence is not proceeded with, the fingerprints must be destroyed and you can ask to witness this. Reasonable force can be used to take fingerprints where consent has been dispensed with.

Generally, the police need to obtain consent before photographing a juvenile. Who gives the consent depends on the age of the child, just as it does for fingerprinting. Consent can be dispensed with where the child is arrested at the same time as others and a photograph is necessary to establish who was arrested at what time and at what place; where the child is charged with or reported for a recordable offence and has not yet been released or brought before a court; or where the child is convicted of such an offence and his or her photograph is not already on record. Even if consent can be dispensed with, the police cannot use force to take a photograph. There is the same right as with fingerprints to have them destroyed and to witness this.

Do not forget the fundamental principle of the criminal law, that your child is innocent until proven guilty. It is for the court not the police to determine guilt or innocence.

The Juvenile Court

If your child is charged or summonsed (this means that he has not been arrested but told by post to appear at court), he (and you) will have to appear at the juvenile court. These courts sit locally throughout the country and cases are heard by magistrates who receive some special training to hear cases involving children. The courts sit in private and although the press can publish details of cases (the facts of the offence and the sentences passed), they are not allowed to publish the names and addresses of children involved or any information which could identify them. The procedure is intended to be less formal than other courts and the bench, usually three people of whom at least one must be a woman, often sit behind a table but on the same level as the child. The child and his parent or parents sit before the magistrates and his advocate, if he is represented, to one side. There will usually also be representatives from the local social services, the probation service and the staff who run the court. The court hears not only cases which arise in the area but also cases sent from other courts which involve children who live in the area.

The procedure is less formal than in adult courts but the experience can often be daunting. Often cases are adjourned or remanded at the first hearing and sometimes at subsequent hearings too. You are entitled to request an adjournment if, for example, you have not had time to consult a solicitor, or if you wish to trace witnesses. The police often request remands and the case will not be heard on the first occasion if your child is pleading not guilty.

The court will either remand your child on bail or in care.

There is a fundamental principle that your child should be bailed unless there is reason to believe that he will not attend court voluntarily for the next hearing or that he will commit more crimes if bailed, or that he might persuade witnesses not to give evidence against him if bailed. A juvenile can also be refused bail if the court thinks it is in his interest, for example if retribution might come from the victim or his family. If there is no reason to suppose any of these things then the court should grant bail without conditions (unconditional bail). If the court believes there should be conditions attached to his bail to ensure his attendance or to prevent the commission of other offences in the meantime, it may impose conditions, for example that you stand as a surety in a sum of money. If your child does not then appear, you may then lose your money. Similarly, a condition can be imposed prohibiting your child from frequenting a certain area where the offence was supposed to have happened.

If the court believes that the situation is so serious that your child will not attend voluntarily and it believes that he is effectively out of control, it can remand him into the care of the local authority so that he will live at a community home until the next court appearance. When the Children Act 1989 comes into force a remand into local authority care will be renamed a remand to accommodation provided by a local authority – the effect will be largely the same. If the local authority felt that he was so out of control as to be uncontainable in a normal community home they could apply for a secure accommodation order whereby your child is held in a special community home where precautions are taken to prevent children leaving, that is, he is locked up.

Children can be detained in such a place only if they have absconded before and if it is likely that their welfare would be at risk if they ran off. Only a local authority can apply for a secure accommodation order and the court cannot make such an order unless there is a vacancy. Such establishments are expensive to run and places are limited. If the court feels that there is no vacancy, or the local authority have not had time to consider the matter and prepare a written report they can, if the offence is one of violence or where an adult might receive a (maximum) fourteen-year sentence (in practice most theft offences) and if your child is a boy of fourteen to sixteen, they can make an 'unruliness certificate' which means your child goes to an ordinary prison or remand home such as an adult would. If bail is refused by the juvenile court and if he cannot be contained in a normal community home, then a bail application can be made to the crown court where it will be heard by a judge.

Not Guilty Plea

If your child pleads not guilty, the court will set a date for the hearing of the trial. The procedure in court is that the charge is read out to your child who then states his plea, guilty or not. Once he has pleaded not guilty, the police officer or lawyer who is presenting the case for the prosecution will call his witnesses, usually the arresting officer or officers and any other witnesses whose evidence assists the prosecution's version of events. If, at the end of the prosecution case, they have not made out their case at first sight, then a submission of no case can be made. The defence has an opportunity to cross-examine each witness on the evidence he has given. The court should do it on behalf of an unrepresented juvenile who cannot do it himself. Once the prosecutor has called all his evidence, it is the turn of the defence. Usually the first witness to give evidence will be your child, though it is possible for a defendant not to give evidence at all and this is sometimes done where the client's evidence is unlikely to assist the defence because, for example, the child will not make a good witness or, frankly, his defence is weak, or the prosecution case is weak and it is therefore unnecessary. The court considers the case after all the evidence has been heard and makes its decision – if the child is convicted, this is known as a 'finding of guilt'.

To obtain a conviction, the prosecution must show that the offence has been committed and that the defendant intended to do it and knew that it was wrong. As mentioned earlier, a child under ten cannot be convicted. Between the ages of ten and fourteen a child can be convicted but the prosecution must show that he was aware that what was done was wrong. It is not necessary for the prosecution to do this with over-fourteens.

Special rules apply to children who give evidence in court either in their own case, or as a witness in someone else's. First, the court must decide whether the child is old enough to give evidence, the point being that if a child cannot understand the duty to speak the truth, then he cannot give evidence. Second, the court must decide whether or not the child will give sworn evidence on oath, that is by swearing on the Bible to speak the truth. In practice the magistrates or their clerk will ask the child questions such as whether he believes in God, and whether he understands the difference between right and wrong. Even if the court decides that the child should not take the oath, the child may still give unsworn evidence if the court is satisfied that the child is of sufficient intelligence to justify the reception of the evidence and understands the duty to speak the truth.

However, unsworn evidence is treated with caution by the court which *must* have corroboration of it from another source before it can find a child guilty. It is not enough for this corroboration to come from another child giving unsworn evidence. Even when a child gives sworn evidence, the court must be cautious about convicting if it is uncorroborated. Indeed the Police and Criminal Evidence Act stresses the importance of obtaining corroboration wherever possible because, it says, juveniles are particularly prone to providing information which is unreliable, misleading or self-incriminating.

The order in which people speak in court and the information which they may give is governed by the rules of evidence which apply to all courts. They are supposed to ensure that all prosecutions are conducted fairly and uniformly and that allegations or defences raised are thoroughly investigated. The basic premise is that the defendant is innocent until proved guilty and the prosecution is under a duty to prove their case beyond a reasonable doubt. A probability of guilt, for example, would not be enough. If your child is aged between ten and fourteen then the prosecution are under a further duty to prove that he knew that what he was doing was wrong. This does not apply to children over fourteen.

If your child has been in trouble before, details of his previous record cannot normally be referred to in the proceedings. This is because there would then be a danger that he might be convicted because of his past rather than because of the current case against him. However, your child's record, if he has one, can be mentioned by the prosecution if he claims not to have one or if he claims that any of the prosecution witnesses are telling lies.

When your child, or any of the other witnesses in the case, gives evidence, the evidence given must be first hand. A witness cannot quote what someone else has said and put it forward as the truth. Usually the person who said the thing must give evidence of it. If there is another child charged with yours, and if he gives evidence against your child, then the court must be cautious about convicting on this evidence if it is uncorroborated.

There are other circumstances in which the court must be careful about accepting evidence. Sometimes a witness has a purpose of his own in giving false evidence, for example to deflect blame from himself. If your child says that it is a case of mistaken identity, and if the identification evidence against him is not strong, then he should be found not guilty unless there is supporting evidence of some sort.

Guilty Plea

If the child pleads guilty in the first place, or 'admits' the charge, then the procedure is the same as if he had been found guilty after a trial.

Your child and you must be given an opportunity to make a statement. The court considers the child's home situation, school record and medical history, if necessary, to enable the child's best interests to be considered. If the information is not available, then the court should adjourn for further inquiries to be made. Often the court will request reports from a social worker or probation officer, and these reports will usually be discussed with you and your child by the writer of them.

Before announcing its decision, the court will often explain to you and your child the sentence it has in mind and allow you to say what you think should happen.

Sentences and Orders of the Court

If your child pleads guilty or is found guilty, the next step is sentencing. The court must have before it, and take into consideration, information as to the behaviour, home circumstances, school record and medical history of the child. If necessary it must adjourn for the information to be obtained; and it is the duty of the local authority to make inquiries and provide this information. This entails a social worker writing a report and visiting you to gain information. You do not have to co-operate with this person but it is advisable to do so. Normally this information is shown to the child, his parents and their lawyer, but there is no rule requiring this to happen. Sometimes people disagree with information contained in these reports and it is important that you or your lawyer points this out to the court. The prosecution will tell the court about any previous findings of guilt and cautions and brief details of your child's background. Again, make sure that it is accurate and say so if it is not.

Both you and your child must be allowed to make a statement to the court if you wish to do so. If you have a lawyer there, he or she will make a speech and suggest the way in which the court ought to deal with the matter from your point of view.

Before they sentence your child, the court must inform you what is proposed and allow you to express a view on that. This is a further opportunity to persuade the court to make the best available order from your point of view.

Once the court has formally sentenced your child, the magistrates must explain to him or her the effect of the order.

There are several different sentences which the court can pass. Some sentences do not even count as convictions and therefore should not be recorded on national police records. For example, the most lenient sentence available is the *absolute discharge* but the imposition of this is very unusual. As the name implies, absolutely nothing at all happens to the offender. Slightly more serious is the *conditional discharge* which can last up to three years. If during this period your child does not re-offend, then nothing happens. If he does, then he will be sentenced for the new matter and the original one.

You as a parent could be *bound over in a sum of money to take proper care of and exercise proper control over your child*. This order cannot last longer than three years and the sum cannot exceed £1000. You do not have to hand over the sum unless your child re-offends and the court orders that you should lose your money. The court can use this penalty only if your child is over fourteen.

Penalties involving the payment of money are common. These can be *fines*, or *compensation orders*, which means that the money goes to the victim of the crime to compensate for injury, loss or damage to property; or *cost orders* in which case the money goes to the court. These orders are paid by parents unless the parents cannot be found or it would be unreasonable to make them pay. Often the courts wish to see the children themselves paying the penalties if they have the means to do so and they specify this in their order. It is very common for financial penalties to be ordered to be paid in instalments and the means of the child and parent(s) have to be considered when setting the level of the penalty and the size and frequency of the instalments.

Children must not be fined more than an adult could be for the same offence and the maximum for a ten- to thirteen-year-old is £100, and for a fourteen- to sixteen-year-old, £400. Compensation can be ordered up to £1000. The court can order both a fine and compensation to be paid.

Costs can also be ordered to be paid in addition both to a fine and compensation. This is often used as an additional penalty by the court if it feels that a person should have pleaded guilty rather than unsuccessfully contesting a charge. Parents can be ordered to pay whatever sum the court sees fit – there is no limit, but children cannot be ordered to pay more in costs than any fine which may have been imposed.

The court can order a *money payment supervision order*. This means that a social worker or probation officer is given the duty of assisting the offender to budget to pay the penalty imposed.

What if you do not agree with the penalty? You can appeal (see later) and they must give you the opportunity of being heard before imposing a sentence of this sort.

If the sum is not paid, the court can bring you back and order your child to be detained either immediately or postponed on condition that the sum is paid. The court can also make your child go to an attendance centre (see p. 218). It can order you to pay if it originally ordered your child to, or it can, with your consent, ask you to guarantee payment by your entering into a recognizance to ensure payment.

It is important to recognize that financial circumstances change, and instalments can be varied later if need be by applying to the court.

DEFERRED SENTENCE

The juvenile court may postpone sentencing for up to six months. The idea behind this is to see how the child behaves during the period of deferment. There is a hearing after the period where reports are read out about the child's conduct during the period. If your child has stayed out of trouble, then often the sentence imposed is a conditional discharge or fine.

SUPERVISION ORDER

These can last for up to three years and your child will generally be supervised by a social worker unless there is already a probation officer working with someone in the family, in which case he or she may supervise. This is really the juvenile equivalent of a probation order. The supervisor's task is to 'advise, assist and befriend' the child. This usually means visits to your home and to the school to discuss your child's progress, behaviour, and so on. It is a requirement of supervision orders that the supervisor is kept informed of any change of address or of employment if your child works. Your child must also keep in touch with the supervisor and receive visits at home.

The court can include the requirement that your child submits to medical treatment if it is satisfied by a psychiatrist that your child needs treatment but not such as to warrant the making of a hospital order (see p. 217). If your child is fourteen or over, he must consent to this.

In recent years supervision orders have been extended in the hope that courts will use them more often as an alternative to care or custody for children. *Intermediate treatment* (IT) has been introduced as a halfway house between the child remaining at home and being removed. This came about when it became clear that 80 per cent of young offenders who go into custody re-offend within two years. The idea behind IT is to help the child come to terms with the community within which he or she lives and to confront their crime. It is hoped that this will lead to an improvement in the number of youngsters who are successfully rehabilitated. The facilities are set up by the local authority with DSS funding and they include a wide range of 'recreational, educational and socially valuable activities'.

The court can delegate to the supervisor the decisions on the extent of participation in IT or it can stipulate the form and manner of IT and insist on it being fulfilled, with punishment imposed in default.

Delegated IT

In delegated IT the court may order your child to comply with the supervisor's directions. The giving of directions is at the supervisor's discretion. These can include living in a certain place for specified periods, presenting him or herself at a specified place on specified dates and participating in specified activities. These directions can be for up to ninety days during the supervision period.

Stipulated IT

In stipulated IT the court may directly order all these requirements instead of delegating them to the supervisor. In addition, the magistrates may direct your child to refrain from certain activities, for example visiting a particular place (but again not for longer than ninety days), and abide by a 'night restriction order'.

The court cannot impose these conditions without being satisfied that the supervisor believes that they are feasible and may secure his/her good conduct or prevent re-offending. It also cannot impose these conditions without your child's consent if he is aged fourteen to sixteen, or yours if he is aged between ten and thirteen.

A night restriction order is really a curfew. The child has to stay at home for specified periods of up to ten hours per night between 6 p.m. and 6 a.m. 'Home' can be one of several specified places, for example if the parents are separated, and your child can go out during the curfew only if accompanied by you, or the supervisor or any other person specified in the order. The curfew cannot last longer than thirty days in the first three months of the supervision order. You must be asked to consent to this type of order and there is no requirement on you (or on the supervisor) to supervise the curfew.

DISCHARGE/VARY SUPERVISION ORDER

If a supervision order is breached, the court may substitute a fine or an *attendance centre order* (see p. 218). This is where the basic requirements are breached, for example, not keeping in touch or notifying a change of address, or where stipulated IT requirements are breached.

If the breach is of a direction delegated to the supervisor then the only sanction is an application to the court to discharge or vary the order. This would usually be made by the supervisor, though it can be made by the supervised person if, for example, the supervision order has outlived its useful purpose. The court can insert any provision which it could have done originally or substitute a care order instead (see p. 219).

CHANGES TO SUPERVISION ORDERS MADE BY THE CHILDREN ACT 1989

When this Act is fully implemented, it will make three basic changes.

1. Supervision orders under the Act may impose requirements on those with parental responsibility for the child and other people with whom the child is living.
2. A residence requirement can be imposed stipulating that the child will live in accommodation provided by the local authority for up to six months.
3. A residence requirement can also stipulate that the child should not live with a named person during that period.

Residence requirements are intended for delinquent children who commit serious offences apparently as a result of their home circumstances. A court will not be able to make one unless it considers that the child has committed a serious offence which would have resulted in a prison sentence if the offender had been over twenty-one. There must have been in force at the time of the offence an earlier supervision order which imposed requirements. There must usually have been a social inquiry report before the court, covering the child's home circumstances. Before the court can impose a residence requirement, the child must be given the chance to be represented by a lawyer.

HOSPITAL/GUARDIANSHIP ORDERS

In the case of youngsters suffering from mental illness, the court may make a hospital or guardianship order providing that it has reports from two doctors. This means that the child can be detained in hospital for up to one year and may be released earlier at the hospital's discretion. Where the situation is more serious, the court can ask the crown court to make the order accompanied by a restriction order, which means that the hospital may not release the child without the Secretary of State's consent.

ATTENDANCE CENTRE ORDERS

Of the types of sentence designed to meet more usual situations, attendance centre orders and community service involve loss of free time for the offender but do not involve locking him or her up. Attendance centres are usually run by the police and the activities are usually of a sporting or PE type. They must be fairly near the child's home, otherwise a court cannot impose the order. The rule is ten miles or a forty-five minute journey for under-fourteens, or fifteen miles or an hour and a half's journey for over-fourteens.

These can be given where a child has breached a supervision order or not paid a fine, as well as being imposed for fresh offences. The number of hours to be spent there are generally between twelve and twenty-four, though the court can impose less or more in special situations. The time spent must not clash with school or work and is not more than three hours per day. They are often on a Saturday and are often timed to prevent the child going to a football match if the offence was connected with hooliganism. If the child does not go or breaks the rules when there, the court can substitute another sentence. The court can also discharge or change an order already made.

FOOTBALL EXCLUSION ORDERS

A juvenile can be banned from football matches if he is convicted of an offence connected with football, that is one which is committed on the way to or from a football match, or at or near the ground. The offence must involve violence or the threat of it towards a person or property; or disorderly conduct or incitement to racial hatred under the Public Order Act 1986; or a breach of the law prohibiting alcohol being consumed or taken to football matches. This penalty cannot be imposed on its own: some other sentence such as a fine or a probation order must be passed at the same time. The court must be satisfied that the ban will help to prevent violence or disorder at football matches. It should not therefore ban somebody if the offence was out of character or is unlikely to be repeated or the offender is unlikely to go to another football match. The minimum ban is three months and there is no maximum – the court decides and sets the length of the ban. The court can order that the juvenile be photographed. If you breach an exclusion order, you can be arrested and fined or sentenced to custody.

COMMUNITY SERVICE ORDER

Community service for juveniles applies to children of sixteen only and consists of socially useful work. The hours which the court may order the child to serve are between forty and 120; twenty-one of these hours must involve manual labour. Again this must not clash with work or school. A child can be ordered to serve community service only if a report has been prepared by a social worker or probation officer recommending him/her as suitable. The order remains in effect until the hours are served but they must be finished within one year. If the child does not attend, the court can give another sentence including a fine.

CARE ORDER

It is possible for a child to be taken into care as a result of committing a criminal act. Children can also go into care because their parents place them in it voluntarily. They can also be put into care by the court because they are neglected or harmed by their parents. The latter two types of care are dealt with in Chapter 9.

The offence has to be one which carries imprisonment for an adult and this applies to over-fourteens only. A child under fourteen can be put into this kind of care only if he/she commits murder or manslaughter. What 'care' means is that more or less all the powers a parent has in law are transferred to the local authority which decides where the child lives. This can be at home, or it can be in a community home, or with foster parents. The court can authorize the child to be locked up in 'secure accommodation' (see above) if it feels it is appropriate. Before making this type of order the court must be sure that the child is in need of care and control which she/he is unlikely to get unless a care order is made. The orders generally last until the child is eighteen unless they are discharged earlier, or unless it is made when the child is sixteen or over in which case it will last until nineteen. A parent can apply for a discharge on his/her child's behalf, and the court has power to substitute a supervision order (see above) if it thinks this would be better. The court cannot make a care order if the child is not represented by a lawyer.

Charge and Control in Care Order
As mentioned above, it is usually the council which decides whether a child lives away from home. However, if a child in care commits another offence for which an adult could be sent to prison, then the court can impose a charge and control

condition, meaning that the discretion of the council as to where the child lives is restricted. This can be for up to six months. However, the council, not the court, still decide where the child lives and it does not prevent weekend home leave if the council permit it. The court can, though, specify particular people to whom the child can go despite the order, for example parents, relatives or friends. The court cannot make such an order unless the child has a lawyer.

CHANGES TO CARE ORDERS MADE BY THE CHILDREN ACT 1989

By the time the Act is fully implemented it will no longer be possible for the court to impose a care order as a criminal penalty. The fact that a child has committed an offence may however be used as evidence by a local authority that a child is suffering significant harm and needs to be in their care. The Act affects the whole of the law on care and is dealt with in detail in Chapter 9.

Existing criminal care orders will end six months after the Act comes into force. This period is intended to give local authorities the opportunity to apply for a new care order or supervision order if that is appropriate. They can also apply for an order that the child should live in local authority accommodation for up to six months. This could be used to take a child away from a home placement and into a children's home or foster home.

MOTORING OFFENCES

Juveniles can be convicted of road traffic offences. A person can hold a licence to drive a moped at the age of sixteen, but cannot hold a licence to drive most other vehicles until reaching the age of seventeen. Most driving offences can be brought against juveniles as well as adults, but because of the age qualification, there is an offence of driving while disqualified by reason of age. If you cannot drive because you are under age you cannot be insured either. This means an additional charge of driving without insurance. All the driving offences which adults can be charged with are also applicable to those under seventeen, for example speeding, drunken driving or taking away a vehicle without the owner's permission. The juvenile court can pass any of the sentences available to it depending on the seriousness of the offence and the circumstances.

Often a fine is imposed, but in extreme cases more serious penalties including custodial sentences will be passed. Motoring offences are typically committed by teenaged boys who become fanatically interested in vehicles. Where this leads them into committing many offences, the court may well make a supervision order with IT. Some areas have motor projects where boys can tinker with old cars, learning about how they work and perhaps driving them. This is not illegal provided it is on private land. It is a way of satisfying their curiosity without getting them into further trouble.

Depending on the offence committed, the court is usually obliged to award penalty points which go on to the offender's licence and may also disqualify him from driving. For drunken driving a disqualification is mandatory. This may seem odd, given that a juvenile cannot hold a licence for the very reason that he is a juvenile. The answer is that the penalty points or disqualification go on record at the Driver and Vehicle Licensing Centre awaiting the day when a licence is applied for.

CUSTODY

Custody is the most serious penalty which the juvenile court can pass. The sentences for young offenders, that is under twenty-ones, are detention in a young offender institution, custody for life, and detention under section 53 of the Children and Young Persons Act (CYPA) 1933.

The defendant must be offered legal representation and there must in most cases have been a social inquiry report on possible alternatives.

If the court decides that it must be custody, the reasons why this is the only appropriate sentence must be stated in court. Young offenders are entitled usually to have one-third of their sentence remitted for good behaviour. Once released they will be under supervision by probation or social services for a period.

Time spent without bail on remand comes off the sentence too. However, if your child was remanded in care prior to conviction and/or sentence, this period will not count towards the sentence, unless the remand was spent in secure accommodation in which case the time spent does count towards the sentence. If the remand was in care and does not count towards the sentence, the court can be asked to take this into account when sentencing by passing a shorter sentence.

Sentences can be *consecutive*, that is where more than one period is imposed then they follow on after one another, or *concurrent*, where the child serves only the longest of the sentences passed.

Detention in a Young Offender Institution
To qualify for this sentence males have to be aged between fourteen and twenty, and females aged between fifteen and twenty.

The maximum sentence which the crown court can impose is the same as the maximum term of imprisonment which an adult could get for the same offence. The maximum which a juvenile court or a magistrates' court can impose is six months. There are two exceptions to this maximum rule: a boy of fourteen can get no more than four months; and a child of either sex who is aged fifteen or sixteen can get no more than twelve months.

The minimum sentence is usually twenty-one days, but for girls aged fifteen or sixteen it is four months and one day. There is a further exception to the twenty-one-day minimum in that a shorter sentence can be imposed where a child is being sentenced for failure to comply with the supervision to which an offender is subject following release from an earlier sentence.

Detention in a young offender institution is meant to be a last resort when no other sentence is appropriate. The court must state in ordinary language why it is satisfied that the offender qualifies for this sentence. The test it must apply is as follows.

1. The circumstances, including the nature and gravity of the offence, must be such that if the offender was twenty-one or over the court would pass a sentence of imprisonment; and
2. the offender qualifies for a custodial sentence, because:
   - he or she has a history of failure to respond to non-custodial penalties and is unable or unwilling to respond to them; or
   - only a custodial sentence would be adequate to protect the public from serious harm; or
   - the offence is so serious that a non-custodial sentence cannot be justified.

Sentences can be concurrent or consecutive either when imposed at the same time or when an offender already serving a sentence is given a further term. Generally the aggregate term of detention imposed by consecutive sentences can exceed the maximum that could have been imposed for one term. This is subject to two exceptions: a boy of fourteen cannot receive a total of more than four months; and a child of either sex who is aged fifteen or sixteen cannot receive a total of more than twelve months.

The offender will usually serve the sentence in a young offender institution, but if the offender is aged seventeen or over, he or she can be placed by the prison department in an ordinary prison or remand centre. This can happen only in the case of an under-seventeen for a temporary purpose, such as assessment of the young person to decide where they should serve their sentence. Where they do serve it depends not on the length of the sentence but on where they are allocated by the prison department.

Custody for Life

This *has* to be imposed in murder cases unless the offence was committed by someone under eighteen (see below), and can be passed in very serious cases where an adult would receive life imprisonment. Only the crown court can deal with these matters. Although the name of the sentence suggests that it lasts for life, it does not. The sentence is usually approximately eight years but it depends upon the authorities. If released on licence (similar to parole), this licence lasts for the rest of his/her life.

Detention under Section 53 CYPA 1933

This covers the rare situation where a child under fourteen is convicted of manslaughter, or a young person aged fourteen to sixteen is convicted at the crown court of an offence punishable in the case of an adult with imprisonment of fourteen years or more as a maximum. It therefore applies only to juveniles, that is under-seventeens, who are convicted of really serious offences, such as arson, rape, robbery or attempted murder. The sentence is sometimes spent in prison, but equally it can be in a community home. It is up to the Home Secretary, who can also decide to release on licence.

FORFEITURE OF PROPERTY

Any property found on your child when he or she was arrested can be confiscated by the court if the offence is one for which an adult could receive two years or more imprisonment at a crown court (in practice most offences), and if the court is satisfied that the property was used in connection with the offence. The type of item covered includes knives, wire-cutters or other tools used to gain entry to a building. Also, if your child is convicted of possession or dealing in drugs, the drugs themselves and any equipment used for dealing – knives, scales, etcetera. – may be forfeited.

There is provision for the proceeds of crime of persons who are convicted of being drug dealers to be taken away, and there are proposals to extend this to other crimes as well.

COMMITTAL TO CROWN COURT

As mentioned above, the juvenile court cannot sentence a child to custody for a longer period than six months on an individual charge, though it can sentence up to twelve months in total on more than one charge. However, in the case of persistent offenders or for offences which the juvenile magistrates view as serious because of the circumstances, they may commit the child to the crown court for sentence. The crown court has higher powers of sentencing and can pass a sentence the length of which is the same as the maximum term of imprisonment which an adult could receive for the same offence. The committal for sentence is virtually certain to be in custody because the juvenile court is likely to be doing this only if it thinks that the child should be locked up for a substantial period. The time counts towards the sentence.

REMITTAL TO OTHER COURTS

The juvenile court can hear cases which have not arisen in its area but which have been sent to it by the juvenile court in whose area the offence was supposedly committed. Also, it is asked to sentence children who have been found guilty by other courts such as the magistrates' court (see below).

The Adult Court

A juvenile can usually only be dealt with by the magistrates' court if he or she is jointly charged with someone who is over seventeen. If the magistrates hear the case against the adult they will also usually hear the case against the child. If, however the adult pleads guilty or takes his or her case to the crown court for trial, then the juvenile can be sent to the juvenile court for trial even if he or she is also pleading not guilty.

The magistrates have a discretion to hear a juvenile's case in three other situations: where the child is charged with aiding, abetting, allowing or permitting an offence committed by an adult; where it is the adult aiding or abetting the child; or where the offence with which both are charged arose out of the same circumstances or they are connected.

Usually the court must remit the child to be sentenced in the juvenile court if it finds him or her guilty. The magistrates' court can sentence him/her only if the appropriate penalties are an absolute or conditional discharge; a fine; or the binding over of the parent or guardian.

PUBLICITY

If a child is tried in the magistrates' court, then the same restrictions on publicity which apply in the juvenile court can be applied and the child's parent(s) can be compelled to attend.

BAIL

If the case has to be adjourned, then the child can be bailed or remanded in custody (if unruly) or care just as in the juvenile court. If the remand is for a short period then the juvenile can be detained at a police station rather than a prison, but this cannot be for longer than twenty-four hours. A magistrates' court cannot make a secure accommodation order.

The Crown Court and Beyond

FOR TRIAL WITH AN ADULT

A child does not have the right to trial by jury but, if charged with murder or manslaughter, the juvenile court will send him or her to the crown court. It can also do so if he or she is aged fourteen to sixteen and charged with serious offences and the court feels that long sentences may be appropriate. The only other situation in which a child can go for trial is if he or she is jointly charged with an adult and the magistrates' court considers it right to send both for trial, or the adult chooses to go for trial. The proceedings at which the case leaves the lower court, whether the juvenile or magistrates' court, are called committal proceedings. If these take place at the magistrates' court then the restrictions on publicity mentioned above apply.

FOR SENTENCE

As mentioned earlier, the juvenile court can commit the child to the crown court for sentence if the circumstances are serious.

Appeals

If your child pleads guilty, and the sentence is heavy, he or she can appeal to the crown court. He cannot appeal against the conviction if the plea at the juvenile court was guilty. If the plea was not guilty, but the court finds him/her guilty then there can be an appeal against conviction. Both types of appeal must be lodged within twenty-one days. The hearing at the crown court is a re-hearing of the matter and is heard not by a jury but by a judge and two magistrates.

If the child is in custody as a result of the sentence, he or she can apply for bail pending appeal to the magistrates' and/or the crown court.

There are two other types of appeal against orders of the juvenile court and both are heard in the High Court. The first is the right to ask the magistrates to state a case for the High Court to consider on the grounds that the magistrates were wrong in law or acted in excess of their powers. This must be done within six weeks. Secondly, the High Court can review the magistrates' orders if they, for example, failed to do something. This is called judicial review. This must be done within three months.

In addition to these 'formal' appeals, the juvenile court has the power to vary or withdraw any sentence within twenty-eight days. It must be the same magistrates who passed the original sentence. Remember also that if bail is refused at the juvenile court, a second application can be made to a judge at the crown court.

Legal Aid

For more detailed information on this subject, please refer to Chapter 13. Briefly, legal aid is available to a child facing a criminal charge. Application forms have to be completed and your child can have the solicitor of his or her choice provided that that person undertakes legal aid work. Sometimes where there is more than one child involved, and they are jointly charged, the court will say that only one solicitor can represent them all unless there is a conflict between them, for example they are blaming one another. This may mean your child has the solicitor chosen by the other child – it is up to the court. Legal aid means that the state pays the lawyer's bills, not you or your child. Please note, however, that the solicitor is representing your child, not you, and therefore his or her instructions will come from your child. Your child may see the case differently from you, and in a conflict between your views and your child's, the solicitor is generally bound to follow your child's wishes.

Rehabilitation

Parents naturally worry that if their child acquires a criminal record it will stay with them for ever, affecting their career and prospects. In fact, under the Rehabilitation of Offenders Act 1974, most convictions are 'spent' after a certain length of time has elapsed since the date of the conviction. This means that to all intents and purposes the record is wiped clean and they need not be mentioned, for example on a job application. It depends on the sentence which was passed. The more serious offences attract custodial sentences. In the case of a young person under seventeen sentenced to between six and thirty months' custody, the conviction will become spent five years from the date of conviction. If the custody sentence was up to six months in length, then the corresponding period is three and a half years from conviction. If sentenced to detention in a detention centre, then the period is three years.

Where an under-seventeen-year-old is fined, the conviction is spent after two and a half years. It is six months after the imposition of an absolute discharge and, in the case of a conditional discharge, a bind over or a supervision order, the period is one year or the period of the sentence if that is longer. A conviction leading to an attendance centre order is spent one year after the order ends, and a motoring conviction leading to a disqualification is spent on the date the ban ends.

In exceptional cases, where young people have been sentenced to custody lasting longer than thirty months, the conviction is never spent.

Chapter 9

Children in Care

The law on child protection and care has undergone important changes recently. In 1987, the government published proposals in a White Paper which eventually became the Children Act 1989. The bulk of this chapter sets out the present law. The final section, called 'Changes in Child-care Law', sets out the new law.

THE MEANING OF CARE

When a child is 'in care' it means that he or she is being looked after by a local authority, who have the legal responsibility which would normally be the parent's.

Children of all ages from babies to teenagers go into care and stay there for widely differing lengths of time. Some stay temporarily, and others for their whole childhood. There are various routes into care (for details see 'Ways of Coming into Care', pp. 246 ff.)

1. The police or social services department can apply to the juvenile court for a place of safety order in an emergency.
2. The social services department of the local authority can apply to the juvenile court for a care order under one or more of four grounds of the Children and Young Persons Act (CYPA).
3. The education authority can apply to the juvenile court for a care order under one ground of the CYPA.
4. One or both parents can voluntarily ask the local authority to take their child into care.
5. If a child has been 'abandoned' and there is no suitable person to look after him or her, the local authority has a duty to take the child into care.
6. The court in most family proceedings, for example divorce, can make a care order.

7. The court can place a ward of court in local authority care.
8. The juvenile court can make a care order on a child who has committed an offence.
9. A child who appears before a court charged with a criminal offence may be put into care until the next hearing, instead of being given bail.

The Role of the Local Authority

Local authorities have wide-ranging duties towards children in their care, and wide powers over them, for example they can decide how a child should be brought up and where he or she should live. Their powers and duties differ according to the type of care.

By law, the child's welfare must be the local authority's first consideration. They have a duty to take notice of the child's views and feelings but children's wishes are almost always over-ridden: most children placed away from home will want to go back, however awful the home situation may seem to an outsider. Local authorities decide what they think is best for the child, and should do this after a careful and objective balancing of all the factors, the main one being protection of the child from physical and emotional harm. Unfortunately, problems caused by increasingly scarce resources and limited budgets are now a major factor in local authority thinking. For some children, going home would be the best thing for them if their families received sufficient social work support, home helps, nursery places, and so on – but fostering might be cheaper. In an ideal world, financial considerations would not come into decisions about the best care for children, but hard-pressed social workers, parents and children know a different reality.

Local authorities' powers, although wide, are not untrammelled. As well as abiding by rules on the day-to-day care of a child, they must re-examine the care order every six months. This review must consider whether the care order should carry on or be discharged. Unfortunately, there is no nationwide agreed procedure for these reviews. Some local authorities understand that the parents and child should be involved in meetings and discussions about the child's future, but others do not even tell the parents the review is taking place. If your child is in care, tell your social worker you want to be involved as much as possible in the review – even if the review does not result in your child coming home, it does give you a formal chance to air your problems and concerns.

For all practical purposes, the local authority becomes the child's parent. Although there is nothing to stop local authorities consulting the parent about day-to-day decisions, by and large they do not – as far as the law is concerned, they have the right to make choices for the child, and you do not.

EDUCATION

The local authority takes over the parent's duty to ensure that the child receives full-time education, suitable to the child's age, aptitude and any special needs he/she might have (see Chapter 4).

HEALTH

The local authority must see that the child gets medical and dental attention and treatment when necessary. Hospitals and doctors – who need parental consent before treating a child – will get this from the local authority and not from you. Consent is often implied – taking a child to the doctor implies you agree to treatment. Children in care must live in hygienic conditions.

Foster parents must agree to regular medical examinations of their foster children and are required to agree to call in a doctor when a child in their care is ill or when the local authority asks them to have the child seen by a doctor.

DISCIPLINE

Staff at residential homes and foster parents can exercise reasonable discipline including corporal punishment (hitting the child). Each local authority can make rules about the extent to which corporal punishment is allowed in foster homes or community homes (children's homes run by the authority). Other punishments – for example, withdrawal of treats or television – can be laid down as well. Staff at children's homes must keep a record of all punishments meted out.

The local authority can make their own rules to limit how foster parents discipline children living with them – if they do not do so, then foster parents have the same powers as parents. These powers are wide: parents are allowed to punish their own children physically as long as this is 'reasonable chastisement'. What 'reasonable' means in this context is hard to define exactly: the line between chastisement and abuse is thin, and depends on the type and extent of the chastisement, whether it caused injury and whether it can be seen as justified. If prosecuted for hitting a child, a parent must be acquitted if the court decides that it was 'reasonable chastisement' and not, therefore, an assault. Similarly, the line between other kinds of punishments and unlawful treatment is variable and complex: depriving a child of food could be a form of torture and a breach of the European Convention on Human Rights, while withdrawing privileges – like sweets – is not against the law.

Some children in care are placed in voluntary homes run by charities and not by the local authority. In such homes, corporal punishment cannot be inflicted on a boy over sixteen or a girl over ten. A child of either sex under ten can be smacked on the hand. A boy aged between ten and sixteen can be caned on the buttocks over his clothing but not for more than six strokes.

Locking Up a Child

Locking up a child in secure accommodation as it is called will only usually be applicable to a small minority of children in care.

Apart from any other considerations, this is an extremely costly business from the local authority's point of view for it generally costs more to keep a child in secure accommodation than to send him to Eton.

It should be done only if absolutely necessary. Homes are not supposed to be like prisons, with children being confined or herded into limited areas.

If the local authority feel that a child must be confined they can do this lawfully only in the following circumstances:

● the child must have a history of absconding – that is, running away – and be likely to abscond from any other sort of accommodation than a lock up;
● it must be likely that the child would be at risk physically, mentally or morally if he or she were to abscond;
● it must be likely that the child would injure him or herself or other people if not locked up.

If these conditions are met then the child may be locked up for up to seventy-two hours continuously, or up to seventy-two hours spread over a period of twenty-eight days. If the seventy-two hour period ends on a weekend, or a bank holiday, then it extends to midday on the next working day.

Local authorities can do this without going to court or even telling the parents, but if they want to hold the child in secure accommodation for longer than seventy-two hours they must apply to the juvenile court for an order allowing them to do so. To get the order they must prove the conditions above.

Parents can go to court and be represented by a lawyer. The child should usually be represented as well, and indeed the court generally cannot make an order unless he or she is.

The court can authorize the child's detention for up to three months. After that, the local authority can apply for further orders of up to six months, proving the grounds again for each new application.

There is a right of appeal from the juvenile court for the child and the local authority to the crown court.

Even though they have an order, the local authority is not supposed to keep a child locked up if the need to do so ceases. They are therefore under a duty to monitor the situation to see whether the grounds have ceased to apply.

If a child is locked up, the local authority must appoint a panel of at least three people to review the case every three months at a minimum. At the review, the views of the local authority, the child and his or her parents are considered. They must decide whether the grounds still exist and whether the child should remain in the accommodation.

The children who are most vulnerable to being locked up are the disturbed: sometimes tranquillizers and other drugs are used as a further method of control. Drugs ought to be administered only on clinical or therapeutic grounds where the child could injure him or herself or other people.

If you believe your child is being sedated or drugged unnecessarily then take it up urgently with the local authority, if necessary with the help of a solicitor, councillor, MP or a pressure group.

Transfer of Rights and Duties of Parents

When a child is in 'compulsory' care, that is, after a court has made a care order or the local authority has passed a parental rights resolution (PRR – see pp. 258 ff.), the local authority then have the parents' rights to decide how the child is to be brought up and treated and how often the parents can visit.

Parents cannot control or challenge decisions made by the local authority, unless the circumstances are so extreme that they then have a case to take back to court. For example, if a child is put into care during wardship proceedings, and the local authority make a patently unreasonable decision, the parents could apply to the High Court for help.

Parents who have placed their children into 'voluntary' care – for example for a short period when the family is under stress or a parent is ill – have more rights. They should be able to choose how often they see the child, subject in practice to fitting in with children's home and foster parents' schedules, and can take the child out of care when they please in the first six months. After this time, removing the child becomes more formal (see below).

In place of parental rights, the parent of a child in compulsory care has certain duties. A parent must keep the local authority informed of his or her address. If they do not, they can be prosecuted and fined, although this is virtually unheard of. Parents can be obliged to contribute towards the maintenance of their child in care (see p. 243).

ACCESS

If a child is in care, a parent will be worried and concerned about seeing him or her. Although the local authority alone generally have the power to decide on this, in some circumstances, detailed below, the court can make specific orders, and the parent has rights to apply for them. In all circumstances, the local authority should act reasonably and as a 'good parent' towards the child. There is a DHSS publication, a code of practice called 'Access to Children in Care' which sets out the ideal way in which local authorities should organize contact between families in this situation.

The code is for guidance only, and does not have the same force as law – a local authority have discretion on access which over-rides the guidance. Their discretion would be upheld by a court if they can show they have used it reasonably in the interests of the child. But the code is useful and there is nothing to stop parents using it (for example by quoting its provisions in letters) to back up their arguments for more or better access. You can find the code in good reference libraries, or get your own copy from HMSO.

The code sets out the general principle that access should be promoted and sustained. This is particularly important in the majority of cases, where the aim is to reunite the child with the family. The 'family' includes brothers, sisters, grandparents, non-custodial parents, putative fathers and other relatives, and not just the parents with whom the child lived.

The code says local authorities should consider including members of the wider family in access arrangements, even if the child was not in regular contact with them before going into care, and even encourages social workers to trace 'lost' family members to set up access with them. The over-riding principle here is the basic one in child-care law – is it in the child's interests? There can be innumerable family reasons why a child has not seen a loved relative, and why they should see them, and ideally the local authority, acting as a 'good parent', should put the child in touch with people he or she needs, building bridges if necessary. However, with the present state of social services' resourcing, with children in some areas not even being allocated a social worker, the good practice of the code may be sacrificed. The code sets out an obvious truth – that personal meetings with the family are likely to be the most satisfactory way of maintaining the relationship, but other forms of contact can help to keep family bonds alive. They give examples of this: letters, telephone calls and exchange of photographs.

The code also says that where access ends, contact like this can be good for the child to remind them where they come from and to keep links open for later life.

In practice, many social workers encourage a child in care who is not going home to keep a family album with photos, letters, drawings, perhaps a family tree, and memories of the old life. Although this may seem an unbearably sad substitute for a family, there is a body of evidence to show that children separated from the natural family have a strong need to understand the past, and know some of their history. Where older children are adopted, there is evidence that they can settle down better if they are encouraged to remember their old families, and younger children who may not have their own memories need to know their origins.

Unfortunately, disputes between social workers and parents about access are common when parents want access to be more frequent and more free. Social workers often restrict access – sometimes for practical reasons where parents' wishes must take second place to those of the people looking after the child. Sometimes access is limited and restricted because the social worker who organizes it does not trust the parent to behave properly with the child or to return them promptly or at all after a trip out. In some cases, depending on the circumstances, access will be supervised – in extreme cases where the parent has abused or hurt the child in the past, it definitely would be supervised to start with, and might be refused altogether. In all cases, the social worker should consider what is best for the child, not what is best for the parent or more convenient for the local authority.

Sometimes social workers stop access altogether, for example when they feel access is damaging for the child, or where there is no prospect that the family will be reunited and they want to make alternative plans for the child, for example adoption.

If a local authority decide either to restrict access or to stop it altogether, parents may be able to challenge this. The law is confusing – what your rights are exactly depends on the route by which your child went into compulsory care, and which court made the order.

Depending on the proceedings, parents may be able to apply to court either if they are not getting access at all, or if they are getting some access, but want the arrangements or frequency of it to improve.

The most common route into care is following care proceedings in the juvenile court. Generally, care proceedings are started when the authorities are concerned about the welfare of the child and the parents' ability to look after or control them properly.

However, other courts have power to make care orders when they have been asked to decide family issues, for example divorce, guardianship and custody between parents. Very rarely, an application for custody of a child brought by a parent ends up with the court making a care order instead. They will do this if, after hearing the parents, they think neither of them is fit to look after the child.

Courts that can make care orders are:

- the High Court in family cases – wardship, divorce, custody, guardianship, custodianship and adoption
- the county court in divorce, custody, guardianship, custodianship and adoption cases. They can make such orders in wardship also, once the case has been started in the High Court and delegated to them. 'Divorce' here means all applications under the Matrimonial Causes Act 1973
- the magistrates' court in custody, custodianship, adoption, guardianship. Magistrates' courts cannot handle divorce or wardship
- the juvenile court in civil and criminal proceedings.

A juvenile court making a care order in civil proceedings has no power to order that access be given to the parent, nor to define any arrangements for it. Once the order is made, then the juvenile court leaves what will happen up to the social work professionals. Generally, the local authority will allow the parent access once a care order is made. The aim with most children will be to return them home eventually, and social workers and parents ideally work together for this. Access can be the subject of a 'contract' with the parents, and increase once the original family problems have settled down. However, in cases where social workers do not feel it is likely the child could ever return home, or fear access would be bad for the child, access is kept at a minimum and may be stopped altogether. If a child is to be adopted then access will almost certainly be stopped by the time the child is placed with prospective adoptive parents.

In all cases where the local authority decide to stop access they must tell the parent this by serving a written notice on the parent that access is being terminated. They must do this even if, for whatever reason, the parent did not get access at all during the case.

This notice must also tell the parent of their right to challenge this decision. After getting notice, the parent has six months to make his or her own application to the juvenile court for access. The parent and the child, if the court makes them a party, can get legal aid for this, depending on their means. The court may decide that you and your child have separate solicitors for this, and can appoint a guardian ad litem to represent the child and investigate all the circumstances (see below for details).

If the parent's application for access is successful, then the juvenile court after making the access order *can* then put conditions on it, and specify arrangements for it. Once the order is made, the parent or the local authority can go back to the juvenile court again to get it varied or discharged. All parties can appeal to the High Court if they do not like the result.

Parents cannot use this procedure if the local authority give them some access but they do not like the arrangements made – it is only for cases when local authorities serve formal notice that access is to stop. Parents who want more access or better arrangements for it can only try and agree this with the social worker concerned.

Even if there is an access order, the local authority can suspend it in an emergency when they fear that access would involve a serious risk of harm to the child. An example of this might be their suspicion that the parent would abuse or abduct the child. They should apply to a magistrate for permission to stop it, but in urgent cases would stop the access and apply after. These applications can be ex parte – i.e. the parent is not told of the hearing until afterwards – and the court can suspend access for seven days. If the local authority then decide to stop access permanently, they must still serve the notice on the parent who can make an application to court as outlined above.

Parents can use this right to apply to the courts for access if care orders have been made by the county court in everything except divorce; the juvenile court in all cases; and the magistrates' court in family proceedings. Very importantly, the parents of children in care following a parental rights resolution, where no court need be involved, can use this part of the law to get access.

The High Court and the county court in divorce and judicial separation cases have far wider powers than the juvenile court. When they make care orders, in any proceedings, they can also order access, and can make detailed arrangements for this although they often leave it to the local authority's discretion, which means they and the parents come to an agreement.

If the agreement does not work, or either side becomes unhappy with the order, they can go back to court for a decision. The juvenile court is not involved at all while the higher court is still dealing with the case. After wardship, if a child is no longer a ward but is still in care to the local authority (because a care order was made in wardship) the parent can then use the juvenile court procedure. Divorce cases technically never end – which may not come as a surprise to those involved – and parents can go back to the county court years later unless their parental rights have been legally ended, say by adoption.

In any hearings for access, whenever or wherever they are decided, the courts make their decisions after hearing the evidence of all the parties on the general 'welfare' principle. This means that the interests of the child are the first and paramount consideration – the child therefore comes first, and access is given, extended or refused basically if the court considers this is good for the child. It is not the parents who have a legal right to see the child, but the child who has the right to see the parents.

The hearings are conducted in the same way as care proceedings generally: in private, with all parties being represented by lawyers if they choose, and all parties giving evidence personally, having witnesses on their behalf, and cross-examining witnesses if they wish to do this.

MEDICAL TREATMENT AND ILLNESS

If your child is under sixteen and in care under either a full or an interim care order, then the local authority can consent to any medical treatment where the parent would normally consent, for example for an operation. They do not have to get the parent's consent to this, but if the child is seriously injured or ill then the parent has a right to be informed. It is likely that a local authority with an interim care order would consult the parents more in an emergency than if they had a full care order. Rights of the local authority in this over-ride the convictions or religious beliefs of the parents – for example, Jehovah's Witnesses who are against blood transfusions would have no rights to prevent one taking place.

Local authorities occasionally take urgent wardship proceedings on just this issue, but the advice issued to medical staff in hospitals is basically that if life-saving treatment is required, it should be given despite the parent refusing consent. (For further details see Chapter 12.) With children in voluntary care, the local authority get only those parental rights that are necessary for the day-to-day care of the child – routine medical care will be the parent's decision, but in practice anything more urgent would be the local authority's decision. It is in any event unlikely that a parent – or indeed a court – would criticize an authority if they overstepped the strict legal position about medical consent if treatment benefited the child.

The Right to Apply for Care Order to be Discharged

When a care order is made, it lasts until a child is eighteen if the child was under sixteen – or until nineteen if the child was past the sixteenth birthday when the order was made. However, a parent can apply to the court which made the order to discharge it. The court should grant the application if satisfied that there is good reason to do so, and that the child will receive the necessary care and control from the parent if returned to live with them. Parents can apply as of right – but have a real chance of success only if family circumstances have changed for the better since the order was made.

Parents can apply for discharge every three months – but will not get legal aid unless the legal aid authorities accept they have a good case. Parents have the same right to apply to the juvenile court if the child is in permanent care following a parental rights resolution.

The child and the parents have a right appeal to the crown court after a care order has been made. The appeal is a re-hearing of the case before a judge and two magistrates – there is no jury. Deciding to appeal might involve balancing the likelihood of success – with legal advice on this – against the possible distress for the child and the parent of going through it all again. It is important to get quick legal advice on whether it is worth appealing as the notice of appeal has to be lodged within twenty-one days. Lawyers should advise on appeal immediately after the case – but make sure you ask them. A legal aid order covers this advice on appeal. For the appeal itself, the child and the parents will need to apply anew for legal aid which can be granted either by the juvenile court or the crown court itself.

What Happens After a Care Order is Made?

ADOPTION

Increasingly these days care means adoption, especially if the child is very young and there seems no immediate prospect of the parent or parents or some other family member assuming responsibility for the child's care and upbringing. Often even older children are considered suitable candidates for adoption if no suitable carer exists within their own family. The rationale behind this is that children thrive best in a family rather than in an institution, and that they should have the security of knowing that they are a legal part of the family they grow up with.

In the past, families with serious problems – for example alcohol or drug abuse or mental breakdown – whose children needed a stable home until their own was sorted out, could rely on having a few years' grace while the child was fostered or in a community home, provided they maintained access and family links. Now, however, local authorities are less inclined to keep children in care for indefinite periods and prefer to work quickly towards rehabilitation. If that fails or seems unlikely to succeed, the local authority will want to set up an alternative long-term plan for the child. Put crudely, the child in care is not in storage while chronic problems are slowly solved and further chances are given to the parents.

Local authorities should of course make it plain to parents what their views on the child's long-term future are – and warn them that if access is not taken, or the parent does not seek recommended treatment, that they could stand to lose their child. If a parent 'fails' in this way, courts are less likely to turn down a local authority's application, for example to place the child for adoption. Conversely, an authority which state they intend to reunite the family, and then fail to attempt this can be – and have been – severely criticized by the courts.

Overshadowing this area of children returning home is the question of the 'status quo'. Briefly, courts are reluctant to order too many changes in a child's life. If a child is settled in a long-term foster home and the parents apply for their return, the court will weigh the likely benefits of going home against the likely harm of uprooting them. The longer a child stays settled somewhere else, the less likely it is the court will return them home.

Another argument for the increase in adoption must be that it is cheaper for local authorities not to have financial responsibility for children in care throughout their whole childhood.

There is also a tremendous demand from childless couples who wish to adopt. The enormous problem with this from the parents' point of view is the finality of an adoption order, which almost always means an end to contact between parent and child. It need not do, and 'open adoptions' where contact continues are legally possible but very unusual. (For more details on adoption see Chapter 2.)

FOSTERING

As part of the push towards children in care having an experience of family life rather than institutional life, fostering has also become a popular means of accommodating a childhood in care. Most local authorities divide foster parents into those who provide short-term care on the one hand, and long-term care on the other. (Foster parents are dealt with in detail in Chapter 7.)

If a child is fostered out and the parents have access, then clearly natural parents and foster parents will have contact with one another and have to co-operate on practical matters. No doubt this works very smoothly in many cases, but there are problems commonly mentioned on both sides. Natural parents often resent the fact that day-to-day decisions on their child's upbringing have been taken over by someone whom they see as an 'outsider'. It can be painful to accept that another person is disciplining, praising and receiving affection from your child. It can be galling to have to fit in with other people's plans and lives in order to see your child. Although as far as possible foster homes should be near to the child's own home, this often does not happen in practice and travel becomes inevitable.

From a foster parent's point of view, natural parents can seem hyper-critical and quick to find fault. Their visits may often unsettle children who were settling in and cause them problems. Often foster parents have other children, either fostered or their own, and it can be hard to meet all the demands on their time from natural parents claiming access and sometimes not turning up when they say they will.

From a local authority's point of view, fostering is cheaper than institutional care, even after the allowances for fostering have been paid to the foster parents.

HOME PLACEMENT

A substantial number of children are placed back at home, although in law they are still in care and thus the legal responsibility of the local authority.

Although this means that the natural parent actually has the day-to-day responsibility for decision-making, the local authority can at any time remove the child without necessarily referring back to the court. If your child is living with you under these circumstances, then you can expect to be under scrutiny and receive visits from your social worker. Co-operation with the social worker is vital.

Although, generally, a juvenile court making a care order cannot order the child lives at home, it can if:

- the child was charged with a criminal offence, found guilty, and a care order was made as a result; or
- care proceedings were brought under the offence ground, the offence was proved; and
- the offence was one for which an adult could be imprisoned.

In these circumstances the juvenile court can order that the child lives with a parent or another relative, or that the child does *not* live at home. The court might order a child to live with a parent who it felt would control the child. Alternatively, it might feel the parent was a bad influence on the child and they should be separated.

The court can make these orders for a fixed period of not longer than six months.

Although it is rare for care proceedings to be brought because a child has committed an offence, it is not so rare for children who appeared at the juvenile court *charged* with an offence which is then proved to be 'sentenced' to a care order. If the only thing apparently wrong with a child is a tendency to minor acts of delinquency, then staying at home is a real option. This illustrates the confusion between 'punishment' and 'welfare' which operates in the juvenile court: the CYPA was originally intended to 'decriminalize' offending children and make courts a way of getting them professional help rather than punishment. However, social policies towards offending juveniles have changed; children are first charged, then found guilty, and then the help option is brought into play through care orders being made.

INSTITUTIONAL CARE

Local authorities run and maintain different types of homes for children.

Community Homes
Once called children's homes these are generally in the area where the child lives. The child goes out each day to attend local schools. The homes are staffed by residential social workers with ancillary help.

Community Homes with Education (CHEs)
These are children's homes, with education on the premises. HMI reports have indicated the educational standards are not good. CHEs are becoming less common.

Assessment Centres
These are units where children live for a short period while their needs are being assessed by a team of experts so that a decision can be made about their future care and education.

Family Resource Centres
These can be day centres where families go for access, to engage in activities,

etcetera. They have an educational function for parents who need help with financial budgeting, child-care, etcetera. Occasionally they include residential facilities for entire families who can, with social work assistance, put themselves together after a crisis.

VOLUNTARY HOMES

These are privately-owned homes, run by voluntary groups or charities. Frequently they are specialist homes dealing with children who are disabled or have other special needs. Although independent of the local authority they must comply with standards and regulations laid down by the government and enforced by the local authority.

Such homes must register with the Secretary of State. Regulations cover the numbers of children who can be accommodated; the standard of equipment and accommodation; and how the home should be run. If a home is not registered or it breaks the rules, it can be closed by the local authority who must visit homes within their area.

Often children are placed in voluntary homes outside the area where they live. If this is the case then their social worker should visit.

PRIVATE HOMES

These are run by private individuals not by local authorities or charities.

SECURE ACCOMMODATION

Secure accommodation is often provided in special units attached to community homes or residential schools. It can be a single room or a designated area comprising a group of rooms. They incorporate special features designed to detain or restrict the child from leaving without permission, in other words the child is locked in.

As mentioned earlier, special rules apply obliging local authorities to apply to court if they wish to detain a child in this way. It is vital to get professional advice in this situation. As many solicitors may not be expert in this area of law try to get a recommendation through a CAB. (This is dealt with in detail on pp. 231–2.)

Maintenance

The local authority are under a duty to maintain children in care. However, a contribution can be demanded from the child's parents if their child is under sixteen, or from the child if he or she is over sixteen. This does not apply if the parents are on income support or receiving family credit.

The maximum contribution is equal to the amount the local authority pay their foster parents. No contribution can be demanded where the local authority have placed the child at home while in care.

The local authority must make their request for money in the form of a written notice. If the parent/s do not agree with the demand, or agree and fail to pay, the local authority can take them to the magistrates' courts.

The court is bound by the same upper limit as the local authority and can make what order it considers reasonable.

Where the local authority are demanding money from the child personally, the same rules apply. An order made remains in force for the duration of the child's stay in care.

The same enforcement procedures apply as in other sorts of money orders.

Thus if the payments are not made the court can grant an attachment of earnings order requiring the payer's employer to deduct the maintenance from their wages. The court can order 'distress' which means taking away property to the value of the debt. As a last resort, it can order imprisonment if no other method of enforcement has worked.

Social Workers

Social workers are the people who implement care orders in practice. Every child in care, under supervision orders, at risk, or otherwise in need should have a social worker allocated to them or to their family. In practice, increasingly, there are not enough social workers to go round, they have heavy case loads, and in some areas have to concentrate on emergencies.

All social workers below a certain grade should have a supervising officer, who is either more qualified or experienced than they are. Generally, social service departments are divided into area offices within the area that the council covers.

Those social workers who work with families in the community are often referred to as field workers. Residential social workers work within their institutions such as community homes. Sometimes a social worker allocated to a particular case will be described as a key worker.

Social workers work in teams. The senior members are referred to as team leaders or seniors. Each area has a manager. The overall head of the department is the director of social services who reports to the social services committee of the council made up of the elected councillors.

The Apparatus

CASE CONFERENCES

Major decisions on individual cases are taken by the case conference. These meetings are convened by the social worker, are usually held at his or her offices, and consist of the professionals who are involved in the case.

As well as social services, these can include the GP, hospital staff, health visitors, school health services, schools, day nursery staff, police and sometimes solicitors. It is unusual for the subject of the conference to be invited to the discussion part of the conference, though he or she may be invited to the end of the meeting where the decision is announced.

CHILD ABUSE PROCEDURES

Local authorities have individual procedures for dealing with cases of suspected child abuse.

Child abuse covers physical and emotional neglect, deprivation, ill-treatment and injuries. Non-accidental injuries are what they say – deliberate physical harm. Accidental injuries can be abuse if caused by neglect or negligence. Child abuse includes sexual abuse, a term which covers a wide range of inappropriate sexual behaviour towards children. (For more information, see Chapter 11.)

If the social services or other agency get reports of a child being abused, perhaps from a neighbour, the police or the NSPCC, then they should invoke their child abuse procedures. Hospitals and casualty departments have their own procedures set by the area health authority; GPs have theirs set by the family practitioner committee; and social services departments set their own.

Commonly, a multi-disciplinary conference is called where all the professionals who deal with the child discuss what to do.

The conference may decide to protect the child first by putting his or her name on the At Risk Register or Child Protection Register. Only case conferences can decide to do this. The register is a list of children who have been or might be in danger of abuse from their parents or others they live with. It is divided into categories such as non-accidental injury, neglect or sexual abuse.

The register is an administrative aid for the social services and other agencies, kept by the social services who must allow other agencies – the police and health authorities, for example – access to it. Parents and members of the public are not allowed to inspect it. How much parents may know about an entry relating to their child depends on the social worker – they have no right to know who gave the information or what it was.

Social workers do not have to tell parents their child is on the register at all, but if at a case conference they decide not to tell, they must minute their reasons for not doing so.

If it is decided to tell parents, the information should include:

● the general nature of information held on the register
● who has access to the register
● the purpose for which it is held
● the arrangement for deregistration.

The registers are meant to protect children and to alert social workers to pay particular attention to the child, and make regular checks that all is well in the family. If a family moves from one area to another, information from the register should be transferred to the new social services, either through the previous social worker handing it on, or the new social worker, if there is one, making inquiries of the old. This does not always happen.

Allegations of abuse that can get a child on the register vary in severity and type. It is possible for children to stay at home when they are on the register – part of the function of the register is to alert professionals to the possibility of harm coming to the child, to monitor it and check whether any injury was symptomatic of continuing problems or a 'one-off' incident.

The information may be old, and social workers feel the family is coping better so that the child is not in immediate danger. However, in cases of sexual abuse, the child is more likely than not to have been removed at the first indication of abuse. If the evidence of sexual abuse was extremely tenuous or ambiguous then the child might stay at home.

There is no set format for the registers which vary from area to area. Periodic reviews are held to decide whether a name should remain on the register or be removed. A decision to take a child's name off the register can be made only by a case conference. If parents were originally told about the entry, they must be told of the deregistration. Parents who did not know remain in ignorance.

The record of the child being on the register is kept for two years, or until the child is five, whichever is the longer. If after this period no caring agency has asked the social services to check the register or has expressed concern about the child's welfare, then the actual entry on the register is destroyed: social workers and others can keep their own records about this period in the family's life, but any one making inquiries of the register itself cannot find out the history that way.

If during this two-year minimum period some agency does make an inquiry to the register or expresses concern to the social services abut the child's health and welfare, then a new case conference can be called, and if worries are strong enough the child goes back on the register.

While no one could argue that there should not be provisions like this that can protect children, parents – who may be the victim of exaggeration, malice or confusion – have no legal right to challenge their child going on the register, nor to refute the information on it, and of course they do not even have to be told they are on it. Social services can make decisions about the child on the basis of confidential information they will not share with the parent, without the parent having any right to challenge this and clear his or her name. In this position, consult a solicitor, who can advise on making representations to the social services.

Erroneous information or entries based on this can be deleted from the register with no repercussions or further monitoring.

Ways of Coming into Care

There are many different pieces of legislation under which children can come into care. These various routes into care are outlined at the start of this chapter (p. 228).

1. Place of Safety Orders (PSOs)

Place of safety orders are an immediate, compulsory and ex parte method of taking children from their homes in an emergency. Ex parte here means that no notice need be given to the parents or child – the first many families will know of this is when a social worker or police officer removes the child.

PSOs can last for up to twenty-eight days – if after that period is over social services or the police are still concerned about the home and child, then care proceedings under the Children and Young Persons Act 1969 can be started.

Some children removed under PSOs are returned home when the order expires, or before if the danger or perceived danger to the child ends.

Armed with a PSO the police or social services can remove the child from your home, take him or her to a children's home, a foster home or a hospital. They may refuse access and not even tell you the child's whereabouts.

Many people are amazed to learn that the court can confer these wide powers by granting orders. When the order is executed and the child removed, the parent is often left reeling. Almost always the police or social services' concern is centred on the child and little support or comfort is given to the distraught and bewildered parent to whom this may have come as a bolt from the blue. This can happen out of office hours and parents feel that there is no one to turn to, no one to whom they can complain and nowhere to seek redress.

A PSO should only be a remedy of last resort, and should be granted only if a child has suffered harm or is in real danger, and it is thought that the parent will not co-operate with the authorities, perhaps by agreeing to place the child in voluntary care.

There are three types of PSO, two of which are granted by a magistrate. Magistrates' orders last up to twenty-eight days, and anyone can apply for them. It is usually the police, social services or the NSPCC who do so, but it could be any person with sufficient grounds and concern about a child.

The magistrate must be satisfied that one of the following conditions applies:

- the child is being ill-treated
- the child's proper development is being avoidably prevented or his health is being avoidably impaired or neglected
- it is probable that the above condition will apply because a court has found that another child of the same household has been neglected or ill-treated
- a person in the same household as the child has been convicted of a serious offence against a child or children
- the child is being exposed to moral danger
- the child is beyond control
- the child is not receiving suitable, efficient, full-time education.

These are some of the same conditions as for care proceedings – but unlike care proceedings there is no hearing where the evidence can be challenged, witnesses can be cross-examined or alternative evidence (for example medical evidence in cases of suspected child abuse) can be called. There is no right of appeal, nor any right to apply to the court for the order to be discharged.

In cases where the court might have used its discretion wrongly or otherwise erred in law it is possible to apply to the High Court to have the decision of the court judicially reviewed. In the vast majority of cases this will not apply, although it is possible that magistrates swept up in a dramatic emergency situation may not always remember to observe all the legal niceties.

However, the High Court is likely to interfere with the magistrates' decisions only if they acted unreasonably in making the order. You may feel that they did, but the point is that if evidence was produced to the court it may be the accuracy of the evidence which you are disputing, and that is not within the High Court's remit on an application for judicial review.

The second type of PSO which a magistrate can grant is contained in the CYPA 1933. The grounds here are different: the magistrate has to be satisfied that the child is being assaulted, ill-treated, neglected or harmed. The order can include a warrant giving the police the power to enter and search the child's home using force if necessary.

There is no right to appeal or apply to discharge. Again, the order lasts up to twenty-eight days. Any concerned person can apply, although generally it is social services or the police.

The third type of PSO is not even granted by a court. Under s28(2) CYPA 1969 a police officer has a separate power to detain a child in a place of safety to an absolute limit of eight days if he has reasonable cause to believe that any of the care grounds set out above applies. This power does not include the right to enter and search premises. If police officers come into the house to remove the child, their entry must be by consent. The child and his or her parent or guardian must be told why the child is being detained as soon as possible.

This must be distinguished from an arrest – the detention is not because the child has in any way broken the law, but because the police believe he or she must be protected.

The custody officer at the police station is responsible for all detained persons including children. If a child is brought in, the custody officer must be told and then should investigate the circumstances. He can either release the child or authorize continuing detention. The detention does not have to be for eight days – and it could be just a matter of hours if the parents satisfy the police the child can be safely returned to them from the station. The police must tell the child and the parent if detention is to carry on, and for the right to apply to court for the child's release.

The parent or person with whom the child lived can apply to a magistrate at the juvenile court for an order for the child to be released. The magistrate has a duty under the Act to order the child's release unless he thinks that release would not be in the child's best interests – but in an emergency situation, where the police have stepped in, the parent is not likely to have all the counter-balancing evidence ready for an urgent application of this sort.

In practice, when the custody officer authorizes further detention the social services will be called in to look after the child. Police stations do not have facilities for young children, and are not proper places for them. When the social services are alerted and take over responsibility from the police, they can arrange somewhere for the child to stay, contact the parents and arrange access. Their powers to decide what to do with the child in the long term are the same as in every other case, except that they cannot release the child home before the eight days of the original order are up except with police consent.

Because criticisms have been made of this area of the law it is going to be radically changed with the introduction of a new form of order called an emergency protection order. (See 'Changes in Child-care Law', p. 265.)

Although the taking of a PSO is often not preceded by a case conference, especially in an emergency, it is usually followed by one. Clearly, the local authority have to decide what to do after the order expires. It is vital that the parent's view be known even if he or she is refused permission to be present. This is a crucial time and a parent in this situation is advised to co-operate with social services and to seek legal advice urgently, preferably from a solicitor on the child-care panel. This is a list of solicitors with expertise in child-care which is published by the Law Society. It can be obtained from them, or consulted at CABs, law centres or social services.

2 & 3. Care Proceedings Under the CYPA 1969 (Including the Education Ground)

This is the most common route by which children are taken into compulsory care. It often follows a place of safety order.

These cases are always heard in the juvenile court, usually started by the local authority, occasionally by the police or NSPCC. Only education authorities can take proceedings on the education ground.

The applicant applies to court which issues a notice or summons telling the child and the parents to attend the court hearing. If the parent and child ignore the summons, the court can through a warrant have them arrested by police and brought to court.

Care proceedings do not have to result in a child going into care: there is a range of orders the court can make, but no order at all can be made unless and until the applicants have proved one or more of the following.

1. The child is being ill-treated; or the child's proper development is being avoidably prevented; or his health is being avoidably impaired or neglected.

2. It is probable that (1) will apply because a court has found that another child of the same household has been neglected or ill-treated.
3. A person in the same household as the child has been convicted of a serious offence against a child or children.
4. The child is being exposed to moral danger.
5. The child is beyond control.
6. The child is not receiving suitable, efficient, full-time education.
7. The child has committed an offence other than homicide.

Ground 1 is the most commonly used: it covers most forms of ill-treatment, physical, emotional and psychological. The court does not have to find who caused the harm, only that it occurred and that it could have been prevented.

The moral danger ground can be used where a parent runs a brothel or works as a prostitute. It is unusual, as in cases of emotional or other damage to the child the first ground would normally apply.

The 'beyond control' ground can be used where the parent does not seem able to control the child, or exert an acceptable degree of parental authority.

The final ground is very rarely used. A child who has committed an offence will usually be prosecuted: after being found guilty the court can then make a care order as the 'sentence'.

These grounds all refer either to past or present harm done to the child – there is a further test which relates to the future, which the applicant *must* prove as well. This is called, by lawyers, the 'care and control test'. The applicant must show that the child is in need of care and control which he or she is unlikely to receive unless an order is made.

'Care' here means adequate parenting; 'control' means adequate discipline. For example, if a parent can convince the court that previous neglect of the child was because of a temporary family breakdown or crisis and that in future their parenting will be satisfactory, they would be entitled to have the case dismissed. Some lawyers do feel that through understandable concern for children juvenile courts perhaps err on the cautious side and do not look closely enough at the future prospects for change in the families they see. Some social workers, on the other hand, might feel that a legalistic insistence on 'technicalities' like this allows some children to slip through the welfare net.

The summons or notice is sent to the people with whom the child lives whether parents, guardians or foster parents.

In addition, whether the parents have been married or not, or when the parents have been married and are separated or divorced, the local authority must notify the non-custodial parent; they must notify any guardian of the child; and any foster parent, grandparent or other person with whom the child lived for at least six weeks within the last six months. This rule has the effect of excluding from full participation the unmarried father of a baby of under six weeks. He and anyone else who does not satisfy the rule cannot participate fully in the hearing but only make representations at the end. Legal aid is not available for this.

Parents can instruct a lawyer to represent the child and themselves, and run the case on the child's behalf – they are presumed to have the same interests as the child. But they should not do this if there is any conflict or possible conflict of interest between them. Parents will generally feel that they know what is best for the child, and think they act in the child's interests – but in most care proceedings it is the parents' ability or power to act in the child's best interests that is the crux of the matter. In cases like this the child should be represented separately from the parents, and be independently advised. If there is a conflict of this kind the lawyer should point it out to the court.

Separate lawyers are not automatically appointed, and where there is a clash of interests between the parent and child, however technical the parent might think this clash is, the court should be asked to make a separate representation order which means that the child and the parent will have different solicitors.

As well as having a lawyer of his own, the child can also have a guardian ad litem. Guardians are appointed by the court to act for the child, either in conjunction with the lawyer, or in some cases on their own without lawyers. Generally children have both. In some courts, lawyers are appointed first, and then they ask the court to appoint a guardian, while in other courts the guardian will be appointed first and then will choose the child's lawyer.

The guardian ad litem is to watch the interests of the child, acting independently from the local authority and the parents in this. He or she prepares a report for the court on what should happen to the child if the case is proved.

The guardian is chosen from a panel of senior experienced social workers or probation officers. Their independence is protected by a rule that they cannot be employed by the local authority which is bringing the case. Guardians investigate the facts, interview the parties and main figures in the child's life, and have access to the local authority's files and records about the family.

The guardian and child's solicitor should keep in close touch – neither is subservient to the other, and ideally should work independently but in co-operation. They both have duties towards the child, which differ slightly. When children are old enough to say what they want, the solicitor and the guardian must pay great attention to their wishes. The solicitor's duty is to be the child's advocate, and put to the court what the child wants them to say. For example, even if a solicitor disagrees with an older child's expressed wish to go home, they must follow the normal professional rules and abide by the client's instructions. The guardian must also put the child's point of view to the court, but can differ from it, and their over-riding duty is to put forward what they believe is best for the child. When the child is too young to express a view, the solicitor takes instructions from the guardian.

The guardian's role in the care proceedings is crucial. It is vital that parents understand this: the guardian's independence from all parties gives him or her a particularly influential position and courts set great store by guardians' findings and views. It is extremely important for parents to co-operate fully with the guardian, giving them full and accurate information. Accuracy is particularly important, because what parents tell the guardian will influence their decision and go into the report.

The case is in two parts: 'proof' stage and 'report' stage.

The court is private, with only court staff, the parties, lawyers and the guardian present. The court can excuse the child's attendance if he or she is under five years old. If the child is over that age then they must attend court and be seen, but the court has the power then to hear the case or part of it in the child's absence. This is frequently the way it is done but a child can express a wish to be present.

The proof stage is like a trial in other proceedings; the report stage is like the sentencing after the case has been decided.

The proof stage is heard first. The applicant argues his or her case first, giving evidence to support the ground on which they have chosen to take the proceedings. They can call any witnesses they choose, in practice mainly social workers and medical evidence. The child and the parent through their lawyers, or in person if they are not legally represented, then cross-examine the witnesses.

When the applicant has called all his or her witnesses, the parents and child have their chance to tell their side of it, argue their case and call evidence in support of it. Some cases can be argued just on the law – that is, it might be apparent that the applicant's case is flimsy, or the evidence they call is not sufficient to prove the grounds used – but most cases must be argued on the facts as well.

It may not always be necessary or advisable for a parent or a child to give personal evidence in the witness box, but this is a difficult decision that can be made only in each individual case. Parents have a right to speak for themselves in these cases, and usually do although they do not have to: it is unusual for children to give evidence personally, although they can do.

Parents can, with the court's permission, make a speech either personally or through lawyers at the end of this stage. Foster parents, grandparents and others with whom the child has lived for at least six weeks in the last six months can also address the court at the end of the evidence but they cannot cross-examine witnesses or give and call evidence.

If the case is proved, then and only then does the court go on to read the reports previously prepared. It is during this report stage that the court decides which order to make.

The guardian's report will be seen by the court only if it finds the case is proved. The court will also then see other reports, for example from social workers, the school and perhaps medical and psychiatric reports. These reports will often contain a great deal of detail and some inaccuracies. The child and his or her parents will usually be allowed to read the reports but have no right to do so. They are, though, entitled to hear a summary of the reports, and in particular to be informed of anything in the reports which influences the court in deciding what order to make. (See 'update', p. xii.)

ORDERS

Interim Care Orders (ICOs)
When the case first comes to court it is unlikely that all those involved will be ready for the final hearing. If the court has to adjourn the case, it can make no order. This means that the child continues to live at home or possibly that the child is placed in voluntary care by his or her parents.

The court can make an interim care order for up to twenty-eight days. This means that during the adjournment the child is in local authority care. The court is likely to do this if it feels that the child might come to harm if left at home. There may be a series of ICOs before the final hearing takes place, but on the first hearing the court can make an ICO only if the child attends court or cannot be there because of illness or accident (or is under five years old).

254 A Parents' Guide to the Law

Whatever the child's age the court can excuse his or her attendance on the next occasion unless the next hearing is the final one.

The parents are entitled to contest the ICO on each occasion. During the ICO the local authority decide on what access to their child the parents will have. The court cannot make orders or directions on this. The local authority also have complete discretion as to where the child lives. An ICO can be discharged before it expires by either the child or the parents on the child's behalf applying to the juvenile court or the High Court.

Full Care Orders

This means the full transfer of the parents' rights to the local authority. It is for an indefinite period, and will run until the child becomes an adult unless either the parents or the local authority ask for it to be discharged earlier. (See p. 232 for the implications of such an order and p. 238 for an explanation of the procedure to discharge.)

Supervision Orders (SOs)

These last for up to three years or until the child's eighteenth birthday, whichever is the sooner. Under an SO the child will usually live at home. The child is under the supervision of a social worker or a probation officer if the child is over thirteen or his or her family already has a probation officer. An SO does not entitle the supervising officer to enter the home or remove the child. If the supervising officer is unhappy then he or she can take the matter back to court and have the SO discharged or made into a care order. The child also has the right to apply to the court to have the SO discharged.

The supervisor's duties are to advise, assist and befriend the child. They should visit the child regularly. The child must notify the supervisors of a change in address, and must keep in touch and allow visits.

The order is made on the child, not the parents. However, if a parent fails to co-operate with the SO by, for example, refusing to allow visits or contact with the child, it is likely that the supervising officer would take the matter back to court and a care order be made if appropriate.

Criticisms have been made of supervision orders. Over-stretched social services departments can take months to allocate a social worker to a family, and over-worked social workers may not visit very often. This can mean that the child is effectively unsupervised. There have also been criticisms over the fact that a supervisor who suspects that a child may be at risk does not have the power to enter the home or remove the child under the terms of the supervision order.

Supervision orders will be changed when the Children Act 1989 is implemented (see p. 271).

Recognizance

The court can order that the parent enters into a recognizance or bindover. This means that the parent makes a pledge to the court to take proper care of the child and to exert proper control. The penalty for not doing so is payment of a sum fixed by the court of up to £1000. The parent must consent to the making of such an order. It lasts for up to three years or until the child is eighteen, whichever is the sooner. It is unusual for these orders to be made.

Hospital and Guardianship Orders

These orders can be made only where a child suffers from a mental illness. Under a hospital order the child is treated in the community and parental powers go to the person appointed guardian – usually the local authority. To make either of these orders the court must have evidence from two doctors as to the seriousness of the illness and must be satisfied that this is the most suitable way of dealing with the problem. Orders last for six months but can be renewed after that without a court order. Applications can be made to discharge them. They are rarely made.

Bindover of Child or Compensation Order

These orders can be made where care proceedings have been brought under the offence condition, which is rare. Accordingly it is also rare for these orders to be made. A bindover means that the child promises to the court to be of good behaviour for a period of time on penalty of payment of a fixed sum. A compensation order means that the child pays money to the victim of the crime to compensate him or her.

APPEALS

Legal aid is available for all three avenues of appeal.

Crown Court

The child or the guardian on his or her behalf or the parents can appeal against the court's finding or order. This must be done within twenty-one days and the appeal takes the form of a re-hearing of the case in the crown court before a judge and two magistrates. The unusual orders of a parental recognizance or a binding over of the child can not be appealed by any of the parties.

High Court

Any party or person can appeal to the High Court on the ground that the finding or order of the magistrates was wrong in law. This does not mean that there is a re-hearing of all the evidence.

Judicial Review

It is also open to any party or person to ask the High Court judicially to review the decision of the juvenile court. Again, this does not mean a re-hearing of the evidence. This remedy can be used where, for example, the magistrates have acted outside their powers or unreasonably.

DISCHARGING CARE AND SUPERVISION ORDERS

Care orders are not made for fixed periods of time and the child, the parents or the local authority can apply to the juvenile court to revoke them. The same applies to supervision orders. On discharging a care order, the court may substitute a supervision order if the child is under eighteen. Likewise, the court may discharge a supervision order and substitute a care order.

The hearing in both cases is similar to care proceedings. It is in two parts with written reports being submitted only after the case has been proved (see 'update', p. xii). Separate representation orders can be made and a guardian ad litem is usually appointed. The applicant must show that it is appropriate for the court to make the order sought and that the child will receive the care and control that he or she needs. Legal aid is available to a parent and a child to apply for the order. You can apply to discharge every three months.

4. & 5. Voluntary Reception into Care

The local authority has a duty to receive a child into care if:

- the child has no parents or guardian; or
- the child is lost or has been abandoned; or
- the child's parents or guardians are unable to look after the child by reason of any circumstances, including illness; *and*
- the local authority believe that intervention is necessary to ensure the child's welfare.

Around 40 per cent of children in care are there because their parents have asked the local authority to take them into voluntary care. This might be because of family illness or other problems which mean that the parents are unable to cope with looking after them. Most children in this situation stay in care temporarily and then return home.

The local authority have a duty to keep the child in care as long as this is in the child's interests, but they also have a duty to try to organize for another suitable person to take over the care of the child – a relative, guardian or the other parent if this would be better than institutional care.

A child cannot go into voluntary care if he or she is over seventeen. Once in voluntary care, a child can remain there until the age of eighteen.

Obviously, the local authority have to provide the child with a home. If the stay in care is temporary this is likely to be in a children's home. If the stay is likely to be longer, or if the child is very young, it is more often in a foster home. If a number of brothers and sisters from the same family go into voluntary care, the local authority will usually try to place them together, but this often does not happen and children may find themselves separated into different foster homes.

Parents have a right to be told where their child is living and should be allowed to visit. They can also take back their child at any time, provided that the child has been in care for less than six months.

If the child has been in voluntary care for more than six months then they must give the local authority twenty-eight days' notice of their intention to take the child back. This does not have to be in a formal style or document – a letter will do.

If the twenty-eight days have passed and the local authority have taken no steps to take over the parents' rights, then the parents can reclaim their child. A local authority can return the child within the twenty-eight days if they want, and are likely to do so if they are satisfied that family problems have improved.

If, however, the local authority are worried about returning the child – perhaps because they consider the family still needs sorting out – they can either take a parental rights resolution (see pp. 258–9) or make the child a ward of court (see pp. 260–64).

FOSTER PARENTS

A child in voluntary care for a lengthy period may well be placed with a foster family. It is important to realize that foster parents can in certain circumstances take over some of the parents' rights, and get rights of their own if they have looked after children for some time. If a child has lived with foster parents for more than three years the foster parents can apply to the court for a custodianship order: they do not need anyone's consent to do this. If the child has lived with the foster parents for one year, they can apply for a custodianship order as long as the parents consent to this. A custodianship order gives the child some legal status in the custodian's home, and gives some parental rights to the custodian – neither the local authority nor the parent can summarily remove the child from the foster home. (See Chapter 2.)

It is also sometimes possible for foster parents to make children wards of court and ask the court to order that the children should not be removed from their care.

PARENTAL RIGHTS RESOLUTION (PRR)

A PRR has a drastic effect on the parental rights of the person against whom it is passed: it takes them over.

To most intents and purposes the local authority which passes a PRR becomes the parent in law – except that:

- the local authority cannot give a valid consent to the child being adopted: this must still come from the parents
- the local authority cannot change the child's religion
- it is unclear whether it is the parent or the local authority whose consent is required for a young person in care aged between sixteen and eighteen to marry.

The social services committee of the local authority can make a PRR on a child in voluntary care if one or more of the following situations apply:

- the child's parents are dead and there is no guardian or custodian
- the child has been abandoned, that is the parents' whereabouts have been unknown for at least twelve months from the date that the child was received into care
- the parent suffers from a permanent disability or a mental disorder that makes him or her unfit or incapable of looking after the child
- the parent's habits or mode of life make him or her unfit to have the care of the child
- the parent has consistently and without reasonable cause failed to discharge a parent's obligations
- a PRR is already in force in relation to one parent and the other wants the child back but now lives or is likely to live with the parent from whom the parental rights have been taken
- the child has been in voluntary care for three years.

This is the only form of compulsory care that is not ordered by a court – it is an iniquity. It will be abolished (see 'Changes in Child-care Law' at the end of this chapter).

The mechanism for a PRR to be taken is as follows: a report will be made by the director of social services based on information from the social worker concerned. The report is put to the councillors on the local authority's social services committee.

The local authority must arrange for the parents' views to be put before the committee. Either they can attend the meeting, or they can put their views in writing. A parent can be represented at the committee meeting but legal aid is not available to provide a lawyer. The child does not attend and there is not the same requirement for his or her views to be considered.

Within seventy-two hours of passing a resolution the local authority must notify the parents in writing and tell them of their right to object. Parents who wish to object must do so in writing within twenty-eight days. The local authority can either then let the resolution lapse or start court proceedings, where they ask the juvenile court to ratify their decision. These proceedings must be started within fourteen days of the local authority receiving the parents' objections. If they are not, then the resolution lapses. Once proceedings have started, the PRR remains in force until the court has decided the case.

The juvenile court has to decide whether or not the PRR continues. In order to continue a PRR, the court must be satisfied that all the following conditions are met:

- that grounds for the resolution existed when it was passed
- that grounds still exist at the time of the hearing
- that it is in the child's interests that the resolution should continue.

The burden is on the local authority to prove their case. Legal aid is available to parents who qualify for it.

The parents are full parties to the proceedings. If the court believes that the interests of the child are likely to be different from the parents' interests, then it can appoint a guardian ad litem to represent him or her.

A parent can appeal from the juvenile court's decision to the family division of the High Court, and so can the guardian ad litem, if appointed.

PRRs can be revoked. Either the local authority can revoke it themselves, in council as they made it, if they feel that being in care is no longer in the child's best interests; or the parents can apply to the juvenile court for revocation.

A PRR ceases to have effect if the child marries, is adopted or freed for adoption.

260 A Parents' Guide to the Law

6. Care Orders Made after Family Proceedings

The court has power in matrimonial proceedings to make a care order if it feels that this is in the child's best interests. 'Matrimonial proceedings' includes divorce, judicial separation and nullity. For further descriptions of these see Chapter 10.

7. Wardship

Making a child a ward of court is a very old procedure whereby the High Court takes over custody of the child. The High Court decides who should look after the child and has very wide powers to decide and direct how the child should be brought up.

In previous centuries wardship was often used by the parents of teenage girls to stop them associating with boyfriends disapproved of by the parents. Nowadays it is mainly used in three situations.

1. In most family proceedings relating to children, only parents may apply to the court to have their views heard. This is not the case in wardship. It is therefore useful to grandparents, other relatives and even family friends who, for example, feel that a child is not being properly looked after by the parents.

2. Wardship is frequently used by one parent to prevent the other parent 'snatching' the child and taking him or her out of the country.

3. In recent years local authorities have been warding children and asking the High Court to make a care order. They do this in circumstances where they might not be granted a care order by the juvenile court, for example, because they cannot be sure of proving that the child will not receive the care and control it needs if the court does not make a care order. Often, local authorities ward children as a way of 'appealing' against the refusal of their application for a care order by the juvenile court. This means they get another bite at the cherry – this course is not open to other parties.

The procedure to ward a child is quick and relatively straightforward. However, it is inadvisable to embark on this without first obtaining legal advice and it is best to be represented throughout by a solicitor. Legal aid is available to cover representation, and advice and assistance on applying for it is available under the green form scheme (see Chapter 13). Wardship is undoubtedly expensive for those whose income or savings put them outside the legal aid scheme. This is compounded by the fact that it is very unusual in wardship for a party to be ordered to pay another party's costs. So you will end up bearing your own costs even if you are successful in the case.

Access to wardship proceedings is wide. Any unmarried child under eighteen who has some connection with England and Wales can be warded. The child need not be British but can be, for example, staying here. The court will not allow a child to be warded if the parents claim diplomatic immunity or where the Home Office is considering deporting the parents. Also, the court will not usually act where a child has been refused admission to the country by an immigration officer. Anyone who is connected with the child or concerned about him or her can ward the child. This can be done at the family division of the High Court in London or at one of the district registries throughout the country. The procedure is straightforward, and a fee, currently £60, is payable. Anyone who has an interest in or is concerned about the child can be joined in the proceedings as a party. The child can be a party as well. A child who is a party will have to be represented by a guardian ad litem. This is the same in all civil proceedings and the term used here means something different from the role of a guardian ad litem in care proceedings. A guardian ad litem in wardship proceedings will not necessarily have to interview all parties and prepare a report for the court, though this may be involved. Usually, in the High Court children are represented by the Official Solicitor (OS).

The OS is a public official appointed by the Lord Chancellor's department. He is a lawyer and runs an office staffed by lawyers and others. One of his duties is the representation of children in wardship and certain other types of proceedings.

Occasionally, children want to make themselves wards of court. In such a situation they will need an adult to act as 'next friend', that is, to initiate the proceedings on their behalf and represent them. This cannot be the Official Solicitor. Anyone in this unusual situation should see a solicitor with experience of this area of law.

When warding a child, it is not necessary to file any documents with the court. The form, or originating application, which is completed at the time must include the child's whereabouts, if this is known.

Once the child is warded, what happens next depends on the circumstances and the reason why the proceedings were taken.

EMERGENCIES

Immediately a child is warded the applicant can go to a judge in the High Court for emergency orders and injunctions. Where the child has been snatched or this is threatened, the judge can order the child's return to the applicant or make an injunction to stop the child leaving the country.

In exceptional cases where the applicant must get an instant order, the judge can make orders before the child is warded on an undertaking to ward immediately. Emergencies are no respecters of business hours – a duty judge can be reached on the phone at night, weekends and bank holidays. A duty officer at the High Court will contact the judge for you.

As in all applications, the applicants must have enough evidence to show that fears of abduction or threat are well founded. In such an application, the judge will normally order that wardship continue and give the directions that would otherwise have been given at the first appointment.

Where there is no need for an immediate hearing before a judge, the normal procedure involves the applicant taking out an appointment for directions to be given by the court. This hearing is often called the 'first appointment' and is usually before an official of the court called a registrar.

This appointment is the first scrutiny of the case by the court, and the first time its legal merits are looked at. When the wardship is taken out the papers are processed by administrative staff who do not look into the case. The application for a first appointment *must* be taken out within twenty-one days of the child being made a ward, although this hearing can take place later. If this appointment is not made, the wardship lapses after twenty-one days and the child automatically stops being a ward. Solicitors as a matter of practice take out the first appointment when they ward the child.

At the first appointment the registrar can continue the wardship and give a timetable for the filing of evidence by the parties and for the hearing of the case. The registrar can make agreed orders where all the parties consent to the order. He or she cannot hear disputes, for example about access, which must be heard by a judge.

By the first appointment the court must have been told the whereabouts of the child and should have been given a copy of the child's birth certificate.

Where there has already been a hearing before a judge, he or she will have scrutinized the case and given directions.

AFFIDAVITS

An affidavit is a written statement sworn on oath by the maker of it. If the person making the statement has no religious belief he or she can affirm it by stating that the contents are true, without reference to religion.

The affidavit is an important document because it sets out each party's case and puts their views and wishes to the court. The affidavits are filed with the court, and each party gets copies of everyone else's. This means that before the case is actually heard, all the important issues and problems are known in advance.

Parties can reply to each other's affidavits and should where allegations about their behaviour are made which need answering.

At the hearing, parties can be cross-examined on the contents of their affidavits, which have the same status as evidence given personally in the witness box. These documents must be prepared carefully, thoroughly and accurately. Legal representation in wardship is particularly important because of this and because High Court procedure is complex and filled with technical pitfalls.

ORDERS THE COURT CAN MAKE

When a child is a ward of court, the court itself has custody of the ward. While the High Court keeps the custody, it can use its wide power to make orders for care and control, or whatever other order is needed to protect the child. It can grant care and control to whomever it believes can best care for the child.

The High Court grants custody to someone only where it also orders that the wardship should cease.

Care Orders
The court can make a care order to the local authority. This differs from a care order made by the juvenile court: not all the parental powers will transfer to the local authority, and as long as the child in care remains a ward the court will retain its supervisory interest.

It can also make orders about access to the child, even if it does commit the child into local authority care. This cannot happen in the juvenile court.

Applications can be made to court by any of the parties for decisions on issues affecting the child. The local authority is therefore continuously answerable to the court for decisions they make about the child.

Adoption
Although the High Court in wardship does not make adoption orders, which are separate proceedings made after a child stops being a ward, the court can make an order permitting adoption proceedings to be started.

Money
In the case of a marital child the court can order that either parent make

maintenance payments to the other or to whomever has care and control of the child.

Supervisory Role
While the child remains a ward of court, no major step can be taken without the court's consent. Permission is needed:

- before a change of address
- before a change in the carer of the child
- before the child goes abroad, even for a holiday (this means out of England and Wales, and includes trips to Scotland, Northern Ireland and Eire)
- before the child has medical or psychiatric treatment (this does not include routine medical or dental treatment)
- before the child can marry
- before the child can be adopted
- before a change of the child's name
- before the child is the subject of publicity.

The court exercises control over education, financial matters and all aspects of the child's life. Any of these issues will be decided on the basis of what is in the child's best interests.

Wardship ceases automatically at the age of eighteen and can be terminated earlier at any time.

8. Care Orders Made by the Juvenile Court

The juvenile court can make a care order as a form of sentence at the end of a criminal case against a child. The young person must be aged between fourteen and seventeen, and the offence must carry imprisonment if an adult commits it. The court has to be satisfied that a care order is appropriate because of the seriousness of the offence and that the child is in need of care or control which he or she is otherwise unlikely to receive. The child must be legally represented.

Criminal care orders have the same effect on the parents' rights as the more usual care order made in the juvenile court in care proceedings. Those rights transfer to the local authority.

9. Remand in Care

If a criminal court refuses bail it will normally remand the child into care.

Effectively, the court hands the child over to the social services to keep in control until the next hearing, even if the social services had no involvement with the child until then. The child lives away from home temporarily, until the next court appearance, perhaps in a short-term foster home or community home. For bail and the other methods of treating children refused bail, see Chapter 8.

The local authority to whom a child is remanded in care by a court then have the legal responsibility of caring for the child on a day-to-day basis, and have such of the parental rights as they need for that.

If the child is found guilty the court may then ask the local authority to prepare reports recommending what should happen to the child.

Changes in Child-care Law

The government published a White Paper in January 1987 covering its proposed changes in the law on child-care and family services. These were translated into law in the Children Act 1989. The aim is to make the law on this subject less confusing and complex and to 'offer a fairer deal both to children and parents'. The Act brings sweeping changes to this area.

Among the guiding principles are:

1. The recognition that the prime responsibility for the upbringing of children rests with parents. The state should be ready to help parents to discharge that responsibility, especially where doing so lessens the risk of family break-down.
2. Services to families and help should be arranged in a voluntary partnership with the parents. Where the child is cared for away from home, close contact should be maintained so that relationships continue and children can return home if appropriate.
3. Parents' rights should be transferred to local authorities only by courts after a full hearing, that is, not by local authority resolution.
4. Emergency powers to remove children at serious immediate risk should be changed. Orders should be for short periods and there should be a right of appeal for parent and child.
5. Where a child is in care, the legal responsibilities and powers of both local authority and parents should be clearly defined, and even where children are taken into care, the parents' parental responsibility is removed only in so far as is necessary to safeguard the child's welfare.

The emphasis is clearly on safeguarding parents' rights and defining them precisely. Parents are to be encouraged to work with social services where their child is away from home. Different provisions leading to compulsory care will be rationalized so that parents know where they stand.

The aim seems to be to change some of the glaring affronts to parents' rights contained in current legislation. For example emergency protection orders will replace place of safety orders and will be appealable in court by parent or child. There will be a presumption in favour of making no order unless it is thought better to make one. There will be a presumption that delay in deciding questions is likely to prejudice the child's welfare.

Voluntary Care

The aim seems to be to encourage parents not to place their children in voluntary care by the provision of support in the home such as family aides to help in the home, day nursery places for young children, and residential facilities to enable a child to stay for periods away from home. Parents are to be encouraged to share care with the local authority, and voluntary care placements away from home are to be seen positively as a way of supporting the family, thereby diminishing the risk of long-term family breakdown. Parents will no longer need to give twenty-eight days' notice to take back their child from care where the child has been in care for more than six months. There should be mutual agreement between local authority and parents on placement, schooling and contact and any changes should be settled by agreement. If agreement cannot be reached on terms which the local authority believe to be in the child's best interests, then the local authority can withdraw their services. Where action to delay or prevent a return home is thought essential to protect the child, the local authority will be able to apply for an emergency protection order.

Local authorities will no longer be able to convert voluntary care into compulsory care by their own resolution. There must be court proceedings.

Where a child has been abandoned, the duty of the local authority to provide accommodation and maintenance remains unchanged. The local authority will be under a duty to take into account the views and wishes of the child in care and, in particular, sixteen- and seventeen-year-olds should be capable of making their own agreement with the local authority from which both sides can withdraw. It is not clear from the proposals what would happen to such a child who did withdraw from an agreement with the local authority. Presumably it would be open to the local authority to take care proceedings, or to take out an emergency protection order, if they felt that the child needed protection and was incapable of judging where his or her own best interests lay. The courts will also be under a duty to ascertain the wishes and feelings of the child before reaching a decision.

Where a child in voluntary care is living away from home, it is proposed that the rights of parents and local authority should be clearly defined. The parents will retain all parental powers and responsibilities except in so far as they are delegated to the local authority to enable them to look after the child. The person who is actually looking after the child will have the responsibilities flowing from actual custody. The local authority's powers and responsibilities must be discharged in partnership with the parents.

The government propose to put local authorities under a special responsibility towards children in care, whether voluntarily or compulsorily, who are living away from home in preparing them for leaving care.

The 'welfare principle' will still apply, that is local authorities should act in such a way as to ensure the child's welfare. The local authority will be under an obligation to safeguard and promote the health, development, education and welfare of the child and in particular to afford him or her opportunities for the proper development of character and abilities. Certain things will be unchanged: the local authority are supposed to take into consideration the child's wishes and feelings and to respect his or her religion and culture. The local authority will have to review the child's position periodically and consider whether to discharge the care order. It is proposed that there be an independent complaints procedure to resolve disputes and complaints which children or parents may have against the local authority.

When children leave care the local authority must assist them to adapt to independence by providing advice and assistance, this to be a continuing process throughout the child's stay in care. The local authority will be under a duty to advise and befriend all those who leave care after leaving school, provided that they need and request this. This previously applied up to the age of eighteen; in future it will apply up to twenty-one.

The legislation will be designed to make clearer the muddle between parents' rights and local authority rights where a child is in compulsory care. A care order will give the local authority parental responsibility and the power to prescribe the parents' parental responsibility but only so far as is necessary to safeguard the child's welfare.

Local authorities will be placed under a responsibility for children who are away from home for long periods, either in hospital or in residential schools. For some of these children, contact with their families reduces, and these provisions are designed to ensure that the health authority informs social services so that the welfare of the children does not suffer.

If a child has been resident for three months in a hospital or nursing home, then the institution concerned must inform social services who can assess whether their help is required.

When either a local authority or a local education authority places a child in a residential school or a community home with education, each must inform the other so that the child's possible need for assistance is not overlooked.

Emergency Protection Orders (EPOs)

Perhaps the most far-reaching change proposed is the replacement of place of safety orders with emergency protection orders. This arises out of concerns over the apparent increase in cases of child abuse. It is proposed that local authorities will have a more active duty to investigate *any* case where harm to a child is taking place or is likely to do so. There will be legal provision designed to ensure that statutory agencies, such as local authorities, and voluntary agencies, such as charities, co-operate with one another and share information. The hope is that if this happens fewer cases will slip through the net.

It is proposed that in future only social services departments and the NSPCC will be entitled to bring care proceedings. The police will no longer be able to, nor will local education authorities in cases where children are not receiving education. Local education authorities will instead be able to apply for education supervision orders, or alternatively, if poor school attendance is coupled with other problems which give rise to care proceedings then social services will be expected to initiate proceedings and consult the local education authority. The logic behind this proposal is that if a care order is made it is the local authority or occasionally the NSPCC who will actually be responsible for the child in care.

The new emergency protection orders are designed to deal with situations where there is 'reasonable cause to believe that significant harm to the child is likely unless he can immediately be removed to or detained in a place of protection'. An order can also be granted if there is a suspicion of significant harm coupled with an unreasonable denial of access to the child. The responsibility for the child during the period of the order will be with the applicant. It appears that, as with place of safety orders, any person will be able to apply. The applicant will have the parental responsibility for the child for the duration of the order.

Other features of emergency protection orders will be:

- parents must be notified of the making of an order
- parents will get reasonable contact unless the magistrate specifies otherwise
- the order will last for only eight days.

In exceptional circumstances the local authority can apply to extend an order for a further seven days but the parents and child can challenge this on the ground that there is no risk to the child which would justify such an extension.

It is proposed that during the initial eight-day period there will be a right to apply for discharge by the parent or child. This can be done after seventy-two hours have elapsed. It is expected that the local authority should apply for an interim care order as soon as possible if they believe that care is in the child's best interests.

Local authorities may be concerned because a child has not been seen or there are difficulties for social services or other agencies in gaining access to the child. EPOs can be applied for in these situations and the local authority must not remove the child if, when seen, this proves unnecessary. There will be a provision requiring parents or other carers to disclose the whereabouts of a child. If entry to the home cannot be gained by agreement, a search warrant will be necessary.

As at present, the police will be able to detain a child without seeking a court order and keep him or her in a place of protection. However, this power will be limited to keeping the child for seventy-two hours. The police are to be encouraged to hand the child over to social services who can then apply for any further orders which may be necessary.

Child Assessment Orders

Another new feature of the law is the child assessment order. This provides that where a social worker or an NSPCC officer believes that the child is suffering or likely to suffer significant harm, *and* the parent has refused to produce the child for examination on request, he or she could ask the court to make a child assessment order.

The order would require the parent to take the child to a clinic or a GP's surgery for a medical examination, and, if the child is under five, a developmental assessment. The order can specify the time and place of the examination and who is to do it. The order can last up to seven days and the assessment take place away from home, but *only* if necessary. Prior notice of the application should be given if reasonably practical so parents can challenge it. They may be appealed against – rules will be issued later. Parental responsibility is not changed – they deal only with the assessment.

Care Proceedings

These will be changed substantially. These are the main features of the new legislation:

● new grounds for the making, and the discharge, of care orders
● strengthened supervision orders
● a new type of custody order (a residence order) for cases where responsibility for the child can be assumed by, for example, a relative rather than the local authority
● more rights for parents to ask courts to decide on access
● wider rights of participation in proceedings
● parental rights resolutions (where a local authority acquire parental rights without going to court) to be scrapped

In future there will be three grounds, each of which must be satisfied before a care order can be made:

1. Evidence of significant harm or likely significant harm to the child.
2. This harm or likely harm is attributable to the absence of a reasonable standard of parental care or the child being beyond parental control.
3. The order proposed is the most effective means available to the court of safeguarding the child's welfare.

The aim of these changes is to widen the scope of cases which the courts can deal with. Previously where harm was 'likely' as opposed to actual, local authorities were using wardship rather than care proceedings in which hitherto the grounds were more strictly defined and related to specific situations such as non-attendance at school or the commission of an offence.

All three tests will need to be satisfied before the court may make a care order. 'Likely harm' is intended to cover 'all cases of unacceptable risk in which it may be necessary to balance the chance of the harm occurring against the magnitude of that harm if it does occur'. The court must judge whether there is a risk and what the nature of the risk is.

The third test is designed to direct the court to all the options, including making no order at all. The local authority will be expected to outline their plans for the child. The court will consider the proposed arrangements for contact and the parties' views on these arrangements.

INTERIM CARE ORDERS

In order to make an interim care order the court must be satisfied on the first two grounds *and* must believe that the power to remove or detain the child is necessary in order to safeguard his or her welfare during the interim period. The court will expect the local authority to outline how they will manage the care of the child during the order. An interim care order will be made for a period up to eight weeks in duration with the local authority having the right to apply for extensions of up to four weeks thereafter if necessary. Thus it should not be necessary for a series of interim care orders to be made prior to the full hearing, which is what tends to happen at present. The idea is that fewer will be necessary. The court can make orders as to contact and medical examinations.

DISCHARGING CARE ORDERS

It is proposed that in proceedings to discharge a care order the test will be:

● is the court satisfied that discharging the care order is in the child's best interests? and
● is the court satisfied that if control is needed it will be provided?

   A residence order can be sought which means the discharge of the care order.

SUPERVISION ORDERS

There have been criticisms of supervision orders. One of these is that conditions can be imposed only on the child, not on the parents. This will be changed and the person with whom the child lives must allow the supervisor reasonable contact. Supervision orders will be 'beefed up' with greater powers being given to the supervising social worker to enter the child's home and to demand to see the child, under a search warrant if contact is refused. Interim supervision orders will be possible for up to eight weeks on the first application and up to four weeks subsequently. Full supervision orders will last one year, but the supervisor can apply to extend for a further two years.

NEW POWER TO MAKE RESIDENCE ORDERS

As part of the options which the court will have, it is planned that the court will have the power to make a residence order to a parent or to a step-parent or to any other person, for example, a grandparent. This will apply where the first two grounds for making a care order apply and a residence order is the most effective means of protecting the child's welfare. If it grants an order in this way, the court will also make a supervision order so that the situation can be monitored unless it decides that this is unnecessary. This is intended to ensure that the local authority work with the family and are able to bring the matter back to court if things are not working out.

NEW POWER TO MAKE CONTACT ORDERS

The changes proposed with regard to access mean that the court which makes a care order can at the same time decide on contact and the arrangements for it. There will be a presumption of reasonable contact to the parents written into the new law. If disputes over contact and the arrangements for it arise after the order has been made the court will be able to determine them. If the local authority want to change access arrangements which are specified in an order then the parent or child will have a right to object. The dispute will then go back to court to be resolved unless the local authority back down, in which case the previous arrangements prevail.

WHO WILL BE INVOLVED IN CARE PROCEEDINGS?

The parents or guardian will be parties. Anyone who is seeking legal responsibility for the child will be able to be a party; this could include a non-custodial parent, a step-parent or a person who could apply for custodianship.

APPEALS

It is proposed that all parties to the proceedings should be entitled to appeal. The court which hears the appeal will be able to make a care order or a supervision order pending the appeal if it believes this to be in the child's best interests. This cannot happen under the present law. This would arise where the original court had refused a care order or had ordered that one be discharged. As a further protective measure, the original court will have the power to stay its decision where this could mean that a child leaves care. This could be at the end of discharge proceedings where the court has decided to grant a discharge of the care order. The original court would be able to stay its decision where there was to be an appeal; this would be for a short period only, the aim being to avoid the risk of unnecessary interruptions in the child's life and to maintain protection which would otherwise cease.

PROCEDURE

The new law aims to make care proceedings more like civil proceedings which is what they are, and to get away from the feeling that a criminal trial is taking place.

Hearsay evidence, that is information which has come to the witness second-hand and is not in their direct knowledge, will be allowed.

The use of guardians ad litem will be extended. The court will appoint one in almost all care and related proceedings including emergency protection orders and child assessment orders.

It will no longer be possible for a local authority to pass a parental rights resolution thereby granting itself the equivalent of a care order by an administrative decision without going to court. *All* cases will have to go to court if the local authority want care.

The Family Court

For some time now it has been felt by professionals working with children and families who come into contact with the law that there should be one court to deal with all the various issues in this field. The government has issued a consultative document on the family court but there are no legislative proposals at present. If such a court is introduced it is envisaged that care proceedings and proceedings on all care-related topics would be heard in that court. This would undoubtedly be better than the present system which spreads these proceedings across magistrates' and county courts and the High Court. The family court may not, however, come into being for some time, not least because it will cost a great deal of money to set it up. It is therefore likely that the new care proposals will at first be based around the existing court system.

Care proceedings will start in the magistrates' court, though they can then be transferred to the county court or the High Court if it is thought appropriate. Wardship will be used only for exceptional cases.

Miscellaneous Changes

- Care orders will no longer be available to the juvenile court as a criminal sentence.
- It is intended that the criteria for allowing children in care to be kept in secure accommodation will be tightened. Regulations will be issued on this, but one new departure is that if a child is not in compulsory care, his

or her parent will be able to remove the child from secure accommodation
- Among the new duties placed on local authorities will be the duty to provide money for alternative accommodation for alleged perpetrators of child abuse who agree to leave the home so that the child does not have to.

Chapter 10

Family Breakdown

This chapter deals with the position when couples, whether married to each other or not, separate or divorce.

Whatever the quality of the adult relationship that is ending, and whatever the tone of the separation itself, the least that can be said about any kind of family breakdown is that it is a major disruption in the life of a child. At worst, it can be a nightmarish trauma for the child; at best, when carefully and sensitively handled by the parents and lawyers concerned, it still turns young worlds upside down.

The courts go some way towards recognizing this and are, where children are concerned, considerably more humane and sympathetic than litigants often expect. In addition, the court itself has duties towards the children in divorce or separation which are explained in greater detail below.

While it is possible for parents – married or not – to separate without going to law at all, it is most common with separating families that either at the time of separation or later, the courts will be involved. The degree of involvement of the courts varies from case to case: parents might have all the practical arrangements sorted out amicably between them, but want these to be confirmed by court order for practical or financial purposes. In other cases parents may be in dispute about major matters and need the court to decide between them because they cannot agree what is to be done.

The Children Act 1989 changes, clarifies and codifies the law relating to children, particularly in care and family law. Until it comes into force, the law remains as described here. We have in this chapter also described the bare bones of the Act, putting the new provisions at the end of the relevant sections. Note that despite changing orders in respect of children following divorce, it does not alter the procedure or rules on divorce itself.

As the Act is not in force we can give no practical advice about how it will work, or the procedures and forms that might be needed. It is meant to unify

family law, speed it up and make it simpler. It does make some radical changes –
how these will work in practice is for the future. It repeals and then re-enacts a
good deal of legislation. One of the best things it has done is to put children's law
in one statute rather than disperse it among many.

When the new law comes into force, the first most obvious change will be in
the language used: instead of the *melange* of parental rights/powers/duties/custody
there will be a new, simple term: parental responsibility. Instead of access orders
there will be contact orders; instead of care and control there will be residence
orders. The principles of these are the same.

If a parent already has an 'old' order under present law about the custody of or
access to the child on the day the new Act comes into force, the old orders remain
valid. They are automatically converted from the old type of orders into the new
type of orders – for example, where a parent had an order giving care and control
of a child on the day the Act comes in, from that date they are treated as having a
residence order made in their favour.

There are two exceptions to this: from the day the new Act comes in, two sorts
of order will cease to have effect entirely. These are declarations that a parent
was an unfit parent, under the Matrimonial Causes Act 1973; and the court's
power to remove a person's authority over a child in cases of incest, under the
Sexual Offences Act 1956.

The Courts and Children in Family Breakdown

However the courts come to be involved, where they are asked to decide on
matters which concern children they will act on a principle that recognizes their
vulnerability in any family breakdown: the welfare principle.

Welfare is defined by the *OED* as the state or condition of doing or being well. It
is a definition capable of covering a very wide range of factors: this normal meaning
of the word is reflected by courts which treat the principle as broad and wide-
ranging. The welfare of the child encompasses physical, material, financial, moral,
religious, educational and emotional factors. The child's emotions and affections
are part of this – and their wishes and feelings about their lives are also taken into
account if they are of an age and understanding that make this appropriate.

This does not mean that if, say, an eleven-year-old child chooses one parent
over another that the parent will necessarily win a custody action, but the child's
choice and views become part of the whole picture for the court to inspect.

The welfare principle is a statutory one, presently found in section 1 of the
Guardianship of Minors Act 1971 which says that:

where in any proceedings before any court the custody or upbringing of a minor or the administration of any property belonging to or held on trust for a minor, or the application of the income thereof, is in question, the court, in deciding that question, must regard the welfare of the minor as the first and paramount consideration.

The revised welfare principle will be from section 1 of the Children Act which says that:

when a court determines *any* question with respect to:
(a) the upbringing of a child
(b) the administration of a child's property or income the child's welfare shall be the paramount consideration.

The Children Act goes on to say that where the court has to make certain orders (including where the child is to live, with whom and about access or contact with the other parent) it must have regard to:

- the ascertainable wishes and feelings of the child concerned considered in the light of his age and understanding
- his physical, emotional and educational needs
- the likely effect on him of any change in his circumstances
- his age, sex, background and any characteristics of his which the court considers relevant
- any harm which he has suffered or is at risk of suffering
- how capable each of his parents, and any other person whom the court thinks is relevant, is of meeting his needs
- the range of powers the court has to deal with the proceedings.

Courts should also avoid delay in settling children's cases; and only make orders at all if it is better for the child to have them made than not to have them made.

The welfare principle extends to the child's own money which affects only a minority of children. But note that when parents are in dispute about their money, whether house, property or income, following separation and divorce, the welfare principle is not the over-riding principle.

'First and paramount consideration' means that the welfare of the child is the most important and over-riding consideration of all. In a case where the welfare principle was discussed, the court said the principle meant more than just treating the child's welfare as the top item in a list of relevant items. First consideration meant it was of first importance, and paramount consideration meant the welfare of the child actually determined the course the courts should follow.

In other words, it is not enough for the court to pay lip-service to the idea of the child's welfare. The decisions they make should spring directly from considering what is best for the child.

Although the new welfare principle drops the 'first' it is not likely to reduce the strength of the principle in practical terms.

Issues Involved in Divorce Cases

It is a truism that divorce or separation involves emotional pain – but this basic fact must be kept in mind, all the time, by lawyers and courts. For parents, disputes about children can be particularly traumatic, especially if they do not fully understand the process by which these actions are decided.

First, it is the welfare of the child which ought to be at the front of the judge's mind: the welfare of the parents is not the main concern, although their wishes and emotions are taken account of because of the importance of parents to their children. It is not the depth of the parents' love for the child which is being judged, but the ability of the parent to provide what the judge considers is the best possible future for the child, bearing in mind all the other influences and circumstances of the family.

Second, it is the judge of the action who decides the outcome of the case. This may seem obvious – but many people assume that custody cases are decided, as are other branches of law, by 'precedent' and set rules. One case with identical or very similar facts to another may have a completely opposite result.

There are no set rules which the court must follow. For example, people often believe that mothers invariably get custody of very young children and girls. This is not necessarily the case now, although in the past it was more true. Over recent years there has been an increase in what one might call 'fathers' rights' where individuals and organizations have lobbied for a change in the stereotyped view that only women can properly care for children.

Some courts in some districts have responded to this social change: others perhaps have lingering old-fashioned views. The ideal position is that the court will decide what is best for the child with a free and open mind after examination of all relevant facts. In practice, the way custody disputes are decided varies from place to place and court to court.

The judge has power to decide the case before the court using his or her 'discretion'. The legal fetter on the judge's discretion is that it must be exercised 'reasonably'. If judges act unreasonably, the theory is that a higher court can overturn the decision made on appeal – while many family cases do go to appeal successfully either on the law or facts, the higher courts tend to give great credence to the fact that the original judge tried the case, heard the evidence and saw the witnesses which they do not.

Third, what the parents say either about their own abilities or the demerits of the other partner is only one part of the whole case. A properly prepared custody or access case can involve reports from experts, social workers, doctors, etcetera, and, crucially, a report from the court welfare officer. Courts pay very great attention to professional opinions about the welfare of children, and seek an all-round, objective picture of the home life and environment of the child.

Consequently, if a court welfare officer or social worker is involved, their reports will carry a lot of weight in the hearing. It is wise for parents to co-operate fully with the experts involved, and particularly with the officer appointed by the court to investigate and report to it.

Some experts make recommendations either in their reports or in evidence as to what should happen to the child – courts take recommendations of this kind very seriously. However, increasingly, court welfare officers will not make recommendations but lay out the facts for the judge to consider. Basically, this is because judgment is the court's job, and not theirs.

Another crucial point about disputes concerning children is that the behaviour of the adults to each other does not have the importance they sometimes wish it did. Crudely, it is the child who matters, not the unhappy adults who have landed up in court. A parent may have been violent and dishonest and caused extraordinary hurt to their partner; they are not precluded from 'winning' favourable orders about the children because of this behaviour. Again, there are no set rules which can be stated either here or in court about this matter: but if a court accepts that the parent's violence was not directed at the child, or came from the stress of the marriage and is unlikely to be repeated, and that he or she is best suited to bring up the child, then it can and does disregard the misery such behaviour caused the other parent.

Fourth, the courts that deal with family cases do not operate in the way most people imagine. The public image of a court tends to come from the criminal law – proceedings there are often reported in detail in the press, or on television, or are the subject of dramas, documentaries or series. They are also public, and anyone who chooses may visit and see, on a good day, the licensed savagery of an experienced defence counsel attacking a police officer, or a prosecutor making mincemeat of a defendant.

Courts which deal with children are – or ought to be – different. Although we do not yet have family courts and the present system is far from perfect, the best sort of magistrates', county or High Court dealing with children cases is run on quiet, civilized and courteous lines.

Whatever the result of the case, generally the parent who 'loses' must, for the child's sake, continue to be involved – and it is bad legal practice for such a parent to be terrorized or intimidated by any of the professional parties involved. Solicitors and barristers tend to present family cases in a courteous and low-key way; this is partly the tradition of these courts, and partly because there is no jury to be won over but a judge who is unlikely to be impressed by dramatic pyrotechnics.

This does not mean that the lawyers should be wet or unconvincing, and the best family practitioners are, like the best criminal practitioners, afraid of nothing, but there is more feeling of working together towards a compromise solution than in other courts. In criminal courts there is one bald issue – innocent or guilty? In family cases the issues are delicate, complicated and far-reaching because they concern the happiness and welfare of children whose lives are being changed through no act of their own.

Dealing with Solicitors

The first question here is, do you need one? Generally, the rule must be that unless you know exactly what you are doing and have the confidence to act for yourself in an emotional situation, getting a solicitor's advice at an early stage is strongly recommended. Detachment as well as confidence and knowledge is needed – solicitors who themselves go through divorce or separation generally instruct other solicitors to act for them.

This apart, it is of course perfectly possible for someone to do their own divorce, and there are helpful leaflets and books on how to do this. But generally, if children or property are involved you should get proper professional advice. This need perhaps only be an initial interview for advice and confirmation that you are on the right lines, with perhaps some warning about potential problems. Where you are agreeing a financial settlement with your spouse it is highly advisable to get independent legal advice. You can find solicitors by recommendation from a CAB or law centre; by word of mouth; from a list provided by the Law Society in your area: or pot luck from the phone book.

However you find a solicitor, it is a good idea when you phone for an initial appointment to ask what the firm specializes in, if anything, and for details about the person you will be seeing.

When using solicitors, remember that you are employing them, and they are not doing you any favours. They are paid for what they do, either initially through the Legal Aid Board (and subsequently by you through the board's charge: see 'Legal Aid', p. 238) or privately by you. You are entitled to proper service, which includes information about their skills if you want this.

At the initial appointment, the solicitor will ask you for a history of the marriage or relationship and the present problems, taking notes on this.

Once the solicitor has the outline, then he or she can give general advice. If after this discussion you want to continue either with that solicitor or with the case itself, you will probably be asked to go to a further appointment when more details will be taken. From a solicitor's point of view the ideal client is one who remembers details with clarity or has kept a diary – or at least has some recollection of who they married and when and how old their children are. This is not just a joke – it is truly remarkable how often clients do not know these facts!

Be prepared to answer detailed and personal questions. Solicitors *must* know a great deal about your family life before they can advise properly on your case. To prepare a proper petition for divorce, applications or proceedings for injunctions, conscientious solicitors like to know when, how and why things happened so that they can prepare as full a case as possible. It is not just nosiness. If there is anything you feel is important which the solicitor has not asked, then volunteer this. The most chilling words a lawyer can hear in court are 'But my solicitor never asked me that', after the client has admitted in evidence to some incriminating behaviour.

Remember here that the solicitor who acts for you in taking on your case takes on duties as well – this includes the duty of confidentiality. This means that the solicitor must preserve your privacy and keep your secrets, sharing these only with the counsel he or she instructs on your behalf if this is relevant to your case.

However, the solicitor owes a duty to others as well as to you including the court itself and the Law Society, and is bound by professional ethics as well as the normal rule of law. This means that the solicitor can never deceive or mislead the court or anyone else on your behalf, however much this deception may seem to be in your interests.

If, for example, you admit to the solicitor that your estranged spouse's petition is correct and you have indeed done exactly what is alleged, this admission although given 'in confidence' cannot be covered up: the solicitor cannot pretend you did not say this or put forward lies in your defence. The basic rule here is that while a solicitor's duty to you prevents him or her disclosing damaging information about you without your consent, he or she cannot pretend to anyone that those facts do not exist.

The most obvious example of this is that if you confess a crime to your solicitor, their duty to you will prevent them from telling the police about this unless you instruct them to do so – but their other duties prevent them indicating to the court that you have never broken the law.

However, and in addition, in family finance cases there is a duty to disclose full information if this is relevant to the matter in hand. Where for example there is a dispute about money, both sides must let each other know full financial details, keeping back nothing even if this affects entitlement to maintenance or a property settlement.

While it is the solicitor's duty not to hide relevant facts, it is also in these circumstances the client's duty to disclose them. Although the solicitor can face professional disciplining for deceiving or misleading the court or the other side, clients themselves can face favourable orders being overturned when the full facts come out. For example, if a client fails to let anyone know about a pools win or inheritance while fighting a case against their spouse for financial support, when the other side do find out they can take the case back to court and apply for the order to be changed. The court will change the order if it decides that the undisclosed facts, if known at the time, would have affected the original decision.

Where children are concerned, the best guideline is partly cynical and partly genuinely concerned with their best interests. It is this: make sure the solicitor knows the facts, even when these might show you up in a bad light. This is cynical, because it looks far better for a client to admit something freely than have it reluctantly dragged out of them in cross-examination from the other side. The genuine worth of this guideline is that where children are concerned courts actually should know the whole circumstances of their lives, warts and all, before they can make a decent and humane decision.

One very practical point here: when marriages or relationships break down, there can be an enormous weight of guilt which increases the usual worries of whether or not one is a good enough parent. An experienced and sympathetic solicitor should understand this and be able to reassure the client that the court will not make its decision on the kind of trivial points that parents often lose sleep over.

While family solicitors should be – in the authors' opinion at least – sympathetic, willing to listen and in tune with the feelings of their clients, in order to make a living they have to take on a large number of cases which necessarily limit the time they can spend putting those virtues into practice. And however sympathetic they are, they have to run a business and make money. Do bear in mind that when you are paying privately the eventual charge will take account of every phone call and appointment you have with the solicitor. If you are legally aided the Legal Aid Board's charge will operate on any eventual capital you receive from the case.

Legal Aid

Legal aid is not available for a straightforward undefended divorce, the procedure of which was simplified in 1973 making it feasible for petitioners to act in person.

If a solicitor is consulted and agrees to do the divorce under the green form scheme, then although he or she will deal with all the paperwork and use their office address for service of papers, the client is still, technically, acting in person.

The client must personally sign the petition and statement of arrangements for the children. Legal aid solicitors get a limited fixed sum for preparation of a divorce under a green form which, although it can be extended to cover particular complications which might arise, does not generally cover very detailed advice about 'ordinary' issues.

If there are disputes about children or money with applications being made to court about ancillary matters, then legal aid is available to cover that. If and when a divorce becomes defended the petitioner can then apply for legal aid.

Divorce Proceedings

Divorce is the legal termination of marriage. Following a final decree the parties are no longer married, are free to marry again, and have no legal relationship left with each other except as parents of the same child or children.

Starting divorce proceedings is the key which opens the door to the courts' wide powers over family property and finance, and custody and access to children. Either party may apply to the court for orders in these areas once a divorce petition has been filed, or even before this if he or she undertakes to the court to file one quickly. These applications are heard separately from the divorce.

For many people the crucial part of the proceedings may be the hearings which determine what will happen to children and how the family assets will be divided, and they might see the divorce itself as relatively unimportant. Technically, the actual divorce is the substantive or main action and the other applications brought under it are 'ancillary' to it. The divorce progresses more or less on paper while the proceedings brought under it can be complicated and time-consuming.

The Procedure

A county court is a civil court and thus has a completely separate jurisdiction from criminal proceedings which are heard in magistrates' and crown courts. Not all county courts are authorized to deal with divorce but those which are can take divorces and matrimonial proceedings from outside their geographical area.

Divorces can be transferred from the county court to the High Court in certain circumstances: if they become defended, involve a ward of court, or have some particularly difficult or complex point which needs the greater expertise of High Court judges. But the majority of divorces begin and end in the local county court.

Divorces are begun by *petition*, which is a printed form with blank spaces for the details needed. The person seeking the divorce is called the *petitioner*, their spouse is the *respondent*.

The details required in the petition are:

- full names of the parties
- date and place of marriage
- date parties last lived together as man and wife
- residence and occupation of the parties
- number of children of the family, names, dates of birth
- details of the education or training the children will receive if they are aged under sixteen or between sixteen and eighteen
- whether there are or have been other proceedings about the marriage, property or the children of the family and details of these
- details of any arrangements made between the parties for the financial support of the petitioner and children
- the ground of divorce and the facts needed to support this
- the *prayer* – this is printed on the form and amended as necessary. It is a list of all the relief for which the petitioner could ask: dissolution of the marriage: ancillary financial orders; custody of the children; and costs to be paid by the respondent.

In addition to the information about children in the petition, a further more detailed *statement of arrangements* about the proposals that will be made for them following divorce must be prepared.

The details required here concern children aged under sixteen, or between sixteen and eighteen who are either still in full-time school education or being trained for a profession, trade or vocation. They are:

● where the children will live, with whom, and in what sort of accommodation

● which school they will attend, or what type of training they will receive

● who presently supports them and whether or not the petitioner will apply for financial orders for them

● the arrangements if any that have been made for access to the other parent and how much access there will be

● whether or not they suffer from any chronic illness or disability or the effects of such. (Medical reports should be attached here. If they are not available at the time the statement of arrangements is prepared they should be obtained from the doctor or specialist treating the child as soon as possible. The illnesses and disabilities referred to are more than the common temporary illnesses of childhood.)

● whether or not the children are under a care or supervision order and, if so, which local authority is involved and when the order was made.

THE GROUND FOR DIVORCE

There is only one ground for divorce, which is that the marriage has irretrievably broken down. 'Irretrievably broken down' means that for one of the parties at least it is broken beyond repair. In order to prove that this is so, the petitioner must prove one of five facts.

1. That the respondent has committed adultery and the petitioner finds it intolerable to live with the respondent
If husband and wife are still living together when the petition is presented, then the adultery has to have taken place within the six months before that, or the petitioner must have found out about an older adultery only within that same period. Any longer, and self-evidently the petitioner did not find it intolerable to live with the respondent and is taken as having condoned and forgiven the adultery. If the petitioner knows the name or identity of the other person then those details must appear on the petition, however sketchy. Where the name and identity are known, then that person becomes the co-respondent and must be served with a copy of the petition which he or she can then defend if they so choose.

2. That the respondent has behaved in such a way that the petitioner cannot reasonably be expected to live with the respondent

The behaviour complained of must also be fairly recent although there are no strict time limits as with adultery. Behaviour petitions are probably the most unpleasant for both parties as the petitioner has to recall details of incidents he or she (although it is generally she as most petitions are brought by women) would prefer to forget, and most respondents hate getting such petitions and have considerable difficulty in accepting the details. The major problem about behaviour petitions is that they can inflame an already difficult situation.

3. That the respondent has deserted the petitioner for a continuous period of at least two years immediately preceding the presentation of the petition

The desertion has to have been against the wishes of the petitioner, and must have been chosen by the respondent – a spouse who has been imprisoned for two years has not deserted unless during that whole period he would not have returned had he been able, nor would a spouse be in desertion if he or she was asked to leave the family home unless they then refused to come back.

4. That the parties to the marriage have lived apart for a continuous period of at least two years immediately preceding the presentation of the petition and the respondent consents to a decree being granted

The respondent must consent in writing to this fact. This is done by his or her signing the *acknowledgement of service* personally and answering the question about consent on that form.

5. That the parties to the marriage have lived apart for a continuous period of at least five years immediately preceding the presentation of the petition

This fact is used by people whose spouses do not consent to a two-year separation when no other fact is available to them. It was referred to as a 'Romeo's charter' when debated in Parliament, but actually is little used, and as much by women as men.

   These are colloquially known as adultery, behaviour, two years, five years and desertion.

SERVING THE PETITION

The solicitor or the petitioner in person prepares the petition on one or more of these facts. The facts have to stand up to examination by the court – and of course by the respondent if he or she is disputing the divorce proceedings. Excessively trivial complaints in a behaviour petition would not stand up to the court's scrutiny nor pass the test of what a reasonable petitioner should be able to tolerate within marriage.

While there can be complications either in preparing, serving or proving the petition in a straightforward, undefended divorce, the procedure has been greatly simplified and is as follows.

The petitioner or the solicitor files at the county court:

- two copies of the petition, plus one for each co-respondent if it is an adultery petition
- the fee (petitioners who are being advised under the green form scheme do not have to pay a fee if a fees exemption form signed by the solicitor is also filed with the other papers)
- two copies of the statement of arrangements for the children
- marriage certificate.

The court sends a copy of the petition and statement of arrangements for the children by ordinary post to the respondent at the address given for him on the petition. They enclose a form called an acknowledgement of service for the respondent to fill in and return to the court.

The respondent fills in the acknowledgement, saying where and when he got the petition, stating whether or not he wants to defend the petition, or to make his own application for custody and access to the children. If two-year separation or adultery is the fact used, he can also consent to it in writing or admit the adultery.

The respondent returns the acknowledgement of service to the court.

The court sends the petitioner or solicitor:

- a sealed photocopy of the acknowledgement of service
- a form which asks for *directions for trial*
- an *affidavit* in printed form with blank spaces to be filled in.

This is the proof stage of the divorce, where the petitioner gives evidence by way of affidavit proving the facts in the petition.

The form of the affidavit depends on what fact was used in the divorce. The petitioner must fill this in, swear it or affirm it before any solicitor, paying a small fee (£3.50 at the time of writing). The petitioner then signs the form asking for directions for trial and returns it to the court.

The next stage is dealt with, on paper, by the registrar at the court. He or she inspects all the documents at the court, and if they are in order certifies that there can be a decree nisi under the special procedure.

The court administration fixes a date for the pronouncement of decree nisi in open court. At the same time they fix the date for the *children's appointment* before a judge.

THE CHILDREN'S APPOINTMENT

This is a private appointment with a judge. The petitioner must go to this – the court tells the respondent of this appointment, and he or she can go if they wish. Lawyers do not attend. Sometimes petitioners feel nervous about this appointment, fearing that it will be like an adversarial trial, but in fact it is informal and, depending on the character and qualities of the judge, friendly.

The judge will have read the statement of arrangements for the children, but expect to be asked questions about these, and financial plans for the children. The judge must be satisfied that the arrangements for all the children of the family are satisfactory, or the best that can be made in the circumstances.

In some rare circumstances he can certify that it would be impracticable to make any such arrangements. When he is convinced that the children are properly considered, he will make a *certificate of satisfaction* to that effect. This is a crucial step in the divorce as no decree absolute or final order can be made unless the judge makes this certificate.

ORDERS FOR CUSTODY AND ACCESS

At this point the judge can make the orders for custody and access which have been agreed beforehand between the parties. He will know from the acknowledgement of service if the respondent has agreed or not with the plans for the children in the petition – and know from the other papers whether or not a respondent has actually applied on his own account for custody or access.

If there is a full-blown or threatened dispute the judge will *not* make orders about custody or access, as these have to be dealt with in a full hearing. If there seems to be apparent indecision or faulty agreement he is likely to suggest that the parties take further legal advice and come back to court.

The judge has power to make whatever orders he or she feels are appropriate for the children's sake at this appointment. In rare cases, what he discovers about the children in the course of this appointment might lead him into ordering a welfare report on them, or making no orders until the parties have seen their respective solicitors.

Once decree nisi has been pronounced, there is a waiting period of six weeks before the divorce can be made final. The petitioner can then apply, on a simple form, for the decree to be made *absolute*. After a few days, the court then sends a copy of this *final order* to both the parties. The petitioner must make an application – it is not done automatically – and until this is done the parties are still married.

Occasionally petitioners, or indeed their solicitors, forget to apply for decree absolute. The simple form of application can be used for up to a year following decree nisi, but if there is a delay of more than a year the court rules require that some explanation is made. This is done by preparing an affidavit setting out why the delay occurred.

If petitioners do not apply for at least three months after decree nisi, then respondents can. In such a case they prepare an affidavit explaining why they are making the application instead of the petitioner: an explanation that the petitioner is refusing to do so without good reason would suffice.

Defended Divorces

Very frequently, respondents' first reaction to getting a divorce petition is to say that they will defend it. This reaction comes from emotions stirred both by the fact of divorce and the contents of the petition.

Very few respondents do in the event defend a petition: either they change their minds voluntarily, or are advised against it. There are good reasons for not defending a petition, not the least of which is cost. A defended divorce must be transferred from the county court to the High Court, takes years to litigate, and before legal aid could be considered must have a good basis for the defence.

As the ground of divorce is irretrievable breakdown of marriage, the defence is that the marriage has not broken down. This is difficult to prove if the petitioner wants to get out of the marriage so much that she or he continues with fighting a defended case.

If a respondent cannot accept the facts in the petition and claims they are lies or in some way wrong – which is a different issue from proving the marriage has not broken down – then he or she could attempt negotiation through solicitors to amend or change the most contentious allegations. It is also possible to make it clear to the other party and the court that a respondent does not accept all the facts as true, but does accept that the marriage has broken down and enough of the facts to support that. Ultimately the respondent can defend the original petition and cross petition with a different set of allegations against the petitioner. If and when the court hears the petitions, it could order a decree nisi on each one, or prefer one above the other.

If a respondent is determined to defend, he or she can put in a defence to the petition right up to before decree nisi is pronounced. The time limit is eight days to do this on the acknowledgement of service.

Judicial Separation

Judicial separation is legal separation, a halfway house between marriage and divorce.

After the single decree of judicial separation has been made, the parties are still legally married but have no duties to cohabit with each other. Because they are still married, neither can marry again, neither lose pension rights on the death of the other, and can claim on their will or intestacy as a spouse.

A decree of judicial separation is given on the petitioner proving one or more of the facts used in divorce. But there is no claim that the marriage has irretrievably broken down, and the prayer in the petition is amended to read 'that the petitioner be judicially separated from the respondent' rather than that the marriage be dissolved.

The parties can apply for the same range of orders after a judicial separation petition has been filed as in divorce, and the courts can deal with property and children in the same way. The same provisions apply for the children's appointment and the judge must make a certificate of satisfaction before any decree of judicial separation is made.

Reconciliation

Families break down because of countless different strains and problems. When married couples have problems, the popular view is that there is only one type of legal solution – divorce. Although there are not a large number of solutions there are alternative methods of sorting out problems which fall short of dissolution of the marriage.

The first step should always be discussion and conciliation. This is available to any couple, married or not, either through RELATE (formerly the Marriage Guidance Council) or through conciliation agencies which are attached to courts or are independent. Conciliation services try to heal the rifts and find compromise solutions to the problems – they do at least hold out the possibility of increased personal happiness for the family.

If conciliation fails, then unless you know what you want to happen, legal advice should be sought. Family solicitors are used to clients coming in to ask advice about divorce, and then making it apparent in the interview that they have a rather different problem.

Filing a petition does not bind anyone to continuing with the divorce. It is not a completely automatic process and petitioners can stop it merely by failing to complete the next stage. If this happens, the court does not send reminders or chivvy the petitioner on – but they do keep the papers on file and, technically, the divorce is still 'live'.

This can cause problems if after a failed reconciliation the petitioner tries, even years later, to start divorce proceedings again. The court cannot accept another petition if one is live on file.

In such a case tell your solicitor or the court about the existence of the previous petition before attempting to file a new one. The old petition can then be dismissed before the fresh proceedings start, or amended to bring it up-to-date.

Custody

The popular understanding of custody is that the person with whom the child lives has custody and full responsibility for and rights over that child. In law, however, there is a division made between the physical presence of children and the legal rights and duties surrounding them. Different terms are used to describe these.

In matrimonial causes – divorce, judicial separation, nullity – the word 'custody' means the full parental legal powers and duties including the power to make decisions about the child's welfare and future, where they live and what they do. 'Custody' in this context includes access to the child. The term 'care and control' is used to describe the day-to-day management and tending of the child by the person with whom he or she lives. These terms are used in all matrimonial causes in the High Court and county court and in wardship.

A different set of terms is used in other proceedings about children. 'Legal custody' is defined in the Children Act 1975 as meaning so much of the parental rights and duties as relate to the person of the child, including the place and manner in which his time is spent. In the same Act 'actual custody' is what people have if they have actual possession of the child's person. These terms are used in custody applications brought under the Guardianship Act, Guardianship of Minors Act, and in applications for custodianship under the Children Act 1975.

When parents are married they share equally the custody, care and control of the child irrespective of how they actually divide the physical and intellectual duties of parenthood between them. They have the same rights and authority over the custody and upbringing of the child as each other and either of them can exercise these rights without the other. This is specifically laid down by s1 of the Guardianship Act 1973 which was passed partly to give married mothers rights equal to their husbands'. The section also says that any agreement between parents for one or the other to give up their rights and authority is not enforceable. This means that a court would not force a parent to give up his or her rights to the other, even where some sort of agreement had been reached to do this.

This is similar to the provision in the Children Act that no parent can surrender or transfer their rights to anyone else. Both these provisions might be of help to women whose husbands consider they are the 'head' of the family and whose authority is absolute.

This equality of parental rights exists unless and until either spouse seeks an order to change the situation.

Under the Children Act 1989 parental responsibility replaces custody/legal custody. 'Parental responsibility' is all the rights, duties, powers, responsibilities and authority which by law a parent of a child has in relation to the child and his or her property.

More than one person can have parental responsibility for a child, and people who are not biological parents can have it as well. When more than one person has parental responsibility, they cannot pass the buck between them – they all have the same responsibilities.

When parents are married at a child's birth they both share it equally – as they share custody at the moment. Either parent can exercise parental responsibility without the other, as now.

No one who has parental responsibility can surrender or transfer it to another as under the present law, but he or she can arrange for someone else to take some or all of the responsibility on his or her behalf. If they do this, they still have liability for any failures in their own responsibility to the child.

When parents of a child were not married at the time of the child's birth the mother has parental responsibility alone – as now. Fathers can apply to court for parental responsibility – as now – but there is a new provision whereby parents can, without going to court, agree that the father should have parental responsibility for the child.

These agreements have to be in writing, in a set form which will be decided by regulations. This is a way of both parents having parental responsibility, without the father having to apply to court for parental rights. This is done at the moment under the Guardianship of Minors Act or the Family Reform Act, both of which will be repealed entirely by the new law.

When the mother agrees with the father that he should have parental responsibility, she is not surrendering her own, but extending it to both. This provision will be particularly useful for parents who live together and do not want to get married but do want both parents to bring up the child in full partnership.

Parental responsibility agreements can be ended. To do this, one of the people who has parental responsibility applies to court under the Act. This could be either parent – practically, it is more likely to be one aggrieved parent trying to sever the other's links with the child rather than a parent choosing to give up their own. The grounds for applications are not defined at the moment. Following normal custody cases, they ought to be decided on what is in the child's best interests, rather than on the problems the parents cause each other.

There is a radical new provision in the Act: a child can apply for a parental responsibility agreement to be ended, effectively choosing to be divorced from his or her parent. Children can make an application of this sort only when they have the court's permission to do so. Permission will be given only if the court is satisfied the child has sufficient understanding to make the application.

Why Seek an Order for Custody?

When married parents separate there is no legal requirement to formalize this with orders from any court. It is possible for couples to live separately for years, bringing up their children more or less in accord, and making their own arrangements about where the children live and who maintains them.

The practical effect of this – as children cannot live in two places at once – is that although both parents would keep the joint custody as in marriage, one of them would have the effective care and control. This necessarily means that the other has surrendered it. The rule that no one can surrender or transfer their parental rights is specifically relaxed in the Guardianship Act 1973 to allow such agreements between separated married couples over the children. Even so, the court has power to over-ride what has been decided if it considers the agreement made between the parents is not in the best interests of the child.

This over-riding power applies not only to verbal agreements but to terms about children in separation deeds. The welfare principle allows courts to re-draft and reset agreements where the child's interests are not properly accounted for – naturally, they would know about this only if one of the parties applied to court in an application. It is always open to an informally separated parent, or one who has made a previous written agreement about custody, care and control, to apply under the Guardianship Acts or indeed in divorce for orders that change an agreement previously made.

Parents apply for custody orders when they need them. The most obvious need is when the parents are fighting about which one the child is to live with. Other less immediate needs might be for the clarity and security of an order, even where parents are rubbing along fairly amicably with an informal agreement between them. Situations can change, and children require a continuity of care that, without an order, could be interrupted by one parent announcing it was their turn now and the child was going to live with them.

Parents also apply for custody orders when they have to – while they may have a choice about whether or not to get orders when they are just separated, there is no choice in divorce. No final decree in divorce and no decree in a judicial separation can be granted unless a judge has made a certificate of satisfaction about the children, and will not do so unless custody, care and control are settled.

This basic rule remains the same under the new Act, although the wording has been changed.

Which Proceedings?

Married parents who cannot or do not want to take matrimonial proceedings for divorce or judicial separation can apply under the Guardianship of Minors Act 1971 for custody and access orders.

For various reasons parents may choose not to dissolve the marriage even when it has broken down. They may not want to take this step just yet, or could have been married for less than a year and are therefore absolutely barred from taking divorce proceedings. In addition, because divorce and judicial separation require the proving of facts to prove irretrievable breakdown, some couples may not be able to petition because none of the necessary facts is available to them.

This could happen where a couple have been separated for under two years; or for more than two years (but less than five) and the respondent does not consent to a divorce; the behaviour of both has been tolerable to each; or the marriage broke down because of the adultery of the party who wants the divorce and the party who could divorce on that fact chooses not to. Under the new law, all such applications to do with children must be made under the Children Act 1989 itself.

MATRIMONIAL PROCEEDINGS

These comprise divorce, judicial separation and nullity. For a description of the procedure used for the main actions see p. 284–8.

The application is for custody, including care and control and access. Care and control is not a statutory term but is generally used to describe who the child will live with, and obviously that point is the main one in a custody application.

It is certainly of greater moment to a parent to have care and control than to have custody – compared to the fact of living with a loved child the theoretical question of possession of the legal rights comes a poor second.

CHANGES UNDER THE NEW LAW

All applications for custody and access will be made under the Children Act 1989 and not under the Matrimonial Causes Act 1973. The sections in that Act which deal with these matters will be repealed. Divorce generally will still be under the Matrimonial Causes Act and the grounds and procedure have not been changed.

The kinds of orders that can be made in family proceedings are:

- residence orders
- contact orders
- specific issue orders
- prohibited steps orders.

They can be found in s8 of the new Act.

A *residence order* is one which settles who the child is to live with. Note here that under the new law a residence order can be made in favour of people who do not actually live together: the order can specify the amount of time the child is to spend with each.

A *contact order* requires the person the child lives with to allow the child to visit, stay with, or have contact with the other person named in the order.

A *specific issue order* is what it sounds like – it is an order where the court settles directions about a particular subject of dispute. Where the problem can be solved by either a residence or a contact order, the courts should use them instead.

A *prohibited steps order* is one which states that no one with parental responsibility can take steps of a kind specified in the order without first getting the court's consent. As with specific issue orders, if the problem can be settled by other orders, it should be.

Between them, these orders cover all the eventualities set out below. The specific changes made follow each section.

The Kinds of Orders That Can be Made

CUSTODY, CARE AND CONTROL TO ONE PARENT

This is the common order when the parents together or the court after a custody action decides which parent should live with the child.

With this kind of order, the parent who does not live with the child still retains some parental rights and is entitled to be involved in decisions about the child. If this does not happen or consultation breaks down and the custodial parent is about to do something the non-custodial parent disagrees with, then he or she can apply to the court under s1(3) of the Guardianship Act 1973. This is available to parents who either are married and living together, or married and separated, or were married and are now divorced. It applies when there is a disagreement between parents about the child's upbringing. The court can make whatever order it thinks is appropriate and direct the parents as to what should be done in the child's interests. The court cannot change the custody or access position or make orders about those subjects.

The equivalent of this order under the new law would be a residence order in favour of one parent, with parental responsibility to one or both.

In cases of dispute between parents the court can make a specific issue order which gives directions about a specific question to do with any aspect of parental responsibility. They should not do this if the problem can be resolved by making a residence or contact order. Nor can they go further in their directions than a court in wardship (for example, they cannot settle a dispute about the child's education which is already the subject of an attendance order under education law).

SPLIT ORDERS

Courts can split off care and control from custody, giving care and control to one parent and custody to the other. But in general, they do not unless there are rare and exceptional circumstances. In one case where the parent with whom the child was to live was a Jehovah's Witness, the court gave care and control only to that parent, with custody to the other who could then give the only valid consent to a blood transfusion if the child needed one.

There are practical reasons for not making split orders. If the parent with whom the child lives cannot in law make decisions about visits abroad, education and medical treatment but always has to get the other parent to do so, then the consequences for the child could be at the very least inconvenient. There could be emotional consequences too – the non-custodial parent could resent the implication that he or she was fit only for the routine care and not the over-all duties.

JOINT CUSTODY

Courts can give custody of the child to both parents, and care and control to one. This is called 'joint custody' and is considered a good idea where the parents are likely to be co-operative and helpful to the child. It is considered unwise where the parents are likely to be argumentative and acrimonious with each other but even so it can be granted in recognition that the absent parent is still very much involved with the child.

Joint custody orders can be specifically applied for by parents who agree this is what they want at an early stage. The petitioner or solicitor alters the petition to read that the petitioner wants an order for joint custody to be made. Or the judge at the children's appointment can be asked to make the order then. Where there has been a dispute about custody and a full hearing before a judge, the order can be made at the end of the proceedings.

The joint custody order entitles the non-custodial parent to play an equal part in decisions about the child, as during the marriage. It formalizes the situation. If consultation fails, the parent can use the s1(3) provision under the Guardianship of Minors Act described above on p. 296.

An additional advantage of joint custody orders is that older children who understand what is happening can find an emotional security in knowing that both parents are still fully legally involved with their lives.

The equivalent of this under the new law is for both parents to have parental responsibility.

UNFIT PARENT ORDERS

The court has power to make a declaration in a decree absolute in divorce or a decree of judicial separation that either party to the marriage is unfit to have the custody of the children of the family. These declarations are rare. The petitioner can apply for such a declaration in the petition. One effect of such a declaration is that the parent who is declared unfit cannot take over custody of the children if the custodial parent dies when they are still minors. Normally, when a custodial parent dies the surviving parent takes over in law, automatically recovering the full parental and legal right and duties.

Unfit parent orders will cease to have effect when the new Act comes in.

HOW LONG DO ORDERS LAST?

Interim orders, including interim injunctions, last until the next hearing or until an alternative time set by the court in making the order.

Final orders last until they are varied, discharged or suspended by the court. If none of this happens, custody and access orders in matrimonial proceedings last until the child is eighteen, or until the death of the parent if earlier.

Under the new law orders can be varied or discharged as at present. Contact and residence orders will cease automatically if the parents live together again for a continuous six-month period. Courts should not make any s8 orders on children who are already sixteen, or which will last till they are over sixteen unless the circumstances are exceptional.

CARE AND SUPERVISION ORDERS

The court can order that a child – as long as he or she is under seventeen at the time – is committed into the care of the local authority. This order can be made where the court considers that there are exceptional circumstances making it either impractical or undesirable for the child to be entrusted to either of the parties in the marriage, or to any other individual. In other words, if there is another person apart from the parents capable of looking after the child, the court can give them custody of the child. Before the order is made, the local authority are entitled to make representations in court.

The local authority concerned is the one for the area in which the child was living before the order was made.

These orders are different from care orders made in the juvenile courts because the court which makes them has power to give directions to the local authority about how the child is treated, including how they should safeguard and promote welfare and where they place the child.

If the court does give directions then the local authority must carry out their duties subject to the court's wishes. If the court makes this kind of care order, parents can ask the court to make directions about matters such as where the child is to live and access, which if accepted would influence what directions were made and therefore how the child was treated.

As with care orders generally, there is nothing to stop the local authority placing the child at home with either of the parents: if this did not work out for the child's benefit, they could remove the child without going back to court for permission.

The court which made the order can vary or discharge it. Parents and the local authority can apply for this to happen if circumstances change.

The local authority must be allowed to give their views about the care order to the court before one is made, and can also apply to the court for a money order against the parents as contribution for the child's upkeep. If they do apply, the parents will have the chance to give affidavit evidence about their means and can put their views about a money order being made against them in that affidavit.

The court is likely to make a care order only when it considers the parents are simply not fit to look after the child properly. These orders are not particularly common.

SUPERVISION ORDERS

The court can make supervision orders either to the local probation office or to the local authority if there are exceptional circumstances making it desirable for the child to be supervised by an independent person.

This order can be varied or discharged like any other order. Otherwise it would last until the child was eighteen.

Under the new law courts will still be able to make a care or supervision order in all family proceedings if the grounds exist, after investigation by the local authority.

Access

Access is the formal word used to describe seeing a child when you do not live together. An appallingly high proportion of children in divorce completely lose contact with the parent who moves out – some figures are as high as 45 per cent. This is effectively abandonment of the child by the parent and is due more to the wishes of the parent who does not visit than to the actions of the court which encourages access whenever possible.

A parent has a right to apply to court for access if this is not being freely given by the parent who looks after the child, whether or not the adults ever lived together, were married or are in the process of divorce. Of course, in most separating families the parents together make amicable arrangements for access, but in a large proportion of cases access is a difficult and fraught subject that eventually has to go to court.

Access itself used to be seen as a right of the parent – now courts see it as being far more the right of the child. What this means in practice is that when deciding access the court will not automatically give it just because the parent applies, but only if the child will benefit. Generally, access is given to parents unless for some serious reason the court thinks they are likely to be an emotional or physical danger to the child.

Only parents who do not live with the child can apply for access. The parent with whom the child lives cannot apply for an order that the other partner visit the child or positively enforce an order that is given. Nor can the child apply for an order that his or her parent visits. The application for an order and enforcement of it are down to the parent in whose favour the order was made.

Unfortunately, when parents separate access can become a battleground whether or not an order has been made. The reasons are obvious, and the solutions common-sensical if difficult to put into practice. The golden rules for the child's sake should be as follows.

FOR THE NON-CUSTODIAL PARENT

● Do what you say and visit when you are meant to. If you cannot, contact the child and the other parent as soon as possible and make alternative arrangements immediately.

● Consult the other parent before you buy the child clothes or presents, particularly if these are expensive and longed for. It is not unreasonable for the custodial parent to resent you buying the bicycle she has been saving up for.

● Bring the child back on time. However painful it may be to think that the child's bedtime routine is now run by the partner from whom you are separated, that is the situation.

FOR THE CUSTODIAL PARENT

● Never deny access unless there is a genuine reason for it, and say what the reason is. Access is not for your convenience, but for the child. If a child is ill and cannot go out, tell the other parent as soon as possible and arrange an alternative.

- Never stop access altogether unless you have an overwhelming reason for doing this. Consult a solicitor before you do.
- Never use the threat of withdrawing access as a way of disciplining the child. However dreadfully he or she may behave, this must not affect the relationship with the other parent.

FOR BOTH PARENTS

- Remember that whatever the problems between you, you are always going to be the parents of the same child, and that relationship is permanent.
- Never ask the child to tell you details about the other parent's personal life, and never criticize the other parent to the child.
- Present a united front before the child, and if possible try to avoid the 'doorstep' situation where the child is handed over like a parcel at the front door. Gritting one's teeth and drinking a cup of tea together is better for the child's sense of security.
- Never ask the child to express a preference between you. The child loves you both and is confused as to why you do not love each other.
- Particular sensitivity is needed if either parent has a new partner: treat this as a delicate area, and do not for example spring a new person on the child without careful consideration and consultation with the other parent.
- Consult, consult, consult.

These are not legal rules – but ignoring them leads to a lot of law.

Types of Access

The access arranged informally between parents can take whatever form and frequency they choose. The only restriction on this is that the court might not approve the arrangements if the parents then go to court for orders to be made. The court has a duty to the child and an independence which can over-ride even where parents are in full agreement with each other. For example, they are likely to disapprove of unsettling arrangements for children, or long access periods which would interfere with the child's education.

REASONABLE ACCESS

When courts make orders this does not necessarily mean the parents are locked in combat; in divorce even where the parties are not in dispute about anything the court must still make custody and access orders.

It is very common for orders to say 'reasonable access' with no other details given. It is left up to the parents to decide what they will do, and they themselves define together what 'reasonable' means. Even where there has been a dispute of some sort, the court is likely to make a reasonable access order, giving parents the opportunity to sort something out between them and leaving the practical details of times and places open for discussion.

DEFINED ACCESS

Where arrangements between the parents are not working out, or where the court accepts they should interfere for the child's sake, they can make a defined access order. This sets out in detail how and where the access is to take place. Generally, the court will only make such orders if there have been quite serious problems, for example where access has been denied or stopped by the custodial parent, or the parents have been unable to agree on the terms on which access is to take place.

Although defined access orders can help parents who cannot agree together in a more flexible way, putting precise details into an order can lead to more dissent about minor points – for example, being five minutes late in returning the child after an ordered time is technically a breach of the order and could be litigated on.

SUPERVISED ACCESS

This is an order for access where someone else, other than the custodial parent, is present throughout to keep an eye on things. Such orders are made when there is some doubt about the parenting abilities or expertise of the non-custodial parent. This need not be sinister – it could be that the non-custodial parent has lost touch with the child over a longish period, and should get to know the child again in controlled and secure surroundings. Although the supervising person can be a professional, the courts prefer that the parents agree on a suitable non-professional person if one can be found. A practice direction recommends that where there is going to be an application for access to be supervised, the parents should have found a suitable person before the case is heard. This can be a mutual friend, godparent or unprejudiced relative. Only when parents cannot find such a person to help should they ask for professionals, for example court welfare officers, to be involved. The professional supervising person can also be a social worker at a family centre or member of staff at a nursery. In such a case they would be able to report back to the court on how things went, either because the court wanted this or at the request of the non-custodial parent in an application to lift the supervision aspects of the order.

Where the local authority are involved, for example in care proceedings or wardship, and they require access to be supervised, they will provide the person to do it. This could mean the parents seeing the child at the children's home with a social worker either in the room at all times, or popping in and out to see how things are going.

STAYING ACCESS

This describes overnight and holiday visits. A staying access order can be combined with a reasonable access order, and might read 'reasonable access to include staying access', leaving the details for the parents to agree together. With defined access orders it is common to make more specific terms setting out how many weekends or weeks per year. When necessary, orders can be even more specific, attaching detailed schedules of when and where the child is to be for months ahead. This can be sensible where for example the parents are unable to agree as a matter of course and their lawyers iron out long-term plans at a hearing.

NO ACCESS ORDERS

The court can, on the application of the parent with whom the child lives, make an order that there should be no access by the other parent. The judge can make this sort of order at the children's appointment without seeing the other parent in court. This could be done where it is very clear that the parent has no interest in seeing the child and is disruptive or otherwise bad news. In this sort of case, where the parent has had no opportunity to put his or her point of view he or she would be able to apply to the court for an access hearing. This kind of order acts as a protection to the petitioner and the children – the other parent could not have access against the petitioner's wishes unless and until the court on hearing all the facts decided this after a hearing.

The court can make a no access order after hearing a disputed case. A judge would do this if he or she believed access to that parent was not in the child's best interests.

CHANGES UNDER THE NEW LAW

Under the Children Act 1989 access is covered by contact orders, which like all the new s8 orders can contain directions about how it is to be carried out, impose conditions on it, have time limits or specified periods imposed on it.

The court has power as well to add other provisions it thinks appropriate. The general principles and advice given on access in this chapter are not likely to be affected by the new law.

Custody and Access: When are Orders Made?

In matrimonial proceedings, the court can make orders for the custody and education of children under the age of eighteen at any time after a petition has been filed. This can be before or after decree nisi, or after a decree absolute of divorce or a decree of judicial separation or nullity.

In emergencies, the court can make orders before a petition is filed with the court if the would-be petitioner promises to file one shortly.

The court can also make these orders when the petition is dismissed and no decree of divorce or judicial separation is made at all. This would apply where a petition was defended and after a trial was thrown out.

When an order is actually made depends on the circumstances of the case. The situation will not change under the new law.

AGREED ORDERS

Where the parents are not in dispute about custody or access and have mutually decided what is to happen, there is no need to apply for orders before the children's appointment when agreed orders can be made by the judge.

This appointment is fixed for the day that decree nisi is pronounced. While no one need attend the court to hear the decree nisi being read out, the petitioner must go to the children's appointment.

The time courts take to get to this stage varies: some courts are backlogged and busy, others process special procedure divorces quickly. A general guide is that in a straightforward special procedure divorce with no hitches, decree nisi can be about two months after the petition has been filed.

ORDERS BEFORE DECREE ABSOLUTE

If there is a problem between the parents, either one of them can apply to the courts for orders as soon as the petition has been filed – or even before if they make an undertaking to file a petition within a short period, usually seven days. An undertaking is a promise to the court, which if broken can be punished as a contempt of court.

The application for custody or access will then be given a first hearing as soon as the court can fit it in. The first hearing will be a preliminary one and although the court will make orders on custody and access before the case has been fully heard, these orders will be 'interim' ones. An interim order is a preliminary order, which lasts until the next hearing. When the case has been fully heard and gone through the procedure described below, final orders can then be made. These last until the children stop being minors or until they are changed by another application to court.

EMERGENCIES

In an emergency, the petitioner or respondent can apply for urgent orders and injunctions at any stage of the divorce proceedings. Injunctions are orders of the court which make someone do or refrain from doing something. They can be heard 'ex parte' or 'on notice'.

On Notice Applications
These are hearings where the other party is told of the hearing in advance and given a chance to appear at court. The amount of notice he or she must be given varies with the type of injunction sought. In emergency applications about custody or access, the period of notice is two full days.

The person seeking the orders and injunctions fills out an application, saying what kind of orders he or she seeks, and prepares an affidavit setting out in detail what the particular problem is. Both these documents must be served on the other party, getting to him or her two days before the hearing is fixed.

Ex Parte Applications
These are used when there is no time to lose, and an immediate order must be made. The other party is not told of the hearing which can take place as soon as the parent, solicitor and court get it organized. For example, if a parent has failed to return a child after access, the custodial parent can go straight to court for an injunction ordering the child's return. The paperwork can be kept to a minimum in a real emergency to save time; affidavits are not absolutely necessary as the applicant can give evidence personally, or can be handwritten by the solicitor outside court rather than typed in the office.

After hearing evidence, orders can be made which would last either until the next hearing or whatever period the judge fixes. Injunctions to stop people doing something can last for fixed periods of some months after which they automatically expire unless renewed. Injunctions ordering people to do something last for a shorter named period. All injunctions can be extended for a further period on a fresh application for this.

ORDERS AFTER DECREE ABSOLUTE

Either parent can return to the court at any time after the proceedings are over if there are problems over custody and access. There is no need to start new proceedings – matrimonial causes stay alive for ever. The application can be to enforce the previous order – for example, if access arrangements have broken down and the non-custodial parent wants these upheld. These applications would either be to ask for the court's direction or, where there has been a breach of the order, to ask the court to commit the other party for contempt.

The application can also be to change the original order, for example where a non-custodial parent now seeks care and control. This latter is called an application to vary, and can be done only if there has been a change of circumstances since the order was made. It is not an appeal or a rehearing but effectively a fresh application for care and control for up-to-date reasons.

Although there is this power to return to court at any time, parents who find the ordered arrangements are not working out should try negotiation first, either personally or through solicitors. Going back to court should be the last resort.

Who Can Apply for Orders about Children in Matrimonial Proceedings?

Under the present law, people who can get custody, care and control and access to children in matrimonial proceedings (divorce, judicial separation and nullity) are the parties to the marriage only. These may not necessarily be the biological or adopted parents of the child, but can include step-parents. Grandparents could get access to a child in custody proceedings under the Guardianship Acts, after a custody order has been made, but cannot intervene in divorce proceedings.

Under the new law, residence and contact orders can be made in the course of any family proceedings, including divorce, in favour of:

- obviously, either parent
- any party to a marriage whether or not it is still going on at the time of the proceedings if during that marriage the child was a child of the family –

this could include a previous step-parent who could apply for a residence or contact order during the ex-spouse's *next* divorce

- any person with whom the child has lived for a period of three years – the three years does not have to be continuous, can be aggregated from within the last five years, as long as the last period of living with the child was within three months of the date of the application for an order
- any person who, where there is already a residence order about the child, has the consent of each of the people in whose favour the residence order was made
- any person who has the consent of the local authority where the child is in care
- any person who has the consent of each of those people who have parental responsibility for the child
- any person who gets the leave of the court to make a s8 application (in deciding whether to give leave the court has to look at the kind of s8 order that would be applied for; the applicant's connection with the child; whether or not the application would be disruptive to the child; and the views of the local authority if the child is in care to them).

In addition, the court has its own power to make any section 8 order, including residence or contact orders, if it thinks it should be made, even where no one has formally applied for one.

The Children Act 1989 introduces a new structure to try to cut down delay in family cases, including a timetable.

Financial Orders in Divorce

Either party to a marriage can apply to the divorce court for financial orders for themselves and the children of the family. In practice, it is women who apply for maintenance as they most commonly bring up the children after divorce.

These orders are made 'ancillary' to the main action, which is divorce, judicial separation or nullity. There has to be a main action before financial orders can be applied for.

Divorce does not make families rich. Sharing the family assets and funding two households instead of one is an impoverishing process, particularly now when there are no tax benefits to sweeten maintenance payments for husbands. Family finance is complicated, and applicants should get legal advice. This section is a run-down of basic principles and the orders that can be made and should be read as a starting point to the whole business.

The court can make:

- maintenance orders where either spouse pays the other maintenance in the form of periodical payments, either temporarily or finally;
- property adjustment orders that transfer property from one to the other and set the terms on which this is to be done;
- lump sum orders which transfer cash from one to the other on such terms as they think appropriate;
- periodical payments and lump sum orders to the children of the family. These can, unlike adults' orders be made at any time.

Basic Principles

The court has wide powers in family finance cases which throw the whole money issues of the family open and redistribute the assets and income according to basic principles. The court must look at all the circumstances of the case, including the welfare of any children under eighteen. Then it must take account of specific areas including the financial needs and resources and earning capacity of the parties, now and in the foreseeable future; the family's standard of living before the divorce; the age of the parties and length of the marriage; any physical or mental disability of the parties; contributions the parties have made to the marriage; and any relevant conduct during the marriage. 'Conduct' means bad conduct – in a few rare cases particularly awful behaviour can be penalized by tougher money orders.

Where the court is asked to make orders for children, it has to apply the same sort of investigative process to the children's own financial and other needs, including their health, education and training, as well as the parents' situation.

HOW IS THE CLAIM MADE?

Financial claims are made in the petition itself, printed on the set forms as part of the 'prayer'. They have to be activated by the petitioner by filing a set form of application at court, giving the other side notice of intention to proceed with the claim. The claims for financial relief should never be scored out by a petitioner acting in person – applications for financial relief can be made later if this is done, but need the leave of the court and lead to complication.

The respondent can apply for financial relief, without leave, in his or her answer to the petition or by filing a set form.

WHEN ARE THE ORDERS MADE?

Courts can only make property adjustment orders, final maintenance orders and lump sum orders in favour of spouses when the proceedings are complete: that is, when a decree nisi in divorce or nullity is made, or a decree of judicial separation is ordered, or at any time after that. But the terms of the orders come into effect only when the divorce or nullity is made absolute, which is a minimum of six weeks later.

Orders in respect of children can be made at any time before a decree is granted.

Maintenance pending suit orders can be made at any time after the petition has been filed and before the main case has been determined.

Parties to a marriage can first apply for financial orders even years later without problem if the claim was originally made in the petition. But courts have a discretion not to hear the case if doing so would be oppressive or unjust to the other side.

CAN ORDERS BE CHANGED?

Maintenance orders can be varied up or down when the financial circumstances of the applicant for variation have actually changed. For example, a husband would be entitled to have a maintenance order reduced if he became unemployed after it was made.

Maintenance orders can also be discharged (ended) on the application of either party.

Orders which give lump sums in cash cannot be reopened. A spouse who gets a lump sum cannot go back to court when it has been spent and ask for more. Nor can a spouse who discovers the divorced partner has become rich after divorce go back to court and ask for some of the windfall. The exception to this is where there has been trickery or deceit about money, when original orders can be set aside by the court and fairer ones substituted.

HOW LONG DO THEY LAST?

Final maintenance orders for adults last until they are varied; the recipient of maintenance remarries; or the payer or payee dies. The exception to death is where the payer had been ordered to secure the periodical payments against investments, in which case they would continue, but this is rarely done and only where there are large assets.

Orders transferring property or cash between the parties being one-off orders last until they have been put into effect.

General Principles

Both partners have to provide full details of their income, outgoings and financial situation generally. This is done by exchange of affidavits: sworn statements which form the basis of the case. Obviously it is in an applicant's interest to be completely informed about the outgoing costs of the household and how much money is spent on the children. The detail required is considerable, and amounts spent should be broken down and not just given in general terms. It is important to remember that maintenance is paid to cover the actual costs of living; there is no punitive or profit element.

There are ways of dealing with parties who do not provide an affidavit of means when required to, which can in difficult cases lead to imprisonment for civil contempt of court. If full disclosure of financial affairs is not made, and the secretive partner benefits, this could entitle the other to have the order changed later on. In any event, not giving full information can lead to mistakes being made or delays while it is sorted out.

All these orders can be made by consent. If the parties cannot agree about the terms of a settlement, there has to be a hearing in private session at court.

At a hearing, both partners can give oral evidence, be cross-examined and call witnesses. Documents proving the financial claims and situation are relied on, and both parties have to produce anything relevant, e.g. building society books, bank statements, wages slips. Production of these details is not just a voluntary act; one of the stages of the litigation is discovery of documents, which compels the reluctant.

Maintenance Pending Suit

This order can be made in favour of either partner, and/or in favour of the children of the family. It is a temporary order to tide the applicant over before the family finances are finally separated and shared out. It does not necessarily reflect the kind of provision that will finally be made, as the court makes these orders often before the full financial situation is known or the long-term financial needs of the parties are clear.

An order for maintenance pending suit can be applied for once a petition has been filed with the court, and usually lasts until the case is finished (that is, decree absolute in divorce; a decree in judicial separation). The court looks at the immediate financial situation of the parties and the children: earnings, outgoings, entitlement to income support and other financial needs. The aim is that the applicant will have enough money to exist until the divorce or separation is sorted out.

These orders should be applied for quickly if they are needed.

Income Orders after Decree

These orders can be made by consent after negotiation between the parties and their solicitors, or after a court hearing.

Once the full financial facts are known the court decides what amounts should be paid to the applicant and children. These amounts must obviously be based on what is available and what is reasonably required. Courts do not set levels of maintenance which would take a man below subsistence level.

As a guideline or starting point, courts can use general rules to help their calculation. A commonly-used guideline is the 'one-third' rule which adds together the husband and wife's income, divides it by three and orders whatever amount is necessary to get the wife's income up to a third of the total. This is for the wife only – there would be additional amounts ordered for the children on top. Wives cannot apply for maintenance once they have remarried, but children's maintenance goes on despite any remarriage.

If the husband has a new family, that is taken into account. If he is living with or married to someone else, with or without children, he is allowed to keep the reasonable costs of maintaining that new household. The new partner's financial situation is also taken into account, inasmuch as if a new wife is earning, then the husband does not have to support the whole new household and has more income to pay towards the old.

The one-third rule works only where the total amount of income is reasonably high. When there is not enough family income to support both the parties and the children, then a claim for income support makes up the shortfall.

The problem about income support being used to supplement maintenance is that any maintenance awarded will become a 'resource' and the income support will be deducted accordingly. Spouses in this situation get no more income than they would if they did not have a maintenance order in their favour. Even where this is the case, courts will still make maintenance orders because they relieve the state of responsibility and shift it on to the ex-partner.

Although there might be no immediate benefit, it is still advisable to get a maintenance order in this situation because:

- the order can be varied upwards later on, e.g. where the recipient can come off income support because he or she is working;
- even a small or nominal order for maintenance keeps the claim alive.

Capital and Property Orders after Decree

Frequently the only capital asset to be considered after divorce is the matrimonial home. The courts have to ensure that children are properly housed, and no one is made homeless. The orders that are made vary with the facts of each case, the value of the property and the new circumstances. Examples of orders that can be made are:

- immediate sale of the house and division of the proceeds in the proportions decided – both partners will then be able to use the money to buy new, smaller properties;
- transfer of the house to one partner, either outright or with an arrangement to buy out the other partner;
- a postponed sale of the house until the children have reached eighteen, and then division of the sale price in fixed proportions.

Where there is other capital – e.g. shares, cash in the bank, property other than the matrimonial home – the court can divide this, again according to each party's needs and the specific circumstances of the case. It is common to use the one-third starting principle here as well. Often the court does a juggling act between income needs and property needs. A fairly common solution is to transfer property to one spouse and reduce income as compensation to the other. For example, a wife could have the house transferred into her name, supporting herself and the children mainly on her salary or on income support.

Clean Break Orders

These are orders which aim to cut the financial links between the parties at divorce, where the wife gives up her right to maintenance for herself in return for a decent property or cash settlement. Her application for periodical payments for herself would be dismissed and could not be reopened. In practice this works only where she can be financially independent of the husband. Applications for children's maintenance are never dismissed in this way: they have continuing rights which are preserved.

Specific Rules for Children's Money Orders

Maintenance orders in favour of children last until they are seventeen. This is pegged to the school-leaving age, and is the birthday after they reach that age.

The court can, however, extend the period to eighteen where the child's welfare requires this. In special circumstances it can be extended beyond eighteen, including where the child is still receiving education or training.

Generally, orders may not be made where the child is eighteen, apart from the exceptions above.

Children of a family can themselves apply for periodical payments and lump sums from either parent, first getting leave from the court to do so.

There is now no tax benefit in making new orders payable to the child him- or herself, and no tax benefits in making covenants e.g. for school fees.

Powers of the Court

The court has wide statutory powers to deal with most financial situations arising from family breakdown, not merely the familiar ones above. There are mechanisms for enforcing orders, and methods of protecting assets from being disposed of by respondents to applications. In case of any doubt, get professional advice immediately.

Separation Agreements

Separation agreements are written contracts between husband and wife which do not affect the validity of the marriage but settle the terms on which the parties are living apart. They can cover any area the parties choose, including the custody of the children and arrangements for access, money, maintenance and property. They cannot remove the right to apply to court for financial orders at a later stage, e.g. in divorce proceedings. But note here that a properly-entered-into agreement with legal advice would not necessarily be discarded by the family court in favour of better terms later.

The court would set the agreement aside if one of the parties was bullied or tricked into making it, and would be reluctant to uphold it if no independent professional advice was taken.

None the less, if separation agreements have financial terms in them, either party can apply to the High Court or divorce county court to have those altered. The court can use its powers under the Matrimonial Causes Act 1973 (s35) where it is satisfied that there has been a change of circumstances since the agreement was made which makes it in some way less than just.

Agreements which contain money arrangements for children can also be altered if they do not take proper account of the child's needs. Where a separation agreement has *no* financial terms in it, the court can under the same section write terms in if asked to do so.

The advantages of separation agreements are that they do not affect the validity of the marriage: people may need a cooling off period to decide if the marriage is to continue or not, and make sensible arrangements while they do this. They can be useful for people who for some reason do not want to divorce although they intend never to live together again.

The Power of the Courts

Magistrates' Courts

Family proceedings in the magistrates' court are heard in the domestic court whose sittings are not open to the general public. The magistrates must be drawn from a special domestic court panel and usually the hearings are separated from the rest of the court's business.

Proceedings can be brought under the Guardianship of Minors Act 1971 and the Guardianship Act 1973 or under the Domestic Proceedings and Magistrates Courts Act 1978. The 1978 Act mainly covers the same ground as the earlier Acts and most proceedings are now brought under it. The Guardianship of Minors Acts remain in force, however, and are considered separately below as they also cover the High Court and the county court.

The Domestic Proceedings and Magistrates Courts Act covers married couples and is designed to cover the legal consequences of a separation where divorce is not required.

If a married couple separates, either party can apply to the magistrates' court for financial provision under the Act. This can consist of maintenance in the form of periodical payments or of a lump sum payment either to a spouse or to a child. It does not involve divorce or judicial separation proceedings. In deciding whether and how to make an order the court must give first consideration to any child of the family. This includes natural children, adopted children and step-children. The court cannot dismiss an application or make a final order on it without deciding whether it should make a custody or access order in respect of any child of the family.

The court can make a *financial order* against a respondent, that is the person against whom the proceedings have been brought, if he has:

● failed to provide reasonable maintenance for the applicant; or
● failed to provide reasonable maintenance for any child of the family; or

- behaved in such a way that the applicant cannot reasonably be expected to live with him or her; or
- deserted the applicant.

The court can also make an order where the other party agrees to this or where the parties have, by agreement, been apart for a continuous period of at least three months and the respondent has been paying voluntary maintenance.

Under the Act the court can make orders as to who should have the legal custody of any child of the family and orders regarding access. It can do this whether or not it makes financial orders and in making these decisions it must apply the welfare principle.

'Legal custody' means 'so much of the parental rights and duties as relate to the person of the child including the place and manner in which his time is spent.' The court can grant legal custody only to one person so it cannot make orders for joint custody, but it can order that the other party retains 'all or such as the court may specify of the parental rights and duties'. These are held jointly with the person given legal custody. Because this type of custody relates to the person of the child it does not give the person who has it the right to administer the child's assets or property. If a dispute arose over the exercise or interpretation of a right, either party could go back to the court for guidance.

If an order for legal custody is made, the other party can ask for an access order to be made. Also a grandparent can ask for access to a grandchild; this applies whether or not the parents were married.

Under the Act, the magistrates' court has power to make orders prohibiting one spouse from behaving violently towards the other or towards any child of the family. These are known as *personal protection orders*. The court orders the respondent not to use, or threaten to use, violence. The court has to be satisfied that this has happened, and that it is necessary for the protection of the applicant or child that an order be made. The court also has the power to order the respondent to leave the home, or to prohibit him from entering the home, if it is satisfied that he has used or threatened violence and that the applicant or child is in physical danger if he remains or goes back into the home. These are known as *exclusion orders*. If the problem is that the applicant has been put out of the home by the respondent, then an order can be made requiring him to allow her to go back and remain. All these orders can be expedited in emergencies, and can, where there is an imminent danger of physical injury, be granted without the respondent being told in advance about the hearing. The court can attach a power of arrest to an order if satisfied that the respondent has physically injured the applicant or child and that he is likely to do so again. This means that if he breaches the order the police can arrest him immediately and must then bring him before a magistrate within twenty-four hours. He can be committed to prison if the breach is a serious one. If it involved a serious assault it is likely that he would be charged with a criminal offence.

In many ways the magistrates' court is similar to other courts which hear family cases. Disputes between parents can be referred back to court and orders can be varied or revoked. The magistrates can make interim orders before the final hearing. Welfare reports can be requested by the court to help them in their decision-making. Like the county court and the High Court, the magistrates' court can order that a child should not be taken out of the country without the court's permission and it can make a supervision order or a care order if deemed appropriate to do so. However, if the magistrates' court does make a care order it cannot order access.

In simple cases, the magistrates' court has the advantage over other family courts in being quicker in dealing with cases. The procedure is easier to understand as evidence is given orally, there are no sworn written statements (affidavits) and the type of legal aid available (assistance by way of representation) is straightforward and is processed much more quickly than its equivalent for proceedings in the county court or High Court.

Perhaps the main drawback is that the magistrates cannot consider the whole picture in family breakdown since they cannot grant divorces or judicial separations. They can make financial orders but not orders to transfer property or divide family assets. They cannot make joint custody orders; in any event, legal custody does not confer the fuller rights implicit in a custody order made in divorce proceedings. This is why solicitors very often advise that applications be made in other courts even when proceedings are just starting and the orders being sought at that stage fall within the magistrates' powers. As the case progresses other types of orders may well be required which the magistrates cannot consider.

CHANGES UNDER THE NEW LAW

The Children Act 1989 makes important changes to this area of law. It changes the orders which courts can make in respect of the care of children and their financial provision. In future all courts – magistrates', county court and the High Court – will be able to make the same orders. The distinction between the parent with custody of the child and the other parent will be less pronounced.

Both parents will have parental responsibility for their child, and family breakdown will not alter that.

There will be a presumption in favour of making no order unless it is thought to be better for the child to make an order. The range of new orders will be:

- a contact order to replace access
- a residence order to settle the arrangements about who the child should live with
- a specific issue or a prohibited steps order which can be used to settle disputes between the parents.

Anyone who has an interest in the child will be able to apply for an order. This can be used by relatives, including grandparents. The concept of custodianship will be abolished.

The courts will have new powers to make financial provision for children. These will co-exist with the powers under the Matrimonial Causes Act and the Domestic Proceedings and Magistrates Courts Act. The same orders can be made whether a child is born to married or unmarried parents.

Applications Under the Guardianship of Minors Acts

These proceedings are about the guardianship and custody of children. They can be brought in the High Court, the county court or the magistrates' court but are usually brought in the county court. This is because the magistrates' court cannot deal with the property of a child, or grant injunctions, and because the Domestic Proceedings and Magistrates Courts Act (DPMCA) has largely taken over the purpose of these Acts in the magistrates' court. The High Court is used only for unusual and complicated cases. The Acts apply to married and unmarried parents. This section deals with married parents; for unmarried parents, see below.

The court can only make orders concerning the parents' natural or adopted children. It cannot consider 'children of the family' such as step-children; step-fathers and mothers needing a court order can apply in other proceedings, such as wardship or custodianship.

The court must apply the welfare principle. It should have regard to the child's welfare and to the conduct and wishes of the parents, but the child's welfare is the paramount consideration.

Under these Acts, the court can be asked to decide which parent should have legal custody of the child. The definition of 'legal custody' is the same as it is for DPMCA applications, that is those parental rights and duties which pertain to the person of the child. The court cannot award this to more than one person and so it cannot make orders for joint custody. The court can, however, order that the other parent retain all or such as the court may specify of the parental rights and duties (other than the right to actual custody) and that these are held jointly with the parent who has legal custody. Thus if a dispute arose over education or religious upbringing, the court could be asked to decide it.

If the court feels legal custody should not be given to either parent, and that a third party, say a relative, should look after the child, it can make a custodianship order in favour of that person. For details of custodianship, see Chapter 2.

If the court decides that neither parent, or anyone else, is suitable to care for the child, it can make a care order to the local authority. If, when making an order for legal custody, it feels that it is desirable for a supervision order to be made in respect of the child, it can make such an order to the local authority or to the probation service. These care and supervision orders can be varied or discharged later on the application of the parent, the social worker or the probation officer.

The court has the power to award access to the non-custodial parent, and also to grandparents. This is one of the comparatively few rights, specifically written into the law, which grandparents have. It does not apply where the child is in care. An order of this sort can be made where one of the parents is applying for legal custody or access. A grandparent can also apply where one or both of the child's parents are dead.

Orders for legal custody or access cannot be made in respect of children who have been 'freed for adoption'. (This is a preliminary application made before an adoption order. For more details, see Chapter 2.) They end when the child reaches eighteen.

The court can order the parent who does not have custody to pay maintenance in the form of periodical payments or lump sums up to £500 to or for the benefit of the child.

In deciding on financial applications the court must have regard to all the circumstances of the case including:

- the income, earning capacity, property and other financial resources of the parents and of the child
- the needs, obligations and responsibilities of the parents and of the child
- any physical or mental disability from which the child suffers.

Before the final hearing, interim orders for periodical payments can be made, as can interim orders for legal custody or access. After the final hearing, orders for legal custody, access or periodical payments can be varied or discharged by the court on the application of either parent. The court must look at all the circumstances including any changes which have occurred since the original order was made.

The court has the power to make orders preventing parties from doing things in certain situations. It can direct that the child should not be removed from England and Wales without the permission of the court. If an application to take a child out of the jurisdiction, whether permanently or temporarily for a holiday, is opposed by the other parent, then the hearing must normally take place in the High Court.

The High Court and the county court can make injunctions against either parent provided that the central purpose of the proceedings is the custody and upbringing of their child. So, for example, the court could order one parent not to assault the child, or remove the child from the legal custody of the other parent. The court could also order one parent not to assault the other parent provided it was clear from the circumstances that the dispute revolved round the child or was affecting him or her. An example might be where the non-custodial parent was using access visits to the child as an opportunity to harass the other parent, or where distressing and violent rows were taking place in the child's presence. The magistrates' court has no power to make injunctions under these proceedings. Injunctions ordering one parent to leave the family home, 'ouster' injunctions, cannot be made under these Acts.

The procedure in magistrates' courts is similar to that under the DPMCA. Evidence from the parties and their witnesses is given orally, and the hearings take place in the domestic court, not open to the public. Procedure in the High Court and the county court differs in that evidence is usually given by sworn statement (affidavit), although in contested cases it is usual for the principal witnesses with whom the child will be in close contact to give evidence in person as well. As in the magistrates' court, hearings are not open to the public and there are restrictions on the press reporting the cases or giving out specific information. All three courts can request reports from the local authority, the probation service or the court welfare officer to aid them in their decision-making.

The Wardship Jurisdiction of the High Court

Wardship proceedings can begin only in the High Court and most wardship cases remain there, although the High Court can delegate the case to the county court if it considers it to be appropriate to do so. Wardship is an ancient procedure and is based not so much on statute law made by Parliament as on case law made by judges in previous cases.

The effect of making a child a ward of court is that custody passes from the parents to the court itself and remains vested in the court as long as the child is a ward.

In family breakdown, wardship can be used in two situations in particular. First, most family proceedings are geared towards parents applying to the court for orders concerning their children; in wardship anyone can apply provided that he or she can show that they have genuine concerns or reasons for doing so. Second, the High Court has wide powers to protect children and to order that they should not leave the country, or that they should be returned to the country if taken abroad. These can be used in snatching or kidnapping cases.

The welfare principle governs these proceedings; that is the welfare of the child is the first and paramount consideration. Any child under eighteen can be warded provided that the child is a British subject or is resident in the jurisdiction of the court, that is in England or Wales. A child whose parent claims diplomatic immunity cannot be warded, nor can a child who has been refused admission to this country by the immigration authorities. A child who is either already in care, or who is about to be the subject of care proceedings, cannot be warded unless the local authority agree to this or take the proceedings themselves.

Anyone who has a proper interest in the child can start the proceedings. One of the features of these proceedings is that they are not confined to parents. Some examples of people who may wish to ward children about whom they are concerned are step-parents, foster parents, potential adopters, relatives, friends of the family or people professionally involved with the family such as guardians ad litem appointed in care proceedings. Where parents are involved, unmarried parents have the same access to the court as married parents.

The party taking the proceedings, the plaintiff, fills in a form known as an originating summons. A fee, currently £60, is payable. The people against whom the order is sought are made the defendants to the action. Commonly these are the parents or other carers of the child, the local authority if they have been involved, and any other person with a close interest in the child, for example the putative father. In some cases the child is made a party; this might apply where an older child is involved who wishes to express a view about his or her future. The originating summons must state the present whereabouts of the child or that the plaintiff does not know this if that is the case. The child's date of birth must be given and the birth certificate must be filed with the court by the first hearing. The connection of each of the parties with the child must be included, and the form contains a warning that it is a contempt of court to take the child out of England and Wales without the court's leave or permission. In addition the plaintiff has to state what order is being sought, for example that the child should remain a ward of court, and/or that the plaintiff should be granted care and control.

The child becomes a ward immediately, even though none of the other parties has had a chance to put his or her views to the court. The summons can be served on the defendants up to twelve months after it is issued; in practice it is usually served as quickly as possible. Once they receive the court papers the defendants must file a form known as an acknowledgement of service with the court within fourteen days. In this form they notify the court of their opposition or otherwise to the proceedings.

The effect of wardship is to freeze the existing arrangements for the child so that no major change in those arrangements can be made without the court's involvement. So, for example, the child's home must not change, nor must he or she go to live with a different person without the court's prior consent to the move. The child can receive routine medical or dental treatment or emergency treatment without the matter being first referred to the court, but the court must be consulted and give its consent to any other form of treatment, such as seeing a psychiatrist, undergoing an abortion or sterilization.

The plaintiff must arrange the first hearing, known as the first appointment, within twenty-one days of warding the child, even if the hearing itself cannot take place until later. If this is not done the child automatically ceases to be a ward after twenty-one days. In an emergency, a hearing can take place immediately or even before the child has been warded. This might apply where the plaintiff fears that the child is in danger and should be removed from home. The court has the power to make injunctions to protect the child, even against people who are not parties to the action.

In a non-urgent case, the first hearing will be the first appointment before a registrar or official of the court who has the power to make orders with which all the parties are in agreement. In cases of disagreement, the matter will be resolved at a hearing before a judge. The registrar gives directions for the future progress of the case. This is a timetable for the filing of evidence. In wardship proceedings, evidence is put before the court in the form of sworn statements or affidavits made by each of the parties setting out their point of view and saying what order they wish the court to make. At this stage the court can be asked to allow the child to undergo psychiatric treatment, if that is appropriate. In some cases, the court may ask the parents or other potential carers to undergo medical or psychiatric examination so that the court can have the benefit of reports when hearing the case.

If the case is contested, the full hearing will take place later before a judge.

Some cases proceed with all the parties in agreement, and there is a series of hearings before the registrar with no need for a full hearing.

The High Court has significant powers. As mentioned above, the court can make injunctions to protect the child against anybody, whether they are a party to the proceedings or not. In emergencies applications can be made ex parte, that is without informing the other parties in advance. There is always a judge available to deal with out-of-hours emergencies, and he or she is contacted by telephoning the High Court.

As long as the child remains a ward, custody remains with the High Court. The court can make orders as to care and control. The person granted care and control has day-to-day care of the child and the rights associated with this subject to the court's direction and supervision. The court should be kept up-to-date with the child's progress, but day-to-day decisions, such as necessary medical treatment, should not need to be referred to the court. The court can grant care and control to two persons jointly, for example both parents where there is no dispute between them. The court can be asked for permission for the child to be known by a different surname. This might be appropriate where care and control is granted to foster parents. The court would be unlikely to agree to this unless rehabilitation with the natural family seemed out of the question. The child's wishes would be taken into consideration if he or she was of sufficient age and understanding. One of the situations in which wardship can be particularly useful is where parents and child are to be reunited, but gradually rather than immediately. The court can order a phased rehabilitation and supervise its progress via a series of hearings before the registrar. In this way, care and control can be transferred gradually.

The court can order access if it believes it to be beneficial for the child to maintain contact with a party who does not have care and control. This person need not necessarily be one of the child's parents. The details of access are usually left to the parties to arrange but where agreement proves impossible the court can define the arrangements and it can order that access should be supervised if it feels that the child needs such a safeguard.

The court can order either parent of a ward to pay maintenance for the child, but an important, and surprising, gap in the court's powers is that it cannot require a parent to pay maintenance for his or her illegitimate child.

The court can decide how a child should be educated, and in which religion, if any, he or she should be brought up.

As under the Guardianship of Minors Acts, the court can make a care order or a supervision order. A care order would be made where the court did not believe it to be in the child's interests to be brought up by any of the parties. A supervision order would be made where the court felt that care and control could safely be committed to one of the parties, but wished the local authority to oversee the situation. Both orders can be varied or discharged on the application of any of the parties. A care order in wardship is a very different animal to a care order made by the juvenile court under the CYPA. In a wardship care order the court ultimately retains control and the actions and decisions of the local authority can be challenged by the parties asking for the court's directions. So, for example, a parent dissatisfied with access to their child in care in wardship could apply to court, a right which they would not have otherwise.

Breach of an order made in wardship is punishable as a contempt of court, and can lead to a fine or even imprisonment. Wardship proceedings are held in private and it is contempt to publish information relating to them. Other matters which can be contempt are: showing the court papers to someone who is not involved in the case without first obtaining the court's permission; concealing a ward's whereabouts from the court; removing a ward from the country without consent; referring a ward for psychiatric examination without consent; or any important step in the ward's life which is taken without the court's leave.

Before custodianship was brought in, wardship was the main way in which a non-parent could make an application to a court about a child. (For details on custodianship, see Chapter 2.) Now that it has been introduced, it will be a more applicable remedy for some people in this situation. It is only available, however, for people with whom the child has been living and so for those who fall outside this category, wardship will continue to be useful.

WARDSHIP IN KIDNAPPING CASES

In family breakdown, wardship is often used where a child either has been or may be snatched or kidnapped. It is possible, however, that parents may use it less often because of the alternative remedies provided by the Child Abduction Act 1984 (of which more later) and because the magistrates' court and the county court have power to direct that a child should not be taken out of the country except with the leave of the court (under the DPMCA 1978 and the GMA 1971). Furthermore, a custody order under the Matrimonial Causes Act 1973 normally includes such a provision. However, in cases which are unusual or complicated, wardship should be used because the High Court has wide powers and has more resources at its disposal for the enforcement of orders and the tracing of missing children.

324 A Parents' Guide to the Law

It is a contempt of court to take a ward out of England and Wales without the court's leave. The court can be asked to make an injunction restraining such a removal. If the ward has a British passport, or is included on a British passport held by someone else, then the court can order it to be surrendered and can notify the Passport Office not to issue a replacement. Whether or not the child has his or her own, or is included on someone else's passport, the police can be asked to institute a 'port-alert'. If the child is under sixteen, it is not necessary to obtain a court order or even ward the child first. Port-alerts are arranged by the police under the Child Abduction Act 1984. This makes it an offence for a parent, guardian or person awarded custody to take or send the child out of the UK without the consent of the other parent, guardian or person awarded custody, or without the court's leave. If the child is aged between sixteen and eighteen and a port-alert is required, then you must obtain an order to restrict or restrain removal or an order which gives you custody.

If there is an order in force, of if the child is a ward, then the order must be produced to the police. A request to the police for assistance should be made to the local police station or to any police station in an emergency. The police should then pass on information about children at risk of removal to the immigration officers at ports and airports. The police will need full descriptions of the child or children and of the person who is likely to remove them, details of the likely destination, the reasons why removal is suspected, and full details of the person whom they should contact if they prevent a removal.

In a situation where a child has been taken, the police can be asked to assist by investigating the removal as a criminal offence, and by instituting a port-alert. The powers of the wardship court can also be invoked if the child is already a ward, or by warding the child as soon as possible. Parties to wardship are required to state the whereabouts of the ward, and the court can order any person who may have information on this to attend a hearing and give evidence. A search warrant can be issued enabling the police to look for the child, and the court's own enforcement officers, known as the tipstaff, can assist in the search.

The High Court has formal arrangements with some government departments, such as the DSS, which enable records that are normally private to be searched in the hope of tracing a missing ward. This could cover records of claims made for welfare benefits.

Normally wardship hearings take place in private but where a ward is missing presumed snatched or kidnapped, the court can adjourn for the press to attend so that the matter can be publicized and a photograph of the child is usually made available to the press.

The High Court can make an order that the person who has removed the child should return him or her, and if this is not done a warrant for the arrest of the kidnapper for contempt of court can be issued. The practical problem facing a parent trying to retrieve his or her child from abroad is, what happens if the kidnapper simply ignores the court orders and warrants; how are they enforced?

It depends on which country they have been removed to. Certain countries have signed conventions and treaties under the Child Abduction and Custody Act 1985. These countries agree to abide by and enforce one another's custody and wardship orders. Some examples of signatory countries are France, Australia and Canada. In this situation the parent seeking the return of the child contacts the Lord Chancellor's Department (LCD) in this country which deals with enforcement. Legal aid is available and the LCD will appoint a solicitor to act from a special panel. The problem is that the vast majority of countries are not signatories. In this situation, all a parent can do is to take proceedings in the country in question. This can be hazardous and expensive. Usually legal aid or its equivalent is not available and the prevailing laws may be on the side of the kidnapper. For example, in some Islamic countries a mother has few rights concerning her children. It is best to contact the Foreign and Commonwealth Office which can supplement advice given by solicitors. There are also self-help groups which may be able to provide advice and moral support (see pp. 404–5).

Where a kidnapped child is brought to the UK having been removed from the person having custody or care abroad, the child can be made a ward of court. The court will then decide whether to hear the case in full or to order that the child should be returned immediately. If there is a foreign court order in force and the child has been brought from a country which is a signatory under the Child Abduction and Custody Act, then it is likely that the court will order an immediate return. In any case, the over-riding consideration is the welfare of the child, although the existence of a foreign court order will obviously be a consideration. The courts have in the past recognized that such cases should be resolved as quickly as possible in the interests of children who may be suffering from the disruption caused by their abduction at a time when they are already suffering the effects of family breakdown. If the party from whom the child has been abducted seeks their return, then generally speaking it is for that party to show that an immediate return is in the child's best interests. The court is concerned with what is best for the child, not with penalizing the kidnapper. Both parties' conduct is, however, one of the factors to be taken into account.

Child abduction can, of course, take place within the UK, but an abducting parent cannot remove a child from one part of the UK to another in order to avoid compliance with custody proceedings or in order to start new proceedings. The Family Law Act 1986 provides that a custody order made in one part of the UK in respect of a child under sixteen is recognized and can be enforced in other parts of the UK. Courts will be able to enforce orders by ordering the disclosure of a child's whereabouts; ordering a child's recovery when that child has not been given up in accordance with a custody order; and ordering the surrender of a passport, either issued to a child, or containing particulars of him or her where the child's removal from the UK has been prohibited.

So far we have dealt with situations of abduction and kidnapping. If one of the parties to wardship proceedings wishes to remove the ward from England and Wales lawfully, then the correct way to go about it is to seek leave from the court. If the application is for permanent removal and it is opposed by any of the other parties, then the court decides in the light of all the circumstances, the child's welfare being the first and paramount consideration. The court must also decide, if the removal is to be permanent, whether wardship should continue or be discharged. It is likely to be discharged where the ward was brought to this country having been kidnapped from another country, and the court orders the child's return. Where the child will continue to have a substantial link with this country, for example through access, the court is likely to continue wardship. The court can require the party granted leave to give an undertaking to return the child, and can insist on security for this by way of a financial bond whereby money is deposited, and forfeited if the undertaking is not complied with.

Applications for leave to remove the child temporarily from the country, usually for a holiday, are likely to be granted provided the court is satisfied that the child will be returned. The party applying can be asked to give an undertaking, or lodge a bond in extreme situations. The court can give general leave so that a special application for each trip is unnecessary. In this situation, the party with general leave lodges with the court before each trip a written consent from the other parties, details of the departure date, the length of the stay, the address abroad and a written undertaking to return the child at the end of the trip. If any of the other parties does not consent then an application for special leave must be made. All applications for leave to take a ward out of the country can be made to the registrar if they are unopposed; they are made to a judge if they are opposed.

CHANGES UNDER THE NEW LAW

The Children Act 1989 will make some changes relevant to this area of the law.
Some of the wide and specific powers which have hitherto been available only

to the High Court will be available to all courts dealing with family law. There will be new orders known as specific issue orders and prohibited steps orders which could be used to clarify the situation with regard to the removal of children from the person with whom they reside.

The general position will be that the written consent of each person who has parental responsibility, or the leave of the court, will be required before a child who is the subject of a residence order can be taken out of the UK. This will not usually apply if the person with the residence order removes the child for less than a month, but the court can make an order prohibiting even this.

Residence, contact, specific issue and prohibited steps orders will collectively be known as section 8 orders, after the section of the Act in which they are covered. Where a person fails to give up a child in breach of a section 8 order, the court may authorize an officer of the court or a police officer to take charge of the child and take him or her to the person in whose favour the order was made. The officer is authorized to enter and search premises where the child is believed to be and to use necessary force to enforce the order.

In addition, where a person breaches a residence order by keeping the child away from the person with whom he or she is to live under the order, proceedings for contempt of court can be brought against them.

The Unmarried Family

A child is 'illegitimate' if at the time of birth his or her parents were not married to one another. There are exceptions to this, for example a child may have been conceived after his or her parents got married but the marriage may have ended by the time of the birth, either through divorce or the death of the father. A child in either of those situations would be legitimate. If parents marry after the birth of their child, the child is legitimated by the marriage.

'Illegitimate' is now the old-fashioned term and the preferred term now for children born to single mothers is 'non-marital'. The Family Law Reform Act (FLRA) of 1987 was passed to abolish most forms of legal discrimination faced by non-marital children, in recognition that no social stigma should be attached to this situation. Increasingly, from a legal point of view, the differences between marital and non-marital children are disappearing.

The mother of a non-marital child has all of the parental rights and duties exclusively. Obviously single mothers can and do treat the fathers of their children as being equal partners in parenthood, but this gives no extra legal rights to the father which they could enforce or which the courts would recognize.

If she dies her rights and duties die with her – but she can ensure the father then has some legal rights and status by appointing him the testamentary guardian of the child by deed or in her will.

Custody and Access

If during the mother's lifetime a father wishes to acquire parental rights and duties he must apply for a court order under the Family Law Reform Act 1987 as these will not automatically be conferred.

Before the court can make an order in favour of the father they must decide that he is the father. If the mother disputes this, blood tests can be used to prove paternity or DNA fingerprinting. If the mother refuses to provide a sample herself or to give her consent to a sample being taken from her child, then inferences can be drawn from her refusal, unless there is a good reason for it.

Under the Family Law Reform Act an unmarried father can apply to the court to share parental rights and duties with the mother. Cohabiting couples will be able to apply together for such an order by agreement.

Fathers can apply for an order where the mother has died without appointing a guardian. If a couple separates, the father will be able to apply for full parental rights. Broadly, an unmarried father can use the court's powers to place himself in the same position as married fathers are automatically.

At present, an unmarried father cannot apply for access to his child in care. The Act does not alter this. This is because he is excluded from the definition of a 'parent' contained in the Child Care Act 1980 and the FLRA 1987 did not remedy this. Nor did this Act change the absurd situation whereby a natural father is allowed to apply for custody of his child in care but the judge is obliged to turn his application down.

These situations will be changed as part of the Children Act 1989.

Maintenance for Non-marital Children

The Family Law Reform Act 1987 provides that applications for maintenance can be heard in the magistrates' court, the county court or the High Court.

The effect is that non-marital children are in the same position as marital children for the purposes of maintenance.

The court hears the case in private. If the alleged father agrees that he is the father, then that proves paternity. If, however, he disputes paternity, then the mother must prove this, normally by giving evidence herself. This is given verbally in the witness box. Her evidence is not enough on its own, it must be corroborated. This could, for example, be evidence from some other person that the couple were cohabiting or sleeping together at the time of the child's conception, or it could be scientific evidence provided by blood tests.

The blood tests presently used in court proceedings cannot prove conclusively that a man is the father, but they can establish conclusively that he is not. It is usually possible for the testers, analysing samples from the mother, the child and the alleged father, to determine the blood group characteristics. The frequency of these occurring is expressed as a percentage of the general population. If the alleged father belongs to a small percentage blood group, then the court is likely to decide on a balance of probabilities that he is the father.

The court can direct that tests take place but it cannot force the man to provide a sample. If he does not, then it is perfectly proper for the court to assume from this reluctance that he has something to hide; in such a case it can take his refusal as corroboration of the mother's evidence that he is the father.

New tests have been developed known as DNA genetic fingerprinting. These tests are very sophisticated genetic tests and can positively establish parentage rather than just exclude it.

If paternity is proved, the court can order the father to pay maintenance for the child by periodical payments – that is, regular instalments – and/or a lump sum. This lump sum for the child could be paid to cover expenses already incurred by the mother in connection with the birth and providing for the child, as well as a sum for the future.

Orders usually last until the child reaches the birthday following attainment of the school-leaving age. At the moment, this is the seventeenth birthday. The order can be extended even after the age of eighteen if the child is receiving education or training or there are special circumstances.

In deciding the level of maintenance, the court must take account of all the circumstances, particularly the income, earning capacity, property and other financial resources of the parents, their present and future financial needs, obligations and responsibilities. Financial resources include entitlement to state benefits. It must also consider the child's financial needs and resources, and any mental or physical disability from which he or she may suffer.

Payments are made to court which then forwards them to the mother. If the father fails to pay the maintenance or gets behind with the payments, the order can be enforced through the court.

Before the 1988 budget which took away tax relief from new maintenance orders, it made financial sense for natural fathers to pay for the upkeep of their children

under a court order. Some cohabiting couples used this provision to advantage.
Now, unfortunately, new maintenance payments do not attract tax relief.

Wardship

The powers of the High Court in wardship proceedings can also be invoked by
unmarried parents. This is dealt with in detail on pp. 319–23 of this chapter.

CHANGES UNDER THE NEW LAW

The Children Act 1989 makes sweeping changes to the law regarding the
children of unmarried parents.

Parental responsibility automatically vests in the mother but the father can
acquire it by making an application to the court or by making an agreement with
the mother. Regulations are expected to be announced covering the form of such
agreements.

The Children Act will supersede the Family Law Reform Act and will
recognize orders made in favour of fathers under its provisions.

The courts will be able to make the same financial orders for non-marital
children as for marital children.

Violence

Injunctions can be applied for by unmarried parents who need to protect their
children, and themselves, from violence on the part of the other parent.

If the couple are not living together then the application can be made in the
county court or the High Court under the GMA (see p. 317.)

If the couple have been cohabiting then a different provision is applicable.
The Domestic Violence and Matrimonial Proceedings Act 1976 can be used by
unmarried couples who have been living together. The Act can also be used by a
married person, even if the couple are separated at the time of the violence. As
the proceedings do not involve divorce, they can be used where the estrangement
may not be permanent, or where it is too early to tell what will happen.

The application is made to the county court. The applicant can ask the court
to make an injunction order against the other party, ordering them not to assault
or threaten the applicant or child. For an order to be made, there has to have
been violence or the threat of it against the applicant or child.

If the couple are living together the court can order that the violent partner be excluded from the couple's home. Where the applicant has left the home because of the violence, the court can order the other party to allow the applicant to re-enter the home and remain there.

The court can attach a power of arrest to any of these orders if the judge is satisfied that the other party has caused actual bodily harm to the applicant or to the child and is likely to do so again. A power of arrest empowers any police officer to arrest the violent partner if he or she breaks the order. The order with the power of arrest must be notified to the police.

This makes enforcement of the order easier and more effective from the applicant's point of view.

Chapter 11

Parents in Trouble

The idea that children have rights of their own distinct from their parents is comparatively new in England and Wales, as is the understanding that children are not the property of their parents and are entitled to society's protection from parental abuse. Similarly, the idea that society itself should not abuse children through economic, sexual or other exploitation is historically recent. It was not until the reforms of the nineteenth century that children as a class were allowed to have much legal or human status independent of their parents and the adult world, nor was the state inclined to interfere with the 'private' nature of family life. For example, the first statute to prevent cruelty to children was not passed until 1879. The position for the children of the rich who were heirs to property was, as ever, different – the courts felt entitled to intercede with the disposition of their property in what later became the wardship jurisdiction.

Society now has adjusted to the idea that it can and must interfere with family life if a child is at risk, and has set up complex mechanisms to protect children from neglect and abuse. These mechanisms can tragically fail to protect children, and can also be exercised inappropriately so that injustice is done to families and children.

Parents' rights do exist – but are far from absolute. Lord Scarman said in the case brought by Mrs Victoria Gillick (see Chapter 12 for more details of this important case) that parents' rights were derived from their duties, and existed only so long as they were needed for the protection of the person and property of the child. Parent's rights must be balanced with the rights of the child and the expectations of society.

This chapter is a summary of the ways in which parents as parents can come into contact with the restrictions and rules of the civil and criminal law.

Offences Connected with Pregnancy and Childbirth

The Criminal Law Relating to Foetuses

Although an unborn child is not a separate legal person at any stage of gestation, there is a considerable body of law concerning the foetus. Abortion is the word used to describe a termination of a pregnancy at any gestational stage.

There are three Acts which deal with this area of law. These are:

- the Offences against the Person Act 1861, which makes illegal abortion an offence
- the Infant Life Preservation Act of 1929, which created the offence of child destruction where an illegal abortion terminates a foetus capable of being born alive
- the Abortion Act of 1967, which legalized abortion when it is performed in certain prescribed circumstances.

There is a vital distinction between these Acts: abortion is legal when it complies with the Abortion Act, but not when it does not and the other two Acts deal with those situations where it is still illegal.

Under the Abortion Act, a termination of pregnancy is legal if two doctors say that pregnancy would put the woman's life or health at risk, or that the injury to her physical or mental health or that of her existing children would be greater than if the pregnancy were terminated; or if there was a substantial risk of the foetus suffering serious handicap.

Under the Act, it is the doctors' decision that counts, and not the woman's choice. The doctors base their decision on their clinical assessment of the woman's health and present, or reasonably foreseeable, circumstances.

There is no gestational time limit referred to in this Act, but there have been attempts in Parliament to introduce one. There are regular attempts to amend abortion law, usually by lowering the time limit (see 'Update', p. xii).

Termination, unless done in an emergency, must take place in an NHS hospital or in a private one approved for performing abortions by the Health Secretary. In an emergency, the doctor performing the operation can dispense with the two-doctor certification but only where the abortion is immediately necessary to save the woman's life or to prevent grave permanent injury to her physical or mental health.

There is a conscientious objection clause for doctors and nurses who do not wish to participate in abortions but in an emergency they have a duty to participate in treatment which is necessary to save a patient's life or to prevent grave permanent injury to her health, whether physical or mental.

ILLEGAL ABORTION AND CHILD DESTRUCTION

If an unborn child is killed it cannot amount to murder or manslaughter. The crimes which cover this situation are: illegal abortion (which is an offence under the Offences against the Person Act 1861) or child destruction (which is contrary to the Infant Life Preservation Act 1929).

Illegal abortion can be committed at any stage of the pregnancy, whereas child destruction can be committed only where the foetus is capable of being born alive. Child destruction is confusingly named; what it actually amounts to is an illegal abortion which takes place when the foetus is capable of being born alive. If the woman is twenty-eight or more weeks pregnant the child is usually regarded as being capable of being born alive, but in the case of a less mature foetus the court would need proof that the child could have been born alive. Foetuses of under twenty-eight weeks show discernible signs of life, but this is not enough – if the medical evidence is that the foetus would be incapable of breathing naturally or without the help of a ventilator, then such a foetus is not capable of being born alive as far as the 1929 Act is concerned.

Although abortion is legal when done in compliance with the Abortion Act, the offences of illegal abortion and child destruction still stand where it has not been complied with and they each carry life imprisonment.

Delivery

The law imposes rules on who can deliver babies. It is an offence for anyone other than a registered midwife or a registered doctor, or a trainee in either profession, to attend a woman while she is giving birth. This does not apply in emergencies, where babies have been known to be delivered by cab drivers and police officers!

This means that a couple cannot choose to do it themselves without professional help. In that situation, the helper rather than the mother would be liable to prosecution.

Concealing the Birth

A mother can be found guilty of the manslaughter of her child if she decides to be alone at the birth in order to conceal it temporarily, and her baby then dies as a result of her negligence (see below).

There is also a separate offence under the Offences against the Person Act of concealing the birth of a child who dies before, at or after its birth by secretly disposing of the body. This crime carries a maximum of two years' imprisonment. A prosecution can be brought against the mother and anyone else involved in concealing the birth. The child has to have reached such a stage of maturity at the time of its birth that it might have been a living child. Merely denying that the birth has taken place does not amount to this offence; there must be an actual and secret disposal of the body.

There are several associated offences.

- It is a crime to dispose of or to destroy a dead body with intent to prevent an inquest being held. This applies where a person dies at any age.
- It is an offence to make a false statement regarding a birth or a death, and this includes the live birth of a child.
- It is against the law to fail to give information regarding a birth or a death when under a statutory duty to do so, for example a mother whose baby has died.

The Killing of Children

'Homicide' is a general term that describes the unlawful killing of a human being. The criminal offence of murder is divided into two parts – a physical and a mental element. The physical element is the unlawful killing of a person who dies within a year and a day of the event that caused the death; the mental element is the intention to cause death or really serious harm.

Manslaughter is committed where death results from an unlawful application of violence which is not accompanied by an intention to kill or to cause really serious harm. The violence could be committed negligently or without thought for the consequences. Manslaughter can also be brought in by a jury as an alternative verdict to murder where a person accused of murder can show that he or she was provoked into committing the violent act that resulted in death.

Similarly, if a person accused of murder argues that they acted in self-defence, if the prosecution can show that the force used was not commensurate with the threat faced, then the jury can convict of murder, but manslaughter is more likely.

Infanticide

This is a particular form of homicide applicable to women who have recently had babies. It is the unlawful killing of a child under the age of twelve months by the mother. The unlawful killing of a child of any age by anyone else would be murder or manslaughter depending on the circumstances. Infanticide is the equivalent of manslaughter which does not carry mandatory imprisonment for life as murder always does. It often results in a prison sentence of five years, sometimes less and occasionally a non-custodial sentence. Infanticide can either be a defence to a murder charge, or a charge on its own. The rationale for this charge is that a woman may be suffering from the effects of giving birth or breast-feeding a child, so that the balance of her mind is disturbed. In those circumstances it would be grossly inhumane to convict of murder.

Murder and Manslaughter

If a child is born alive, but dies as a result of substances or injuries that it received in the womb, it may be murder by the person who administered them.

Furthermore, if a person, intending to procure an abortion, does something which causes a child to be born so prematurely that it cannot survive and it dies because it was born too soon, the person who causes it to be born prematurely and puts it into a situation where it cannot live is guilty of murder.

A mother can be guilty of murder if she decides that she wishes her child to die and after it is born she leaves it to die. This would not necessarily be infanticide – it would be up to the jury to assess whether the woman was disturbed by the effects of childbirth or nursing a child. She can also be guilty if she resolves to conceal the birth by methods which will probably end in its death and they do so. She can in this situation be found guilty of murder even though she had no intention to murder her child.

She would be guilty of manslaughter if she decided to be alone at the birth because she wished temporarily to conceal the birth and the child died as a result of her negligence. This applies even if she has no intention to kill the child.

A mother cannot, however, be convicted either of murder or manslaughter simply because near the time of delivery she deliberately abstains from taking the necessary precautions to preserve the life of her child after its birth and it dies as a result. The rationale for this is that she must be guilty of negligence towards the child after it was born.

If a baby is fatally and deliberately injured while it is being born, this may be murder if the child is born alive and dies of the wound.

For a person to be prosecuted for the murder or manslaughter of a newborn baby, it is necessary to show that the child has been fully born and it must be breathing and its blood circulating independently. It must be functioning independently and not through its mother's body, though it can still be connected to its mother by the umbilical cord.

Assorted Offences

The Children and Young Persons Act 1933 contains a litany of unusual offences which it is possible for adults to commit in relation to children. Although the numbers of prosecutions for these offences are small, nevertheless they remain on the statute book and can be invoked.

ALLOWING PEOPLE UNDER SIXTEEN TO BE IN BROTHELS

It is an offence for a person who has the custody, charge or care of a child or a young person between the ages of four and sixteen to allow him or her to reside in or to frequent a brothel. The penalty is a fine or up to six months' imprisonment.

CAUSING OR ALLOWING PERSONS UNDER SIXTEEN TO BE USED FOR BEGGING

This includes busking for money. It carries a fine or up to three months in prison.

GIVING INTOXICATING LIQUOR TO CHILDREN UNDER FIVE

This is an offence carrying a fine unless it is done under doctor's orders or in an emergency, including where the child is ill. This would presumably cover giving brandy for shock or purely medicinal purposes.

SELLING TOBACCO TO UNDER-SIXTEENS

It is an offence to sell tobacco to people who appear to be under the age of sixteen, and it carries a fine. If a cigarette machine is used extensively by under-sixteens then the owner of the vending machine or of the premises can be ordered to prevent it being used by them or to remove it. A police officer or a park-keeper, in uniform, is under a duty to seize any tobacco or cigarette papers from someone who appears to be under sixteen and can dispose of them.

TAKING PAWNS FROM UNDER-FOURTEENS

It is an offence, punishable by a fine, for a pawnbroker to take an article in pawn from a person who appears to be under fourteen.

VAGRANTS PREVENTING CHILDREN FROM RECEIVING EDUCATION

This offence defines a vagrant as someone who habitually wanders from place to place. This is a wide definition and could include gypsies or travellers. It is an offence for such a person to take with him or her a child who is over five but under school-leaving age and to fail to ensure that the child or young person receives efficient full-time education suitable to his or her age, ability and aptitude. This need not mean school (see Chapter 4 for details of education other than at school). Only an education authority can bring this charge against a person. They will in practice be likely to liaise with social services as to whether care proceedings should be brought (see Chapter 9).

EXPOSING CHILDREN UNDER TWELVE TO THE RISK OF BURNING

A person of sixteen or over who has the custody, charge or care of a child under twelve is committing an offence punishable with a fine if he or she allows the child to be in a room containing a fire or any other sort of heating appliance *and* the child is killed or suffers serious injury because the person has not taken reasonable precautions against the risk of the child being burnt or scalded. The person concerned could also be prosecuted for an offence under section 1 of the Children and Young Persons Act (see below) which is a more serious offence.

FAILING TO PROVIDE FOR THE SAFETY OF CHILDREN AT ENTERTAINMENTS

Where entertainments are provided for children in a building and the number of children attending is more than 100, there is a duty on the person providing the entertainment to station wherever necessary a sufficient number of adult attendants, who are properly instructed, to prevent more people, including children, from being admitted than the building can properly accommodate.

The attendants must control the movements of those attending while entering and leaving the building and take all other reasonable precautions for the children's safety.

Failure to comply is punishable with a fine, and if the building is licensed it can be revoked. A police officer or a local authority official can enter to see that these provisions are being obeyed. None of this applies to any entertainment given in a private house, for example a children's party.

Neglect as a Criminal Offence

Neglect is both a criminal offence and a ground for care proceedings. For details of care proceedings, see Chapter 9. This section deals with neglect as a crime.

Section 1 of the Children and Young Persons Act 1933 makes it an offence for anyone over the age of sixteen who has the custody, charge or care of a child under sixteen to assault, ill-treat, neglect, abandon or expose the child. This offence tends to be referred to as cruelty. In all these instances, the treatment must be wilful, that is, intentional. The treatment has to be in a manner likely to cause the child unnecessary suffering or injury to health (including injury to or loss of sight or hearing, or limb or organ of the body, and any mental derangement). It is also a crime if a person causes or procures another to assault, ill-treat, neglect, etcetera. the child.

The offence can be committed by anyone who is the parent or guardian of a child or who is legally liable to maintain him or her. Equally, it can be committed by anyone into whose care a child is committed by the person who has custody, or anyone who has actual possession or control of a child.

The sentence for this crime can be up to six months' imprisonment if the matter is dealt with by a magistrates' court, or up to ten years' imprisonment in the crown court. The length of the sentence will depend on the actual injuries and the circumstances in which they occur. What might be described as deliberate wickedness on the part of a parent will be dealt with more severely than family disasters where parents cannot cope or are out of their depth, sometimes against a background of unemployment or inadequate housing.

A parent can be found guilty of neglect if he or she fails to provide adequate food, clothing, medical aid or lodging for the child; or fails to obtain it for the child from some other person or body, for example, social services. It is also specified to be neglect if an infant under three suffocates while in bed with a person over sixteen who has been drinking.

A child does not actually have to be harmed for an offence to have been committed. It is the likelihood that it could have happened which is important. So there can still be a prosecution if someone intervenes to protect the child. Equally there can still be a prosecution for cruelty if the victim dies, whether or not there is sufficient evidence to charge the defendant with murder or manslaughter as well.

The Act says that nothing in the section referring to this crime should be construed as affecting the right of a parent or a teacher or any other person having the lawful control or charge of a child to administer punishment. The legal textbooks are full of gruesome Victorian cases of fathers and school masters beating pathetic children to death and then seeking to justify their behaviour by saying that it was punishment for misbehaving or for stealing. Chastisement must, however, be reasonable and appropriate. See Chapter 12 for parents and punishment, and Chapter 4 for teachers and punishment.

It is unlikely that parents would be prosecuted for failing to call medical assistance for their child unless they should have realized that the child needed medical help or unless they were reckless as to whether or not it was needed. For neglect to be proved on the ground of failing to provide medical aid the court must be satisfied that the child did need medical aid *and* the parent was aware that the child's health would be at risk if it was not provided or the parent's unawareness was due to his or her not caring whether or not the child's health was at risk. It has been held to be wilful ill-treatment for a child to be put to bed after a fall without receiving medical attention or treatment.

Refusing to allow an operation to be performed has been held by a court to amount to neglect if the circumstances are such as to make the refusal unreasonable. Neglect can be deemed even if medical aid is not supplied because of religious objections.

Abandonment means leaving a child to his or her fate, for example a father was convicted for leaving his children in the house alone after phoning the NSPCC, but a father was acquitted after leaving his five children at a juvenile court on the basis that this was not likely to cause them unnecessary suffering or injury to health. A father was acquitted of wilful exposure when he exposed his eight-year-old son and five other boys to risk by taking them on to a baulk of timber on a disused section of the London docks and punted them in deep water. None of them was harmed.

Parents who are jointly charged with a crime under this law are in one way in a different position from other co-defendants – one parent may have a duty to intervene in the ill-treatment of their child by the other whereas a stranger would have no such duty in law. Normally to prove a crime against 'passive' co-defendants, the prosecution must show that the person aided or assisted in the commission of the crime by the other. If a man and a woman are jointly charged with neglect, the man can be found guilty even if he was not the prime mover in the offence if he saw what was going on.

There is under the Offences Against the Person Act 1861 an offence of abandoning or exposing an infant under the age of two so that its life is endangered or its health is, or is likely to have been, permanently injured. It carries up to five years' imprisonment. Although this offence is still on the statute book, it is rarely used because it has largely been superseded by section 1 of the 1933 Children and Young Persons Act described above.

Assault and Battery

The offences of ill-treatment and cruelty contained in section 1 of the Children and Young Persons Act 1933 apply only where the victim is under sixteen. If a young person over the age of sixteen is injured by a parent or by anybody else then a charge may be brought against the perpetrator under the Offences against the Person Act 1861.

An *assault* can mean an act by which a person intentionally or recklessly applies unlawful force against another – however slight the force. It can also include a situation where a person intentionally or recklessly causes the victim to fear immediate unlawful personal violence or actually to sustain such unlawful personal violence. So an assault includes a situation where someone strikes out but misses, or throws something but misses, or simply points a weapon when the victim is within reach of it, or does any other act indicating an intention to use violence against another person. There must be some hostile act to constitute an assault; a threat or a gesture which could be taken as a threat or a compulsion. Words on their own are not enough for this charge.

Battery is the actual application, whether intentionally or recklessly, of unlawful force, however slight, to another. It includes beating and wounding, but also any kind of touching, however trifling, done in an angry, rude or hostile way. The fundamental principle is that every person's body is inviolate. There are, however, exceptions to this high-sounding rule. Some are clearly a matter of common-sense, such as jostling in crowded places, and touching a person to engage his or her attention; whereas other exceptions are more contentious, such as smacking children to correct them. The physical punishment of children must be reasonable and moderate in the manner, instrument and quantity of it to amount to a defence to assault (see Chapter 12).

Within the law of assault there are different offences to deal with the degree and severity of the violence inflicted.

These start with *common assault* which is defined as unlawfully assaulting or beating a person. It carries a fine, but if the victim is a woman or a girl of any age, or a boy under fourteen, and the magistrates take the view that the offence cannot be sufficiently punished by a fine, they can imprison for up to six months or pass an increased fine.

The next most serious assault is that which causes *actual bodily harm* (ABH). As its name implies, this type of assault must involve some actual bodily injury. It need not be either permanent or serious; nor does it need to be physical – an assault which causes a hysterical and nervous condition is one which causes ABH. It carries up to five years' imprisonment.

The most serious type of assault results in *grievous bodily harm* (GBH). Within this category there are two offences – *unlawful wounding*, and the more serious offence of *wounding with intent*. Grievous bodily harm means really serious bodily injury, but it need not be permanent or dangerous. The wound can be of any sort but the skin must be broken. So a kick with a shoe might result in GBH if the skin is broken. *Wounding with intent*, the more serious of the two offences, means deliberately causing GBH, and it can carry life imprisonment. *Unlawful wounding* is the less serious offence. It also involves causing GBH but without intent to do so. However, the wounding must have been malicious. Confusingly, this does not mean that the assailant must have felt spite or ill-feeling towards the victim, but that he or she must have recognized that their unlawful conduct was likely to subject the victim to risk of harm. The offence carries up to five years' imprisonment.

Child Sexual Abuse

In their guidance to doctors on diagnosis, the Department of Health defined child sexual abuse thus:

> The involvement of dependent, developmentally immature children and ado-
> lescents in sexual activities they do not truly comprehend, to which they are
> unable to give informed consent; or which violate social taboos of family roles.

Sexual abuse tends to be thought of as vaginal or anal penetration, but in fact it encompasses all those activities in which children 'are used for the sexual gratification of older people'. This does include vaginal and anal intercourse and attempts at these types of intercourse, but it also includes oral intercourse, the introduction of objects or fingers in the anal or vaginal orifices, the fondling of genitalia and the involvement of children in pornography.

All of these activities amount to criminal offences; they vary in the degree of seriousness and this is reflected in the differing sentences which they carry. Nowadays, most types of child sexual abuse are taken very seriously by courts and custodial sentences can be expected.

In terms of seriousness, rape, buggery and incest are at the top end of the scale.

Rape is vaginal intercourse without the victim's consent. The lack of consent must always be proved even where the victim is under sixteen (this being the age at which a girl can legally consent to sexual intercourse). Strangely, when a rape charge is being tried by a court, it is not automatically assumed that a girl under that age cannot consent. It depends on the circumstances. The prosecution must prove either that she physically resisted or if she did not that her understanding and knowledge were such that she was not in a position to decide whether to consent or resist. Where the victim is quite young, in practice the prosecution need not prove much more than her age. There is another offence of unlawful sexual intercourse with a girl under sixteen. With this offence, it is immaterial whether or not she consents. A man who commits the offence of having sexual intercourse with a girl under thirteen can face life imprisonment. Again it is immaterial whether or not she consented.

In the case of *buggery*, however, the issue of consent is treated differently. Buggery is anal intercourse without the victim's consent where the victim is over the age of twenty-one; if the victim is under twenty-one it is still an offence even if the victim consented to it. This is because the activity of buggery is illegal unless it takes place in private between consenting adults over the age of twenty-one. The victim can be male or female.

Incest is committed when a man or a woman has sexual intercourse with a close family member. In the case of a man, with his daughter, granddaughter, sister or mother: in the case of a woman, with her father, grandfather, brother or son.

Moving down the scale of seriousness, there are the offences of indecent assault and indecency with children. *Indecent assault* can be committed by a person of either sex on a victim of either sex. A boy or a girl under sixteen cannot in law give consent which would prevent an act being an indecent assault. This offence covers activity such as inappropriately touching or fondling a child, penetrating the vagina or anus with an object or a finger, or oral intercourse where the older person is the perpetrator rather than the recipient. There must be an element of indecency in the behaviour and the application of unlawful force however slight, for example touching.

Indecency with children covers acts of gross indecency with or towards children under fourteen. This is used in practice where there has been inappropriate touching or masturbation, including situations where the older person has invited contact and passively allowed the child to continue. In such a situation it is arguable that there is no indecent assault but the behaviour would be covered by this offence.

DIAGNOSIS

Child sexual abuse is obviously a very difficult and delicate area. Diagnosis is still a very inexact science, and it is usually impossible to make confident and categoric pronouncements as to what has or has not happened. The main 'witness' for the prosecution may be too young to give reliable evidence, or may simply deny that there has been sexual abuse. That cannot and should not be the end of the matter – a parent occupies an immensely powerful position in the life of his or her child, and the child often has an overwhelming desire to please the parent. Accurate diagnosis is further hindered by the frequent absence of corroborative evidence of a medical or any other nature. There are important issues of child protection at stake on the one hand, and equally vital issues of justice and liberty of the subject at stake on the other hand.

Because child sexual abuse is a wide area when properly defined in all its manifestations, there are bound to be difficulties in future for the social services and the NSPCC in trying to sort out genuine cases which merit investigation from those where innocuous behaviour has been wrongly and suspiciously interpreted. Reports of abuse are increasing all the time and the NSPCC now receive substantially more allegations of sexual abuse than ever before.

There is a thin line between what might be described as 'minor' sexual abuse – inappropriate touching – and the perfectly natural, affectionate and often very sensual horseplay which takes place in families. Behaviour can easily be misinterpreted.

This whole area has been the subject of publicity because of events in Cleveland where a surprisingly large number of children were diagnosed as the victims of sexual abuse, and were removed from home and taken into care. The social services department were relying on the evidence of paediatricians using a procedure called the 'anal dilatation test' to achieve their diagnoses. Following press reports and the involvement of a local MP, a judicial inquiry was set up. In subsequent court hearings relating to the children some have been allowed home.

There is widespread controversy in the medical world about the reliability and value of this test. Done properly it consists of examination of the anal region by separating the buttocks and by the introduction of two or more fingers by the examining doctor into the subject's anus. The subject may be asked to 'squeeze down' on to the fingers. Some doctors believe that certain reactions by the subject can indicate that he or she has been subjected to anal intercourse. These include the relaxation of the muscles around the anus so that it is seen to relax rather than contract when the buttocks are separated, a slight contraction of the anus being the 'normal reaction'. The test's advocates believe that children subjected to buggery learn to relax the anus to lessen the pain involved. The test's critics point out that the anus can relax rather than contract if the subject is doing his or her best to co-operate with the examining doctor; or has had previous examinations of this type; or has been using enemas or suppositories; or is constipated. Furthermore, if the test is not done properly, that is gently, any force used in separating the buttocks can produce an appearance of dilatation.

Sometimes soreness and splits around the anal area, diarrhoea and constipation are suggested to be further symptoms indicating that a child has been penetrated. Obviously there can be other explanations for these symptoms, such as poor hygiene or bowel problems causing irritation and scratching in that area.

All these indications can be found in cases of anal penetration but the test in isolation may not be reliable. There should be other abnormal physical signs such as thickening of the skin on the verge of the anus, a reduction in the skin folds around the anus, a change in the skin pigmentation, increased stretch in the muscles, and a marked reduction in the power of the muscles to 'squeeze down'.

Practitioners have found that even when the test is correctly performed, 'positive' results can be found in patients who have not been penetrated or in patients who wish to defecate, and they point out that the test has never been recognized as reliable in the absence of other physical findings.

DEALING WITH CASES OF ABUSE

A system needs to be established whereby serious allegations of child sexual abuse can be properly investigated without subjecting the child and his or her family to numerous examinations and interviews which inevitably invade their privacy. Professionals involved may have to learn to accept that because of its nature this problem is peculiarly difficult to detect and they must face the possibility that there will be some unresolved cases where we will never know what did or did not happen.

Before proceedings which may break up a family are initiated, there could be multidisciplinary involvement so that the case does not merely rest on one, possibly suspect, medical diagnosis. A case conference can be a useful forum for the exchange of information. Social services can seek the views of teachers, nursery staff, health visitors and GPs who know the family and see them at first hand.

In cases where it seems clear that sexual abuse has occurred, alternatives to the removal of the child with all the misery that that entails need to be investigated. One obvious alternative is removal of the alleged abuser rather than the victim. It is important that children are not made to feel that it is their fault that the abuse has occurred and their fault that the family has been split up.

It is planned to reduce the stress and anxiety placed on abused children who must give evidence against their abusers. Already in some cases children have been allowed to give their evidence from behind a screen so as not to encounter the accused, and sometimes judges order that their courts be made less formal by abandoning the wearing of wigs and gowns by barristers and judge, and by having social workers in court to comfort children who become distressed. Arrangements are being made so that children can give their evidence on a live video link so that their evidence could still be tested by cross-examination but in a setting less frightening to the witness, and not in the presence of the alleged abuser. It is possible also that the rules of evidence will be amended so that a child's evidence need not necessarily be corroborated by other evidence in order to be accepted by the court. It may also be possible in future for children to give evidence by pre-recorded video, with an informal hearing involving cross-examination which will also be videotaped.

Pornography Involving Children

It is an offence to:

- take, or allow to be taken, indecent photographs of children
- distribute or show or advertise the sale of photographs of this type
- possess such photographs with a view to distributing or showing them.

This is covered by the Protection of Children Act 1978. A child under this Act is classed as someone under sixteen. The police can apply for a warrant to enter premises, search for and seize this type of material. The court will forfeit it if the case has been proved.

These offences carry up to three years' imprisonment or a fine or both.

It has recently also been made an offence simply to possess such photographs, even if there is no intention to sell them or show them to other people.

Liability to Maintain

Married Couples

FAILURE TO PROVIDE MAINTENANCE

Either party to a marriage can apply to the county court or the magistrates' court for a maintenance order on the ground that the other party to the marriage has failed to provide reasonable maintenance for the applicant, or has failed to provide or make a proper contribution towards reasonable maintenance for any child of the family. This is the case even if the couple are separated to the point of having been granted a decree of judicial separation (see Chapter 10). They must, however, still be married to apply – this legislation is intended to be used where there has been a marital breakdown which falls short of divorce. There is nothing to stop it being used where a couple are still together though such an application would be unusual. The court can, in an emergency, grant interim orders where there has not been enough time to go into everything thoroughly but there is an immediate need.

SOCIAL SECURITY LAW

Social security law also places spouses under a duty to maintain one another and the children of their family.

DIVORCE

Where there is a divorce, the county court or the High Court can make orders regarding ancillary relief, that is orders sorting out money and property which are ancillary to the divorce. Maintenance, for example, can be ordered to be paid to either party to the marriage by the other party and to children of the family. Child maintenance orders usually end when the child becomes an adult or is self-supporting, but spouse maintenance orders last until the recipient remarries or dies. If the recipient cohabits with a new partner, the court may well reduce the maintenance, but it does not end automatically.

Unmarried Couples

MAINTENANCE

Where a couple are not married there is no duty on either of them to maintain the other, but either one of them can be ordered to maintain any child that they may have. Proceedings can be brought in the magistrates' court, the county court or the High Court.

SOCIAL SECURITY LAW

Men and women are under a duty to maintain their children. In the case of a man, he is under a duty only when he has been adjudged to be the putative father of the child in court proceedings. An unmarried couple are not under a duty to support one another but while they live together only one of them can claim income support on behalf of both of them.

Parental Liability

The age of criminal responsibility is ten years old. This means that children of ten or older who commit crimes can be charged and made to appear in the juvenile court. Children who are below the age of ten and who commit crimes cannot be charged.

Vicarious Liability

There is a principle in law under which people are liable to others in negligence even if they themselves did not directly cause the injury. This is called vicarious liability. It is mainly used when someone is employed and in the course of his or her work causes injury to someone else through negligence. It can also be used against parents whose children cause injury while acting on behalf of the parent and carrying out their instructions.

For example, a father sends his fourteen-year-old son to buy paraffin from a local shop. The boy carries this home but drops it by mistake down a manhole where it ignites against a blow-lamp causing injury to a workman. Is the father liable to the workman? If this was a reasonably foreseeable accident then the answer is yes. The father would *not* be liable if his son had for example abandoned the paraffin and gone off somewhere else; or deliberately poured it down the manhole to see what would happen; or taken the route past the road works when advised not to by the father.

Basically, when children and young people are used as agents or 'employees' by their parents, the parents can be liable for the negligent acts they commit.

When a child causes injury to another person when the parent was fundamentally to blame – for example by inadequate supervision or allowing dangerous games to be played – then the parent is liable for their own negligence and lack of foresight.

There is a government proposal, unpublished at the time of writing, to make parents liable to prosecution for failing to prevent their children committing crime. The proposed new offence of failure to prevent child crime would be punishable by fines and would apply only to parents of children up to the age of sixteen. It has been stated that legal action would be taken only where it could be shown that the parent knew or could be reasonably certain that the child was going to commit a crime. A guilty verdict should be returned only where the parent could reasonably have prevented the crime and where a prior formal police caution had been given to the parents about their duties to their children.

This would mark a major departure in English law where it is generally the case that a person cannot be held responsible for someone else's crimes, and it remains to be seen whether the proposal will make it to the statute book, and if it does in what form.

Under existing law it is not possible for a parent or any other adult to use a child under ten to commit crime for them relying on the fact that that child cannot be prosecuted. In that situation the parent would be guilty of using the child as his or her agent and the parent, not the child, would be liable to prosecution.

Fines Ordered Against Children

The liability is the parent's. A juvenile court can order a fine of up to £400 against a fourteen-year-old or older. For an under-fourteen, the maximum is £100. The court will order that the parent need not pay the fine only if he or she cannot be found or if it would be unreasonable for some reason for the parent to pay. An example might be where the child is in care, or living away from home.

Children's Debts

A debt usually arises where someone has contracted to buy goods or services and then does not pay for them. Contrary to popular belief, a contract or agreement can be verbal only, nothing need be in writing. An example would be going into a shop and asking to buy something. Obviously children do this all the time. Often, in practice, there is no difficulty if the child then changes his or her mind.

What happens, though, if a difficulty does arise, perhaps because the goods were expensive and had to be ordered? Is the parent liable to pay for them, is the child, or neither of them?

The simple answer is that a child can sue to enforce a contract but cannot be sued by the other party, because under-eighteen-year-olds are not considered to be fully liable for their actions in making agreements and are deemed to need protection. If the parents are involved in the agreement, however, then it can usually be enforced against them instead of their child.

There is a rather old-fashioned exception to this rule, involving contracts for 'necessaries'. The idea is that a child should be bound by agreements to purchase goods which are necessary to him or her. What is 'necessary'? The cases all involve items such as food, clothing, medicine and educational expenses. None is particularly relevant to today's teenager and in practice this area of law now does not arise very often.

How does this law affect young people? The rule that contracts for non-necessaries can be enforced against the child only if his or her parents were involved in the transaction means that retailers and suppliers often insist on a parent being involved as a guarantor. Credit is rarely available to under-eighteens because of the risk to the lender who cannot enforce payment, so again guarantors are required. This could cause difficulties for under-eighteen-year-olds who wanted to start their own businesses, for example.

Can a Child Sue a Parent?

The answer to this is yes. Indeed, it is quite common for children to sue their parents for damages for injuries sustained in car accidents where the parent was driving the car. In this type of situation, the parent will generally be able to look to their insurance policy to cover them.

In general, there is nothing to stop a child suing a parent through another adult called a 'next friend'. This can be for any kind of legal situation where the parent has been negligent.

Children in Courts

If a parent has to attend court, can he or she take the children too, for example because there is no one else to look after them?

The 1933 Children and Young Persons Act contains a prohibition against children being present in court during criminal proceedings unless they are 'infants in arms', or their presence is required as witnesses. In this context a child means someone under fourteen. Any child present in court when not allowed to be by the Act can be ordered to be removed.

Although the Act says that 'infants in arms' can be in court, it is usual for courts to ask that babies and toddlers be taken out of court because of the difficulty of keeping them quiet! It is rarely possible for the court to provide someone to keep an eye on the child outside the courtroom and so it is best to make alternative arrangements and not to take them to court.

Prisoners' Rights

These are governed by the Prison Rules and by the standing orders made under them. However, on issues such as visits, letters and leave quite a lot of discretion is exercised by individual prison governors. It is therefore advisable to inquire of the prison concerned as to what their arrangements are. We set out below the general position.

Visits

The number of visits which a prison inmate can receive depends upon whether or not he or she has been convicted.

Unconvicted prisoners who have been remanded in custody, that is refused bail, are entitled to have as many visits as they want, although in practice this is unlikely to be more than one a day. Each visit is limited to three adults. In addition, it is usually possible for them to be accompanied by up to two children up to the age of ten or eleven. Children of any age can visit prisoners but they must generally be accompanied by an adult if they are under sixteen. The visits generally last at least half an hour, though the length of the visit is sometimes reduced if there are a lot of visitors. They take place within the sight of a prison officer. The prison governor cannot stop visits by way of a punishment, but if a prisoner is confined to his or her cell as a punishment then visits can be postponed until this has been completed.

Convicted prisoners, that is prisoners who are serving their sentences or waiting to be sentenced by a court, are entitled to far fewer visits. The Prison Rules say that a prisoner is entitled to only one visit every four weeks. In practice however most prisons allow more visits than that, perhaps two a month. The prisoner has to send out to his visitor a visiting order which is their permit to be allowed into the prison. Children of any age are allowed to visit provided that they are accompanied if they are under sixteen, and the same rules apply to the maximum number of visitors allowed on any one visit as for unconvicted prisoners above.

A governor has the power to stop a prisoner from seeing anyone considered to be 'unsuitable'. A prisoner who feels that this is unreasonable can write to his or her MP. If a prisoner is in Category A, that is a top security prisoner, then all his or her visitors must be approved by the Home Office. If a prisoner is confined to his or her cell as a punishment, then their visits can be deferred until this has been completed. Visits take place within the sight of prison officers, and sometimes the governor may decide that the visit must be within the hearing of an officer as well. The prisoner and his or her visitors may be banned from touching, embracing or kissing if the prison officer in charge has reason to think that prohibited items may be passed over.

The prisoner can ask to be allowed an extra letter instead of a visit. The governor may allow a prisoner an additional letter or visit where this is thought to be necessary for his or her welfare or for that of the prisoner's family. The board of visitors (officials who regularly visit the prison) may allow a prisoner an additional letter or visit in special circumstances, and they can direct that a visit should last longer than usual.

While prisoners of either type *can* receive visits from their children, they do not have a right to receive visits from their children. Proceedings to force the other parent, or a local authority if the child was in care, to bring the child to the prison would be unlikely to succeed.

Letters

Again the rules differ according to whether the prisoner is convicted or unconvicted.

Unconvicted prisoners can write and receive as many letters as they like. The postage on two letters a week will be paid for by the prison. Further letters can be sent provided that the prisoner pays for the stamps either from his or her own funds or from prison earnings. Letters concerning a prisoner's defence will be sent at the prison's expense if the prisoner has no money. Similarly, if the prisoner has urgent domestic matters the governor can allow a further letter to be paid for by the prison. All the letters which a prisoner sends or receives are read by a prison officer and can be censored, except letters between the prisoner and his or her lawyer, provided that these refer only to the prisoner's legal matters.

Convicted prisoners have fewer rights. They can send one letter a week at public expense, and receive one letter a week. They can send one extra letter a week but they must pay for the postage out of prison earnings. These letters cannot be withheld as a punishment. In practice many prisons allow more letters, perhaps three or four a week, both in and out. The governor can allow an extra letter instead of a visit, and the board of visitors can allow an additional letter in special circumstances. All letters, except legal letters, can be read and censored. The governor can stop a letter on the grounds that its contents are objectionable or that it is too long. The prisoner must be given an opportunity to rewrite an outgoing letter that has been stopped.

There is no objection in normal circumstances to prisoners, whether convicted or not, from writing to or receiving letters from their children. Letters out will however almost certainly be stopped if the child is a witness against his or her parent accused of assault or abuse of any sort.

Leave

Convicted women prisoners may be allowed temporary absence under escort to visit their children or other relatives. This does not apply to Category A prisoners. This will not normally be granted more than two or three times a year.

COMPASSIONATE LEAVE

This can be granted to convicted prisoners of either sex where a death or illness has occurred. It does not last for long, perhaps a day or two, or up to a week, and whether it is granted and for how long depends on the circumstances. The prison authorities will look at how close the relationship is between the prisoner and the person who has died or is ill, how long a sentence the prisoner is serving, and how far through the sentence they are. Leave involving an overnight stay is, for example, unlikely to be granted early in a sentence because of the greater risk of the prisoner absconding.

Whether the prisoner is accompanied by a prison officer depends upon whether they are serving their sentence in an open or a closed prison – if it is a closed prison they will normally be accompanied, if it is an open prison they may not be. Whether parents who are prisoners can expect to receive leave where their child is ill is likely to depend on how seriously ill the child is, and how close a relationship he or she has with their parent. A prisoner who was living with and looking after his or her child before going into prison is perhaps more likely to be granted leave than one whose child was living apart from his or her parent with only sporadic contact.

Babies in Prison

The rules which govern how prisoners are treated are the Prison Rules of 1964. Rule 9(3) states:

> The Secretary of State may, subject to any conditions he thinks fit, permit a woman prisoner to have her baby with her in prison, and everything necessary for the baby's maintenance and care may be provided there.

Clearly, therefore, women can have their babies with them in prison. Men prisoners cannot, even if they are single parents. Many people believe that too many women are sentenced to imprisonment when they have committed offences which could be dealt with by a non-custodial sentence. In 1988, 50 per cent of women prisoners had committed offences involving theft, handling or fraud. These are obviously serious offences, but they are arguably less serious than offences of violence, robbery or sexual crimes. Yet only twenty-six per cent of that year's female prison intake had committed such offences.

When women are punished by imprisonment, their children are punished too. Over half the women in gaol have dependent children. Most of them end up being looked after by family, friends or being taken into care. This disrupts family ties and results in financial hardship. Many children do not see their mothers very often because of the stress and the travelling involved in visiting. In 1988, only 129 women were allowed to have their babies with them in prison, yet only 16 per cent of those women had committed offences involving violence or robbery.

There are, in England and Wales, only forty places for pregnant women, and only thirty-four places for mothers and babies. Whether babies are admitted depends on the prison governor's discretion and on the availability of places in the mother-and-baby units at the time. These places are sought after because there are so few. Priority is given to women on remand, that is women who have not been convicted but have been denied bail while awaiting trial.

Pregnant women in prison are generally accommodated in the prison hospital wing, or in a room or cell with other inmates. They are not allowed to be on their own, so that help can be called if necessary. Their ante-natal treatment is often outside the prison in an NHS hospital, to which they are taken. Except in an emergency, their babies are generally born outside the prison, again in NHS hospitals. They will be accompanied to the maternity hospital by a prison officer, who will remain at the hospital to guard them until their return to prison. This usually takes place as soon as possible after the birth.

A mother in this situation is not necessarily eligible to have her baby with her in a prison mother-and-baby unit. If the child will be more than nine months old by the mother's earliest release date from a closed prison, or more than eighteen months old by her earliest release date from an open prison, then it is likely that the baby will not be allowed to remain with her. If separation is to take place then it is likely to happen when the baby is four weeks old if the mother is breast-feeding. If she is not then it will happen before. The baby can be cared for by family or friends, but if not then the alternative is care by the local authority.

Obviously, prison is hardly the best place for a baby to grow up. Indeed it is probably one of the most artificial situations that a baby can find itself in. In 1982, roughly half of the women eligible for a place in a mother-and-baby unit declined to have their children with them because of the units' regimes and what they viewed as the stigmatizing effect of imprisonment. The alternative of separation is, however, traumatic for both mother and baby.

While in a mother-and-baby unit, a mother is liable to disciplinary action like any other prisoner. This can result in her being separated from her baby. However, an offence against discipline is usually insufficient ground on its own for removing a baby from the prison. This has to be done on the decision of the prison governor exercising the Home Secretary's power on a delegated basis. When such a step is contemplated the mother should be warned of the likely outcome should she fail to alter her behaviour, be allowed to have her say and be given an opportunity to mend her ways.

Chapter 12

Health and Safety

Children's Health

The National Health Service (NHS)

Parents have the primary responsibility for their children's health. If a parent wilfully neglects a child's health needs and this is discovered, the neglect can be a ground for care proceedings, or the parents can be charged with criminal offences.

The National Health Service has the practical responsibility of caring for the health of the population, including children, and is given duties and powers by the law to do so.

Under the main act governing the NHS, the National Health Service Act 1977, it must provide health services for England and Wales. These services include the provision of hospital accommodation, medical, nursing, dental and ambulance services, contraceptive services, and facilities for the diagnosis, prevention and treatment of illness and the aftercare of the sick.

In addition the NHS should provide specific services for the care of children and mothers. The Act states this in general terms as being 'such other facilities for the care of expectant and nursing mothers and young children as he [the Secretary of State for Health] considers are appropriate as part of the health service'.

The NHS also has responsibility for providing medical and dental inspections for children at local authority maintained schools.

The Act sets out the duties and what should be provided in general terms, which are subject to what the Secretary of State for Health (who with his government department runs the NHS) considers is 'necessary to meet all reasonable requirements'. In one important way, this vagueness is essential for a flexibly-run health service: if the NHS were to be tied down to an exact and specific provision of services then any treatment, however valuable, if not specifically included in the legislation could be unlawful.

On the other hand, a disadvantage of the generalized duties is that patients cannot point to any Act enshrining their full rights to health care and demand the specific services it provides for themselves or their children.

Another limitation on the ideal of a free, nationwide and comprehensive health service is that NHS services can be lawfully limited by the money and resources available to them, as long, that is, as their services meet 'all reasonable requirements'. That is, the NHS has no legal obligation to provide the best care for all that money can buy regardless of the financial costs. What is a 'reasonable' requirement, as is usual with the word, depends on the facts and circumstances of each case as eventually defined by the courts should a case be brought against the Secretary of State for failures under the Act. The NHS and the Secretary of State can allocate their limited funds to the areas and services they choose, and as long as the allocation is not seriously unreasonable it is within the law.

At the time of writing, the government have plans to alter radically the financial management of the NHS which may result in the restructuring of how medicine is paid for and distributed.

England and Wales are divided into geographical areas which have regional and district health authorities responsible for the provision of medical services, hospitals and treatment in their area. Each local area has a family practitioners' committee which controls GPs and clinics.

Doctors, dentists, nurses and other health professionals have their own organizations responsible for their professional conduct, which is also regulated by statute.

In England and Wales the NHS is charged with promoting 'a comprehensive health service designed to secure improvement in the physical and mental health of the people of those countries and in the prevention, diagnosis and treatment of illness' and to provide services to do all this.

Comprehensive health care means that everyone living in England and Wales is entitled to have a GP and to receive hospital treatment if they need it. This should be free for residents of the UK.

GENERAL PRACTITIONERS

Doctors can choose whether or not to accept someone on their list of registered patients, and it may not always be possible to have the doctor of one's choice if, for example, his or her patient lists are full or the practice is limited to a geographical area. In emergencies, however, GPs must treat patients who do not have another doctor in the area.

If a person cannot find a doctor to accept him or her as a registered patient, then the family practitioners' committee has a duty to find a doctor to take them on.

Once a patient is accepted, the doctor has professional duties towards him or her. Doctors must:

- treat patients with reasonable care and skill, having a duty of care towards them – this most crucial duty includes making such home visits or referrals to specialists as is reasonably necessary
- obtain patients' consent to medical treatment
- see patients who come to the surgery
- provide alternative care for them if absent or on holiday
- provide free advice and treatment with some exceptions, for example writing out certificates for some purposes
- preserve confidentiality and give out no information about the patient's condition unless with consent, or to other health professionals for the purpose of treatment.

HOSPITALS

Hospitals which have casualty departments have a duty to treat people in an emergency even if they are registered with a doctor in the area.

They can refuse treatment, for example where the doctor who first sees the patient forms the clinical judgment that he or she is not in immediate need and refers the patient back to the GP. If the clinical judgment was wrong, and the patient – adult or child – suffers as a result, he or she might have a negligence claim against the hospital.

Other than casualty treatment, patients are referred to hospitals by their GPs. While there is no general right to insist on a referral, bear in mind that a doctor's failure to refer when it is medically necessary could also be negligence.

A surprising proportion of unreferred visits to casualty follow a recent examination of the patient by a GP. With children, illnesses can flare up so suddenly that parents should never feel intimidated or feel they are second-guessing the GP.

The Child in Hospital

The best hospital practice now involves the parent being treated as part of the medical and nursing team, helping with nursing and feeding, having unrestricted visiting hours day and night, and being welcome to stay overnight near the child. However, hospital practice varies from region to region.

It is not the law that parents should be involved in their child's care in hospitals, but government recommendations made in 1959 set out that:

● parents should be allowed to visit as often as they wish, and allowed to help with the child's care
● parents should be encouraged to settle the child in over the first few days
● parents should be allowed to settle the child to sleep
● parents should be allowed to be with the child immediately before and after an operation
● parents who work should be allowed evening visits
● parents, particularly the mothers of young children, should be encouraged to stay overnight
● visits by brothers and sisters should also be encouraged.

The recommendations also detail the facilities that ideally should be offered to parents, including the use of showers and kitchens.

These recommendations were made following a study of how children were treated in hospital. At the time of the study it was common for hospitals to see parents as intruders who upset their children and the nursing regime. The National Association for the Welfare of Children in Hospital (NAWCH) is a pressure group which has been effective in changing entrenched attitudes and improving conditions. In 1982 they surveyed a large group of wards where children were nursed and found 49 per cent of them allowed unrestricted, twenty-four-hour access. The rest varied between allowing nearly unrestricted access, to a few wards where parents were allowed only up to four hours visiting a day.

In a 1986 follow-up of the 'worst' wards from the original group, significant improvements in attitude were found. There were still wards which did not allow the parents to see their child around the time of an operation, or imposed visiting hours, but the majority had changed their policy.

The problem here for parents is that a doctor's reasons for banning a visit or restricting access might seem compelling – the risk of cross-infection for example, or problems caused by high-tech nursing in special care units. But the 1959 recommendations also say there should not be a general rule restricting visits immediately before or after an operation or where children have infectious diseases.

While consultants are entitled to ban access on medical grounds, parents should remember that this ought to be the exception rather than the rule, and argue accordingly. Where they need further advice or support, the NAWCH can help.

Complaints can be made to the health ombudsman about access or other aspects of the child's care.

Education in Hospitals

Children who are in hospital for a considerable period should continue to receive an education. Section 56 of the Education Act 1944 empowers local education authorities to provide an education for children in hospitals. This can either be done individually or in hospital schools. The teacher ideally should work as part of the medical team in co-operation with the hospital. It is the hospital's responsibility to alert the education authority if a child is going to be in hospital for some time, but parents can also do this.

HEALTH BENEFITS

For entitlement to free prescriptions and dental treatment, see Chapter 6.

Consent to Medical Treatment

THE LAW

Technically, any deliberate physical contact made without permission is an assault on the person, and doctors and health workers need the consent of the patient to examine and treat him or her.

Consent to medical examination and treatment has to be valid; that is patients should know and understand what they are letting themselves in for, and be able to understand the risks of the treatment. The law assumes that adults have sufficient intelligence and understanding to give an effective consent and make decisions about their own bodies, and gives a specific right to anyone over sixteen to consent to or refuse medical treatment on their own behalf. This is contained in s8 of the Family Law Reform Act 1969.

The position for children under sixteen is different. Although they do not have the automatic right set out in the above Act, there is no legal assumption that under-sixteen-year-olds can *not* give proper consent to their own medical treatment. Whether or not they do depends on the age of the child and the degree of understanding they have, and is a question for the doctor to decide.

The Gillick case was important in this area. In that case, a mother tried to get court orders forbidding doctors in her area from providing contraceptive treatment and advice for any of her daughters aged under sixteen. Her arguments, briefly, were that doctors who gave contraceptive advice to girls under the age of sixteen – the 'age of consent' to marriage and therefore sexual intercourse – were effectively aiding and abetting a crime; and that as a parent she had an undisputed right to consent to or refuse medical treatment on her daughters' behalf until they were sixteen.

She lost the case at the High Court, won at the Court of Appeal, and lost at the House of Lords. The Lords rejected the argument that she had full rights of control over her children until a fixed age when they suddenly got rights of their own. The Lords took an organic view of growing up and getting the power to make decisions. In Lord Scarman's words, which at the least amount to a charter for co-operation between parent and growing child:

> Parental rights clearly do exist and they do not wholly disappear until the age of majority . . . but the law has never treated such rights as sovereign or beyond review and control. The principle of the law . . . is that parental rights are derived from parental duty and exist only so long as they are needed for the protection of the person or property of the child.

Where a child is very young the Gillick case would have no practical effect. Parents have to make the decisions when children cannot. For older children of, say, fourteen, the parent and child are likely to discuss the medical problems together and give a kind of shared consent. Where a child refuses treatment which the parent wants them to have, the doctor would have to decide between them.

In an emergency where life-saving procedures are needed, his or her decision is made easier because necessity is a defence to an assault. A doctor could provide treatment or operate without consent to save life because a court is not likely to convict of assault in those circumstances.

A more likely situation is where the child wants treatment and the parent either does not know about it or would refuse consent. The provision of contraception is the most obvious example of this.

THE PRACTICE

Giving consent is often implied rather than formal. Taking a child to a doctor's surgery or the casualty department of a hospital is an implied consent to examination and treatment.

Patients are asked to sign a consent form before surgery. Parents sign this on their children's behalf. Before giving consent to surgery, patients or their representatives should be told what the risks of the surgery are so that they have enough information on which to make up their minds.

How much information is 'enough' is controversial. In a leading case on consent where a woman suffered terrible injuries as a result of a risky operation, her lawyers argued, among other things, that as the doctors had not spelled out all the risks to her beforehand she could not have made a proper informed consent to the surgery. They argued therefore that the operation was in fact assault and battery. The House of Lords did not agree, deciding that inadequate disclosure of the risks did not vitiate consent to treatment.

The present position is that there is no rule that consent must be 'informed' in the UK – unlike America – and that doctors can decide how much to volunteer and how much detail to go into about risks and dangers. In practical terms it is likely that a concerned surgeon faced with anxious parents will give as much helpful information as possible. The rule for parents here is, ask for all the information you want; keep on asking until your queries are answered; get a second opinion if the position is not clear. Doctors may assume parents know that, for example, all operations carry a risk of post-operative infection of the wound: do not be afraid to ask 'obvious' questions.

EMERGENCIES

In emergencies, for example a child run over and attending hospital without the parent, the need to save life over-rides the need for consent. Doctors will go ahead and do what is necessary to save life regardless of whether consent is given or not. They would then face any subsequent court action, in the reasonable belief that no court would then criticize them.

REFUSAL OF CONSENT

Patients generally have a right to refuse treatment for themselves with two exceptions:

- if they are carrying a notifiable disease (one of the highly infectious or contagious diseases which when diagnosed have to be recorded at the Public Health Laboratories); or
- if they are detained as a mental patient under the Mental Health Acts.

These restrictions on refusal apply to children as well as adults. However, a parent who refuses routine treatment for a child under sixteen could be guilty of neglect, and the local authority could take action (see Chapter 9).

Following Gillick, there is an argument that in such a case the child's consent is equally valid if they understand and can appreciate the situation.

Parents who refuse treatment for their child might do this either out of a religious belief, for example being a Jehovah's Witness; out of gross negligence or fear of what an examination or treatment might find; or out of a genuinely held belief that treatment would not benefit the child.

If parents refuse medical treatment for their child and no other valid consent can be got, then doctors and hospitals can none the less go ahead and treat the child if he or she needs a life-saving procedure.

The DHSS (now the DSS) issued guidelines in 1967 setting out what should be done where the parents refused their consent to either an operation or a blood transfusion. The medical services can call in the social services, either to ward the child or to start care proceedings but the DHSS did not advise this, preferring that doctors and consultants went ahead using their clinical judgment. They advised that there should be full discussions with the parents; that the consultant should get a written opinion from a colleague supporting his view that the patient's life was in danger if the treatment was not given; and if possible a written explanation from the parents saying they refused consent while knowing the danger the child was in. The DHSS thought that if this was done the consultant would be in little danger in a court.

THE COURTS AND CONSENT

A child can be warded where there is any problem about parental consent to treatment, either where the parents refuse it or cannot decide what is best.

In cases like this, the doctors or other concerned people make the child a ward of court so that a judge can make the decision and give consent or not after hearing the facts of the case.

In a case in 1981 parents of a Down's syndrome child born with a defect which needed life-saving surgery refused consent because they felt the child's life would be so disadvantaged it should not be prolonged. The doctors had a conflict of opinion, and the wardship court was brought in to make the decision. In this case they held that the child's best interests required the operation to go ahead, and that there was no reason to assume that the child's life even with Down's syndrome would be so miserable that it should not be saved. In other words, they came down on the side of life and hope, appreciating that Down's syndrome on its own need not bar a child from having a constructive and happy life.

Where a child is already a ward of court, the court itself must give consent to medical treatment before it is carried out. This does not apply to routine medical and dental treatment or to emergency life-saving treatment although this should be notified to the court as soon as possible. It applies therefore to any treatment which is not routine nor done in an emergency – what is routine is a matter of fact, and in case of any doubt the court should be contacted. When an under-sixteen-year-old ward asks a doctor for contraceptive advice or contraception, the doctor is responsible for getting the court's consent.

Where any child, ward or not, is to have a sterilization operation, then the courts must be involved and give consent before the operation can be carried out.

LIFE-AND-DEATH DECISIONS

In tragic cases where children are born with terminal handicaps which cannot be ameliorated, decisions have to be made about whether or not their lives should be prolonged. Cases like this do not usually reach the courts, as the parents and doctors between them would decide on how much treatment to give a child who, in the normal course of events, would die. This is like any other case where the relatives of a terminally ill patient decide what treatment is to be given, but becomes more emotive where a child is involved.

The case of Baby C in 1989 received a lot of publicity and raised important issues about the treatment of the terminally ill. The baby was born with hydrocephalus of a particularly serious kind and medical evidence showed that she had no hope of recovery. An operation to relieve pressure on the brain had been carried out soon after birth, and she was receiving full medical and nursing care. The child had been made a ward shortly after birth. The decision to ward her was made before she was born for social reasons before anyone knew of her handicap, but once she was warded the court had to be involved in her treatment.

The High Court was asked what future treatment should be given. The issue here was really whether or not the hospital should prolong her life by medical intervention, for example giving antibiotics for any future infections, or whether they should only ease her passage.

The judge decided the hospital need not prolong her life but should give treatment to ease her distress and suffering, allowing her to die peacefully. He made an order ruling out treatment by antibiotics and intravenous or nasal feeding. The Court of Appeal later changed the order in its details, allowing the hospital to make the choice about what treatment was necessary to relieve suffering, which could include drugs if this would help.

The Court of Appeal made it clear that in a case like this the courts can decide whether or not life-prolonging treatment should be given or withheld but must make their reasons for this clear. It is also clear that such decisions can be made by parents and doctors where the court is not involved.

Criminal Liability

In a famous criminal case in 1981 Dr Leonard Arthur was charged with murder, later reduced to attempted murder following the death of a three-day-old Down's syndrome baby in his care. The baby had been rejected by his parents after birth.

In this case, the prosecution accepted that Dr Arthur was a devoted and respected paediatrician who had the interests of his patients and their parents at heart – the issue was whether or not his actions, which were supported by other paediatricians, were criminal.

The prosecution alleged that Dr Arthur had ordered nursing care only, and had prescribed a sedative drug which was given in sufficient doses to accomplish the death of the child. Nursing care meant caring for the child without medical intervention if illnesses developed after birth.

The defence argued that Dr Arthur had allowed nature to take its course, and the drug was prescribed to relieve suffering only. The jury unanimously acquitted Dr Arthur. In the period before the trial, other cases of the sort had been investigated by police but after Dr Arthur was acquitted no further prosecutions were brought.

CONTRACEPTION FOR UNDER-SIXTEEN-YEAR-OLDS

The DHSS (now the Department of Health) issued guidelines to doctors about contraceptive services to under-sixteen-year-old girls which take account of the Gillick case.

The basic fact is that doctors can provide girls under sixteen with contraceptive advice and services without informing their parents. However, before doing so the doctor:

- should take special care not to undermine parental responsibility and family stability
- should try to persuade the girl to tell her parents or guardians about wanting contraception, or to let the doctor tell them

- and if this persuasion fails, should provide advice and contraception only if satisfied:

    1. that the young person could understand his advice and had sufficient maturity to understand what was involved in terms of the moral, social and emotional implications

    2. that he could neither persuade the young person to inform the parents or to allow him to inform them

    3. that the young person would be very likely to begin or to continue having sexual intercourse with or without contraceptive treatment

    4. that without contraceptive advice or treatment the young person's physical or mental health or both would be likely to suffer

    5. that the young person's best interests required the doctor to give contraceptive advice, treatment or both without parental consent.

Doctors make decisions about providing contraception as above in their clinical judgment. The only bar to this is that where an under-age girl is a ward of court (wardship lasts until eighteen), the doctor *must* get the court's consent first.

If Things Go Wrong

If a parent is concerned that their child has either not received the correct treatment or the wrong treatment, they have various options to follow:

- complaints to the health ombudsman
- complaints to the family practitioners' committee
- legal action in the courts.

LEGAL ACTION

Health authorities and doctors can be sued for negligence in the same way as other professionals who have a duty of care towards their clients or patients.

Medical negligence law is complicated and parents should go to lawyers experienced in it. Action for Victims of Medical Accidents can recommend such lawyers. The complications of medical negligence law are in the conduct of it, in the procedure, negotiations and assessment of the medical facts – but the principle upon which a case is brought is the same as in negligence generally. The first question is, has an injury been done to the patient? Then, was this injury the result of negligence by the doctors or health professionals responsible for the treatment?

Doctors owe a duty of care to their patients. The duty is to exercise reasonable care and skill and the ordinary competence of other doctors of the same level. It is not a duty to be better than any other specialist, nor to guarantee success.

This point is important: whether or not a doctor has been negligent is decided by comparing what he or she did against what would generally be done by reasonably competent doctors of the same professional level, taking the current state of medical knowledge into account. To use an analogy – by present day standards sawing someone's leg off without anaesthesia or antiseptics would certainly be on the negligent side; but reasonably competent surgeons in the eighteenth century knew no other way.

Evidence

In cases of medical negligence the patient is entitled to get the medical reports and case notes from the health authority at an early stage before any writ or summons has been issued. This is different from other personal injury cases where the plaintiff cannot see the other side's evidence before a case has started.

If the health authority do not choose to hand the notes over after the solicitor asks them to do so, then the solicitor can issue a summons in court and seek an order that the notes are disclosed to them.

Seeing the notes gives patients and their lawyers an opportunity to find out what clinical treatment was given and what decisions were made by the doctors in the case. It is difficult for a patient to remember, know or understand what was done even when conscious, and in cases of surgery going wrong the patient can have no idea at all what happened. The lawyers can then show the notes to medical experts of their choice. The experts then advise the lawyers on whether or not the treatment given was in line with what reasonably competent doctors would decide.

The medical notes and documents give an indication of whether or not there is a case to be brought. If a case is started, it is then the plaintiff's responsibility to prove that his or her condition was caused by negligence, and show the court that on the balance of probability the injuries suffered were as a result of the treatment given.

There is an exception to this: in cases where the injury done was so massive that it 'spoke for itself', for example, where the wrong leg was amputated, the burden of proof shifts so that the doctor concerned must show he was not negligent, rather than the patient showing he was.

Medical negligence cases require medical expertise and the use of experts is crucial. Like most professions, doctors appear to close ranks against outside criticism or complaint – one reason why experienced lawyers should be used in these cases is that they know which consultants and experts to approach for reports and advice.

Time Limits

A child can sue for personal injuries, including those caused by medical negligence from the moment of their birth, when they become a legal person.

The right to sue extends back to injuries suffered before birth, during gestation or labour. A child can therefore sue through an adult 'next friend' for injuries caused by medical negligence during labour.

The time limit for adults to sue for medical negligence is three years – for children time does not start to run against them until they are eighteen, from which date they have a full three years in which to take action.

Despite this wide time limit parents should seek legal advice at an early stage if a child has suffered injury.

Obtaining Treatment: Can the Courts Intervene?

There have been two recent cases where parents brought High Court actions in an effort to force a health authority to provide medical treatment for children. Both these cases concerned children with heart defects which needed surgery which was not being provided at the time the actions were taken.

The cases were applications for judicial review, a procedure whereby the High Court can scrutinize the decisions made by public bodies and order them to change their decision if it was made unreasonably, unlawfully, unfairly or in breach of their duty.

In both cases, the parents tried to challenge the health authority's decision not to operate on the child. The Court of Appeal turned down both the applications.

What these cases mean for parents in the same tragic position is that

● the courts will not intervene where there has been no 'fault' on the part of the health authority in how they acted towards the patient or how they made their decisions
● the court cannot arrange waiting lists or change how health authorities allocate their resources unless they behaved improperly.

However, members of the public *can* continue to use the courts' power to review health authorities judicially if they act in bad faith or otherwise improperly.

Health and Safety

Where a child is injured or hurt, a parent's first concern is probably not what legal remedy is available for the injury but the child's immediate need for treatment and consolation.

Legal remedies exist either to prevent such an injury happening again, or to get money to compensate the child for serious damage or hurt suffered.

What can be done depends on whether the injury was accidental or deliberate, and by what or by whom it was inflicted.

Accidental Injury

When someone is injured accidentally as a result of someone else's action or inaction they can claim financial compensation if they can prove that they suffered an injury and that the other person did something which caused that injury and was at fault in doing so.

The branch of law concerned here is negligence, which is a 'tort' – i.e. a civil wrong. It is nothing to do with criminal law, and the payment of money at the end of a successful case is intended to compensate the injured person for their injuries and the financial loss they have suffered, or are likely to suffer in the future. Compensation of this sort is neither a punishment nor a fine for a wrong done.

In ordinary life, negligence means a lack of proper care in doing something. In law, the tort of negligence revolves around what is called a 'duty of care'. If someone owes a duty of care to another person, which they fail to carry out by what they do or do not do, and that other person suffers an injury as a direct result of this, then they have been negligent.

Practically everyone owes a duty of care to others. More technically, duties of care arise from the common law, or from statute, or from contracts between people.

COMMON LAW DUTIES

This is the law decided by judges and courts. In a negligence case much loved by law students for its absurdity, a manufacturer of ginger beer managed to deposit a decomposing snail in a bottle. The unfortunate person who drank it became ill. In the subsequent case battle raged about whether or not the manufacturers owed any duty of care to the customer. It was decided they did – on the basis that people owed a duty of care to everyone whom it was reasonably foreseeable their acts or omissions would affect.

This is also called the 'neighbour' principle: a neighbour in law is not just the person living next door, but everyone who should reasonably be considered as likely to be affected by one's acts or omissions. For example, if someone throws a bath out of the window as a quick route down to the bins, and it falls on someone's head and injures them, the bath thrower has broken a duty of care to his neighbour as it is reasonably likely that people would be using the road outside and likely they would be hit.

The duty of care does not go on for ever, as there will come a point when someone is injured and it was *not* reasonably foreseeable that they would be. For example, A drives a car and knocks down B, C sees the accident and goes into shock, collapses and is taken to hospital. C is D's mother – D is a nurse at the hospital and hearing that his mother has been brought into casualty collapses in turn. Because he is ill, he fails to collect E from the airport. E worries herself into a fit. When E's husband F receives a phone call saying his wife is ill, he has a heart attack and dies. Does A owe a duty to all of them? He certainly owes a duty to B – all drivers have a duty to other road users; he owes a duty to C on the same principle and through the likelihood that witnessing an accident would shock; he might owe a duty to D – but he does not to E or F as the damage to them is not reasonably foreseeable.

STATUTORY DUTIES

These are duties imposed on people through an Act of Parliament; for example, duties on employers to run safe workplaces. Statutory duties are different from common law duties in one important way. Usually, someone suing in a negligence case will have to prove that a duty of care was owed to them, that it was broken by a wrongful act and that damage resulted directly from this. Where there is a breach of statutory duty the job is easier. The person suing must show:

- that there was a statutory duty
- that it was broken
- that they suffered injury as a result.

They do not have to prove blame – once a statutory duty is shown to have been broken, then the wrong is shown too.

CONTRACTS

Duties of care arise through contracts between people as well. The relevant example for this chapter is in private health. Where say a surgeon is paid privately and not under the NHS he or she owes a contractual duty of care to the patient, as well as the common law duty of care owed by all medical practitioners to their patients. In practice, a lawyer would sue such a surgeon under both duties.

SUMMARY

Proving that someone owes a duty of care to you or your child is probably the easiest part of a case as the principles are well laid down. For example, teachers and schools, hospitals, doctors and dentists, car drivers, the occupiers of premises, all owe the duty.

What might be less obvious is that parents themselves, when driving a car, owe the same duty of care to their child passengers as they do to all other road users; that parents owe a duty of care to visitors in their house and could be liable if another child suffered injury there; that people owe a duty to take care of themselves; and that children themselves owe a duty of care to other people.

DUTY TO TAKE CARE OF ONESELF

People cannot sue themselves for negligence, but there is a common law duty to take reasonable care of one's own safety. This is also common-sense: if an accident happens and the injured person is trying to lay the blame on someone else, it is only fair to see how much the injury was self-inflicted. This does not mean that a pedestrian must creep along the pavements jumping into doorways whenever a car comes near, but it does mean that he or she should keep to the pavements and not walk in the middle of the road. If he did, and was injured, he has no one to blame but himself.

In a less obvious case, who was to blame for the accident can be divided between the people involved: this is called *contributory negligence*. A judge can decide, after hearing all the evidence, that although the person being sued (the defendant) was to blame, he or she was not completely to blame, and the person suing (the plaintiff) was partly to blame for his or her own misfortune. The judge can decide percentages of blame: for example negligence by the defendant was 60 per cent; negligence for his or her own safety by the plaintiff, 40 per cent. The judge then decides the damages that would be owed if there was no contributory negligence by the plaintiff and awards the plaintiff only 60 per cent of that amount.

In principle, children can be contributorily negligent, but they are not judged by the same standards as adults, and how much they must take care of their safety depends on their age and what is reasonable. They are judged by the standards of children of their own age – for example, it is reasonable to expect that a young person of fifteen will not walk into a busy road without looking, but it is also reasonable to expect that younger children might do just that.

CHILDREN'S DUTY OF CARE TO OTHER PEOPLE

Whether or not a child owes a duty of care to his or her 'neighbour' depends on the circumstances of the case and in particular on the age of the child. In some cases, injury caused by a child can be blamed on the adults who should reasonably have prevented it. For example, if a young child at school is allowed to use sharp scissors without supervision and accidentally hurts a class-mate with them, then the teacher might be liable in negligence to the injured child if the court decided the unsupervised use of dangerous implements was a breach of the school's duty of care to *all* pupils in the class.

In practical terms, suing children for their negligence is worth considering only if either the child or, more probably, the parents have cash or are insured.

For parental liability for acts committed by their children, see Chapter 11.

WHO PAYS?

If the court orders that compensation – the legal word for which is 'damages' – must be paid, it is paid by the person judged to have caused the injury.

Where that person was insured against accidents of the sort which caused the injury, then the insurance company pays on their behalf. This is the case in:

- car accidents, when third party liability insurance is compulsory
- accidents at work
- accidents caused by employees of an insured business or firm
- accidents at a school or educational institution.

Where there is no insurance policy covering the accident then the person found responsible for it must pay the damages personally. There are two important exceptions to this rule: where a road accident is caused by an uninsured driver the Motor Insurers' Bureau (MIB) will pay damages for injury which are ordered by the court after a case against the driver has been brought and won; where the accident was caused by a driver who cannot be traced and therefore cannot be sued (hit-and-run cases), the injured person can apply to the MIB directly which will estimate and make an award of compensation.

The MIB agreements which make the above payments possible make rules on procedures and time limits for applying to them, but lawyers in accident cases such as these will deal with the MIB for parents.

Other than MIB cases, it does not make economic sense to sue a person who has no money to pay damages. In legal slang, the impoverished are 'men of straw'. In other words, you cannot get blood from stones.

Before legal aid can be given, the Legal Aid Board checks that the person to be sued is insured or has funds to pay any damages. Legal aid might be granted despite the other party having no cash, where for example money was not the main or only point of the action, but generally it would be refused.

Are Lawyers Needed?
The short answer is yes.

Personal injury litigation is a thicket of procedure, rules and time limits, and we advise parents whose children may have a claim of this sort to get legal advice quickly. We do not recommend that parents conduct cases on behalf of their children personally.

This section provides only an outline of the law so that parents can be aware of action they can take for their children, and of their own liabilities and duties in this field.

MUST SOMEONE BE TO BLAME?

Not always. Although proving that someone else was at fault and that the fault caused the injury is the central core of personal injury law, there are some types of harm for which Parliament has laid down 'strict liability'. Under the Consumer Protection Act 1987 manufacturers or suppliers whose products cause injury can be made to pay damages without proof of negligence. The Act also contains defences to this to be used by the defendants. However, in most personal injury cases there is no right to compensation unless it is proved that someone was to blame for it.

There is increasing pressure from lawyers and others to force the government into considering 'no fault compensation' systems where a person who was injured and suffering from the effects of that could be given financial help without having to litigate and win a case.

There may be some legal changes in future on this as under pressure from medical and legal organizations the government intend to set up a pilot study into no-fault compensation in some limited cases – but at present in most cases blame must be allocated before damages are paid.

For children particularly, the burden of proving someone was to blame for their injuries and disabilities can end in genuine tragedy. A child seriously injured when young can have a whole lifetime of pain and difficulty but if it cannot be shown that the injuries were the direct result of an identified wrongful act or omission and from no other cause the child cannot be compensated. The severity of the injury or the need for lifelong medical care cannot affect this, however sympathetic the court may be to the child's position.

Personal injuries are not just wounds as a result of an accident, but include the effects of diseases (for example asbestosis and other industrially contracted illnesses), medical accidents, harmful drugs lawfully prescribed, and any physical or mental disability or disablement if caused by another person's act or failure to act.

HOW THE CLAIM IS MADE

The financial claim is made by suing the person who caused the injury in an action for damages for personal injuries. The action starts either in the High Court (by issuing a writ) or in the county court (by issuing a summons).

The county court deals with smaller claims where the damages are likely to be under £5000, with the High Court being used for larger or more difficult cases. There are proposals at the time of writing this book to lift the county court ceiling to £50,000, the powers that be feeling that the county court has greater speed and economy which should be available for more cases.

However, all cases regardless of how much they are worth can start in the High Court and in practice some personal injury lawyers prefer to do this because although it is more expensive there are advantages to the plaintiff in using the High Court.

The actual conduct of the litigation is the lawyer's responsibility, and a blow-by-blow account of what happens in a personal injury case is not the purpose of this chapter. The main common-sense rules for parents in these cases are the usual ones:

● choose a lawyer who knows the field, either through personal recommendation or by referral from a CAB or law centre
● make sure you give all the information the lawyer asks for as quickly and accurately as possible
● if you do not understand what is happening, then ask
● bear in mind that although a busy lawyer will not have time or funds to spend writing letters about everything routine that has happened, you have rights to know how the case is going and he or she should keep you

informed; litigation does not finish overnight and long delays are part of it – your lawyer should not add to the usual delays by sitting on things

● lawyers *must* consult you on major things, like offers of settlement made by the other side.

SETTLEMENTS

Most personal injury cases never get to court and are settled before trial; after negotiation the defendant agrees to pay damages to the plaintiff. Where there is a decent offer, this is the best way of dealing with it because trials are extraordinarily expensive and winning them might not be certain.

In adult cases, offers can be accepted without going to court at all. However, in children's cases the court *must* be involved and approve the settlement made between the lawyers. When an agreement about the amount of damages is made between the parties, a private hearing is fixed before a master (High Court) or registrar (county court) who either approves of the settlement or does not. If it is approved, he or she makes an order to that effect. In the rare cases when it is not approved – where for example the agreement was far less than the going rate for injuries of that kind – then either the parties renegotiate a settlement or, if they cannot agree, a hearing before a judge is fixed to settle proper damages.

People under eighteen are not allowed to control their own damages which are paid into court, and invested by the court, for release when the child is eighteen. Interest is paid on the invested money. Where income or capital spending is needed in the child's interests, the court can order some or all of the cash to be released as the need arises.

WHO CAN SUE?

Any living person can sue irrespective of their age; but anyone under eighteen, even if they are married and socially independent, must sue through an adult called their 'next friend'. This is generally a parent, although it does not have to be. If the child is suing a parent, the 'next friend' must be another adult.

Where children are sued, an adult must conduct the case for them, instructing lawyers and taking decisions in the same way a 'next friend' does. This person is called a guardian ad litem. Note here that the guardian in personal injury cases is not the same as a guardian in care cases – but any adult willing to take on this responsibility. Generally it will be the parent.

TIME LIMITS

There are time limits within which action must be taken. For an adult, the basic time limit in cases where injury was caused is three years from the date he was injured. Within three years of the accident or injury the adult must have issued a writ or summons in a court.

This strict time limit could operate unfairly on some people, for example where an injury did not make itself obvious until more than three years from the event which caused it. Because of this, the rule was modified by statute and now is: three years from the date of the accident or event which caused the injury, *or* three years from the date the injured person first knew his injury was significant *and* knew the injury was attributable to the act or omission of an identified defendant.

The court has a wide discretion to let people sue, even when they are well out of time – it depends entirely on the facts of each case, the behaviour of the person who wishes to sue (for example did he carelessly just let it slide or fail to do anything in his own interests?), and also on the behaviour and situation of the proposed defendant.

The court must think about the defendant's interests also – and the possible unfairness to him of being sued many years after an event. The basic rule here is that despite the court's discretion, people who have suffered an injury must get legal advice as soon as the injury occurred or is noticed.

For children the time limits are different. The three-year time limit starts running when the child becomes eighteen, ending three years later unless extended by the court on the usual rules above. This means that a child can sue through the next friend at any time between the event which caused the injury and his or her twenty-first birthday.

This is a protection for the child, who should not be penalized for the failure of parents or guardians to take action on his or her behalf for an injury suffered during childhood. Once an adult, they have the same time limits as any other injured person in which to take action on their own behalf.

Despite this protection, parents whose child is injured should act promptly for them: not only should the child be compensated promptly for harm done, particularly in cases where money is needed to provide extra care or otherwise improve life, but delay can affect the eventual success of a case. For example, witnesses might become unavailable or forgetful, and physical evidence could be destroyed.

Pre-natal Injury

Only living persons can sue for damages for personal injury, and the law defines a living person as one who has been born.

An unborn child has no rights to sue for damage or injury suffered while in the womb – but after birth can then sue for any injuries caused before or during birth. In some circumstances children can sue if they have suffered physical damage as the result of an injury done to the parents even before their conception.

The right to sue for pre-birth injuries was created by Parliament in 1976 in the Congenital Disabilities Act. This Act followed the thalidomide cases, where children had been born with serious birth defects after their mothers had been prescribed the drug thalidomide during pregnancy. The cases were settled by agreement after the drug company which manufactured and distributed the drug agreed to accept liability and pay compensation for the children's pre-natal injuries. Before this Act a person or company could not have been made liable in a court for injury caused before birth.

The Act provides where a child is born disabled as a result of an 'occurrence', and a person other than the child's mother is under this section answerable to the child in respect of the occurrence, the child's disabilities are to be regarded as damage resulting from the wrongful act of that person actionable at the suit of the child (s1). The word 'occurrence' here is wide enough to cover any kind of event that could cause injury.

Under this section the child cannot sue the mother – even if the child was born disabled as a result of something she did or failed to do during her pregnancy. Any other person including the father can be sued.

The Act defines 'occurrences' as being events which affected *either* parent in their ability to have a normal healthy child; or which affected the mother during her pregnancy; or which affected the mother or the child during the birth if this resulted in the child being born with disabilities he or she would not otherwise have had.

An occurrence which could affect either the mother or the father in their ability to have a normal healthy child could be the administration of a drug to either parent which interfered with their reproductive systems and did genetic damage. It could also include the father infecting the mother with a sexually-transmitted disease capable of harming the foetus.

Occurrences which affected the mother during pregnancy could include the prescription of drugs that harmed the developing baby and a physical attack on the mother which hurt the child inside.

An occurrence affecting the child during birth would cover a medical accident during labour.

People who are responsible for occurrences which cause damage to a child are liable to the child for this if they would have been liable to the parent: in other words, the child's right to sue comes from the wrongful act done to the parent. This is so even if the parent did not suffer any actual damage personally. For example, if thalidomide was prescribed now, children could sue the makers of it for the damage it caused them, even though thalidomide had no bad effects on their mothers. This Act extended the 'duty of care' to foetuses: this duty is to take reasonable care to prevent likely damage to them from one's acts or omissions.

The normal provisions of negligence law apply to pre-natal injuries: generally someone must still be at fault in doing or allowing the 'occurrence'; the occurrence must have caused physical damage to the child, the damage must be directly caused by the occurrence and be proved as such.

Knowledge of the pregnancy makes no difference to liability. If for example a car driver negligently knocks a woman down on a zebra crossing and her unborn child is injured as a result, the driver is still liable to the child even if he or she had no idea the woman was pregnant.

ACTION

By the Child

A child cannot sue his or her mother for injuries caused by her acts or failures to act during pregnancy – apart from one important exception: women who drive motor vehicles when they know or ought reasonably to know they are pregnant are liable to the unborn child for injury caused by their negligence.

Care Proceedings

What the mother did or did not do during her pregnancy can be taken into account in care proceedings after the birth.

In a care case in 1986 the mother was a registered drug addict and had taken drugs during her pregnancy. Her baby was born with drug withdrawal symptoms. The local authority took care proceedings within a few weeks of the birth, on the grounds that the child's proper development was being avoidably prevented or neglected or its health was being avoidably prevented or neglected. They argued that the mother's abuse of her own body during pregnancy had led to the child's development and health being impaired.

The words of the statute are in the present tense and say development 'is being' impaired. Although the mother continued to take drugs after the child was born, in strict fact the behaviour complained of – drug-taking *during* pregnancy – was ended when the child was born. The case eventually went to the House of Lords who upheld the care order, deciding that the juvenile court which made the care order was entitled to take account of the mother's treatment of the child before birth; and that as 'development' and 'health' are continuous concepts, the words 'is being' are continuous as well and in such a case the court can look not only at the present, but at the immediate past and into the future if the future is likely to be similar to the past.

This case shows the court's willingness to extend parental responsibilities towards children before they become legal 'living persons'.

Wardship

A local authority – or indeed anyone with an interest in the child – could ward a child immediately after birth if concerned that the mother's behaviour or lifestyle was not good for the child. This could be based only on the mother's treatment of her pregnancy, even where there were no grounds for care proceedings to be taken.

It is not possible to ward a child before he or she has been born – a local authority did once try, but the court threw it out.

FOETAL 'RIGHTS'

Although the Congenital Disabilities Act introduces the idea that a foetus can be owed a duty of care, inheriting this as it were through the mother or father against whom some wrong act has been committed, this does not extend foetal rights as such.

Because children can take action on their own behalf only after they have been born, this does not give unborn children rights to a healthy life or indeed life at all. This is particularly relevant in cases concerning termination of pregnancies.

Accidents at home

Home is a dangerous place. According to the Royal Society for the Prevention of Accidents (RoSPA), statistics from 1986 showed there were 3 million accidents in the home that year, of which nationally the under-fives suffered 477,000, with children over five but under fifteen suffering 300,000. These were accidents serious enough to require hospital treatment.

Children fall down stairs, are burnt by fires, choked by carbon monoxide fumes from inadequate heaters, trip over giant teddies, fall over flexes and generally encounter serious dangers in what is meant to be their safe haven.

The death-rate for children in the home is alarming: in 1984 171 children under five died as a result of accidents at home, with sixty-four deaths in the five to fifteen age group.

Yet the home is not a regulated areas.

Parents' responsibility for their own children's safety in the home is a general one. It comes from the normal duties to look after children without neglect which if ignored so that the child's development suffers can lead to the involvement of the social services (see Chapter 9).

There is a specific statutory provision about fires: if a child under the age of twelve is left alone with an unguarded fire and is burnt as a result the parent can face criminal prosecution.

The local authority have powers under the 1961 Home Safety Act to educate people in home safety. but these powers are discretionary. This means that local authorities can choose whether or not to carry out education programmes about safety in their area.

RoSPA can advise on safety in the home. Much of it is common-sense: for example, stair gates for the young; guarded heaters; good ventilation; advising the child about safety; keeping dangerous substances and medicines out of reach; and reduction of obvious dangers in the house or garden.

CIVIL LIABILITY

Under the Occupiers' Liability Act 1957 the occupiers of premises owe a duty of care towards their visitors.

The duty is 'in respect of the dangers due to the state of the premises or to things done or omitted to be done on them'.

'Premises' means practically every kind of structure or place capable of being occupied at all: it covers buildings, unbuilt-on land, fairgrounds, tents, boats, building sites, as well as houses, flats and shops.

An occupier is someone who has control over what goes on in the premises. Whether or not someone is an occupier in this sense can be tricky and would have to be decided on the facts – but some obvious examples are:

- families living in their own or rented houses occupy them
- people running businesses occupy the place they use for this

● local authorities who own recreational land occupy it
● education authorities occupy the school buildings they use.

Landlords who rent out the whole of a flat or house and do not keep control of any part of it are not occupiers, the tenant is. But landlords such as local councils who keep control of the common parts of a block of flats are occupiers of those parts. In one case a young child who fell between wide banisters on a staircase successfully sued the local authority who had kept control of the passageways.

This Act is of particular relevance to parents whose premises seem to be endlessly full of other people's children and friends. To be on the safe side, it is best to assume that every danger at home could affect a visitor and lead to one's liability to that visitor.

A danger is anything which causes harm to someone else even if it was not immediately obvious it was going to. A rotten floorboard hidden under a rug is a danger; tiles falling off roofs and hitting passersby are dangers; slippery floors, un-nailed down stair carpets, collapsing garden walls are all the kind of dangers which can lead to accidents and injury.

Warning people of known dangers is essential: pointing out that the floorboards by the window are unsafe and should not be trodden on can absolve the occupier from any liability. If a visitor then insists on jumping on them, it is effectively his or her own fault if they go through. The warning should be strong enough for the danger in question: saying the stairs are a bit tricky when half of them are missing would not be good enough.

Written warning notices can remove or restrict the occupier's responsibility for accidents on the premises.

CHILDREN IN PARTICULAR

Children are allowed to have less sense than adults. While adults should take care to avoid obvious dangers (and have any damages they were awarded reduced by their own failure to take proper care of their own safety if they did not), children are not expected to have the same degree of reasonable caution.

The Occupier's Liability Act specifically provides that occupiers must be prepared for children to be less careful than adults.

In addition, children do seem to be irresistibly drawn towards danger without understanding the risks of it – they tend to see the physical world more as a marvellous playground than as a source of injury. This propensity is recognized in law. Occupiers have a duty to guard children from hidden traps on their land which could attract and lure them into taking risks.

What constitutes a trap of this sort depends on the thing itself and on the age and understanding of the child concerned. The sorts of things which courts in previous cases held were hidden traps have included: a pretty plant with poisonous berries on it in a public park, a lorry laden with sugar, a municipal paddling pool which had broken glass in it, a tree which could be climbed so that children were then in reach of a live electrical cable above it.

The law does of course recognize that accidents happen – and this Act does *not* make occupiers responsible for every disaster that happens on their premises. If an accident happened without the occupier being responsible for it, where there was no obvious or hidden danger to a child, then there is no liability. For example, in one case a young child was injured playing on a pile of stones heaped on the ground: the court found this was not a trap.

Warnings for Children

Where there is something dangerous on land then any warning given to a child is not effective unless the child can understand it, and occupiers should tailor their warnings to the age of the children likely to be concerned. For example, a written warning about a chute in a playground would be no use at all to a child who could not read.

Parents' Responsibility

Occupiers of land are entitled to assume that parents will look after their children and the parents' responsibility to do so is not removed by other people's duties towards children. It is a shared responsibility.

Whose 'fault' it actually was when a child is injured is decided on considering all the circumstances, including the age of the child, whether or not he or she was accompanied – and if not accompanied whether this was reasonable of the parents – any warnings that were given and the nature of the danger.

For example, while it is probably reasonable for parents to assume that a public park is safe for a six-year-old to play in on her own, the occupier of a building site is reasonable in assuming a two-year-old would not be playing there or coming in unaccompanied. The occupiers of land do not have a greater duty to the children than the parents do.

Trespassers

A trespasser is someone who goes into buildings or on to land when they are not invited to. The 'invitation' can be implied – for example, where the occupier of land knows that children use a part of the land as a known short cut and makes no effort to stop them doing this he would probably be taken as inviting them to carry on using it.

But occupiers of land still have a duty towards trespassers even where there has been no invitation of any sort. This is humane common-sense, particularly with children who might climb over a fence or wander off without knowing they were trespassing at all.

The duty owed to trespassers is less than that owed to lawful visitors. It is a duty to be humane – to take such steps as common-sense or common humanity would dictate. It amounts to a duty to keep children away from dangers on the land, either by warnings or fences or, where young children are likely to roam around the land, taking steps to keep them away, for example boarding up a dilapidated house.

This common law duty was created by judges in a case where a young boy fell on to a live rail after wandering on to British Railways' property. If the duty to warn children off is ignored or not responded to adequately, the owners of land where a trespassing child was injured would be liable in damages.

PROTECTION FOR OCCUPIERS

1. Where possible make sure there are no dangers on your own premises.
2. Warn your visitors of any dangers if they cannot be made safe. Tailor your warnings to the age and understanding of your visitors.
3. Remember children are in a special position and need greater care taken of them than adults.
4. Insure against the risks of being sued under the duty of care this Act imposes. Normal household insurance covers liability to visitors under this Act. When a house is mortgaged, the building society or other mortgagee normally insists the property is insured, and the policy includes claims made against the occupiers of it. But it is possible to have no insurance at all if a house is either free of mortgage, or a rented flat. If this is the case, get a policy.

Accidents at School

At school the teachers are in loco parentis (that is, in the place of a parent) and the local education authority and its staff owe the children the same duty of care as a reasonable parent does.

The duty is to take reasonable care for the children's safety and to prevent damage from foreseeable injury while at school. As well as this common law duty, schools owe the normal duties under the Occupiers Liability Act, and are highly regulated under the Health and Safety Acts and Regulations.

THE HEALTH AND SAFETY AT WORK ACT 1974

This Act sets out the duties employers, employees and the general public have in respect of health and safety at work. Regulations made under the Act set out detailed provisions for dealing with potentially hazardous materials and situations.

The Act's aims are to secure the health and safety of workers, give protection to the general public from risks caused by people at work, and to control dangerous substances.

Employers have general duties to ensure as far as they can that workplaces, methods of working and materials worked with do not present risks to the health and safety of the employees or to members of the public who are likely to come into contact with them.

Everyone who employs more than five people must have a written safety policy, setting out the business's policy for the health and safety of its employees and the arrangements for carrying this out. The employer should bring this policy to the employees' attention.

The Health and Safety Commission gives guidance and advice to employers. They advise that employers should be particularly careful where children are likely to be affected by their activities, giving building sites as an example of highly dangerous but fascinating places.

The Act appoints inspectors who have power to go into workplaces and investigate breaches of the Act and regulations. They can order that an activity at work is stopped if it causes a risk of serious personal injury; require the employer to fix safety hazards within a fixed time, and start a prosecution under the criminal law. The sanctions are fines and imprisonment.

EDUCATION

Schools and educational establishments have to comply with the Act and regulations made under it. The local authority or board of governors which employ the school staff must prepare the written policy and bear the general duties of all employers. It is the actual employer who has the legal duties under the Act: while for practical reasons health and safety can be delegated to each local authority head teacher, the liability under the Act stays with the authority itself.

The safety policy should not be limited just to employees, but include the arrangements made to protect the health and safety of visitors, pupils and students: employers have a specific duty to protect all lawful visitors to the site and anyone likely to be affected by the work going on there.

A proper safety policy for schools should include details on safe systems of work, first aid arrangements, the reporting of accidents, school security, and emergency procedures in case of fire or other immediate dangers.

The Health and Safety Commission and the DES advise schools on safety and give guidance on subjects like using materials in science lessons, safety on field trips and PE.

What Parents Can Do

If there is an obvious danger to a child at school parents should feel free to point this out to the head teacher, and ask that it be made safe. Where schools are patently failing to look after the safety of the children in their care, a concerned parent can contact the Health and Safety Executive and report this.

Note here that bad discipline can be a danger to children at school, and bullying pupils are certainly a risk to the health and safety of their victims. Bullying and victimization of children in schools is a serious problem, made worse by children staying silent about it for fear of the consequences. If you know bullying is a problem in your child's school, consider discussing this with the head teacher who can use his or her disciplinary powers, including exclusion of the bullying pupil. If discipline in a school has broken down badly, LEAs can step in as a last resort.

Deliberate Injury

Causing deliberate injury to a child is a crime, and those who perpetrate it can be prosecuted under a host of offences ranging from common assault to homicide. With one exception, laying hands on a child in a hostile way is an assault even where no physical injury is caused by this.

The exception is that parents who strike their children have a defence under the criminal law that the chastisement was moderate and reasonable. This defence comes from the idea that parents have rights and authority over the child and are through these entitled to exert physical power over them. The defence is *not* a 'right', but in practical terms means that a mild 'disciplinary' assault on a child would not be prosecuted by the police if it came to their notice.

As usual, reasonableness is a matter of degree and fact. Unfortunately for children, the reasonableness or otherwise of being hit is unlikely to be tested unless and until someone else steps in and court proceedings are started.

Since the Gillick case where the House of Lords defined parents' rights more as duties towards the welfare of the child than as power to control them, there is a strong argument that parents are entitled to discipline their children only if in some way this is for their welfare: genuinely their welfare that is, and not merely what the parent would like to think is good for them.

On this argument, shaking or slapping a young child who has run on to a road to impress on him or her that she must not do this might be genuinely reasonable and in the child's interests, when doing this out of rage at something spilled on a carpet would not be. From the criminal law point of view, a parent doing this for either motive could successfully use the defence, although it is difficult to imagine a prosecution for this.

This situation may change – several European countries have outlawed physical punishment by parents, and there is pressure to do the same in the UK.

PROTECTION FOR CHILDREN FROM VIOLENCE IN THE HOME

There is a range of remedies that can be used to protect children in the home.

Naturally, the younger a child is, the more dependent he or she is upon the intervention of adults to protect them from family violence. Older children and young people have greater power to seek help on their own account by approaching a trusted adult or professional agency.

Where one parent is violent either towards the children or the other parent, both civil and criminal law can be used.

Criminal Law

Anyone who is the subject of violence can go to a police station and report the crime. It used to be regrettably common that police would dismiss allegations of violence against women by their partners by saying it was 'domestic' and that women should use the civil law instead.

If this happens now, any woman whose complaint is not taken seriously should immediately:

- ask to speak to the senior officer in charge
- consider making a complaint to the police complaints authority or the local equivalent
- take legal advice from the citizens' advice bureau or a solicitor.

We say 'women' advisedly – while some men are the victims of domestic violence the overwhelming majority of abusers are male.

The police are extremely unlikely not to investigate allegations of violence and abuse against a child or young person. The recent publicity given to child abuse has had one welcome effect: young people are more likely to be listened to now than ever before.

Crimes of violence range from common assault to murder, with sanctions varying according to the seriousness of the crime. The law exists to punish the wrongdoer and deter others – which may not be precisely what the victim of the violence needs.

Victims of violence need it to stop. In serious cases the violent partner might be remanded in custody and therefore removed from the home but in the majority of cases, if charged, will be released on bail.

Being arrested, charged and then released to return to the home might be a salutary lesson for the violent partner or parent but does not guarantee safety for the family. In some ways therefore, the remedies under the civil law are more effective.

Civil Law
Courts can:

- order the defendant not to assault the partner or the children
- order the defendant to leave the shared home
- send the defendant to prison if he breaks a court order of this sort
- award damages for assault to the victim.

All these civil law remedies can be used in conjunction with criminal proceedings: it is not an either/or option. For details of this, see Chapter 10.

CHILD SEXUAL ABUSE

Generally there is a far greater awareness of sexual abuse now than ever before and the professionals who deal with children (such as doctors and teachers) ought to be both more able to recognize a troubled child, and more willing to believe what the children confide in them.

Doctors have an important role in diagnosing sexual abuse and in the current climate ought to have the possibility of abuse in mind when they see warning signs in a child. The DHSS guidance to doctors sets out the physical and emotional warning signs they should look out for. For more information about this, see Chapter 11.

Doctors should also consider the family setting, particularly where another child in the family has been abused; or the child is inappropriately exposed to adult sexual behaviour; or a father or step-father suffers from alcoholism or has an aggressive personality disorder. They are particularly advised to consider emotional signs in association with any physical symptoms. Obviously some signs are an extremely strong indication the child has been abused, while others might just raise the suspicion they could have been.

Doctors have a general duty of confidentiality towards their patients, adult or child. But where a child is abused physically or sexually the General Medical Council has said that it is not only permissible to disclose information about it, but that there is a positive duty to do so.

What Should the Parent Do?

Probably a parent's first reaction to the mere thought of their child being sexually abused is that it is not happening, it is not possible. But there is ample evidence that children simply do not lie about this.

Sexual abuse is not always by family members. Where parents suspect or know their child has been abused by an outsider, they should get proper professional advice from a doctor, social worker, health visitor or police officer trained in dealing with abuse cases.

What the parents should *not* do is take the law into their own hands and go after the alleged abuser: however 'natural' it may feel to wreak revenge on a person who has hurt one's child, it is against the law.

Where a parent suspects sexual abuse within the family, they should not, for the child's sake, pretend it is not happening even though the consequences could involve the break-up of the family. It is not invariable that sexually abused children are removed from their home, and it is possible for families to recover. But parents must seek help, particularly for the child who could suffer long-term psychological or emotional damage without it.

COMPENSATION FOR VICTIMS OF CRIME

The Criminal Injuries Compensation Board (CICB) can compensate adults and children if they have suffered injuries by outsiders as a result of crime.

The crime must have been reported to the police although there need not have been a conviction for it.

The CICB investigates the circumstances and gets medical reports and police reports before it decides whether or not to make an award and, if so, how much to give.

Consumer Protection

Manufacturers and suppliers of consumer goods have responsibilities to the public which can be enforced by both the criminal and the civil law.

Criminal Liability

Goods offered for sale must be reasonably safe and not likely to cause harm or danger to the consumer who uses them properly and for the purpose for which they are intended. If they are, the manufacturer or supplier can be guilty of criminal offences under the Consumer Protection Act 1987.

Under this Act, there is a general safety standard with which goods must comply if they are not already legislated for in other Acts.

Very many goods are already covered by specific safety standards, and many categories of goods – such as controlled drugs, food and water – have their own Acts to cover safety and health requirements.

The general safety standard in this Act covers goods which have not been already dealt with elsewhere, as it is impossible to have detailed regulations for each product made in a consumer society.

The general safety requirement is that goods must be reasonably safe having regard to the circumstances. The circumstances include what the item is for, how it is being marketed, what warnings or instructions come with it, how it measures up to published standards of safety, and how it could have been made safer.

Published safety standards can be either voluntary and advisory, or compulsory with the force of law. Where there is a voluntary standard that deals with the safety of a product, then that is the minimum standard required under the 1987 Act – manufacturers cannot say that a push-chair that acted like an ejector seat in a James Bond film was nearly up to the BSI standard and therefore was reasonably safe.

If an article breaches this general safety standard, the person who makes it, sells it, or even just has it on offer for sale, can be prosecuted, fined and/or imprisoned. Prosecutions are brought by local trading standards officers. Parents with complaints about unsafe goods should feel free to contact them: approximately 5 per cent of their work deals with children's products.

Civil Liability

Anyone injured as a result of a defect in a product can sue the producers and in some cases the suppliers of it. This is an area of the law where the injured person does *not* have to prove negligence on the part of the maker of the product.

The law is fairly simple: where anyone suffers damage either wholly or partly as a result of a defect in a product, the producers or importers of the product are liable. The product has to be supplied in the way of business, as part of a consumer/trader transaction. It does not apply to lending or borrowing goods among friends, or even giving them away.

Where the consumer cannot immediately identify the producers, he or she can ask the supplier to tell him who they were. If the supplier either refuses or does not give the information in a reasonable period of time, the supplier then becomes liable for the damage.

Products have defects if they are not as safe as the consumer was generally entitled to expect. In deciding this, a court takes account of all the circumstances including what the product was for, what it was meant to be used for, when it was supplied, and any warnings or instructions for use.

The producers of the product – or the supplier – have defences laid out in the Act. They can say:

- It wasn't me, because I did not in fact supply or produce the goods
- I did supply it, but there was no defect in it
- I supplied it, but not for profit and not in the course of business
- There was a defect in a larger product of which mine was a part – i.e. I only made the nails for the climbing frame, and they were fine, but the wood was rotten so don't blame me
- There was a defect in the thing I made, but when I made it no one in my position could have been expected to know it was there under the scientific and technical information available at that time.

This last defence means that manufacturers can escape liability for damage caused by their products if they can show that at the time they were made or developed there was no way in which the damage could have been reasonably foreseen.

Time Limits

Normally, time limits for personal injury mean action must be started within three years from the date of the injury, which can be extended at the court's discretion; actions for damage to property must be started within six years. All actions under this Act must be brought within three years, but this runs for children from the date they become adults at eighteen. However, there is an absolute cut-off point for all claims of ten years from the date the product was supplied. This is so even if ten years after the product was supplied the victim of it was still a child and under normal law could sue until he or she was twenty-one. The right of action is snuffed out, and no action can be taken under the Act.

Minimum Amounts
The Act cannot be used for small claims. In order to sue under it, the compensation claimed must be more than £275.

Causation
Despite the strict liability of manufacturers, the person suing must still prove causation, that is that the defect caused their injury or loss either wholly or partly. This becomes more difficult in drug cases (see below).

DRUG CASES

The usual arrangement with products is that manufacturers can put them on the market without any prior licensing or government safety tests. If they are found to be dangerous, the government through the DTI can ban them, get them taken off the market or bring criminal prosecutions under this Act.

Drugs are treated the other way round: they cannot go on the market unless they have been previously licensed by the Medicines Control Agency and tested for safety, quality and efficacy. The parts of this Act which deal with quality control do not therefore apply to medicines and prescribed drugs.

Product liability does apply. That is, anyone injured by taking a prescribed drug after the date this Act came in can sue the manufacturers without having to prove negligence. They still have to prove *causation*, and show that the damage suffered actually came from the drug itself.

Proving causation can be extraordinarily difficult in drug cases, particularly when major drug companies can afford to produce volumes of scientific evidence, experts and research perhaps not available to the plaintiff. The manufacturers of a drug can also use the defence that scientific and technical understanding at the time meant they could not reasonably have foreseen the adverse effects of the drug.

How the Act will work in practice on drug cases is uncertain. Certainly there is one apparent major flaw in it – the ten-year cut-off rule. With most products it is common-sense that they will be used within ten years of the date of supply and defects will be discovered then. This applies particularly to children – there is probably no recorded case of a child keeping a new toy unopened for more than three minutes! But the effects of drugs can be hidden and undisclosed and need not make themselves apparent for years. For example, it is possible that a drug could be given in early childhood which adversely affected reproduction and fertility. In the nature of things, this would not be discovered until at least puberty. The victim then would not be able to use this Act and would have to rely on the normal law of negligence, with all the accompanying problems of proving someone was at fault, which the Act was designed to simplify.

VACCINATIONS CASES

Vaccinating children to give protection against illness is a common medical procedure, recommended by the government and child health practitioners. It is not compulsory, and parents can choose whether or not to have it done.

The advantages of vaccination are obvious – smallpox, once endemic in England, has been eradicated. However, vaccination against illnesses can itself cause illness or damage to a child, particularly where there are contraindications (medical reasons why the vaccine should not be administered to a particular patient). Examples of contraindications are: for rubella (German measles) vaccine, pregnancy is an absolute contraindication; and epilepsy, asthma and fever are contraindications for most vaccines.

In the case of the whooping cough vaccine, there was so much adverse publicity about the risk of it causing neurological and brain damage in the 1970s that the take-up rate for vaccination went down significantly. In 1979 the Vaccine Damage Payments Act was passed, which provided that the government would pay compensation (now up to £20,000) to any child who had suffered physical injury as a result of any vaccination.

Claiming Vaccine Damage Act payments does not affect any civil action for negligence later taken by or on behalf of a child.

In a major test case heard in 1988, a child sued the doctor who administered the whooping cough vaccine, claiming that this caused brain damage. The vaccine's makers, the Wellcome Foundation, were joined in at their request, wanting to protect the reputation of their product.

After a lengthy trial with much medical evidence on both sides, the judge found that on the balance of probabilities the vaccine had not caused the damage to that child. Causation was the problem here – the drug company argued there was not a direct enough link between the vaccine and the damage.

The judge did find that the vaccine used was capable of causing brain damage to some children who had contraindications to it. But he also found that the child in this case had not proved causation and that her injuries were not a direct result of the vaccine she had received. Any other case brought on vaccine damage would have to get over this hurdle: drug companies have so much at stake in these cases that they are likely to fight tooth and nail against liability, unless it becomes more to their advantage to make a generous settlement than to fight to avoid this.

The problem that ordinary people have is the cost of funding such actions. The potentially enormous legal costs of proving that a drug was not only capable of causing damage but did cause damage to a particular child cannot realistically be borne on one legal aid certificate. This is partly because the Legal Aid Board can refuse to carry on funding an action if it considers the likely costs of the case will amount to more than the likely compensation awarded. In other words, it might cost £1 million to prove the case but if the damages were likely to be less than that, legal aid could be withdrawn. This is so even if other children in the same position would benefit from the decision.

Chapter 13

Legal Aid

No one needs be deterred from seeking legal help because they cannot afford to pay for a lawyer. Lawyers are costly but there is an extensive system of legal aid.

The legal aid system was introduced after the Second World War and has been extended until it now covers most, though not all, areas of law.

Most types of legal aid involve the filling-in of forms, some more complicated than others. It is, however, possible to obtain legal aid in order to have a solicitor help you to apply for legal aid itself! The various types of legal aid are covered in detail below.

Forms for legal aid can be obtained from solicitors who do that type of work. They can also be obtained from the juvenile or magistrates' court for criminal cases and some types of care case (if the local authority want to take your child into care).

While it is often a good idea to consult a solicitor, there are certain situations in which people almost always need a solicitor, and the law recognizes this by saying that legal aid should be granted as long as the person applying has fairly limited means. These are where:

- young people have been refused bail
- the court is thinking of sending a young person to detention centre or youth custody
- the court is thinking of making a care order as a criminal penalty (when the Children Act 1989 comes into force this penalty will be abolished)
- the court is thinking about making a charge and control order which prevents a child staying at home while in care
- the court is thinking about making a secure accommodation order which means a child can be locked up
- a young person is sent for trial on a murder charge.

When choosing a solicitor, it is best to aim for one who specializes in the problem you need help with. Most solicitors are knowledgeable in several fields of law, but do not cover all aspects. It is best to ask around. If you do not know anybody who has experienced the same problem then consult your local CAB or law centre, or ask a social worker. If none of this works then consult the Legal Aid Regional Directory at your library which tells you which solicitors do particular types of work. Beware, however, because a listing in this guide is not a guarantee of competence. In child-care law each area now has a panel or list of solicitors of proven expertise. It is therefore obviously worth consulting this if you need help in that field, and your CAB or local social services department will have a copy.

The Fixed-fee Interview

The simplest form of legal aid, which needs no form-filling, is the fixed-fee interview. You get half-an-hour of advice for £5. Solicitors who are prepared to do this are listed in the regional directory (obtainable at libraries) or you can ask when making the appointment. Not all solicitors do this, so check in advance.

The Green Form Scheme

For those requiring more advice, there is legal advice and assistance, commonly known as the green form scheme. You can obtain advice and help from a solicitor for most matters. This includes consultations in the solicitor's office, letters being written and telephone calls made for you, and help in preparing a case for court. It does not cover representing you at court. It can be used, however, to assist you to apply for the correct type of legal aid to be represented in court. Initially you are entitled to two hours' worth of work. If your case involves more work than this – for example to obtain a barrister's advice on a particular legal point – your solicitor can apply for the limit to be increased. It is not usually possible to obtain a second opinion or consult a second solicitor about the same problem under the green form scheme, but the second solicitor can ask for permission for you to do this. If you are on social security or low pay, help under the green form scheme will usually be free. At your first interview the solicitor will ask for details of your income, capital and dependants, and will then work out from a form whether you need to pay any contribution. This is on a sliding scale depending on your means. The solicitor will ask you to pay the contribution as soon as possible. You normally have to be sixteen or over (have reached compulsory school-leaving age) to sign the form. For a child under that age, his or her parent or guardian will usually sign.

It is important to note that if as a result of the help you receive, you are awarded money (damages), or recover or preserve some property over which there was a dispute, then normally *you* have to pay the solicitor's bill rather than legal aid paying it. This can mean having to sell the property involved to do this. This does not apply if the property is your home or the money is maintenance or welfare benefits. Also, your solicitor can apply for this rule to be relaxed if it would cause you grave hardship or distress or would be unreasonably difficult to do.

Advice at Police Stations

A different form of legal aid applies to advice given to people at police stations. This is available to children or adults and is free regardless of the recipient's financial situation. There is no need to sign a form. If the police apply to a court to extend the length of time they can hold a person, then this type of legal aid covers representation at court by the solicitor. It is known as advice and assistance at a police station. Remember that all police stations should now have a duty solicitor on call to assist those who request to see him or her. If you do not want to use the duty solicitor and either do not have a solicitor or do not know how to contact him or her out of office hours, then ask to consult the list of local solicitors which the custody officer should have.

Civil Legal Aid

Civil legal aid is available to take or defend proceedings in the High Court or the county court. You may wish to do this on your own account or on your child's behalf. A person under eighteen has to act through an adult, called the 'next friend' if the young person is bringing the action, or a 'guardian ad litem' if the young person has an action brought against him or her. There is only one exception to this – a person under eighteen who sues in the county court for money owed. These adults must themselves act through a solicitor and can apply for legal aid. Civil legal aid covers the representation at the hearing either by a solicitor or a barrister and the preparation leading up to it.

The application is made in writing, on a long form which asks for full details of the proposed case and on an accompanying form which asks for full details of the applicant's means. These are complicated and it is best to do it through a solicitor who should have stocks of the forms. This work can be done under the green form scheme and you can find a solicitor in the same way as suggested above.

Once completed, the application forms are submitted to the Legal Aid Board which decides whether or not to grant it. Be prepared for this to be a lengthy process – it can take months. In emergencies, however, legal aid can be granted in days or even over the telephone. Ask your solicitor for advice about this.

When your application is being considered, it will have to pass two tests. First, there must be reasonable grounds for taking, defending or being a party to the case. For example, an application will be refused as unreasonable if the advantage to be gained does not outweigh the cost involved or the point at issue is trivial. Second, your income and capital must fall within certain limits which are periodically reviewed and which take into account outgoings, financial commitments and dependants. The resources of a married couple are pooled unless they have a contrary interest in the case.

Under-eighteens make their application through their 'next friends' or guardians ad litem, often in practice their parents (see 'Update', p.xii). If the child is over sixteen then only their finances count, if he or she is under sixteen then it is their resources plus those of the person responsible in law for maintaining them and with whom they are living, unless that person has a contrary interest. An example of this would be a child suing his or her parent following a road accident to obtain damages from their insurance company. If the under-sixteen-year-old is in care and away from home then it is his or her own finances which count.

The financial resources of the 'next friend' or guardian ad litem are not included unless they are responsible for the maintenance and living with the young person. However, they can be called upon to pay the young person's legal aid contribution.

The assessment of your finances is undertaken by the Department of Social Security who may ask to interview you. They will decide how much disposable capital and income you have.

Disposable capital means all your savings and the value of your belongings, but they will exclude the value of your home, your furniture, your clothing and the tools of your trade.

Disposable income means your annual income from all sources, less tax and other stoppages, employment expenses (such as fares to work and childminding fees, rent or mortgage payments, and rates). There is also a set amount deducted for each of your dependents (this is reviewed from time to time).

Based on the limits in force at the time, you will qualify for free legal aid, or not qualify at all because your resources are above the maximum limits, or qualify with a contribution either from capital or income. If it is from capital, you must pay it in a lump sum; if from income you may pay it in instalments.

If your finances change while you are receiving legal aid you must notify the legal aid office and they may increase or decrease your contribution.

Sometimes if the Legal Aid Board is not sure about the merits of your case, that is if it feels more information is needed before it is able to give you unrestricted access to legal aid, it grants a limited certificate. A common limitation is to obtain specialist advice from a barrister on the merits of your case and the amount of damages you might expect to recover. If the opinion received is favourable, your solicitor can then ask that the limitation be lifted.

If your solicitor advises that the limitation imposed is unreasonable or indeed if you are refused legal aid altogether, you can appeal. This must be notified to the legal aid office within fourteen days and your appeal will be heard by the area committee, a group of local lawyers. You can be present and address the committee or you can have a representative do this for you who can be a lawyer. However, legal aid is not available for this so you must expect to pay.

As with the green form scheme, there is provision for the Legal Aid Board to recover the costs of providing you with legal aid from any damages which you receive or any property which you recover or preserve. It really depends on whether or not you win and if costs are awarded to you.

Generally the person who loses the case is ordered to pay the winner's costs, although in some cases, such as those involving the welfare of children where all parties were acting in the child's interests, there may be no order for costs. This means that everyone pays his or her own, or the state does if the person is legally-aided.

If you win and the other side has to pay your costs then the Legal Aid Board should return to you any contribution you paid. If you win and you do not get costs then the Legal Aid Board can look to you to pay your costs out of your damages. This can mean that if your claim is small there may be little or no benefit to you in having legal aid. If as a result of taking the case, you recover or preserve some property, you may have to bear your legal costs out of the value of it. There are some exemptions to this and in some circumstances the repayment of the costs to the Legal Aid Board can be postponed by a charge or mortgage being taken over the property if it is a house or flat. This area is complex and you are advised to seek advice from a solicitor.

Obviously there are risks involved and your solicitor should be asked at the start to assess the risk involved to you and advise you accordingly.

There is additionally some risk that, if you lose, you will be ordered to pay costs to your opponent even if you were on legal aid. Costs can also be ordered against an under-eighteen-year-old or against his or her 'next friend' or guardian ad litem. How much you end up paying depends upon your means and the way in which you have behaved in relation to the case, for example if you have added to the costs by refusing to accept a reasonable settlement. Regarding means, these are the means of the same person whose resources were assessed for legal aid originally.

Legal aid can be revoked, for example if you fail to pay your contribution, or if you fail to co-operate with the DSS in an assessment of your means after getting emergency legal aid or if you are found not to be eligible after receiving emergency legal aid. This can mean you repaying the Legal Aid Board for your solicitor's costs.

Criminal Legal Aid

Despite its name, criminal legal aid does not solely cover criminal proceedings. It covers criminal proceedings in the juvenile, magistrates' and crown courts, but it also covers care proceedings in the juvenile and crown courts.

Applying for criminal legal aid is considerably simpler than applying for its civil counterpart, but studies have shown that there is less consistency in its granting and refusing on a nationwide basis. The difference lies in the fact that criminal legal aid is considered by the court itself, rather than by the Legal Aid Board.

The applicant completes a form available from solicitors' offices or from the court. The form is sent to the court which grants or refuses it. Incidentally, in these proceedings, under-eighteen-year-olds do not act through an adult but apply directly themselves for legal aid. The application is decided on two factors: the finances of the person concerned and whether it is in the interests of justice to grant legal aid. Where the application is on behalf of a child, the critical age is sixteen. Below that age, the parents' means are those considered; above that age, usually the child's own. Disposable capital and income are calculated using similar guidelines to those described above in civil proceedings. The green form scheme is available for assistance from a solicitor in completing the forms.

There are rules laid down to set out situations where legal aid should always be granted provided the person qualifies financially. Basically these are the situations where a person's liberty is at stake – where a person has been remanded in custody or care before sentencing or where he or she has been refused bail, where a young person has been committed to trial for murder, where the court is thinking of a sentence involving custody, or where the court is thinking about making a care order as a sentence for a crime (this will not be available for the court once the Children Act 1989 comes in), or a charge and control order preventing a child in care from staying at home, or thinking of locking up a child in care.

Apart from these serious situations, the court follows guidelines in deciding when to grant legal aid. These are included in the form you fill in. They cover the following situations.

1. Where the person could be sentenced to custody, for example where a previous sentence has been breached.
2. If he or she is in danger of losing their job or suffering serious damage to their reputation.
3. If a substantial question of law is involved or the case is a complicated one, for example one of mistaken identity.
4. If the person cannot follow the proceedings because of a disability or because he or she does not speak English.
5. If the case involves expert cross-examination of a prosecution witness, or defence witnesses have to be traced and interviewed.

The court can order the person to pay a contribution towards legal aid, either out of capital or income. If the defendant is found not guilty then the contribution can be returned. You should tell the court if your means change during the case.

Legal aid can be extended to pay for representation by a barrister if the solicitor advises that this is necessary. Your solicitor can also obtain permission to pay the expenses of expert witnesses or private detectives if this is necessary to prepare your case. A legal aid order always includes the giving of legal advice on an appeal so that your solicitor can assist you to apply for the appropriate form of legal aid for that.

It is important to remember the principle that you have a free choice in whom you instruct to be your solicitor, even if you are on legal aid. However, this is modified in situations where more than one defendant is charged with the same crime and there is no difference in their interests. The court can then make them all have the same solicitor so as to save public money.

The Duty Solicitor Scheme

It is also worth remembering that if your case is a straightforward one and you do not wish to go through the process of applying for legal aid, then you can always ask the duty solicitor at court to act for you. He or she can also represent you if there has not been sufficient time to sort out a solicitor. This is a free service, operated at most magistrates' and juvenile courts. The solicitors who run this service are local solicitors who take it in turns to be on duty. They must have a certain amount of experience in order to be allowed to be on the rota, but it is always pot-luck as to whether you get someone with whom you feel happy and who is experienced in dealing with the crime involved. For serious matters it is usually best to arrange a solicitor in advance.

There is a limited right of appeal against a refusal of legal aid. It applies only where

- the charge is one in which an adult could be tried in the crown court;
- the application was refused on the interests of justice ground rather than on financial means; or
- the legal aid application was made at least twenty-one days before the date when it is understood that the trial (or the committal if the case is going to the crown court) will actually take place.

The appeal should be made within fourteen days of refusal. It follows, therefore, that there is no right of appeal if the offence is one for which an adult could be tried only in the magistrates' court or if the refusal is on financial grounds. Remember, though, that you can reapply if circumstances change or if you omitted to mention an important piece of information on the form.

Assistance by Way of Representation

The final type of legal aid is based on the green form scheme and is known as assistance by way of representation (ABWOR).

It covers domestic proceedings in the magistrates' court such as maintenance proceedings. It also covers proceedings before mental health review tribunals – where a mental patient is asking to be released from hospital – and it covers some sorts of care proceedings in the juvenile court.

Financial eligibility is as for green form applications. The green form is completed at the solicitor's office and the solicitor then applies for it to be extended into ABWOR by applying to the Legal Aid Board.

Under-eighteens do not need 'next friends' or guardians ad litem to act for them, and usually apply for this legal aid on their own finances.

It is possible for your solicitor to obtain authorization to instruct a barrister if the Legal Aid Board agree that the case merits it.

With any type of legal problem for which legal aid might be available, the basic advice is to find a solicitor who specializes in the field in which your problem lies, and to inquire when making an initial interview as to the availability of legal aid and any likely financial contribution you might have to make.

Your Child at Eighteen

Eighteen is the age of legal majority, that is the beginning of adulthood.

- An eighteen-year-old can vote.
- He or she can marry without parental consent.
- Eighteen-year-olds can buy and drink alcohol in a bar.
- They can work in a bar serving drinks.
- They can see a Category 18 film and buy videos with an adult classification.
- They can serve on a jury.
- They can make a will.
- An eighteen-year-old has complete contractual capacity. This means that he or she can own land, buy a house or a flat, apply for a mortgage, sue and be sued in his or her own right, enter into binding contracts and administer a deceased person's estate.
- If a child or young person under eighteen has a case to sue somebody for causing them personal injuries then they have until three years after their eighteenth birthday to start proceedings.
- They can apply for legal aid to take civil proceedings in their own right whereas under-eighteens usually need an adult to apply on their behalf. (Different rules apply for criminal legal aid, see Chapter 13.)
- They can open a bank account in their own right without a parent's signature.
- They can claim income support.
- They can apply for a passport without parental consent.
- They can change their name without parental consent.
- They can hold a licence to drive a medium-sized goods vehicle, that is one which weighs up to 7.5 tonnes (they can hold a licence to drive a car at seventeen).
- They can join the armed forces without parental consent.
- If adopted, an eighteen-year-old can apply to see his or her original birth certificate on application to the Registrar-General.
- It is impossible to adopt someone who has reached the age of eighteen.
- If a child is a ward of court he or she ceases to be one at eighteen, and it is not possible to make someone a ward of court once they have reached the age of eighteen.

- A child who has been in care ceases to be at the age of eighteen, unless the care order was made after their sixteenth birthday in which case it expires when they reach nineteen.
- An eighteen-year-old can go into a sex shop.
- He or she can go into a betting shop and place a bet. They can also work in a betting shop. They can take part in bingo (an under-eighteen-year-old can go into a bingo hall but not take part in the game).
- They can pawn goods at a pawn shop.
- They can be tattooed.
- They can donate blood.
- They have to pay for dental treatment unless one of the exemptions applies, for example they are in full-time education or pregnant.
- They have to pay the community charge or poll tax.
- In the eyes of the criminal law, a young person becomes an adult at seventeen. However, between the ages of seventeen and twenty, a person is treated as a young offender where sentences of detention in custody are concerned. They can be sentenced to detention in a young offender institution. The maximum term is six months in the magistrates' court, but in the crown court the same maximum applies to them as would apply to an adult offender of twenty-one or over. The minimum sentence is twenty-one days. They would usually serve their sentence in an institution for young offenders, that is males between the ages of fourteen and twenty, and females between the ages of fifteen and twenty. The prison department can, however, direct that they serve their sentence in an ordinary prison or remand centre. (For further details, see Chapter 8.)

Despite eighteen being the age of majority there are still some rights which are not acquired until the age of twenty-one. These are as follows:

- standing for election as an MP, or local councillor
- applying for a licence to sell alcohol
- holding a licence to drive a heavy goods vehicle or a large passenger vehicle
- applying to adopt a child.

A man can, at the age of twenty-one but not earlier, consent to a homosexual act in private without breaking the law, provided he and his partner are both over the age of twenty-one. Gay relationships between women are not illegal at any age but if one partner is under sixteen, or is over sixteen but does not consent, then the older woman could be prosecuted for indecent assault.

Useful Addresses

The following organizations can offer useful help and advice.

Action for Victims of Medical Accidents, Bank Chambers, 1 London Road, London SE23 3TP. Tel: 081-291 2793.

Advisory Centre for Education (ACE), 18 Victoria Park Square, London E2 9PB. Tel: 081-980 4596.

British Agencies for Adoption and Fostering, 11 Southwark Street, London SE1 1RQ. Tel: 071-407 8800.

Centre for Studies on Integration in Education (CSIE), 415 Edgware Road, London NW2 6NB. Tel: 081-452 8642.

Child Poverty Action Group, 1–5 Bath Street, London EC1V 9PY. Tel: 071-253 3406.

Children's Legal Centre, 20 Compton Terrace, London N1 2UN. Tel: 071-359 6251.

Commission for Racial Equality, Elliott House, 10–12 Allington Street, London SW1E 5EH. Tel: 071-828 7022.

Divorce Conciliation and Advisory Service, 38 Ebury Street, London SW1W 0LU. Tel: 071-730 2422.

Education Otherwise, 25 Common Lane, Hemingford Abbots, Cambridgeshire DE18 9AN. Tel: 0480 63130.

Equal Opportunities Commission, Overseas House, Quay Street, Manchester M3 3HN. Tel: 061-833 9244.

Family Rights Group, 6–9 Manor Gardens, Holloway Road, London N7 6LA. Tel: 071-272 7308/4231.

Family Welfare Association, Central Office, 501–5 Kingsland Road, London E8 4AU. Tel: 071-254 6251.

Health and Safety Executive, Baynards House, 1 Chepstow Place, London W2 4TF. Tel: 071-229 3456.

National Children's Bureau, 8 Wakely Street, London EC1V 7QE. Tel: 071-278 9441.

National Foster Care Association, Francis House, Francis Street, London SW1P 1DE. Tel: 071-828 6266.

Relate (National Marriage Guidance), Herbert Gray College, Little Church Street, Rugby CV21 3AP. Tel: 0788 73241.

Release, 169 Commercial Street, London E1 6BW. Tel: 071-377 5905. Advice on the legal aspects of drug problems; 24-hour emergency number: 071-603 8654.

Reunite, P.O. Box 158, London N4 1AU. Help for parents of kidnapped children.

Royal Society for the Prevention of Accidents (RoSPA), Cannon House, Priory Queensway, Birmingham B4 6BS. Tel: 021-200 2461.

Women in Prison, 25 Horsell Road, London N5 1XL. Tel: 071-607 3353 and 071-609 7463/8167.

Table of Statutes

Index

suspension, 107
verbal chastisement, 103
governors, 67, 68, 100
grammar, 64
grant maintained status, 107–10
HIV positive pupils, 101
homosexuality and, 94, 100
independent, 64, 91–4
assisted places scheme, 85, 102, 155–6
Children Act 1989, under, 92
control of, 92–3
corporal punishment at, 102
standards in, 93–4
leave of absence, 83–4
leaving age, 198
maintained, 60–61, 67–8
meals, 152–3, 156
middle, 63–4
music and ballet, 156
nursery, 61–2, 75, 77
opting out, 107–10
organization of, 66–8
political indoctrination, 94, 100
refusal of place, appeals against, 70–74
secondary, 64
sixth-form colleges, 64
special, 61, 74, 81, 95, 98–9
tertiary colleges, 65
transport to and from, 83, 110, 153–4
truancy, 82, 84, 93
uniforms, 149, 153
voluntary, 61
aided, 61, 67, 69
controlled, 61, 67–8
special agreement, 61, 67, 69
Welsh, 69, 95
see also education
search warrants, 178–9, 248, 324
secure accommodation orders, 210, 231–2, 242, 273–4
separation
agreements
custody and, 315
financial arrangements, 313–15
judicial, 290, 294
care orders in, 236–7, 260
proceedings, 314
see also divorce
severe weather payments, 144
sex
age of consent, 198

shops, 403
sexual offences, 343–4
see also abuse, sexual
sick pay, statutory (SSP), 54
sickness and invalidity benefit, 125
single mothers
income support and maintenance, 135, 137
lone-parent premium, 132
one-parent benefit, 135, 143, 147
young, 135–6
sixteen, children's rights at age, 198–9
social fund, 131, 134, 138–40
family credit and, 147
'passport benefits', 149
social security see child benefit; family credit; income support; National Insurance, benefits
social services
adoptions and, 23, 37–8
childminders and, 47
help from, 156–7
see also local authorities; social workers
social workers, 243–6
access and, 234–5
case conferences, 244
child abuse procedures, 244–6
custody cases, 279
field officers, 243
fostering and, 179
key workers, 243
reports for court, 213
supervising officers, 243
solicitors
confidentiality of, 281
dealing with, 280–83
see also legal aid
Spastics Society, 80
sperm banks, 9–10
specific issue orders, 295, 317
starting credits, 127–8
statutory duties, breach of, 370
step-parents
adoption and, 21, 27, 36–7
care proceedings, in, 272
custody by, 36
guardians, as, 6, 8–9
maintenance orders and, 165
supervision orders, 88, 215–17, 271
Children Act 1989, under, 299
wardship cases, in, 322–3